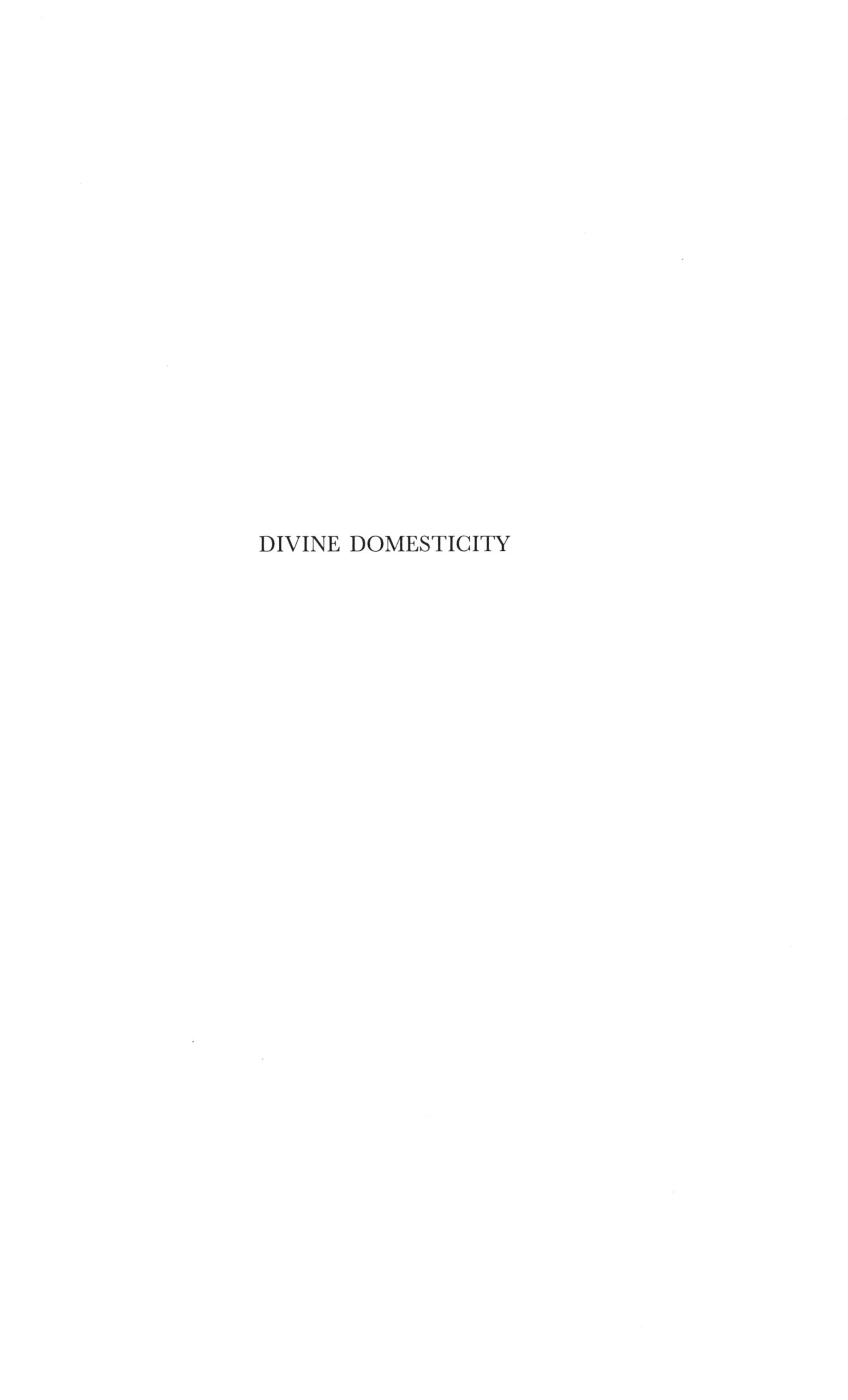

DIVINE DOMESTICITY

STUDIES IN THE HISTORY OF CHRISTIAN THOUGHT

VOLUME LXXIV

MARJORIE O'ROURKE BOYLE

DIVINE DOMESTICITY

DIVINE DOMESTICITY

AUGUSTINE OF THAGASTE TO TERESA OF AVILA

BY

MARJORIE O'ROURKE BOYLE

E.J. BRILL
LEIDEN · NEW YORK · KÖLN
1997

The paper in this book meets the guidelines for permanence and durability of the Committee on Production Guidelines for Book Longevity of the Council on Library Resources.

Library of Congress Cataloging-in-Publication Data

Boyle, Marjorie O'Rourke, 1943–
Divine domesticity : Augustine of Thagaste to Teresa of Avila / by Marjorie O'Rourke Boyle.
p. cm. — (Studies in the history of Christian thought, ISSN 0081–8607 ; v. 74)
Includes bibliographical references and indexes.
ISBN 9004106758 (cloth : alk. paper)
1. Home—Religious aspects—Christianity—History of doctrines.
I. Title. II. Series.
BR115.H56B68 1996
261.8—dc20 96–30781
CIP

Die Deutsche Bibliothek - CIP-Einheitsaufnahme

O'Rourke Boyle, Marjorie:
Divine domesticity : Augustine of Thagaste to Teresa of Avila / by Marjorie O'Rourke Boyle. – Leiden ; New York ; Köln : Brill, 1996
(Studies in the history of Christian thought ; Vol. 74)
ISBN 90–04–10675–8
NE: GT

ISSN 0081-8607
ISBN 90 04 10675 8

PRINTED IN THE NETHERLANDS

CONTENTS

ACKNOWLEDGMENTS

I wish to thank Heiko A. Oberman for accepting the manuscript for publication in the series, Studies in the History of Christian Thought. William Bouwsma, Louis Dupré, and Margaret L. King generously read work in progress. My family was ever supportive of the project.

PROLOGUE

Divine Domesticity is a cultural analysis of the home during the Christian centuries, when home was believed to be heaven.

The metaphorical focus of the book is what the word *focus* literally meant: the hearth as the familial place. An interior designer, distinguished for his restorations of historic houses, has designated the fireplace as the dominant architectural focus of all habitation. "The word hearth, and all it implies, is deeply rooted in our romantic thoughts about the home. . . . Nearly everyone prefers a room that has a fireplace to one that does not." He supposed this idea "a legacy from the caveman, who also expected to arrive home and find a fire waiting for him."[1] Yet if the preference was a prehistoric legacy, it was not transmitted directly. Only with the nineteenth century did there emerge a "cult of domesticity." In prior Christian societies the home was "mundane, mundane because it had no transcendent functions."[2] Believers did not prefer to come home to a room with a lit fireplace, did not prefer to come home at all; but deliberately chose to slam the door shut on the home as a spiritual place. *Divine Domesticity* analyzes the phenomenon.

The religious rejection of the home was not sanctioned by scripture, which revealed a God intimately involved as an architect, builder, and renovator of human housing. His own house, in the phrase "the house of God," was equated with the Israelite people and then in common usage with the Christian community.[3] In the gospel of Jesus of Nazareth the home was an important place. His very call to ministry came not from the general public but from close kin. He taught parables about houses and householders, to the ordinary details of storage and sweeping. He preached not only in the local synagogue but also in his own home, where the crowd became so dense that the companions of a paralytic boldly removed its roof to lower his pallet into the scene. Jesus entered the homes of others to heal them and he sent those he cured home. He ate supper in the homes of friends, who welcomed him. He dined notably at a wedding feast, for which he supplied his hosts amphoras of excellent wine, and notoriously in the houses of the socially impure, to the contempt of the religious establishment. His final

---

1 *Mark Hampton on Decorating* (New York: Random House, 1989), p. 49.

2 Glenna Matthews, *"Just a Housewife": The Rise and Fall of Domesticity in America* (New York: Oxford University Press, 1987), p. 6.

3 "House of God" in *Theological Dictionary of the New Testament,* ed. Gerhard Friedrich, trans. and ed. Geoffrey W. Bromiley (Grand Rapids, Mich.: Wm. B. Eerdmans, 1967), 5:121-22, 125-28, 130-31.

gesture to his disciples was to eat a Passover meal in an ordinary urban home. The promise at that meal was that "if someone loves me, he will keep my conversation, and my Father will love him, and we will come to him and make our home with him" (John 14:23). What was the fortune of that promise of God at home with people? Who believed it? Did any even hear it?

Divine Domesticity investigates the traditional belief of the divine indwelling—God living in persons—not by systematic theology but as cultural history. Diverging in method from the history of doctrine, it ventures to understand doctrine as history. The analysis proceeds, then, not by speculation on faculties of the soul but by research on actualities of housing. What did people experience about home? And how did that experience shape their understanding of the divine indwelling? Because the prime consideration for housing was not style but site, geography precedes architecture, or nature before culture. With its orientation on the land, the research studies the housing room-by-room and the household in its relationships from parents to slaves.

The book examines four cultural constructs for human dwelling: the inn, the sanctuary, the villa, and the castle. The inn and the castle are searched by in-depth analysis of the textual constructs of their singular architects, Augustine of Thagaste and Teresa of Avila. The sanctuary and the villa are explored through exemplary authors, from Bernard of Clairvaux to Erasmus of Rotterdam, as commonplaces of medieval and renaissance convictions. The research is a lesson in alterity, an ugly neologism but a brute fact: the past as "other." A continuity of human experience—the home as basic—cannot be historically assumed. *Divine Domesticity* discovers a fundamental cultural disparity of values between modern comfort at home and the exilic asceticism that once dominated western civilization.

CHAPTER ONE

INN

Domestic architecture since the neolithic period allocated a space for fire. It featured not only portable braziers but also fixed hearths, now defined on sites by a border of stones or the ashes of burnt matter.[1] The domestic hearth once symbolized in Indo-European culture the basic social unit. Through the rituals and ceremonies performed about it, the hearth expressed the religious ideology of the kinship group, bonding its members historically and collaterally, and grounding it to the home it occupied. Archaeological excavations, linguistic and literary evidence, all confirm the hearth as the center of the household. As Ovid explained the Roman calendar, "The hearth (*focus*) is so named from the flames, and because it fosters (*fovet*) all things; in early times it stood in the first room of the house." The hearth served as the altar, since its fire, as descendent from the sun and its cosmic forces, designated it for worship. There was invocation of tutelary powers and sacrificial offering. In Latin the hearth was personified as Vesta, "the living flame," although no image was ever graven in her temple. The cult of fire dated to the nomadic period, with its kindling and tending perhaps a factor in the construction of permanent dwellings. Some ancient historians affirmed that. Vesta's perpetual fire was the original symbol of Rome as settlement, then empire.[2]

The nuclear family was the paradigm, grouped around the head of household as the officiating priest at the private cult of the hearth. Its ceremonials were directed toward the ancestors, offerings of libations to the dead on established dates with traditional rites, in exchange for tutelary power extended to the living. The flame was associated with ancestor worship: the word *foculus* for "hearth" meant also "family" and "grave". From generation to generation it was as a cosmic center the contact between the living and the dead. The same hearth that united the family to its past created bonds in the present and into the future. As focal to daily life, its cult marked rites of

---

[1] Polymnia Metaxa Muhly, "Minoan Hearths," *American Journal of Archaeology* 88 (1984):107-22.

[2] Angela Della Volpe, "From the Hearth to the Creation of Boundaries," *Journal of Indo-European Studies* 18 (1990):158-60, citing Ovid, *Fasti* 6.301-2; *Ovid's Fasti*, trans. James George Frazer (Cambridge, Mass.: Harvard University Press, 1967), p. 341. For Vesta without an effigy see *Fasti* 6.295-98. For background see Jean Pierre Vernant, "Hestia-Hermes: The Religious Expression of Space and Movement in Ancient Greece," in *Myth and Thought among the Greeks* (London: Routledge & Kegan Paul, 1983), pp. 127-75.

passage, birth, and marriage. The infant was received into the family by being carried ritually about the fire. At nuptials the bridegroom kindled his own flame, while the bride brought fire from her familial hearth for an ignition symbolic of the marital union. Like the infant she performed a ritual of circumambulation about the hearth. A guest was admitted to the family circle only if he placed himself first at the hearth. The household flame was perpetual, extinguished only with the termination of the family. Like the family circle, the hearth was traditionally round in shape, a replica of the disk of the sun. It was singular in that design; temples and altars to all other deities were square or rectangular. At the center of the domestic enclosure, the round hearth symbolized the circumscribed space of the household, the sacred space that fostered human life.[3]

Firewood could be purchased in the marketplaces of the Roman empire, with bread, wine, oil, and the other staples of life. Augustine as bishop of Hippo Regius acknowledged that in preaching.[4] Yet he symbolically removed the altar from the hearth to the church in rejection of the traditional social metonym for the home, "altar and hearth."[5] Fire as a sensible manifestation of the divine was only produced through the agency of angels, he believed. It was an angel who had appeared to Moses in the burning bush. The flashes of lightning on Sinai during the giving of the commandments, the pillar of fire guiding the Israelites in the wilderness, were not true theophanies but only transitory material forms produced by creatures—angels—in the service of the Creator. Even the Pentecostal manifestation of the Spirit in tongues of fire was through such subject and submissive creatures. By temporal motions and forms the fire upon the apostles displayed the coeternal substance of the Spirit with the Father and the Son; but it was not the Spirit. The Spirit as fire was only creaturely, like the ancient examples.[6]

By physical law fire tended upward. A person inflamed and elevated by the gift of the Spirit was set on fire to ascend steps. His destination was vertical, not lateral: not the domestic enclosure but "the house of the Lord" as the eternal abiding place.[7] When an ardor of fraternal love inflamed Augustine, it did not inspire him to bond in kinship but in friendship. His tendency, his conversation, his embrace were not for the natural brother but for the spiritual brother, the man who endured keen torments for the beauty and stability of the faith. It was the staunch believer he loved with "a chaste and brotherly love."[8]

The elemental fire that had centered society in religion was extinguished,

---

[3] Della Volpe, "From the Hearth to the Creation of Boundaries," pp. 161-65, 176, 166-69.
[4] Augustine, *Sermones* 167.3.
[5] Cicero, *Contra Sallust* 59.5.
[6] Augustine, *De Trinitate* 4.21.31; 2.13.23; 2.13.25; 4.21.30; 2.6.11.
[7] Augustine, *Confessiones* 13.9.10.
[8] Augustine, *De Trinitate* 9.6.11.

its hearth displaced. In that dark Augustine and some companions stole pears from a neighbor's tree and, merely sampling them, threw loads in disgust to swine.[9] Their action displayed their contempt for the land and its produce: a waste of fruit. The gourmand Apicius had supplied a recipe for pears poached in cinnamon and wine.[10] The agronomist Varro had recommended boiling them into a jam. Pears, he advised, should be stored in earthenware jars covered with pitch and placed upside down in a hole with earth heaped upon them. Others preferred that they should be picked before fully ripe at the waning of the moon, their stems smeared with pitch, and stored in freshly tarred casks made air-and watertight with lead and plaster.[11] Yet the notorious theft of pears was Augustine's personal enactment of the concupiscence inherited from the original sin of Adam,[12] which he maturely assessed as "social necessity."[13] The theft was symbolic criticism of the seamy education in sophistry that bore, or stole, its wanton fruits on holiday from school[14]—more damnably, of an institution that promoted its corrupt nurture: the home.

The pear tree was in the neighborhood of the familial vineyard, in the vicinity of Thagaste (Souk-Ahras), a small interior town of mountainous terrain in Africa Proconsularis near the Numidian border.[15] Of the curial rank,[16] Augustine's father was necessarily a landowner,[17] although his fields were not a twentieth of the patrimony of the church at Hippo.[18] Land was

---

[9] Augustine, *Confessiones* 2.2.4.

[10] Apicius, *De re coquinaria* 4.2.35. See also Jacques André, *L'Alimentation et la cuisine à Rome*, Études et commentaries, 38 (Paris: C. Klincksieck, 1961), pp. 75-76.

[11] Varro, *De agri cultura* 15.16.56; 15.18.61-62.

[12] Commonly acknowledged, but considered "banal," e. g. Gerald Bonner, "Augustine's Doctrine of Man: Image of God and Sinner," *Augustinianum* 24 (1984):496; or "scrupulous over a peccadillo," e. g. John Freccero, "Autobiography and Narrative," in *Reconstructing Individualism: Autonomy, Individuality, and the Self in Western Thought*, ed. Thomas C. Heller, Morton Sosna, and David E. Wellbery (Stanford, Calif.: Stanford University Press, 1986), p. 23. For the theft as derivative from original sin see Hugues Derycke, "Le vol des poires, parabolé du péché originel," *Bulletin de littérature ecclésiastique* 88 (1987):337-48; William J. O'Brien, "The Liturgical Form of Augustine's Conversion Narrative and its Theological Significance," *Augustinian Studies* 9 (1978):57-58; Leo C. Ferrari, "The Pear-Theft in Augustine's Confessions," *Revue des études augustiniennes* 16 (1970):233-42; Robert J. O'Connell, *St. Augustine's Confessions: The Odyssey of Soul* (Cambridge, Mass.: Harvard University Press, Belknap Press, 1969), pp. 47-50; Kenneth Burke, *The Rhetoric of Religion: Studies in Logology* (Boston: Beacon, 1961), pp. 93-101.

[13] Augustine, *De civitate Dei* 14.11.

[14] Marjorie O'Rourke Boyle, "Augustine in the Garden of Zeus: Lust, Love, and Language," *Harvard Theological Review* 83 (1990):117-39.

[15] See Claude Lepelley, *Les cités de l'Afrique romaine au bas-empire: Notices d'histoire municipale*, 2 vols. (Paris: Études augustiniennes, 1979-81), 2:175-76; B. H. Warmington, *The North African Provinces from Diocletian to the Vandal Conquest* (Cambridge: Cambridge University Press, 1954), p. 103.

[16] Possidius, *Vita* 1.

[17] A. H. M. Jones, *The Later Roman Empire 284-602: A Social, Economic and Administrative Survey*, 3 vols. (Oxford: Basil Blackwell, 1964), 2:737-57.

[18] Augustine, *Epistolae* 126.7, cited by Othmar Perler, *Les voyages de saint Augustin*

the principal source of wealth for the curia, whose total property was considerable.[19] North African towns, except for a few coastal cities as mercantile, were agricultural settlements in which the populace earned from— probably worked on—the land.[20] Records of taxation suggest that agriculture, rather than commerce or industry, contributed the bulk of the national income.[21] Rural and urban areas were economically symbiotic. The tendency of socioeconomic development was that fewer people possessed more, through the formation of imperial estates from private holdings, and through the concentration by marriage and investment of hundreds of families and thousands of acres in north Africa.[22] Even with the imperial confiscation and concentration of land, which a law of A. D. 422 rare for its exactness of figures records as one-fifth of Proconsularis,[23] property in the private ownership of the senatorial and curial classes extended into large estates.[24] Augustine testified to wealthy landowners.[25] At the beginning of the fifth century a saint Melania owned an estate near Thagaste vaster than the territory of the town.[26] These large estates were divided into small lots, commonly rented to tenants, who paid a share of their crop and also worked five days annually on the land of the principal lessee, an arrangement supervised by imperial procurators.[27]

When the Romans conquered that land, they secured very fertile areas that had been farmed methodically for generations.[28] The archaeological evidence for agriculture indicates the most important plants as the Mediterranean triad yielding grain, wine, and oil. The cultivation of the grape and the olive required different soil conditions from cereals and pulses, and they were harvested later than such crops. An area of mixed land could yield two additional harvests with the same number of laborers. The development of polyculture was as important for the emergence of civilization in the Mediterranean region as it was for irrigation in the Near East. There was a spiral of development, as the demands of population exploited crops of vines and olives toward a higher level of production, which could support

(Paris: Études augustiniennes, 1969), p. 124.

19 Warmington, *North African Provinces*, p. 65.

20 Ibid., p. 55.

21 Jones, *Later Roman Empire*, 2:1039, 841-50, 855-58; M.I. Finley, *The Ancient Economy* (London: Chatto & Windus, 1973), p. 139.

22 Ramsay MacMullen, *Roman Social Relations 50 B. C. to A. D. 284* (New Haven, Conn.: Yale University Press, 1974), pp. 49-51, 38-39.

23 Warmington, *North African Provinces*, p. 63.

24 Ibid., p. 64; Geoffrey Rickman, *The Corn Supply of Ancient Rome* (Oxford: Clarendon, 1980), p. 111.

25 Warmington, *North African Provinces*, p. 64, citing Augustine, *Epistolae* 56; 89; 35.2; 105.3; *De civitate Dei* 22.8; *Epistolae* 58.

26 Warmington, *North African Provinces*, p. 64.

27 Rickman, *Corn Supply of Ancient Rome*, pp. 112, 111.

28 Ibid., p. 108.

more people, a proportion of whom could work other than in agriculture.[29] The vineyard remained primary, but its produce was as vulnerable as it was valuable. Agronomists warned that farmhouses should not be built near a main road because of depredation by travelers; isolated ones featured towers for observation and strong walls with sturdy gates.[30] A farm, wrote Varro, should be situated at the foot of a mountain facing south in safety from neighbor brigands.[31] Augustine's theft of pears, in which neighbor stole from neighbor, was a detail of the large-scale theft of property in the late empire, by which ownership of the land was arrogated by a few. In the current hyperbole half of Africa was owned by six lords. In the latter half of the fourth century there emerged the predatory aggression long latent in the Roman peace. Contemptuous of the market of legitimate buying and selling, men resorted to armed violence with spears and stones to seize property. The impunity of the aggressor depended on influence established in the system of patronage and clientele, which involved Augustine's father, and on connections with individuals who could sway the legal process. In minor conflicts, such as stealing pears, brute strength mattered. Agricultural aggression was attested in the case from Egyptian papyri of the poor farmer whose sown fields were devoured by cattle let loose on the corn by several sons of wealthy men. The absence of owners from their land exposed the vulnerability of property.[32] A farmer needed to hire guards for posting and patrolling crop and equipment, as protection against theft and against marauding cattle or sheep from the pasturages.[33]

Augustine and his crowd, shaking down pears under cover of dark without retribution, imitated the social shakedown of the defenseless. The theft revealed the fundamental economic weakness of the empire: too few producers fed too many idlers.[34] Augustine and his companions were a gang of otiosity. His familial vineyard was a metonym for the culture of leisure centered in the villa.[35] In the Roman provinces of the empire the villa was the most distinctive feature of its rural settlement.[36] The villa was distinguished

---

[29] Kevin Greene, *The Archaeology of the Roman Economy* (London: B. T. Batsford, 1986), p. 72.

[30] MacMullen, *Roman Social Relations*, p. 4.

[31] Varro, *De agri cultura* 1.7.1; 1.16.2.

[32] See MacMullen, *Roman Social Relations*, pp. 6-12, without reference to Augustine.

[33] Naphtali Lewis, *Life in Egypt under Roman Rule* (Oxford: Clarendon, 1983), pp. 120-21.

[34] Jones, *Later Roman Empire*, 2:1045.

[35] By the sixteenth century *vinea* denoted for Romans not "vineyard" but "villa", a cultivated terrain with a residence to which all social classes retired in the summer custom of *villegiatura*. David Coffin, *The Villa in the Life of Renaissance Rome* (Princeton: Princeton University Press, 1979), pp. vii-viii; Claudia Lazarro, *The Italian Renaissance Garden: From the Conventions of Planting, Design, and Ornament to the Grand Gardens of Sixteenth-Century Italy* (New Haven, Conn.: Yale University Press, 1990), pp. 109-11.

[36] Greene, *Archaeology of the Roman Economy*, p. 88. For a Christian estate in north Africa see Jean Peyras, "Le fundus auficianus: Étude d'un grand domaine romain de la ré-

in the history of architecture from the farmhouse or the cottage by its unique ideological design. This ideology was established in the contrast of the country with the city, as in Horace's familiar tale of the cousin mice. The rural refuge of the villa was not intended to accommodate agricultural functions but to manifest values lacking or debased in the city. As the place of social interaction, the city was necessarily mundane and temporal; while the country, offering confrontations with the brute forces of nature and encounters with its sensuous beauties, inspired human responses.[37]

The essential features of the ideology of country living, in opposition to urbanity, were its simplicity and informality, its salubrious air and opportunity for sport, its scope for intellectual and artistic achievements and for conversations with friends, and the enjoyment of the natural and cultivated landscape in varying seasons and conditions. The factor of pleasure distinguished the residence from the farmhouse, the estate from the farm. The villa could only be maintained by privileged persons, whose income was not dependent on the rigors and risks of laborers who lived permanently in the country, wresting a living from the soil and enduring the tedium of isolation. Farmers, whether peasants or slaves, as bound to the land, unlikely experienced the charms of rural life praised in the literature on villas. The villa was a concept through which persons whose position of economic and social privilege was based in urban commerce and industry expropriated rural land, often with the care of the laboring class of slaves.[38]

Economically there were two categories of villas: the self-sustaining agricultural estate with produce for its own use and surplus for sale, and the retreat dependent for construction and maintenance on surplus capital earned in urban centers. The grander villas on the margins of the Roman empire were more complex in type and scale than those on the Italian peninsula. As isolated, they had to function as social and administrative units, often substituting for towns and often spawning towns. Their economy was typically dependent on production. The villa, unlike the farmhouse, whose design was marked by the gradualism of agricultural change, strained to be up-to-date stylistically. It was usually more innovative than other architectural types, because the requirements of leisure were less defined. Two models were established in the Roman era: the compact-cubic, which was a foil to the natural environment; and the open-extended, which was integrated with

---

gion de Mateur (Tunisie du nord)," *Antiquités africaines* 9 (1975):181-222.

37 James S. Ackerman, *The Villa: Form and Ideology of Country Houses*, Bollingen series, 35-34 (Princeton: Princeton University Press, 1990), pp. 286, 12. See also Harald Mielsch, *Die romische Villa: Architektur und Lebensform* (Munich: C. H. Beck, 1987). For pastoral values in the urban villa see Alfred Frazer, "The Roman Villa and the Pastoral Ideal," in *The Pastoral Landscape*, ed. John Dixon Hunt, Studies in the History of Art (Washington, D. C.: National Gallery; Hanover, N. H.: University Presses of America, 1992), pp. 48-61.

38 Ackerman, *Villa*, pp. 36, 9, 36, 10.

it. These styles reflected the ideology that promoted the villa: the lure of nature, whether expressed in a response of distance or engagement; the contrast of nature and culture; the prerogatives of privilege and power; and pride, whether of nation, region, or class. The signifiers ranged from the siting and form of the entire building to its details and characteristics. There were several classes of villa: the *villa urbana*, the dwelling of the proprietor; the *villa rustica*, the dormitory of the foreman and slaves, centered on a large kitchen, with stables and pens for the animals; and the *villa fructuaria*, the structure for processing and storing wine, oil, and grain, usually incorporated into the *villa rustica*.[39]

Excavations of rural north Africa evidence few traces of residential rooms for landlords, so that they probably visited their estates or farms intermittently at the harvest to oversee production.[40] Augustine's family owned a villa, at least a storehouse for the produce of the vineyard and a dormitory for its laborers. The principal residence of the family was probably in town. Augustine did not share the Roman enthusiasm for villas, unless they were philosophical places, like the retreat at Cassiciacum upon his conversion.[41] He did not ambition like Pliny, the younger, to inquire about a villa "into every corner of the place. . . indulging the love I have for all the places I have largely laid out myself or where I have perfected an early design." He did not set "my entire house before your eyes" with vivid description. For he could not confess to its mental and physical health, which Pliny enjoyed, nor praise it for a "profounder peace" than any other place.[42]

The "idleness" of the villa was introduced to Augustine in his sixteenth year by "domestic necessity." On holiday from school, he began to be with his parents.[43] Although the Romans had no precise word for the nuclear family—*familia* was more complex in including servants—that was the dominant type. The triad of father-mother-children was the center of primary social obligations.[44] In that familial situation Augustine confessed that the

---

39 Ibid., pp. 15, 18-24, 30, 42.

40 Greene, *Archaeology of the Roman Economy*, pp. 132-33.

41 See R. J. Halliburton, "The Inclination to Retirement—the Retreat of Cassiciacum and the 'Monastery' of Tagaste," Texte und Untersuchungen, 80, *Studia patristica* 5 (1962):329-40.

42 See Pliny, the younger, *Epistulae* 5.16.42; 5.16.43-44; 5.14.46; 5.16.45; *Letters and Panegyricus*, trans. Betty Radice, 2 vols. (Cambridge, Mass.: Harvard University Press, 1969), 1:353, 355. For his villas see Helen Tanzer, *The Villas of Pliny the Younger* (New York: Columbia University Press, 1979); Institut française de l'architecture, *La Laurentine et l'invention de la villa romaine* (Paris: Moniteur, 1982); and for the identification of his Laurentine villa, Eugenia Salza Prina Ricotti, "The Importance of Water in Roman Garden Triclinia," in *Ancient Roman Villa Gardens*, ed. Elisabeth B. MacDougall, Dumbarton Oaks Colloquium on the History of Landscape Architecture, 10 (Washington, D. C.: Dumbarton Oaks, 1987), pp. 182-84.

43 Augustine, *Confessiones* 2.3.6.

44 Richard P. Saller, "*Familia, domus* and the Roman Conception of the Family," *Phoenix* 38 (1984):355; Suzanne Dixon, *The Roman Family* (Baltimore, Md.: Johns Hopkins Univer-

bramble of lust towered above his head, while there was no hand to uproot it. His father viewed him at the public baths "ripened to puberty" and restless with assuming manhood. Rejoicing at the prospect of grandchildren, he declared the event to Augustine's mother. His father's was a "wine-bibbing" (*vinulentia*) joy, in which intoxication the world was oblivious of its Creator and loved the creature instead, from an invisible wine flowing from a will perverted and inclined to the dregs.[45] The Roman family was vigilant for the signs of male puberty, which onset was formally celebrated at a household feast or postponed to the collective feast of the Liberalia, on which day boys donned the toga of a man. The father especially rejoiced at puberty, for he would testify at marriage to his son's virility.[46] By the era of Augustine, in distinction to classical practice, it was puberty, rather than citizenship, that made a boy an adult.[47] Yet the perversity of his father's symbolic intoxication already stirred in the common waters of the public baths. It had not been the custom of republican austerity for fathers to frequent the baths in the presence of their pubescent sons.[48] The baths were typical of the works Augustine's father supervised in the curia, since they were built from contributions by prominent local citizens with combined motives of philanthropy and politics. In north Africa the baths were an important part of daily civic life, but differently so from those throughout the Roman empire, because they lacked the gymnasium as an intellectual institution. They offered only recreational exercises, perhaps an occasional public banquet with athletic contests. The local baths were noneducational, leisurely.[49]

Social laxity extending to familial relations was the context in which Augustine freely stole pears. The vineyard and the pear tree were rural neighbors (*vicini*) in a society in which urban associations by street (*vici*)

---

sity Press, 1991), pp. 2-4.

45 Augustine, *Confessiones* 2.3.6; alluding on brambles to Horace, *Epistulae* 14.4-5; and on Hercules among them, to Theocritus, *Idyll* 13.64-65. For the pathetic fallacy see Thomas G. Rosenmayer, *The Green Cabinet: Theocritus and the European Pastoral Lyric* (Berkeley: University of California Press, 1969), p. 184.

46 Aline Rousselle, *Porneia: On Desire and the Body in Antiquity*, trans. Felicia Pheasant (Oxford: Basil Blackwell, 1988), p. 59; Dixon, *Roman Family*, pp. 101-2.

47 Thomas Wiedemann, *Adults and Children in the Roman Empire* (London: Routledge, 1989), p. 139. For puberty in general see Emiel Eyben, *Die jonge Romein: Volgens de literaire bronnen der periode ca. 200 v. Chr. tot*, Verhandelingen van de Koninklijke Academie voor Wetenschappen, Letteren en Schone Kunsten van België, Klasse der Letteren, 81 (Brussels: Paleis der Academiën, 1977), pp. 41-61.

48 See Jérôme Carcopino, *Daily Life in Ancient Rome*, ed. Henry T. Rowell, trans. E. O. Lorimer (New Haven, Conn.: Yale University Press, 1940), p. 254; Maurizio Bettini, *Anthropology and Roman Culture: Kinship, Time, Images of the Soul*, trans. John Van Sickle (Baltimore, Md.: Johns Hopkins University Press, 1991), pp. 10, 12; Eyben, "Fathers and Sons," in *Marriage, Divorce, and Children in Ancient Rome*, ed. Beryl Rawson (Oxford: Clarendon Press for the Humanities Research Center, Australian National University, Canberra, 1991), p. 137 and n. 127.

49 See Fikret Yegül, *Baths and Bathing in Classical Antiquity* (Cambridge, Mass.: M I T Press for the Architectural History Foundation, 1992), pp. 44-45, 184-249, without reference to Augustine. For moral opposition and ambiguity see also pp. 40-42, 314-20.

were vital for collecting a mob, organizing a census, or rallying the populace. At the crossroads youths competed in games with a sense of civic participation, overseen by the lares in the niches of the corners.[50] Augustine related how before robbing the tree he and his companions had prolonged their game in the streets. The social streets of the town of Thagaste, he confessed, coincided with the immoral ways of the city of Babylon, in which he "wallowed in its mud as if in cinnamon." Augustine was tautly attached to the civic "navel" by an invisible enemy seducing his seducible self. His carnal mother, from whose umbilical cord he had been physically severed, had fled from this center of Babylon. But, he complained, she quite stupidly still frequented the rest of it, as if she were not its hard-core citizen but its moral suburbanite. True to her name Monica admonished (*moneo*) Augustine to modesty; yet she failed to allow him the boundary of conjugal affection for his lust. She failed to care because she feared that his hopes of a liberal education would be shackled by wifely fetters.[51] Monica's admonishment to chastity was as ambitious for his rhetorical career as it was pious. For the preservation of a virile voice, "strong, rich, flexible, and firm," Quintilian in his manual on oratory prescribed "abstinence from sex."[52] It was as a potential orator that the Roman child was principally of pedagogic interest, and the mother was a formative influence in grammar and morality toward that end.[53] The attainment of that education both parents of Augustine too strongly designed for him. Augustine blamed his father for thinking nothing about God, inanity about him; his mother, for esteeming the pursuit of erudition no detriment to, and even an aid for, attaining God.[54] She erred, he revealed, because it was in the school of curiosity at Madauros that he learned to imitate Jupiter in fornication.[55]

Such were, he recalled, "the customs of my parents."[56] Parental roles were seldom distinguished by gender in Roman society: both father and mother were firm disciplinarians of the traditional morality, both were involved with and affectionate toward their children.[57] Moralists warned against parental indulgence of adolescent sons, however. They advised fetters and restraints. Boys in their prime were prodigal and restless, needing a curb. Parents who foolishly failed to take the reins with a firm grasp pro-

---

[50] See MacMullen, *Roman Social Relations*, pp. 68-69.

[51] Augustine, *Confessiones* 2.3.8. For some criticisms of his mother see also O'Connell, *St. Augustine's Confessions*, pp. 106-7.

[52] Quintilian, *Institutiones oratoriae* 11.3.19; *Institutio oratoriae*, trans. H. E. Butler, 4 vols. (New York: G. P. Putnam's Sons, 1921), 4:253. On the breaking of the voice see Eyben, *De jonge Romein*, pp. 688-90.

[53] Dixon, *The Roman Mother* (London: Croom Helm, 1987), p. 3. For youth and eloquence see also Eyben, *De jonge Romein*, pp. 292-338.

[54] Augustine, *Confessiones* 2.3.8.

[55] See Boyle, "Augustine in the Garden of Zeus," pp. 119, 123-26.

[56] Augustine, *Confessiones* 2.3.8.

[57] Dixon, *Roman Mother*, pp. 3-4, 131, 233.

vided sons a license for evil.[58] In Augustine's family laxity prevailed. His parents relaxed the reins for his playing (*ludere*) beyond the proper measure of gravity to the looseness of varied affections, he wrote. Play was not just athletic but also sexual. Augustine and his companions of the streets may have prolonged their sport (*ludum. . . producere*), but that verb also means "to beget", "to procreate".[59] The *ludus* was the period of sexual sporting between puberty and youth.[60] Bisexual initiation and experimentation were tolerated. Forbidden was adultery, which undermined a household. Forbidden also, by imperial edict, was a free male, even in the urban brothels, assuming the passive position in a homosexual act. It was unpardonable for a soul assigned to the "sacrosanct dwelling place" of a male body to adopt female poses.[61] Yet, although there was strong bias against passivity for the adult male citizen, boys and slaves could indulge in it if the relationship was voluntary. Sexual issues for the Romans were proprietary: the avoidance of violating personal rights and social rights incurring retribution, and the enhancement of prestige or wealth. Sexual passivity was popularly associated with political impotence, since boys, slaves, and women, who played that role, were excluded from the structures of power.[62] Augustine confessed to "sterile seeds" of lust in transgression of the bonds of friendship. The "overturners" in Carthage whom he frequented were more than a rowdy gang: their overturnings preyed on the modesty of the ignorant, he wrote. Augustine's experience with them was of "flagitious loves," his designation for shameful passionate acts against nature. He admitted his shame at hanging on their company as immodest (*impudicus*),[63] a typical description for illicit sex,[64] a euphemism for homosexual passivity.[65] The precise

---

[58] Eyben, "Fathers and Sons," pp. 125-32.

[59] Augustine, *Confessiones* 2.3.8; 2.4.9.

[60] Eyben, *De jonge Romein*, pp. 469-72; idem, "Fathers and Sons," pp. 127-28.

[61] Peter Brown, *The Body and Society: Men, Women, and Sexual Renunciation in Early Christianity*, Lectures on the History of Religions, 13 (New York: Columbia University Press, 1988), pp. 28, 30, 383; idem, "Bodies and Minds: Sexuality and Renunciation in Early Christianity," in *Before Sexuality: The Construction of Erotic Experience in the Ancient Greek World*, ed. David M. Halperin, John J. Winkler, and Froma I. Zeitlin (Princeton: Princeton University Press, 1990), p. 490; Paul Veyne, "L'homosexualité à Rome," *Communications* 35 (1982):26; Eyben, *Die jonge Romein*, pp. 475-79. For criminal fornication (*stuprum*) see Jane F. Gardner, *Women in Roman Law and Society* (London: Croom Helm, 1986), pp. 121-31. For the toleration of homosexuality and bisexuality see John Boswell, *Christianity, Social Tolerance and Homosexuality: Gay People in Western Europe from the Beginning of the Christian Era to the Fourteenth Century* (Chicago: University of Chicago Press, 1980), pp. 58-59, 63-71, 73, 87.

[62] Boswell, *Christianity, Social Tolerance and Homosexuality*, pp. 62 n. 4, 74-75; Veyne, "La famille et l'amour sous le haut-empire romain," *Annales* 33 (1978):50-51, 56. For moral and social censure see MacMullen, "Roman Attitudes to Greek Love," *Historia* 31 (1982):484-502.

[63] Augustine, *Confessiones* 2.2.2; 3.3.6; 3.1.1; 3.8.15.

[64] J. N. Adams, *The Latin Sexual Vocabulary* (London: Duckworth, 1982), pp. 128, 132.

[65] Veyne, "L'homosexualité à Rome," p. 29; idem, "La famille et l'amour," p. 51.

meaning of *impudicitia* in most texts, those involving the case of a male, was the adoption of the passive position in homosexual relations.[66]

Of the theft of pears Augustine revealed that "the jest was almost in a titillated heart: that we deceived those who did not reckon we would do these things and were forcibly adverse to them." Monica had instructed him against fornication and especially warned him against adultery.[67] Criminal fornication included adultery and incest, and sex with unmarried or widowed women, or with unwilling boys.[68] Augustine also confessed his deed as contrary to divine law. That was no hagiographical topic of a saint bewailing a peccadillo. The theft of pears allegorised the theft of persons. The fruit and the animal to which he thrust it were potent symbols.

The neighborliness of the pear tree to his family vineyard reverted to the classical archetype, the grounds of the palace of king Alkinoös. The excellent garden was that magnificent site in Homer's *Odyssey* to which all literary gardens deferred.[69] In its spacious fenced orchard "there is the place where his fruit trees are grown tall and flourishing." Among them were perfect pears whose fruit never spoiled or failed through the seasons. "Pear matures on pear in that place, apple upon apple, / grape cluster on grape cluster, fig upon fig. There / also he has a vineyard planted." In that enclosure grapes of a fruitful vineyard ripened while others were picked or trodden. "Such are the glorious gifts of the gods at the house of Alkinoös."[70] The pear as the prime tree to produce its fruit symbolized the harvest. The mosaics of Roman north Africa frequently display baskets full of pears.[71] Among its varieties was one called "pride" because it ripened rapidly and was the first to be picked.[72] The pear was sacred to the goddess of the harvest, Demeter,[73] whose Roman cult as Ceres was prolific in north Africa.[74]

---

66 Rousselle, "Personal Status and Sexual Practice in the Roman Empire," trans. Janet Lloyd, in *Fragments for a History of the Human Body*, ed. Michel Feher with Ramona Naddaff and Nadia Tazi, 3 vols. (New York: Zone, 1987), 3:318.

67 Augustine, *Confessiones* 2.9.17; 2.3.7.

68 Gardner, *Women in Roman Law and Society*, pp. 121-31.

69 See A. Bartlett Giamatti, *The Earthly Paradise and the Renaissance Epic* (Princeton: Princeton University Press, 1966), pp. 34-35; Pierre Grimal, *Les jardins romains*, 2d ed. rev. (Paris: Presses Universitaires de France, 1969), pp. 64-65, 69-72.

70 Homer, *Odyssey* 7.114-26, 132; *The Odyssey of Homer*, trans. Richard Lattimore (New York: Harper & Row, 1965), p. 114.

71 Thérèse Précheur-Canonge, *La vie rurale en Afrique romaine d'après les mosaïques*, Publications de l'Université de Tunis, Faculté des lettres, 1re série, archéologie, epigraphie, 6 (Paris: Presses Universitaires de France, n.d.), p. 61.

72 Pliny, *Naturalis historia* 15.15.56. For *pirum* see André, *Lexique des termes de botanique en latin* (Paris: C. Klinksieck, 1956), pp. 251-53.

73 Kurt Lembach, *Die Pflanzen bei Theokrit*, Bibliothek der klassischen Altertumswissenschaften, n. f. 2-37 (Heidelberg: C. Winter, 1970), p. 137, and for the fruit, pp. 137-39.

74 See recently Barbette Stanley Spaeth, "The Goddess Ceres in the Ara Pactis Augustae and the Carthage Relief," *American Journal of Archaeology* 98 (1994):94-100. When the martyr Perpetua was led into the arena at Carthage, she was supposed to vest as a priestess of Ceres. *Passio sanctarum Perpetuae et Felicitatis* 18.

In a bucolic poem celebrating her bounty the pear emerged as a sexual symbol. The poet Simichidas and his companions walked in Theocritus's "Thylasia" from the city of Cos to a farm in the country to be guests for a holiday. Encountering the goatherd Lycidas, the poet exchanged songs in contest. Lycidas with intense passion invented a homosexual wooing. Simichidas sang a serenade about a man inflamed in his bowels and bones for an unwilling boy: "and truly riper than a pear was he." That pear was an erotic metaphor for a person mature for sex; its comparative form indicated that the boy was no longer attractive as a partner. Their poetic contest concluded in the festival of the harvest honoring Demeter. "All things were fragrant of rich harvest and of fruit-time. Pears at our feet and apples at our side were rolling plentifully, and the branches hung down to the ground with their burden of sloes."[75] To be ripe was to be at the prime for love, like fruit ready to fall to the ground. Male fruitage meant bloom or ripeness for love; female fruitage meant virginity. To pluck a female's fruit from the tree was her defloration.[76]

Ancient folk beliefs and customs related the pear to wooing, procreation, and childbirth. Numerous erotic tales in medieval literature seized this symbolism. From the vantage of the pear tree the husband spied on his wife's adultery beneath its foliage; or he even unwittingly boosted her into its limbs, and so into the arms of her lover, as in the ruse of Geoffrey Chaucer's "The Merchant's Tale." The heroine of "Comoedia Lydiae" was seduced in a pear tree. In Chrétien de Troyes's *Cligès* she placed her bed beneath a pear tree, whose falling fruit aroused her to the presence of her lover. In a variation on Eve, Adam, and the apple, the female in Messire Thibaut's *Roman de la poire* offered the male a pear, at whose succulent bite he was overcome by passion. The pear was a symbol for male genitals "grafted" into the female's from the bawdy medieval song "I haue a new garden" to William Shakespeare's *Romeo and Juliet*.[77]

---

75 Theocritus, "Thylasia" 1.120; 1.143-46; *Theocritus*, trans. A. S. F. Gow, 2 vols. (Cambridge: Cambridge University Press, 1950-1952), 1:65, 65-67. For Demeter see lines 31-34, 155-57. For the symbolism of the pear see S. Hatzikosta, *A Stylistic Commentary on Theocritus' Idyll VII*, Classical and Byzantine Monographs, 9 (Amsterdam: Adolf M. Hakkert, 1982), p. 177; and for the idyll, Gilbert Lawall, *Theocritus' Coan Pastorals: A Poetry Book* (Washington, D. C.: Center for Hellenistic Studies, 1967), pp. 9-11, 74-117; G. O. Hutchinson, *Hellenistic Poetry* (Oxford: Clarendon, 1988), pp. 201-12; Halperin, *Before Pastoral: Theocritus and the Ancient Tradition of Bucolic Poetry* (New Haven, Conn.: Yale University Press, 1983), pp. 120-24. For pastoral landscape as literary convention see also J. Vara, "The Sources of Theocritean Bucolic Poetry," trans. Joanna Weatherby, *Mnemosyne* 45 (1991):333-44.

76 Anne Carson, "Putting Her in her Place: Women, Dirt, and Desire," in *Before Sexuality*, ed. Halperin et al., pp. 145-48.

77 Karl P. Wentersdorff, "Imagery, Structure, and Theme in Chaucer's Merchant's Tale," in *Chaucer and the Craft of Fiction*, ed. Leigh A. Arrathoon (Rochester, Mich.: Solaris, 1986), pp. 50-52, 62 n. 55. He also cites "Pamfilio's Story" in Boccaccio's *Decameron*, and naked Cupid hiding in a pear tree in Edmund Spenser, *Shepeardes Calendar*, March 4.5.4-11.

The pastoral with its pears derived its strength from a nature exclusive of society, which it implicitly criticized. The genre originated in a period of social disillusionment as a prominent feature of literature. The republican philosopher Plato sheltered at the wall during the storms of the city-state. His *Phaedrus* displayed the pastoral in its indulgence of nature and in its criticism of society. It censured a prime phenomenon of a corrupt society—sophistry, and its condemnation was uttered in a setting remote from town, in a landscape beneath a plane tree.[78] The philosopher beneath a plane tree[79] contrasted with Augustine the sophist in a pear tree. Social criticism was an important element of the pastoral convention, as Vergil's contribution to the genre. Pastoral served a moral purpose. In a typical pastoral landscape its characters were at rest.[80] "Leisure" (*otium*) was derived from leave from military duty, a vacation,[81] like the rustic picnic concluding Theocritus's idyll.

The vineyard and the pear of Augustine's scene were symbols on north African mosaics of the season of autumn, and so of its harvest.[82] Such a Roman landscape was more amenable than the reality of the wild. The countryside was characterized by its activities of honest toil, vintage, harvest, and the rustic celebration when the ploughman returned home.[83] As Horace praised the gatherer, "When Autumn in the fields has reared his head crowned with ripened fruits, how he delights to pluck the grafted pears." The pears were picked to honor "father Silvanus, guardian of boundaries."[84] Yet Augustine was not honoring boundaries but lacking them. He morally invented an unpastoral scene to extend his criticism of the city of man beyond the human constructions of urbanization to the country of man as naturally rotten. The classical rural landscape was characterized by human activities. Augustine and his companions retraced the commonplace antithesis of the city and the country, like Simichidas and his companions, who walked from the city of Cos to a farm in the country for the celebration of the harvest festival.[85] They were also on holiday, moving in the same urban-to-ru-

---

Some of these references are also cited in Paul Piehler, *The Visionary Landscape: A Study in Medieval Allegory* (London: Edward Arnold, 1971), p. 101 and n. 22; Adams, *Latin Sexual Vocabulary*, p. 29. To them add Juan Ruiz, *Libro de buen amor* 154.

78 Adam Parry, "Landscape in Greek Poetry," *Yale Classical Studies* 15 (1957):14-17; and see Clyde Murley, "Plato's Phaedrus and Theocritean Pastoral," *Transactions of the American Philological Association* 71 (1940):281-95.

79 See Cicero, *De oratore* 1.28-29.

80 See Rosenmayer, *Green Cabinet*, pp. 6, 17, 67.

81 Jean-Marie André, *L'otium dans la vie morale et intellectuelle romaine des origines à l'époque augustéenne* (Paris: Presses Universitaires de France, 1966), p. 10.

82 David Parrish, *Season Mosaics of Roman North Africa*, Archaeologica, 46 (Rome: Giorgio Bretschneider, 1984), pp. 38-40; see also Précheur-Canonge, *Vie rurale en Afrique romaine d'après des mosaïques*, pp. 53-60.

83 Nicholas Purcell, "Town and Country and Country in Town," in *Ancient Roman Villa Gardens*, ed. MacDougall, p. 202.

84 Horace, *Epodes* 2. 17-19, 21-22; *The Odes and Epodes*, trans. C. E. Bennett (Cambridge, Mass.: Harvard University Press, 1964), p. 365.

85 See Lawall, *Theocritus' Coan Pastorals*, p. 9.

ral direction, but restlessly on the prowl. Augustine confessed not rest but fatigue, sexual lassitude.[86] That was the medical sign of debauchery, in which the vital spirit, from which the brain formed the psychic spirit, drained away in the sperm. Fatigue, not desire, impelled the aristocratic clientele to their physicians.[87]

The typical time in pastoral was noon, when the sun burned too hot for comfort and all nature seemed suspended.[88] Augustine and companions acted in unpastoral time, at the dead of night.[89] Sexual temptation was considered stronger in the dark, and Romans made love with the lights off just before going to sleep, as recommended by physicians.[90] The particular hour of the dead of night was classically associated with hiding in the wood.[91] Night outdoors in the Roman empire was lit only by celestial lamps. There were in cities and towns no burning oil lamps or candles in sconces, no lanterns above the lintels, except during the resplendence of festivals. The populace fled home, shut the gate, barricaded the door, and closed the shutters. The rich might sally forth for dinner accompanied by torches carried by slaves and pass the night watch on patrol. Ordinary persons did not venture outdoors without reluctance and apprehension. A satirist advised making one's will first; the legal digests recorded murderers, housebreakers, and footpads abroad. Night was not only dark but also noisy, even in Thagaste. By imperial decree, extending from Rome to every city and town in disregard of its municipal statutes, no vehicles were permitted from sunrise to dusk except for the carts of building contractors. So at night beasts of burden and carts with drivers and escorts filled the streets with a racket of hooves, feet, and wheels. Being in the streets Augustine was necessarily in the mud, for even the city of Rome was unpaved.[92] Secondary roads in north Africa were unmarked, often unrecognizable, especially at night and in the wood,[93] so that a nocturnal trek from the city to the country forebode danger.

The presence of animals marked a scene as pastoral. A pastoral animal was typically a companion in a desegregation that made it a sibling of humans.[94] Humans harmonized with beasts; the emotions of herdsmen like Lycidas compared with the feelings of animals, like goats frisky for love.[95]

---

[86] Augustine, *Confessiones* 2.2.2.

[87] See Rousselle, *Porneia*, p. 15. For *lasso* see Adams, *Latin Sexual Vocabulary*, p. 196.

[88] Lawall, *Theocritus' Coan Pastorals*, pp. 67, 76, 88-89.

[89] Augustine, *Confessiones* 2.4.9.

[90] Rousselle, "Personal Status and Sexual Practice," p. 303.

[91] Vergil, *Aeneid* 3.587.

[92] See Carcopino, *Daily Life in Ancient Rome*, pp. 47-51.

[93] A.-G. Hamman, *La vie quotidienne en Afrique du nord au temps de saint Augustin*, new ed. (Paris: Hachette, 1985), p. 84.

[94] Rosenmayer, *Green Cabinet*, pp. 131, 138.

[95] Lawall, *Theocritus' Coan Pastorals*, p. 7.

Animals as mere embodiments of sexual instinct were at the periphery of the genre,[96] however. In his initial confrontation with nature, over which Adam was given dominion (Gen. 1:28-30), Augustine herded animals to the center of his unpastoral criticism. He compared himself as itchy with lust to a cattle infested with scabies.[97] That was a very contagious disease of cattle and sheep due to an acarine parasite, although Roman agronomists erroneously diagnosed its cause as the cold and the wet.[98] Females have gotten under Augustine's skin, for the cold and the wet were their humoral dispositions in classical medicine. The soundest human condition for the perception and discipline necessary to intelligence was hot and dry: to be male. Emotions were wet, especially the erotic liquid that poured, dripped, heated, softened, melted, loosened, cooked, boiled, and dissolved. Women as emotional creatures, wet and cold,[99] were prone to infect a poor brute like Augustine with the itch.

They intruded on his muddy scene as pigs. Animal behavior was a classical comparison for human vice, as in an imperial edict thundering against those who "rushed into illicit unions in the promiscuous manner of farm animals or wild beasts, driven by execrable lust, with no regard for decency or righteousness."[100] Behaviorally pigs are indeed like people. As carnivores they solicit and enjoy bodily contact with other members of their family circle. Pigs huddle together, perhaps in relation to their method of reproduction, for their litters are large. Both sexes root out molds and wallows for rest, and in them the female builds a nest from twigs and grasses in which to farrow. The mother communicates with her piglets by nuzzles and vocalizations.[101] Pigs are also prolific. Sows in antiquity had litters of a dozen or more, although good breeders limited them to eight.[102] For a healthy farrow it was important that the boar be as lustful as possible in copulation.[103]

In Augustine's unpastoral scene throwing pears to pigs was a metaphor for sexual intercourse. The word "pig" was colloquial for the female genitals. As Varro explained in *De agri cultura*, "Our women, and especially

---

96 Rosenmayer, *Green Cabinet*, p. 141.

97 Augustine, *Confessiones* 3.2.4, 9.1.1.

98 Thomas Fletcher Royds, *The Beasts, Birds, and Bees of Virgil: A Naturalist's Handbook to the Georgics*, 2d ed. rev. (Oxford: Basil Blackwell, 1918), pp. 15, 22-23.

99 See Carson, "Putting Her in her Place," pp. 137-45; Brown, *Body and Society*, pp. 10, 18; Rousselle, *Porneia*, p. 59, all without reference to Augustine. See also G. E. R. Lloyd, "The Hot and the Cold, the Dry and the Wet in Greek Philosophy," *Journal of Hellenic Studies* 84 (1964):92-106; and for warmth as the essential factor in sexual differentiation, Jan Blayney, "Theories of Conception in the Roman World," in *The Family in Ancient Rome: New Perspectives*, ed. Rawson (London: Croom Helm, 1986), pp. 234-35.

100 Cited by Gardner, *Women in Roman Law and Society*, p. 36.

101 Janet Clutton-Brock, *Domesticated Animals from Early Times* (London: Heinemann/British Museum [Natural History], 1981), p. 73.

102 K. D. White, *Roman Farming* (London: Thames & Hudson, 1970), p. 317.

103 Columella, *Rei rustica* 7.9.1.

nurses, call that part which is in girls the mark of their sex *porcus*, as Greek women call it *choeros*, meaning thereby that it is a distinctive part mature enough for marriage."[104] At least one prostitute was called Sucula, "little sow," as attested by the electoral endorsement of an aedile.[105] In renaissance Italy the most common animal insult for women as sexual creatures would still be "sow."[106] Augustine and his companions did not literally throw pears at pigs. Pelting with fruits was classically proverbial. As Erasmus compiled its usage in his *Adagia*, it was "a phrase used of those who try to get what they want in return for gifts, or who give presents to a loved one to arouse love in return," or simply, "when an attempt is made to secure someone's affections, and an invitation is issued."[107] Before civilization Venus joined lovers: the male raped the female or bribed her with "choice pears."[108] Augustine and his companions projected and thrust (*proicio*) their male genitals at female genitals. The theft of pears was property but the essential social property of sexuality.

Theft was a classical delict. Since the decimviral legislation, a minor who damaged another's crop, as by pasturing animals on it stealthily by night, was subject to flogging or to payment of damages. In its development, if he were legally independent, he would be charged as an adult with capital punishment. If he were in his father's power, injurious proceedings would be instituted against the father, who could either surrender his son to the victim or defend the action and pay damages. The youth under the age of twenty five had no special position or protection in liability or penalty in delictal law.[109] Augustine's father would have been answerable in court for his son's misdeed, if it were literally theft. There was one sexual offense defined as theft that involved his imagery of fruits and animals. That concerned the notion of slaves as livestock. Like other properties, slaves legally produced "fruits," abstractly as profits for their owners. The produce of the females was children, as comparable to the yield of plants and the increase of animals. Under the law of usufruct those children were "fruits" be-

---

[104] Varro, *De agri cultura* 2.4.10; trans. Harrison Boyd Ash (Cambridge, Mass.: Harvard University Press, 1960), p. 357. Although my discovery was directly from Varro, the philology is also noted, although without reference to Augustine, by Adams, *Latin Sexual Vocabulary*, p. 82, who gives Greek parallels; and by Jacques André, "Recherches étymologiques sur certains noms de plantes latins," *Latomus* 22 (1963):299-300. For women as animals see Amy Richlin, "Invective against Women in Roman Satire," *Arethusa* 17 (1984):70-71.

[105] Cited by Sarah B. Pomeroy, *Goddesses, Whores, Wives, and Slaves: Women in Classical Antiquity* (New York: Schocken, 1975), p. 201.

[106] Peter Burke, *The Historical Anthropology of Early Modern Italy: Essays on Perception and Communication* (Cambridge: Cambridge University Press, 1987), p. 97.

[107] "Malis ferire" in Erasmus, *Adagia* 2.4.70; *The Collected Works of Erasmus*, trans. R. A. B. Mynors (Toronto: University of Toronto Press, 1991), 33:226.

[108] Wentersdorf, "Imagery, Structure, and Theme in Chaucer's Merchant's Tale," p. 51.

[109] J. A. C. Thomas, "Delictal and Criminal Liability of the Young in Roman Law," *Recueils de la Société Jean Bodin* 38 (1977):10-12, 23.

longing to the slaveholder.[110] Masters had legal right to their slaves for sexual relations, or abuses.[111] Neighbors did not. The delictal theft as fornication by Augustine and his companions perhaps concerned the slaves of a neighboring household.

As a bishop Augustine justified the institution of slavery: owning slaves was a right and like other property rights it was determined by the political authority and subject to its laws. Yet he believed that the relationship of authority and obedience was tainted since the fall of Adam by the lust to dominate others. "The most conspicuous and everyday example of the power of one man over another is the power of a master over his slave. Nearly all households have this type of power," he wrote. While he considered the subordination of slavery a punishment for original sin, he taught that a master was to love a slave as a brother. It was detestable to hold him as a beast, to possess him as an animal; he should consider his good.[112] Slave boys were abused by their masters, either castrated or delayed in their sexual development by mechanical, physical, or magical techniques. Girls could be chosen and raised to be concubines, attaining legal status at age twelve.[113] Augustine raged against the compounded sin of fornication between masters and slaves. It was not an illegal act, however, not fornication in Roman jurisprudence. Augustine posited a conflict between the human and divine laws. He preached that a master's resort to an enslaved concubine was as sinful as his resort to a prostitute. As he posed the case: "'The woman whom I keep is my own serving maid. May I no longer do what I please in my own house?'" No, replied Augustine. Go to hell and burn in everlasting fire.[114] Wickeder still would have been the offense of neighbors, who lacked even legal rights to sexual relations with slaves not of their own household.

Augustine's encounter with the pigs parodied Odysseus's entry into manhood as a feast and a boar hunt.[115] Agricultural metaphors were common

---

110 Gardner, *Women in Roman Law and Society*, pp. 209-10. For slaves and animals as property of their master see also Peter Birks, "An Unacceptable Face of Human Property," in *New Perspectives in the Roman Law of Property: Essays for Barry Nicholas*, ed. idem (Oxford: Oxford University Press, 1989), pp. 61-73.

111 See William D. Phillips, Jr., *Slavery from Roman Times to the Early Transatlantic Trade* (Minneapolis: University of Minnesota Press, 1985), pp. 24-25; Keith R. Bradley, *Slaves and Masters in the Roman Empire: A Study in Social Control*, Collection Latomus, 185 (Brussels: Latomus, 1984), pp. 116-18.

112 Gervase Corcoran, *Saint Augustine on Slavery*, Studia Ephemeridis "Augustinianum," 22 (Rome: Institutum Patristicum "Augustinianum," 1985), pp. 55-86, 30, 32, 22, citing Augustine, *Enarrationes in psalmos* 124.7, 34.

113 Rousselle, "Personal Status and Sexual Practice," pp. 313-14, 312. On the sexual access of masters to domestic slaves see also Phillips, *Slavery*, pp. 24-25.

114 F. van der Meer, *Augustine the Bishop: The Life and Work of a Father of the Church*, trans. Brian Battershaw and G. R. Lamb (London: Sheed & Ward, 1961), pp. 135, 181, citing Augustine, *Sermones* 224.3; Corcoran, *Saint Augustine on Slavery*, pp. 10, 29-30.

115 For Odysseus and for other examples of the youthful pursuits of males in agonistic

for sexuality, with the field, meadow, orchard, or garden for the female; and the instruments that worked the land, like the plough, for the male. Eating was a sexual metaphor, and to enjoy fruit was its pleasure. Theft was a frequent metaphor in amatory poets like Catullus, Vergil, and Ovid for illicit intercourse such as adultery or incest.[116] Another comparison implied in Augustine's criticism was the tilling of the land as juxtaposed to the culture of the mind: just as a field could not be fruitful without cultivation, so a spirit would be fallow without learning.[117] Pigs were illiterate and unteachable, the antithesis of human culture, as in Cicero's phrase "products of the sty, not of the school," or the adage "the sow teaches Minerva."[118] Augustine portrayed himself as so deeply penetrating the grove of sexuality that he was metamorphosing to vegetation, daring to "grow to wood (*silvescere*) in various and shady loves."[119] The wood (*silva*) was primal matter, or chaos,[120] in which he was formless.[121] There in the wood he encountered pigs—women—who epitomized primal formlessness: *mater* was from *materia.* The mud in which pigs wallowed was a female place, for women were dirt, as matter out of place.[122] The proper ground for raising pigs in antiquity was wet, even muddy. As Varro wrote, "At the time of breeding they are driven into muddy lanes and pools so that they may wallow in the mud; for this is their form of refreshment, as bathing is to human beings."[123] Pigs loved to wallow in mud, root in marshes, and dig for worms; at pasturage they behaved filthily.[124] The companions of Odysseus were metamorphosed by woman as Circe into such swine.[125] Augustine, only cleansed superficially at the public baths, wallowed in the mud of the civic streets with a pleasure that identified him also as porcine.

The sexual meaning of "pig" Varro traced to the Etruscan custom of the bride and bridegroom at the beginning of the nuptial rites first sacrificing a

---

activity see Judith P. Hallett, *Fathers and Daughters in Roman Society: Women and the Elite Family* (Princeton: Princeton University Press, 1984), p. 296; for hunting in youth see also Eyben, *De jonge Romein*, pp. 139-40.

116 Adams, *Latin Sexual Vocabulary*, pp. 82-83, 113, 138-41, 198, 167-68, 254.

117 Rosenmayer, *Green Cabinet*, pp. 182, 320-321 n. 11.

118 "Sus Minervam" in Erasmus, *Adagia* 1.1.40, citing Cicero, *In L. Pisonem* 16.37 and other references; *The Collected Works of Erasmus*, trans. Margaret Mann Phillips (Toronto: Univer sity of Toronto Press, 1982), 31:88-90.

119 Augustine, *Confessiones* 2.1.1.

120 In Chalcidius's translation of Plato's *Timaeus* at 123, "matter" became *silva*.

121 Augustine defined chaos as formless in *De Genesi ad litteram* 1:2.

122 For women as dirt see Carson, "Putting Her in Her Place," pp. 158-60; Richlin, "Invective against Women in Roman Satire," p. 73. For female foulness see also idem, *The Garden of Priapus: Sexuality and Aggression in Roman Humor* (New Haven, Conn.: Yale University Press, 1983), pp. 26-30.

123 Varro, *De agri cultura* 2.4.5; 2.4.8; trans. Ash, p. 355.

124 Columella, *Rei rustica* 7.9.1; 7.9.7.

125 For Augustine on Circe see Bernhard Paetz, *Kirke und Odysseus: Überlieferung und Deutung von Homer bis Calderón*, Hamburger romantische Studien, 33 (Berlin: Walter de Gruyter, 1970), pp. 40-43.

sow.[126] Pigs were bred for food and for sacrifice; their slaughter in cult was as important as at the butcher. Oaths, treaties, and promises were commonly sworn in Roman society on a pig. Varro strained to derive "pig" in Greek from the verb "to sacrifice", since the initial victims were swine. They were sacrificed not only in the nuptial rites, but also to the lares, the household gods. A sow was included in the *suovetaurilia*, the most solemn of all offerings. Pigs were especially sacrificed in the initiatory rites to Ceres, the *porca praecidanea*, the entrails offered to her before harvesting the common crops.[127] As goddess of the harvest she ensured the fertility of the fields and also as goddess of marriage, the fecundity of women. It was to Ceres that imperial women were most frequently assimilated to promote fertility and nurture, thus the Roman birthrate. Her priestesses were the only women besides the vestals who administered a state cult, a religion devoted to agrarian prosperity.[128] Before Ceres the pig, like the pear, was sacred to Demeter, who may have taken its form. In ritual it was either dropped by its tail into a crevice to rot or prepared and consumed sacrificially. The Eleusinian mysteries revered it as its cultic animal.[129]

The pig is still prestigious in Mediterranean locales where the vestiges of pre-Indo-European culture remain. The animal belongs in the substrates of its cultural history, since the Egyptian god Set, the eldest god who suffered degradation by upstart divinities, identified with the pig. In a north African context the Roman associations of the pig with fertility and harvest darken, for Set was the personification of evil. Swineherds were the most despised class in Egypt, forbidden to enter any temple. They were unmarriageable except among themselves, with the innuendoes that intermarriage occasioned. A person who touched a pig had to bathe in a river to cleanse its taint. The once sacred animal became abominated.[130] Pigs were used for

---

126 Varro, *De agri cultura* 2.4.10. On the porcine sacrifice at marriage see also Carcopino, *Daily Life in Ancient Rome*, pp. 81-82; J. P. V. D. Balsdon, *Roman Women: Their History and Habits* (London: Bodley Head, 1962), p. 183. For ritual and verbal association in anthropology between eating animals such as pigs and sexual intercourse see Edmund Leach, "Anthropological Aspects of Language: Animal Categories and Verbal Abuse," in *New Directions in the Study of Language*, ed. Eric H. Lennenberg (Cambridge, Mass.: M I T Press, 1964), pp. 42-44, 50-51.

127 J. M. C. Toynbee, *Animals in Roman Life and Art* (London: Thames & Hudson, 1973), pp. 16, 164, 134-35; White, *Roman Farming*, p. 320; Carl Otto Sauer, *Agricultural Origins and Dispersals: The Domestication of Animals and Foodstuffs*, 2d ed. (Cambridge, Mass.: Massachusetts Institute of Technology Press, 1969), pp. 33, 38; Friedrich Zeuner, *A History of Domesticated Animals* (London: Hutchison, 1963), pp. 263-64. For the *porca praecidanea* see also Henri Le Bonniec, *Le culte de Cérès à Rome: Des origines à la fin de la république*, Études et commentaires, 27 (Paris: C. Klincksieck, 1958), pp. 148-57.

128 Pomeroy, *Goddesses, Whores, Wives, and Slaves*, pp. 184, 214.

129 Sauer, *Agricultural Origins and Dispersals*, pp. 37-38; Marcel Detienne, "The Violence of Wellborn Ladies," in idem and Vernant, *The Cuisine of Sacrifice among the Greeks*, trans. Paula Wissing (Chicago: University of Chicago Press, 1989), pp. 134-35; Pomeroy, *Goddesses, Whores, Wives, and Slaves*, pp. 215, 217.

130 Hellmut Epstein, *The Origin of the Domestic Animals of Africa*, 2 vols. (New York:

treading seed into the soil and trampling out the grain on the threshing floor[131] but they were taboo to be eaten.[132] Augustine conflated the porcine traditions to blame sex as evil ritual. All sin, he deliberated on pelting pigs with pears, mimicked worship perversely.[133]

North Africa had a plentiful supply of wild tusked boars and sows. They were also kept in private parks for hunting—for sport or for provision, as in the capture depicted on a Carthaginian mosaic. Capture alive portended display in the amphitheater, perhaps in a sparring match with a bear.[134] Domestic pigs all descended from this single species, *sus scrofa*, the wild boar that is still common in the area.[135] Before Islam the pig played a predominant role in the north African economy.[136] Smaller kinds of pigs were reared and maintained on farms for consumption and for breeding.[137] "Who of our people cultivates a farm without keeping swine?" Varro asked rhetorically. As he moralized, it was lazy and expensive to purchase pork at a butcher's shop.[138] The agronomist lavished more attention on swine than on any other domestic animal. Pork was the preferred meat of the Romans,[139] the richest and most nourishing according to the physicians.[140] The populace was freely rationed five pounds of it.[141] Most of the animals were dispatched either as mature or suckling pigs to the butcher in town for preparation as pork, ham, and sausages.[142] The roast was the customary main dish at a feast,[143] since "the race of pigs is expressly given by nature to set forth a banquet."[144] Trimalchio's dinner party in Petronius's *Satyricon* featured an elaborately garnished sow stuffed with live birds that flew out

---

Africana, 1971), 2:37, 342-43. (The pig had been sacred to Isis, whose devotees wore amulets in the shape of a sow.) See also Mary Douglas, *Purity and Danger: An Analysis of the Concepts of Pollution and Taboo* (London: Ark, 1984), p. 55.

131 Lewis, *Life in Egypt under Roman Rule*, p. 131.

132 H. S. Smith, "Animal Domestication and Animal Cult in Dynastic Egypt," in Peter J. Ucko and G. W. Dimbleby, *The Domestication and Exploitation of Plants and Animals* (London: Gerald Duckworth, 1969), pp. 312-13.

133 Augustine, *Confessiones* 2.6.13-14.

134 Toynbee, *Animals in Roman Life and Art*, pp. 131, 132-33, 134. The boar with reference to the hunt typified winter in north African seasonal mosaics. Parrish, *Season Mosaics of Roman North Africa*, p. 26.

135 Clutton-Brock, *Domesticated Animals from Early Times*, p. 71; Sauer, *Agricultural Origins and Dispersals*, p. 35.

136 Epstein, *Origin of the Domestic Animals of Africa*, 2:330.

137 Toynbee, *Animals in Roman Life and Art*, pp. 132, 15.

138 Varro, *De agri cultura* 2.4.3; trans. Ash, p. 353.

139 White, *Roman Farming*, pp. 316, 320-21; Sauer, *Agricultural Origins and Dispersals*, p. 38.

140 Rousselle, *Porneia*, p. 16.

141 Jones, *Later Roman Empire*, 2:702-3.

142 Toynbee, *Animals in Roman Life and Art*, pp. 132, 15.

143 Sauer, *Agricultural Origins and Dispersals*, p. 38; Zeuner, *History of Domesticated Animals*, p. 263.

144 Varro, *De agri cultura* 2.4.10; trans. Ash, p. 357.

when it was carved.[145]

In Proconsularis the land except for woods was converted to pasture for breeding stock,[146] as Augustine mentioned in connection with wealth.[147] His encounter with pigs had verisimilitude, but only that. The pig was indeed associated with the vine and the pear. The catalogue of the groves in which it pastured included the tendrils of vines and emphasized wild pears.[148] Pastured on mast, pigs were fattened for the table on beans and grains but for prime condition on pears, apples, figs, and nuts.[149] They were also fed on the farm the dregs of wine and grapes,[150] whose vines their manure was used to fertilize.[151] Yet pears literarily thrown by Augustine were as useless to the animals as they were to the humans who picked them. In captivity pigs did not require feeding at night. Swine were also inaccessible at night, even to a gang. There were in antiquity two methods of husbandry for pigs: large herds roamed in forests tended by a swineherd armed with a stick or they were kept in sties to exit at the sound of a horn for their spread of barley.[152] But even the pigs pastured in the forests returned to the sties at night.[153] Swine were not penned together but separated in colonnaded sties, for fear that the sows would lie on top of one another, causing abortions.[154] For Augustine's deed to have been literal, he and his companions would have had to open each sty individually to toss a pear to each pig. More improbable yet would have been circumventing the swineherd in whose charge they snored. When Odysseus, whose wanderings Augustine in his *Confessions* imitated, approached his own farm, four noisy, vicious dogs who guarded the pigs beset him. And the ancestral swineherd Eumaios had constructed around their yard high walls of quarried stone topped with a hedge of wild pear.[155]

Eumaios in welcoming Odysseus sacrificed a pig at his domestic hearth to its goddess Hestia. He observed the ritual of throwing a hog's hair into the fire and praying, laid the first raw cut from all the limbs, then threw it into the flames with a sprinkling of barley meal. He set aside a cooked por-

---

145 Toynbee, *Animals in Roman Life and Art*, p. 132; Carcopino, *Daily Life in Ancient Rome*, p. 268.

146 Warmington, *North African Provinces*, p. 64.

147 Augustine, *Sermones* 239.6; 311.14.13; *Enarrationes in psalmos* 38.13; 53.7, cited by Marie Madeleine Getty, *The Life of the North Africans as Revealed in the Sermons of St. Augustine*, Catholic University of America Patristic Studies, 28 (Washington, D. C.: Catholic University of America Press, 1931), pp. 8-9.

148 Columella, *Rei rusticae* 7.9.6; see also 7.9.8.

149 White, *Roman Farming*, pp. 318-19.

150 Varro, *De agri cultura* 2.4.17.

151 White, *Roman Farming*, p. 321.

152 See Clutton-Brock, *Domesticated Animals from Early Times*, pp. 74, 75, 74.

153 Vergil, *Georgics* 2.520 and see in the edition pp. 173, 220-21.

154 Columella, *Rei rusticae* 7.9.9.

155 Homer, *Odyssey* 14.23-24, 7-10. For Eumaios as the archetypal swineherd see Varro, *De agri cultura* 2.4.1.

tion as an offering, sacrificing the prime cuts to the hearth and the gods with a libation of sparkling wine.[156] The anti-hero Augustine was also ritualizing pigs, but unlike Odysseus, or Aeneas, who slew a prodigious white sow with thirty piglets when he landed on the Italian coast.[157] Augustine was also landed, and in the archetypal site of an orchard, but undefined by borders. Like the females he frequented, he was formless, unbounded. The brambles of lust surpassed the limits of his head, with its faculty of judgment. But no one in his family uprooted the brambles from his mind,[158] as a bailiff from the land.[159] Augustine and his unpastoral companions had homes, and that was their shame; for the family provided them no boundaries, and so they stole the property of neighbors. Augustine was denied marriage as a boundary (*terminus*) to his lust.[160] That was the stone or wooden stake as a phallic symbol[161] marking boundaries in rural agricultural practice. Familial fields were separated from other domains by an enclosure, a swath of uncultivated soil several-feet wide. By law it was consecrated ground. The father of the household traced its outline on appointed days, driving sacrificial victims before him as he sang hymns. On route he placed markers garlanded with herbs and flowers next to a dug hole. A fire was lit, a victim sacrificed. Its blood flowed into the hole, followed by glowing coals to consume offerings of grain, cake, fruit, wine, and honey. When the ashes were merely warm, the boundary was ritually set in place. Its violation by the touch of human or beast was sacrilegious, requiring the expiation of an immolation.[162] Such was marriage as the limit to the field of his sexual ploughing that Augustine's mother denied him.

Friendship also failed him as a different boundary, the *limes*[163] or system of permanent defenses along the frontiers of the Roman empire. The word denoted not only the material barrier to exclude barbarians—either natural like the Rhine on the boundary of Gaul, or artificial like Hadrian's wall in Britain—but also the forts, camps, and roads behind the line, and the outposts and signal towers in advance of it. The *limes* was an in-depth system of defense. The outposts and barriers controlled movement on the frontiers and delayed attack until reserves could be moved forward from behind the line. A substantial barrier effectively protected settlement from the frequent

---

156 Homer, *Odyssey* 14.414-56. Edward Kadletz, "The Sacrifice of Eumaios the Pig Herder," *Greek, Roman and Byzantine Studies* 25 (1984):99-105; A. Petrapoulou, "The Sacrifice of Eumaeus Reconsidered," ibid. 28 (1987): 135-49.

157 See Toynbee, *Animals in Roman Life and Art*, p. 131.

158 Augustine, *Confessiones* 2.3.6. For *caput* as a frequent euphemism for glans see Adams, *Latin Sexual Vocabulary*, pp. 72, 80, 212 n. 1.

159 Horace, *Epistulae* 14.4-5.

160 Augustine, *Confessiones* 2.3.8.

161 Adams, *Latin Sexual Vocabulary*, p. 23.

162 Della Volpe, "From the Hearth to the Creation of Boundaries," pp. 172-73, 174, 175.

163 Augustine, *Confessiones* 2.2.2.

small, but destructive, raids. North Africa had a long southern frontier without natural barriers. The task of defending it, too enormous for the regular imperial army, was entrusted to the *limitanei*, men granted land there on the condition that they would defend it when called upon. Originally they were probably veterans from the troops already garrisoning the frontier, and their sons; later, the very barbarians. Their organization was paramilitary.[164] The model may have informed the monastery that Augustine established as a fortification against the encroachment of the human city. In his dichotomous mentality he drew strict boundaries. Friendship was the boundary, "the luminous limit," like the torches and flares on the north African frontier, that failed to check his lust. In lust he was plunged into the dark. Flowing down erotically from God, he wandered off the highway from divine stability and he became for himself a boundary-line (*regio*) of necessity.[165]

Necessity, not as indigence but as connection, compelled Roman society. Augustine imitated the original sin of Adam by stealing the pears not autonomously but socially. In his examination of conscience he would not have done the deed alone: he did it for applause.[166] Adam's sin he defined as "social necessity." (A current euphemism for the penis was "the necessity".)[167] Augustine's sexual sinning began at home where he was living with his parents "from domestic necessity." His father Patricius could ill afford financially to further his rhetorical education, but needed to borrow money from an aristocrat, an investment in his son's talent universally extolled with praises.[168] Yet Patricius was the generic Roman father, the *pater* as applied since archaic formulas to the most venerable and ancient gods of Rome. His anonymous name derived from the paternal litany: the *patronus* who protected the client; the *patres* as the council of elders; the *patres familiae* as the individual heads of household; the *patricii* as the aristocracy; their possessions, the *patrimonium*, the legal status of fatherhood and the inheritance of male property; their authority, the *patria potestas*, the father's legal power of life and death over his household; and finally, their collective action, *patro*, "to behave like a father", which denoted bringing to completion, achieving one's desires, and sexually reaching orgasm.[169] Patricius was the male stereotype.

Augustine regarded the household in traditional terms as originating in copulation and descending from the father in a chain of power. The domi-

---

164 Warmington, *North African Provinces*, pp. 20, 23-24.
165 Augustine, *Confessiones* 2.10.18.
166 Ibid. 2.9.17.
167 See Adams, *Latin Sexual Vocabulary*, pp. 61-62; Brown, "Bodies and Minds," p. 482.
168 Augustine, *Confessiones* 2.3.5.
169 For the terms see Hallett, *Fathers and Daughters in Roman Society*, pp. 26, 27-28; Adams, *Latin Sexual Vocabulary*, pp. 142-43.

nant relation in the home was father-to-son, strongly bilateral in economic dependency and firmly established in discipline.[170] Patricius's remarkable borrowing of educational funds as a token of paternal faith in his son was, however, but a parody of Horace's praise of his own father. That satirist had declared that, if his life was stainless and guiltless, and if he was loved by his friends, "I owe this to my father." Although his father, as the son of a freedman "poor with a starveling farm," refused to send Horace to the local school for the sons of grand centurions, he more boldly took him to Rome to be educated among the sons of knights and senators. From Horace's attire and retinue anyone would have supposed the expense was paid from ancestral wealth. Horace praised his father as a faithful guardian who accompanied him among all his teachers (by implication, not abandoning him to pederasty). "He kept me chaste—and this is virtue's first grace—free not only from every deed of shame, but from all scandal."[171] Augustine's shift from the school at Madauros to that of Carthage mimicked Horace's social climb but hardly praised his father's virtue. He frankly blamed him as unchaste: unfaithful to his wife and unconcerned about his son's chastity. In providing educational funds that wealthier fathers denied their sons he ensured that Augustine became a dissertator; or rather, he complained, a deserter from the divine culture of God as the true and good lord of the field of his heart.[172]

Nor did his father alleviate him, as Horace's had, for a life "free from the burden of unhappy ambition," so that he could live "not by a father's fame, but by blamelessness of heart and life."[173] Proconsularis was the highest ranking of the African provinces, its proconsulate subordinate directly to the emperor. It was the place for the senatorial aristocracy to be launched in their careers. The curial class, in which Augustine's initial biographer located his father, had the local responsibilities for communal finances and for maintaining roads, bridges, and public buildings. Certain offices by custom or law required large expenditures for public amusement. The imperial administration added to that numerous further charges, especially the assessment and collection of taxes, with personal responsibility for any deficit. The men of the curia also arranged the imperial postal service and supplies for the army; in Africa they also collected the annual produce shipped to

---

170 Brent D. Shaw, "The Family in Late Antiquity: The Experience of Augustine," *Past and Present* 115 (1987):11-12, 19-26. See also Bradley, "Child Care at Rome: The Role of Men," in idem, *Discovering the Roman Family: Studies in Roman Social History* (New York: Oxford University Press, 1991), pp. 37-55; and for morals and family life, also Gilbert Charles-Picard, *Civilisation de l'Afrique romaine* (Paris: Plon, 1959), pp. 278-89.

171 Horace, *Saturae* 1.6.66-88; *Satires, Epistles, and Ars poetica*, trans. H. Rushton Fairclough (New York: G. P. Putnam's Sons, 1929), p. 83. See also Bernard Stenuit, "Les parents d'Horace," *Les études classiques* 45 (1977):125-47.

172 Augustine, *Confessiones* 2.3.5.

173 Horace, *Saturae* 1.6.129; 1.6.64; trans. Fairclough, pp. 87, 81.

Rome as taxation.[174]

Formidable laws prevented any social movement of that class before twenty-five years of dutiful service and progression through its ranks. In a political commonplace the restriction was essential to the state. The curials fled from their oppression, also motivated by personal ambition. The majority of officials of the higher and lower grades of the liberal professions were recruited from that class. The curial office was hereditary. Its hereditary obligation debarred young men, even the wealthy, from social advancement. To remain in the curia meant at most advancing to the class of principals. Desertion to the army was common, and bribery to obtain honorary titles granting immunity or entry into the senatorial class was practiced. Laws multiplied to obstruct those methods, only to be evaded. The determination of the municipal aristocracy to liberate themselves and their descendents from profitless labor and unhonored position was reflected in Patricius's financial debt to advance his son Augustine in a career of rhetoric.[175] Because of their service to the community, public professors were exempt from municipal charges.[176] As a rhetor Augustine would have been released from the paternal inheritance of the curial class.

The epideictic rhetoric of his *Confessions*, in the classical genre for praise and blame,[177] was not documentary evidence of social history. His evaluation of his family was moral, not empirical, and he criticized its household as typical. Augustine's familial portrait of the immoral landowner and his son indicted a fundamental disorientation of place in the Roman empire. The land was the primal creation, the paradise, corrupted by Adam's sin of "social necessity." Original sin was perpetuated by Roman civil servants and perpetrated by Augustine as a decurion's son. The curia, to which Augustine's father belonged, was a class of landowners. Although its members formed a single juridical class of privilege and obligation in a broad socioeconomic range, qualifications were origin or domicile in the city, free birth, and property—normally land. The amount of land varied from city to city, so that the richest inhabitant of a town like Thagaste could be impecunious compared to a decurion of the city of Carthage.[178] In north Africa the curia was a plebeian association in which officers paid for

---

174 Warmington, *North African Provinces*, pp. 2, 47.

175 Ibid., pp. 47-50. For the desertion of curias see also Lepelley, *Cités de l'Afrique romaine*, 1:243-92; for Augustine on a curial see *De cura pro mortuis agenda* 12.15, and on the curia, *Enarrationes in psalmos* 75.1; and also Tadeusz Kotula, *Les curies municipales en Afrique romaine*, Travaux de la Société des sciences et des lettres de Breslau A, 128 (Breslau: n. p., 1968), pp. 135-37.

176 Lepelley, *Cités de l'Afrique romaine*, pp. 177, 228-30.

177 Boyle, "The Prudential Augustine: The Virtuous Structure and Sense of his *Confessions*," *Recherches augustiniennes* 22 (1987):129-50.

178 Jones, *Later Roman Empire*, 2:737-39, and in general, pp. 737-57.

privilege and probably for membership.[179] Yet Augustine's portrayal of his father Patricius as too penurious further to educate his son was not a financial statement; but, in parody of Horace's satire, a moral indictment of his father as unchaste and ambitious.

Since the curial office was hereditary, Augustine demonstrated himself on the land to be his father's heir in vice: rapacious of persons and of property. The symbolism of the theft of pears was symbiotic, like the city and the country: pears for sexuality, sexuality for produce. Their theft implied a scene of nonrecognition between son and father. When Odysseus returned home from his voyages, he stood on the familial estate under a great pear tree observing his aged father Laertes dig around a plant. As proof of his filial identity, he showed him the scar from a wound made by the white tusk of a boar. Then he related all the trees his father had given him as a small boy, as he trotted after him through the orchard begging for things. There were thirteen pear trees, he remembered. Odysseus joyfully reunited with Laertes in embraces and tears.[180] That scene of affective recognition contrasted with the insipid separation of Augustine from his father in illicit sexual embraces and the tears their recollection evoked. In the orchard neighboring his familial vineyard Augustine reverted to the uncivilized state, when in the late Stone Age wild fruits like pears were gathered.[181] The harvesting of pears, once necessary for human survival, Augustine perverted into a gratuitous prank. He had better fruit at home; those he picked were surplus.[182] Augustine as son imitated Horace's cameo of the foolish prodigal who donated what he despised. As a host he pressed on his guest the pears he would otherwise leave for the swine to gobble up—a generosity that elicited only ingratitude.[183]

If Patricius his father was the ordinary civil servant, Monica his mother was the ordinary domestic servant. A double of her husband's desires, she was ambitious; unlike him, she was chaste.[184] That chastity was stereotypical; for the exclusive cult of the Roman matron was the personification of the virtue in which Monica instructed Augustine: Pudicitia, the goddess reserved to those patricians who married once and faithfully. Such women were eulogized on funeral inscriptions as *pia*, *pudica*, *casta*, *domiseda* (a faithful, modest, chaste homebody), with their sole ancient activity as *lanifica*, weaving and spinning. Those were the most frequent stylizations; they demonstrated the persistence of the female model. As the tomb of a Claudia

---

[179] Richard Duncan-Jones, *The Economy of the Roman Empire: Quantitative Studies*, 2d ed. (Cambridge: Cambridge University Press, 1982), pp. 277-83.

[180] Homer, *Odyssey* 24.220-344.

[181] Jane Renfrew, *Palaeoethnobotany: The Prehistoric Food Plants of the Near East and Europe* (London: Methuen, 1973), pp. 139-141, and for grapevines, pp. 125-31.

[182] Augustine, *Confessiones* 2.6.12.

[183] Horace, *Epistolae* 1.7.14-21.

[184] Augustine, *Confessiones* 9.13.37.

declared, "She kept house (*domus servit*)."[185] Augustine's only variation on the model distinguished his mother by the phrase "she served the Lord" (*dominus servit*).[186] Monica learned that divine service by obedience to her husband.

Raised modestly and soberly, but subject to her parents, rather than to God, at the ripe age for marriage she was handed to a man "as if to a lord." Anxious to convert her husband to chastity and Christianity, she tolerated the injustices of the bedroom without dissention. She criticized the marital complaints of beaten and disfigured matrons, reminding them tongue in cheek that the matrimonial contract reduced them to the status of handmaidens, so that they should not presume to be haughty with their husbands. She shared with them her secret of coexistence with a wrathful spouse: to avoid opposition in word or deed, biding the opportune moment of his change of mood to explain one's offensive behavior. Her respect also won the confidence of her mother-in-law and, through her intervention, that of her husband; and eventually, his conversion.[187] Although wifely toleration of a husband's infidelity was socially expected,[188] Augustine did not praise his mother's patience. He rejected the double standard of sexual morality. As a bishop he counseled wives to "jealousy." He commanded them emphatically not to suffer the unchastity of their husbands but to appeal it to the ecclesiastical authorities. In everything else wives were to be subject to their husbands but in chastity they were to defend their own cause.[189]

Augustine defined his mother as being in the formal possession (*mancipium*) of the Lord.[190] That was the original term for the absolute legal authority of the male head of a family group. It was divided into the right of the head of household over his wife (*manus*), his power over his descendants (*patria potestas*), and over his slaves (*dominica potestas*).[191] Monica was "servant of thy servants" by the witness of her holy conversation. The wife of one man, she rendered mutual duty to her parents, managed her household faithfully, and had the testimony of good works. She nurtured her children, laboring with them spiritually. To the converted Augustine and his companions, who were living in community, she served as

---

[185] For Pudicitia see Eva Cantarella, *Pandora's Daughters: The Role and Status of Women in Greek and Roman Antiquity*, trans. Maureen B. Fant (Baltimore, Md.: Johns Hopkins University Press, 1987), p. 115, and for the stereotype, pp. 132-33; Balsdon, *Roman Women*, p. 207. See also Elizabeth P. Forbis, "Women's Public Image in Italian Honorary Inscriptions," *American Journal of Philology* 111 (1990):493-512.

[186] Augustine, *Confessiones* 9.18.17.

[187] Ibid. 9.9.21.

[188] Balsdon, *Roman Women*, p. 215; Rousselle, "Personal Status and Sexual Practice," p. 303.

[189] Augustine, *Sermones* 392.4-5, cited by van der Meer, *Augustine the Bishop*, p. 182, without reference to Monica.

[190] Augustine, *Confessiones* 9.9.21.

[191] Cantarella, *Pandora's Daughters*, pp. 113-14.

the mother and daughter of them all.[192] Although women played public roles as benefactors, personally and visibly,[193] Augustine failed to distinguish Monica's good works. The conversation that commended her socially beyond the family was but standard praise for a female. Even the matrons with whom she conversed were that staple of satire, gossipy complainers.[194] Roman women were rarely occupied in the professions or trades. Beyond the management of the household, although not actually doing its housework unless poor, they devoted themselves to the arts or to sports as a pastime. Or they merely paid social calls, strolled idly (the men shopped for the groceries), attended spectacles, dinners, and the baths. They were profoundly indolent,[195] and it was quintessential that Augustine's introduction to the culture of idleness was at home on holiday with his mother. Monica as wife, mother, and manager was a stock character.

The linguistic formations that associated *pater* with power, ownership, and achievement had no analogy in terms derived from *mater*. The *matrimonium* was the legal status of motherhood but, unlike the *patrimonium*, it designated no transferable property.[196] Roman matrons were not authentic individuals but anonymous fractions of the family.[197] They were so silent as to lack names of their own. "Monica" would have been derived from her paternal or gentile affiliation, Monicus;[198] yet, in a *Confessions* populous with names so typical of their roles as to be virtually incredible,[199] Monica like Patricius was a stereotype. Augustine exploited *moneo*, as meaning "to remind", "to advise", "to instruct", and also, from her dreams and visions, "to predict". The memorial part of his *Confessions* commenced and concluded with Monica the reminder.[200] The authoritative Roman father had no counterpart in the tender Roman mother. Her part was not intimacy or indulgence but vigilance and discipline. Mothers were praised by moralists and biographers for instilling in their children, especially their sons, traditional virtue. They were particularly praised for diverting their sons from inappro-

---

192 Augustine, *Confessiones* 9.9.22; 9.13.37. For the social roles of mother and daughter see Hallett, *Fathers and Daughters in Roman Society*, pp. 211-62, 62-149; and for eulogies of women, Balsdon, *Roman Women*, p. 46-47.

193 MacMullen, "Women in Public in the Roman Empire," *Historia* 29 (1980):212.

194 See Balsdon, *Roman Women*, pp. 57, 272-73, without reference to Monica. For satire on women see also Richlin, *Garden of Priapus*, pp. 67-68, 133-34, 173-77, 194-95, 202-7.

195 See Carcopino, *Daily Life in Ancient Rome*, pp. 180-83, 171; Balsdon, *Roman Women*, p. 271.

196 See Hallett, *Fathers and Daughters in Roman Society*, pp. 28, 216-17, without reference to Monica.

197 Finley, "The Silent Women of Rome," in idem, *Aspects of Antiquity: Discoveries and Controversies* (London: Chatto & Windus, 1968), pp. 129-42.

198 For the names of women see Hallett, *Fathers and Daughters in Roman Society*, pp. 77-83; Cantarella, *Pandora's Daughters*, pp. 121-24; Balsdon, *Roman Women*, pp. 17-18.

199 E. g., Adeodatus ("gift of God"), Alypius ("winged piety"), Faustus ("ominous"), Firmianus ("firmament"), Nebridius ("priest of the mysteries").

200 For *moneo* see Augustine, *Confessiones* 2.3.8.; for her visions, 3.11.19; 6.13.21.

priate courses in life.[201] Monica was modeled on the paragon Cornelia, the singular wife famous for her sons, to whose education she was so devoted that they earned the reputation of virtue from nurture rather than nature.[202] It was commonplace for wellborn Roman women to be portrayed as crucially involved in arranging their children's education and marriage. Although wives could not expect much emotional support from their husbands, they did so focus on their children.[203] Even when Augustine literally deviated from her female sex by pronouncing Monica a "virile" woman, he reverted to a common topic.[204] Its graphic description, on which Augustine preached, was Perpetua's dream in prison that when she was stripped naked for martyrly combat in the Carthaginian arena she became male.[205]

Monica's gift for peacemaking was from God as "an inner teacher in the school of her breast." By her concern for the chastity of her husband and son, in her was being laid the foundation of a divine temple and the beginning of its holy habitation.[206] Literally God had laid in her the warp of a web, an allusion to the typical female task of weaving. The parallel metaphors, textile and architectural, for the divine activity within her located Augustine's mother classically. Roman matrons were not housewives; domestic chores they delegated to a slave, the wife of the chief steward whom they managed. Yet they were expected to spin and weave. Homeric queens to household matrons were commemorated on tombstones as "woolworkers." The attendants at a Roman wedding carried a spindle and distaff in escorting the bride to her new home. Customarily the matron worked while seated at the hearth. Since it was located in the center of the principal room of the house, it signified her complete involvement in the household.[207] Roman women were also active in the construction industry, however. Their names stamped on bricks and pipes recorded their involvement in building, from the ownership of a brickmaking or stonecutting company by an upper-class woman to the actual making of those materials and the construction of buildings by lower-class women. The best known female at Pompeii was

---

201 Dixon, *Roman Mother*, pp. 2, 3, 233, 236.

202 For Cornelia, without reference to Monica, see Hallett, *Fathers and Daughters in Roman Society*, pp. 7, 247; Cantarella, *Pandora's Daughters*, p. 130; Pomeroy, *Goddesses, Whores, Wives and Slaves*, pp. 149-50, 161; for mothers and children, Hallett, *Fathers and Daughters in Roman Society*, pp. 243-62; and for maternal involvement in the education of sons see also Balsdon, *Roman Women*, p. 203.

203 Hallett, *Fathers and Daughters in Roman Society*, pp. 4-5, 243-45.

204 Augustine, *Confessiones* 9.4.8. Elena Giannerelli, *La tipologia femminile nella biografia e l'autobiografia cristiana del ivo secolo*, Istituto storico italiano per il Medio Evo, Studi storici, 127 (Rome: Sede dell'Istituto, 1980), pp. 18-25.

205 *Passio sanctarum Perpetuae et Felicitatis* 10; Augustine, *Sermones* 280-82. See also Shaw, "The Passion of Perpetua," *Past and Present* 139 (1993):37-41.

206 Augustine, *Confessiones* 9.9.21; 2.3.6.

207 See Pomeroy, *Goddesses, Whores, Wives, and Slaves*, pp. 30, 199, 169; Cantarella, *Pandora's Daughters*, pp. 132-33; Balsdon, *Roman Women*, pp. 184, 207, 270-71.

Eumachia, a businesswoman whose family manufactured bricks. She donated to the town porticoes, colonnades, a crypt, and a tomb for herself.[208] When God laid in Monica the warp of a web, he also laid a foundation. Yet it was the foundation of his temple, not his house.

The divine house was not domestic but ecclesiastical; the divine habitation, not secular but sacral. Augustine ventured stability with the conversion of the episcopal residence in Hippo Regius, a dependency across the street from the basilica, into a monastery.[209] It was a household of priests, deacons, and subdeacons under his jurisdiction and a common rule. As the secular clergy in community, it united pastoral ministry with monastic discipline. Its members were required to renounce their property, either to the church or to their family. "He who is ready to live with me will possess God," Augustine promised.[210] The monastic foundation involved his own separation from his familial household. Although at ordination Augustine was granted clerical immunity from the hereditary curial role of his father, he was legally obliged to substitute a relative or to hand over to the curia at Thagaste sufficient property in compensation.[211] Entry to the clerical class, as rejecting the duties of the curial class, necessarily disinherited him from the familial lands and buildings that were its status. The monastic rule attributed to Augustine enjoined its members to live "unanimously in the house" (Ps. 67:7 Vulg.),[212] a repetition of his phrase for his early community in Milan.[213] Its members, who dwelled in that house, were not themselves the houses of God, however. They were ordered to lived in universal concord, honoring God mutually in each other because they were rather his "temples" (*templum*).[214]

The episcopal complex at Hippo Regius was a large block of buildings between the baths and the forum. It comprised the basilica, the palace where Augustine lived with his brethren, a hostel for pilgrims, a convent for women, and secondary structures.[215] The movement of Augustine from the home to the basilica replicated the history of the worship of the Christian community. Next door to his basilica was a peristylar house, formerly used as the church, from which the assembly originally evolved. By the fourth century the basilica was the stylistic norm for a hieratic and established

---

208 Balsdon, *Roman Women*, p. 200.

209 For the buildings see Hamman, *Vie quotidienne en Afrique du nord*, p. 43.

210 Van der Meer, *Augustine the Bishop*, pp. 199-217, citing Augustine, *Sermones* 355.6.

211 For the vicissitudes of the law of clerical immunity see Lepelley, *Cités de l'Afrique romaine*, 1:177, 279-92; Warmington, *North African Provinces*, p. 46. Although Warmington wondered how Augustine escaped being recalled to the curia on his father's death, p. 50, Augustine would have been legally underage for the position, the minimum for which was twenty-five years.

212 Augustine, *Praeceptum* 1.1.

213 Augustine, *Confessiones* 9.8.17.

214 Augustine, *Praeceptum* 1.8; cf. 4.6.

215 Van der Meer, *Augustine the Bishop*, pp. 20-25.

church. It was monumentalised by Constantine's policy of patronage for Christianity, deliberately adapted to its ascendant social position. The basilica as an architectural type did not develop from previous patterns of building churches, however. It was imposed upon them from the standard forms of public architecture, such as civic halls and imperial palaces. The first basilica, the Lateran as the see of the papacy, was constructed from a donated imperial palace.[216] The original Christians were accused of atheism precisely because they lacked temples and altars, as a north African apologist before Augustine observed. Practical factors against distinctive churches were the insufficiency of common funds for public building, the small size of the congregations, and the necessity of privacy against both the threat and the reality of persecution. A theological factor was the displacement of the temple with the community as the very place of worship. With the abolition of the temple as a sacred place, there was no pro-fane as "outside" the temple.[217]

The apostolic community in Jerusalem had gathered "from house to house" (Acts 2:46, 5:42, cf. 12:12), or simply, "at home." The domestic setting conditioned its assembly, worship, and organization. Paul's discussion of the Eucharist (1 Cor. 11:17-34) was architecturally and socially located as an assembly around the common table of a home, like a typical dinner. In that earliest period Christians met in the houses of their wealthier members, in the dining room or another large available room. There was no specialization of domestic architecture for religious use. There was yet no Christian architecture. From there, the community, while still meeting in private homes, began to acquire property, which it renovated. The structure of the buildings was still within the local tradition of domestic architecture but it was adapted for communal worship. Larger buildings were gradually introduced. With the reconstruction of the Lateran, the basilica emerged, although the pattern of revising existing structures continued. The Christian community originated, then, as an urban phenomenon in the home of a host and patron, a home without distinctive religious features of spatial articulation or architectural adaptation. The house remained in domestic usage while serving an informal assembly. Christians also met in a hall or warehouse but most commonly in a house; in major cities there were probably several such cells.[218]

---

[216] See L. Michael White, *Building God's House in the Roman World: Architectural Adaptation among Pagans, Jews, and Christians* (Baltimore, Md.: Johns Hopkins University Press for the American School of Oriental Research, 1990), pp. 23, 4, 18. See also in general Paul Corby Finney, "Early Christian Architecture: The Beginnings (A Review Article)," *Harvard Theological Review* 81 (1988):319-39.

[217] J. G. Davies, *The Secular Use of Church Buildings* (London: S C M, 1968), pp. 1-4, citing Minucius Felix, *Octavius* 32. See also F. V. Filson, "The Significance of the Early House Churches," *Journal of Biblical Literature* 58 (1939):105-12.

[218] White, *Building God's House in the Roman World*, pp. 4, 103, 17, 19, 20, 24, 104-5.

The organization and mobility of the group depended on the hospitality and patronage of its homeowners. There developed social conventions such as "extending the right hand in fellowship" and "greeting with a holy kiss." The writing of letters between groups not only transmitted information but also secured hospitality, as in the request to prepare the guest room (Philemon 22). The reception and mission of persons revealed a social network. The houses also were the local place of communal worship around the common table in the dining room. The meal was the bond of fellowship, the sign of social relations. Only with the numerical growth of Christianity, and not before the middle of the second century, was the Eucharist separated from the meal. Formal ritual replaced the casual dining of the domestic church; the meal was preserved only symbolically. With the diminishment of dining, less food was necessary; so the voluntary offering for the communal table was reduced. The offertory was invented to symbolize individual contributions to the meal, although the very practice of the meal had changed. A stylized Eucharistic liturgy was separated from the informal communal meal by the beginning of the third century. There was also separation of the clergy from the laity, with a more formal arrangement for seating that relegated the women and the children to the rear of the assembly.[219]

Before their aggrandizement in scale and style, Christians had been similar to other groups in the urban context of the Roman empire: collegial associations, philosophical schools, the synagogue—all of which employed domestic settings, indeed the very household. Architecturally Christians used, purchased, and renovated houses; socially they maintained extended household relations. A search and seizure during the great persecution at the beginning of Augustine's century recorded a church in north Africa at Cirta as such a renovated house. Its plan had a library and a dining room. Furnishings included jars and barrels: in storage were gold, silver, and bronze implements, and adult apparel probably for charitable distribution.[220] A practice still in Augustine's era, in such major cities as Rome and Alexandria, was communion before breakfast privately in the bedroom of the house. Husband and wife took the Eucharistic hosts from a container brought home from the celebration of Mass at an altar, although there were differences of opinion about whether daily communion after sexual intercourse was appropriate; some felt unworthy.[221]

A Roman centurion had once confessed unworthiness because of ritual impurity to have Jesus of Nazareth enter his home to heal his servant. The Roman rite perpetuated his demurral, "Lord, I am not worthy to have you come under my roof" (Matt. 8:8), by incorporating it before the liturgical re-

---

219 Ibid., pp. 106, 119-20, 138.

220 Ibid., pp. 143, 140, 122.

221 Van der Meer, *Augustine the Bishop*, pp. 176-77.

ception of communion by priest and people. The alteration of Jesus' location from house to soul, from a material architectural place to an immaterial spiritual space was universalized in theology and piety. Yet the gospel had appropriated the home as an important place for his ministry. The very call of Jesus to ministry came not from the general public but from close kin: in the synoptic gospels from a maternal cousin, in the Johannine version from his own mother. He taught parables about houses and householders to the details of storage and sweeping. Knocking persistently on the door of a neighbor's house to borrow a loaf of bread moralized constancy at prayer. The act of the good shepherd upon finding his lost sheep was to return home with it. Jesus also sent the cured demoniacs, blind, and paralytics home. He even entered homes to heal the sick, like the mother-in-law of Peter, the prototype of the papacy; or the fainted girl needing nourishment. Jesus preached not only in the synagogue but in his own home, where the crowd became so thick that the companions of a paralytic boldly removed its roofing to lower him into the scene. He ate supper in homes, like that of his friends Martha, Mary, and Lazarus, who welcomed him. He dined notably at a wedding feast, for which celebration he supplied his hosts amphoras of excellent wine, but notoriously in the homes of the socially impure to the contempt of the religious establishment. His final gesture with his disciples was to eat a Passover meal in an ordinary urban home. The promise at that meal was that "if someone loves me, he will keep my conversation, and my Father will love him, and we will come to him and make our home with him" (John 14:23). Augustine quoted that verse in his consideration on the Trinity. But rather than attending to the topic of place—believers as divine homes—he speculated on whether by his words Jesus excluded the Holy Spirit.[222] The hominess, even homeliness, of the gospels Augustine converted into an allegory of opposition between domesticity and philosophy. In his exegesis of Jesus' visit to the home of the sisters Martha and Mary scriptural revelation was transformed into philosophical ideal.

Augustine considered the human states to be pilgrimage and dwelling. He appointed them to terrestrial and celestial places by developing their opposition through the biblical sisters. Leah and Rachel represented temporal labor versus eternal contemplation. Leah was the "action of human and mortal life, in which we live by faith, doing many laborious things, uncertain of the outcome to those for whom we care." Rachel was the "certain and delectable contemplation of the truth." Yet he did not oppose them sexually, as matron and virgin, for both were wives. Although Leah was not lovable in herself, she was tolerable as a means to Rachel and she became approved in her children as a useful servant of public life.[223] Their gospel

---

222 Augustine, *De Trinitate* 1.9.18; cf. 7.6.12.

223 Augustine, *Contra Faustum Manichaeum* 22.52-58.

counterparts, Martha and Mary were opposed as labor and leisure, feeding and being fed, many and one, charity and intelligence, present and future, burden and blessing, temporal and eternal. Both sisters were favored, amiable disciples; both were innocent and praiseworthy. Yet, while one was good, the other was better. "What Martha does, there we are. What Mary does, this we hope."[224] Mary prefigured the eternal life of contemplation for a soul at rest from occupation, absorbed in truth in the word of the Lord. Martha was occupied with necessary but transitory work that would be abolished when that need was removed: by its reward of an enduring rest in contemplation requiring only enlightenment by and enjoyment of God.[225]

The only human home Augustine ever lauded was the villa at Cassiciacum to which he retreated upon his conversion with his mother, his brother Navigius, and several friends. There they aspired to the ideal of living leisurely. Yet there he rejected domesticity for philosophy. Upon the death of a friend, Augustine's fatherland had become a punishment and his father's house, an extraordinary calamity. His companion Nebridius also relinquished a fine rural estate belonging to his family, and even his own home to pursue philosophy. Augustine, introduced to philosophy through Cicero's *Hortensius*, "burned" for wisdom.[226] He was attaining the classical condition of maleness: to be hot and dry. For that achievement he was relinquishing the state of wetness: the embryonic fluid in which he was born; the wretched infancy of dribbling mouth and runny nose and tears for the breast; the waves of temptation as a schoolboy, with weeping for poetic fictions that sucked him into whirlpools of immoral practices and swept him onto the flood of human customs, an irresistible tide that washed people out into the great and fearful sea, on whose oceanic bed of skepticism he drowned.[227] He was separating from the female, departing from domesticity.

He cited the conclusion of *Hortensius*, which urged a dedication to philosophy for a speedy departure from earth to eternity, to "a better home."[228] Augustine confessed that he came across the book during his regular course of studies;[229] and in the schools the rhetoricians did debate about Hortensius. He was an elderly bachelor orator who asked Cato to lend him his wife Marcia to beget children. Cato agreed, Marcia obliged, and the Romans

---

224 Augustine, *Sermones* 169.17; 179.3-6; 104.

225 Augustine, *De Trinitate* 1.10.20. For background see Daniel Csanyi, "*Optima pars*: Die Auslegungsgeschichte von Lk 10, 36-42 bei den Kirchenvätern der ersten vier Jahrhunderte," *Studia monastica* 2 (1960): 5-78.

226 Augustine, *Confessiones* 6.14.24; 4.4.9; 6.10.17; 3.4.7. For youth and philosophy see Eyben, *De jonge Romein*, pp. 339-67.

227 For liquid metaphors in the *Confessions* see Boyle, " Prudential Augustine," pp. 137-41, 145-47. The bottom of the sea is the heart of the ungodly. Augustine, *Enarrationes in psalmos* 64.11.

228 Augustine, *De Trinitate* 14.19.26, citing Cicero's lost *Hortensius*.

229 Augustine, *Confessiones* 3.4.7.

quarreled about it. The marital exchange was a contentious subject, from accusations of greed to justifications by ethnological precedent. Quintilian reported the topics for pedagogic declamation as the thesis, "Was Cato right in transferring Marcia to Hortensius?"; and generically, "Whether it was an honorable act on the part of Cato to make Marcia over to Hortensius, or whether such an action is becoming to a virtuous man."[230] Augustine was thus introduced to philosophy through a domestic dispute.

In his conversional *Soliloquia* with God he determined to flee the conjugal bed, for a man's mind was confused by a woman's flattery and her bodily touch.[231] Augustine had lived since his profession as rhetor with a sole woman, not in a union recognized as legitimate, he confessed, but in one a flickering flame had traced out. He experienced in it the difference between a marriage contracted for procreation and a pact of libidinous love in which an offspring was born against the vow.[232] The assumption in concubinage was that the woman would not bear children.[233] Concubinage was in Roman society an acceptable and acknowledged sexual relation of endurance between unmarried partners. It was one of social disparity, however, with the male as superior. The woman was "concubine", but there was no term for the male partner. She had the virtues of a wife but not her status. The intentions of the male toward her were crucial. Although marriage was contracted by the will of both partners, the intentions of one partner might be concealed, as when Aeneas informed Dido, begging him not to abandon their union, that he had never mentioned marriage.[234] As an impediment to marriage, the woman with whom Augustine was accustomed to sleep was torn from his side, like Eve from dormant Adam (Gen. 2:21-23). His heart, to which she cleaved, was cut and wounded and it bled. The woman returned to Africa, vowing never to know another man, and leaving with him his natural son by her.[235] Her vow imitated Dido, utterly weary of the nuptial bed, promising to remain faithful to the memory of her first love yet smitten with Aeneas on his arrival at Carthage.[236] Augustine's concubine was a fickle fe-

---

230 See Cantarella, *Pandora's Daughters*, p. 131; Hallett, *Fathers and Daughters in Roman Society*, pp. 57-58; Balsdon, *Roman Women*, p. 190, all without reference to Augustine. Quintilian, *Institutiones oratoriae* 3.5.11; 10.5.13; trans. Butler, 1:403; 4:121.

231 Augustine, *Soliloquia* 32.

232 Augustine, *Confessiones* 4.2.2. For marriage for procreation see Dixon, *Roman Family*, p. 67; also Danielle Gourevitch, "Se marier pour avoir des enfants: Le point de vue du médicin," in *Parenté et stratégies familiales dans l'antiquité romaine*, Actes de la table ronde des 2-4 octobre 1986, Paris, Maison de sciences de l'homme, ed. Jean Andreau and Hinnerk Bruhns, Collection de l'École française de Rome, 29 (Rome: École française de Rome, 1990), pp. 139-51.

233 Dixon, *Roman Family*, p. 93. For the status of the illegitimate child see Rawson, "*Spurii* and the Roman View of Illegitimacy," *Antichthon* 23 (1989):10-41.

234 Treggiari, "Concubinae," *Papers of the British School at Rome* 49 (1981):59, 61; see also Balsdon, *Roman Women*, pp. 231-34.

235 Augustine, *Confessiones* 6.15.25.

236 Vergil, *Aeneid* 4.1; 4.15-16.

male, as unreliable in her vow of constancy to him as she had proved in her obligation not to become pregnant.

She was anonymous, like all literary ciphers. Naming depended on social recognition and accord. In tragedy, namelessness was a condition of being stripped of identity, like a ruler deposed of his title,[237] as she was of her status. She must have been of a class eligible to be the concubine of a free male but ineligible to attain the status of matron: prostitutes, actresses (mimes), and their daughters, or freedwomen who were not the concubines of their former masters. Although only a small number of concubines were denied the status of mother of the family,[238] Augustine had an impressive exemplar for his repudiation of her in Constantine. When Constantine became at nineteen the emperor, he was required to repudiate his concubine Minervina, mother of his son Crispus, and to marry an underage girl of nine.[239] By imitation Augustine as rhetor at Milan, the imperial seat, associated himself ambitiously with imperial values. His own name portended that.

When he repudiated his concubine he resorted to a prostitute. Although his mother had arranged marriage for him, the girl was two years underage.[240] A female was legally eligible for Roman marriage at twelve. Although some wed as mere girls, from the only evidence—commemorations on tombstones—most married later, at seventeen to eighteen years. The legal minimum for males was sixteen, Augustine's declared age in this episode; but most of them married much later, at twenty-seven or twenty-eight. Rare exceptions were among males of the senatorial class seeking office, who may have married in their early twenties for political advantage. This wide gap in ages between husband and wife had implications for reproduction, relations, widowhood, remarriage, and the devolution of property.[241] From north Africa there is no trace of a custom of male marriage before twenty-five years of age. A father had to survive to be at least sixty to see his son wed and and producing grandchildren; yet his prospects were poor, since the rate of mortality for males soared at fifty.[242] Augustine's father died to be survived typically by his younger mother. Augustine's blame of her for not marrying him at the legal minimum of sixteen exaggerated his lust. Maternal author-

---

[237] See Anne Barton, *The Names of Comedy* (Toronto: University of Toronto Press, 1990), pp. 153-54, without reference to her.

[238] For the legal status of these women see Rousselle, *Porneia*, pp. 81, 82, 85; Gardner, *Women in Roman Law and Society*, pp. 56-60; and for disqualifications, Rawson, "Roman Concubinage and Other *de facto* Marriages," *Transactions of the American Philological Association* 104 (1974):282.

[239] See Balsdon, *Roman Women*, p. 167, without reference to Augustine.

[240] Augustine, *Confessiones* 6.13.23.

[241] Shaw, "The Age of Roman Girls at Marriage," *Journal of Roman Studies* 77 (1987): 42-44.

[242] Saller, "Men's Age at Marriage and its Consequences in the Roman Family," *Classical Philology* 82 (1987):28-29, 30.

ity depended on national custom and personal character, on familial habits of affection and financial considerations. A mother was expected to fret over a son and to exhort him to proper achievement; he was expected to defer to her desires within limits and to attain their mutual satisfaction. A widow typically assumed responsibility and credit for her son's education. She became involved in the choice of his marriage partner, which could be a source of conflict. Her authority derived partly from her power of economic disposition.[243] Augustine was educated at his mother's expense,[244] so that her expectations for his career mattered.

Yet as a neophyte at the villa of Cassiciacum he determined not to marry. His episcopal residence at Hippo Regius was devoid of women. None lived there, none was a guest there: not even his widowed sister, a prioress; or his brother's daughters, who were nuns. Although his family was above suspicion, their female attendants or visitors were not. Augustine feared temptation and scandal. As a bishop he refused to be interviewed by women, or even paid their respects, unless other clergy were present in the room as witnesses, even if the matter for discussion was strictly personal. Woman he judged created for procreation only. For any other task, whether tilling the soil or consoling loneliness, a man was a far superior laborer or companion.[245] His nameless sister, absent from his *Confessions*, was relegated to a convent next door to the episcopal residence, where she supervised the nuns.[246] Augustine's banishment of females from his house contradicted the culture. The differentiation of domestic space by gender was virtually undetectable in Roman experience. Romans did not segregate women, and the matron moved in the midst of males both in physical space and social occasion.[247]

Among the amenities of Roman civilization was a blazing hearth, offering a contented resignation in leisure to the human lot.[248] Homes lacked fireplaces and chimneys. The hearth on which roared a huge fire funneled its smoke through a hole in the roof, but it was welcome with its soot against harsh rural winters.[249] Even a rascally usurer praised a modest wife "piling

---

243 See Dixon, *Roman Mother*, pp. 172, 5, 177, 202-3, 233.

244 Augustine, *Confessiones* 3.4.7.

245 Possidius, *Vita* 26.1-3; Augustine, *De Genesi ad litteram* 9.3.5; 9.5.9; cited by Bonner, "Augustine's Attitude to Women and Amicitia," in *Homo spiritalis: Festgabe für Luc Verheijen OSA zu seinem 70. Geburtstag*, ed. Cornelius Mayer and Karl Heinz Chelius (Würzburg: Augustinus, 1978), pp. 259-62; van der Meer, *Augustine the Bishop*, p. 215.

246 Van der Meer, *Augustine the Bishop*, p. 223. For her see Possidius, *Vita* 26.1.

247 See Andrew Wallace-Hadrill, "The Social Structure of the Roman House," *Publications of the British School at Rome* 56 (1988):50-51.

248 Carcopino, *Daily Life in Ancient Rome*, p. 74.

249 Veyne, "The Roman House," forward, *A History of Private Life*, 5 vols., Vol. 1: *From Pagan Rome to Byzantium*, ed. idem, trans. Arthur Goldhammer (Cambridge, Mass.: Harvard University Press, Belknap Press, 1987-91), p. 315.

high the sacred hearth with seasoned firewood."[250] In urban dwellings braziers burned, not radiating heat to the corners of a room, but a least warming those who drew near to their comfort.[251] Thousands of homes from Roman north Africa are extant, although only a small percentage are excavated and even fewer published. Stylistically they were very similar, distinguished only by size and opulence, or by accommodation to some difficulty of the terrain or neighborhood.[252] Although Augustine's home, where he lived with parents of good social standing in the upper echelons of wealth,[253] is unknown, its ideology was clear. The urban homes of the ruling class revealed its private life but also its social status. As Vitruvius, the sole extant architectural author, explained, the floor plan of a house was associated with the social status of its owner. The axial plan, which singly aligned the vestibule, the courtyard, and the dining room, was widely used in north African domestic architecture, with the total design shaped by the master's social requirements.[254]

Roman domestic architecture and decor since the republic displayed the owner's personality, a social necessity in a competitive society. Although there was moral counsel of moderation, by which the lord conveyed his own dignity to the house, the norm was visibility, not privacy. It was displayed in richness, even extravagance, with the amplitude and opulence of a house an index of the status and wealth of its inhabitants. Domestic architecture was obsessed with social rank, not merely in the distinctions between houses, but also in the spaces within a house. The house was a public focus of power where social contracts were made, providing the basis for public activity outside the home. The architecture articulated space to provide a fitting context for the differentiation of public and private activities. Business was regularly conducted at home, from the emperor receiving the reports of his procurators to the craftsman receiving consumers in the shop that formed part of his living quarters. In a system of clientele there was the obligatory salutation in which the patron received his dependents and friends and con-

---

250 Horace, *Epodes* 2.43; trans. Bennett, p. 367.

251 Veyne, "Roman House," p. 315.

252 Yvon Thébert, "Private Life and Domestic Architecture in Roman Africa," in *From Pagan Rome to Byzantium*, ed. Veyne, p. 329; Hamman, *Vie quotidienne en Afrique du nord*, p. 63; Charles-Picard, *Civilisation de l'Afrique romaine*, p. 211 and on homes in general, pp. 210-23; A. G. McKay, *Houses, Villas and Palaces in the Roman World* (London: Thames & Hudson, 1975), pp. 222-37.

253 Shaw, "Family in Late Antiquity," pp. 8-10, also disputes the legend of Augustine's domestic poverty but on the basis of his father's curial status. He locates him in the lower ranks of a regional upper class.

254 See Thébert, "Private Life and Domestic Architecture in Roman Africa," pp. 319-21, 383, 384, 392. For the house as a symbol of status, with a crowded home prestigious, see also Saller, "*Familia, domus* and the Roman Conception of the Family," pp. 349-55. See in general *Roman Art in the Private Sphere: New Perspectives on the Architecture and Decor of the Domus, Villa, and Insula*, ed. Elaine K. Gazda with Anne E. Haeckl (Ann Arbor: University of Michigan Press, 1991).

ducted business. Callers ranged from peers in his circle to lesser friends, lowly dependents, tradespeople, and slaves. There were numerous and subtle degrees of privacy, in which increased privacy indicated higher privilege. Public activity was clustered around the entrance. Private entertainment lay beyond it, past barriers of corridors and slaves posted at thresholds.[255]

Homes incorporated aspects of public buildings, such as columns in peristyles, to delineate the space as prestigious; or curved walls and ceilings, such as the room ending in an apse, to emphasize interior space by framing it. Architectural forms associated with public buildings absorbed palatial and sacral forms into homes. The decoration of walls with architectural motifs alluded to the public buildings outside the house that provided the social context within which it operated. The interior distinction was not between public and private space in the modern sense but between the degrees of access that the house afforded to outsiders. Any real privacy must have been remarkably difficult. The master received intimate friends in his bedroom, and slaves circulated constantly. Bathing and defecation were public events. A house was visually transparent through its heart along a central axis from the entrance framed by doorways and columns. Architecture was designed to impress visitors. The Roman house invited passersby and it placed its occupants on show. The sole distinction was between invited and uninvited visitors, in imitation of the contrast between leisure and work.[256]

The principal innovation in Mediterranean dwellings was the Greek invention of the peristyle, a central courtyard surrounded by colonnades, around which were disposed the various areas of the house. The elites of north Africa were magnetized by this style, for it enhanced their prestige by incorporating into their private houses an architectural composition whose scale had been reserved for public monuments. The traditional Italic house with atrium was not built there. Every wealthy residence had at its center a peristyle open to the heavens, admitting air and light into its adjacent rooms. The peristyle, whose courtyard made it the ideal place for displaying architectural ideas of magnitude, was allotted as much available space as possible: in the most ambitious homes vast dimensions. In north Africa it was used for receiving guests, the ordinary clients paying respect to their patrons and receiving their dole. Its construction could emphasize its utility by floors of packed earth and a well with holes for cisterns. The colonnade was decorated charmingly, even in lesser versions with several potted plants, a fountain—if only a semicircular basin with holes in its lip, and a pool—if only a few inches deep. The peristyle perfectly embodied the complexity of the private. Embellished with a combination of architectural and natural ef-

---

[255] Wallace-Hadrill, "Social Structure of the Roman House," pp. 44-45, 46, 47, 52, 84, 53, 55, 56, 58, 59, 85.

[256] Ibid., pp. 59-68, 68-76, 81, 82-84.

fects, it was a space in which a variety of activities transpired: from solitary pursuits to great receptions befitting the master's social station, to the work of the servants for whom it served as passageway, work area, and water supply.[257]

Among the features of a north African home that would have disturbed and offended Augustine's faith was this center, the peristyle, for it was the location of the domestic chapel.[258] Houses derived a sacred aura from the household gods.[259] In an association of house and altar, "house" was *penates*. Clients daily participated in its cult. Religion was accorded a principal role to the master, establishing his power, to which subordinates presented offerings. Domestic worship would have been regulated by Augustine's father, and he was a pagan. Overtly Christian motifs were extremely scarce in the late mosaics of wealthy north African homes. Its provincial and municipal notables, remote from the central government and its dictates, maintained classical culture and traditional religion into the fifth century.[260] Cities and towns retained in a secularized form the imperial, provincial, and municipal priests. Some north Africans juxtaposed on their epitaphs symbols and formulas attesting to their Christian faith and to their civic title of flamen. There existed a laicized imperial cult in which the city was not formally pagan but not fully Christian: two societies.[261]

An important domestic room for meeting with visitors was the hall with a broad corridor of access, where the master performed his social duties. It served as his office and doubled as a lecture hall. The decor was fine, with his name often spelled in mosaic on its floor, and with cultural allusions in mosaic of the muses, theatrical masks, and poetic portraits.[262] The use of masks on walls suggested a backdrop for action: scenery as in the theater, which transported the domestic actors to the luxury, grandeur, and publicity of the stage.[263] Augustine was hostile to the spectacles of theater, amphitheater, and circus. He criticized their immorality as a school of vice, especially the lascivious representations of the theater that assimilated the role

---

[257] Ibid., pp. 325-26, 357-64. See also R. Rebuffat, "Maisons à peristyle d'Afrique du Nord: Répertoire de plans publiés," *Mélanges d'archéologie et d'histoire, École française de Rome* 81 (1969):659-724; 86 (1974):445-99.

[258] See Thébert, "Private Life and Domestic Architecture in Roman North Africa," pp. 363-64, without reference to Augustine.

[259] Saller, "*Familia, domus* and the Roman Conception of the Family," p. 350.

[260] See Thébert, "Private Life and Domestic Architecture in Roman Africa," pp. 363-64. 377, 397, without reference to Augustine.

[261] Lepelly, "Saint Augustin et la cité romano-africaine," in *Jean Chrysostom et Augustin*, Actes du colloque de Chantilly, 22-24 septembre 1974, ed. Charles Kannengiesser, Théologie historique, 35 (Paris: Beauchesne, 1975), pp. 36-37.

[262] Thébert, "Private Life and Domestic Architecture in Roman Africa," pp. 373-74; see also Kathleen M. D. Dunbabin, *The Mosaics of Roman North Africa: Studies in Iconography and Patronage* (Oxford: Clarendon, 1978), pp. 131-36.

[263] Wallace-Hadrill, "Social Structure of the Roman House," pp. 70-71.

of the mime to the prostitute. Those comedians he did enjoy he wished had dedicated their talents to a better cause. He complained of the success of the theater to fascinate crowds with frivolity and degradation, so that even Christians thronged the spectacles, rather than the churches. Augustine criticized the evergetes, like the aristocrat Romanianus who had underwritten his own rhetorical education, for financing the shows in ambition for popularity and prestige. While the patrons were prodigal in spending enormous sums on play, the poor went hungry. When a converted Augustine sold his patrimony, he determined that the curia of Thagaste should receive nothing; so he distributed the sum to the indigent.[264]

The dining room of a house was especially distasteful to him. It was frequently the most spacious and sumptuous of the reception halls in which owners received guests. It served socially, with meals as a discharge of obligation. The central space was decorated with a motif, often oceanic, since fish, costing three times the price of meat in north Africa, was the distinction of a rich table. Luxury was associated with the ceremonial of dinner, a display of the host's wealth. In north Africa, as at Rome, the dining room was the space where the master demonstrated who and what he was. Banquets were symbols of power and wealth, with social significance in serving wine of good quality and spectacular platters of food. The meal gathered the entire family, and its room was the setting for important domestic affairs and announcements. There were openly displayed the bonds of domesticity: of marriage, family, household, and friendship. In the dining room space was coded. The place of seating or reclining signified rank, with the couches and their places hierarchically ordered to the master's seat on the right side of the central couch. Guests were seated and served by specialists.[265]

The charm of conversation, since dinner was an occasion for philosophy, was diverted by music and comedy. North Africans favored dancers and courtesans with their meals, and gluttony was a common detraction. The dining room played a cardinal role in domestic socializing, with a code governing relations. It was all-the-more revealing a room because it was a dangerous place. Banquets occasioned the most audacious acts, as guests showed off, although they were expected to behave, under risk of expulsion. Augustine in his episcopal refectory refused wine to swearers.[266] He praised in his *Confessions* the interior justice that did not judge by human custom but by divine law, in contravention of household rules. He ridiculed the ex-

---

264 Lepelley, *Cités de l'Afrique romaine*, 1:376-80, 298-303, 177. For episcopal Augustine on poverty and wealth see also van der Meer, *Augustine the Bishop*, pp. 137-40.

265 Thébert, "Private Life and Domestic Architecture in Roman Africa," pp. 364-69. See also John H. D'Arms, "Control, Companionship, and *clientela*: Some Social Functions of the Communal Roman Meal," *Echos du monde classique/Classical Views* 28 (1984):327-48.

266 Thébert, "Private Life and Domestic Architecture in Roman Africa," pp. 370-71.

traordinary specialization of servants for dining, who contended over one servant mishandling a goblet that was the job of another, while the shame prohibited at the table was done behind the manger.[267]

The dining room was a social occasion for sin. The pig and the pear that were served at a Roman dinner with wine—all prime products—were perversely involved in Augustine's imitation of the original sin of social necessity. He condemned himself for devouring platters of creatures when he was starving for the Creator. While hungry for inner food, he chewed visual spectacles, like the prodigal gnawing on husks meant for swine. Corporeal food was phantasmagorial, dreamy dishes that did not nourish but vanish. Daily people repaired their bodily decline by eating and drinking; but only until death, when God would destroy their very stomachs to supply a wonderful satiety with himself. Augustine confessed to a daily struggle by fasting against the sensuality of the food and drink necessary to sustain the body. Hunger and thirst were intended to be sufferings rescued by food and drink as consolations. Although sustenance should only be medicinal, he thought, under the pretext of health the temptation to gluttony and drunkenness was insinuated. What sufficed for health did not suffice for pleasure; from uncertainty about satisfaction there developed greed. Drunkenness was not a personal problem for him, but gluttony sometimes was. Augustine, in imitation of the porcine critic in Plutarch's morality, was unable to avoid that concupiscence, as he was in his decision to avoid sexual indulgence. Usually temperate, he was sometimes at table carried beyond necessity to indulgence.[268] That cupidity he had inherited, imbibed with his mother's milk. To it he opposed sucking on the divine milk, the maternal breastfeeding of God. That fountain was wisdom incarnate as Christ, divine nourishment for human infancy.[269]

In the morality of nursing Augustine associated his mother with the conservative philosophy that blamed the degeneracy of the state on women farming out their infants to wet nurses.[270] In his eulogy of Monica she was, like her husband and son, stained by the produce of the vineyard, from her

---

[267] Augustine, *Confessiones* 3.1.1; 3.6.10; 3.10.18; 4.1.1; 3.6.11; 3.7.13. For specialized slaves for dining see Carcopino, *Daily Life in Ancient Rome*, p. 71.

[268] Augustine, *Confessiones* 10.31.43-47. See Plutarch, "Bruta animalia ratione uti, sive Gryllus," in *Moralia* 98B-C.

[269] Augustine, *Confessiones* 4.1.1; 7.18.24; *Enarrationes in psalmos* 30 (2/1).9; 33(1).6; 109.12; 119.2; 54.24; 67.22; 120.12; 130.9-14.

[270] For the morality of nursing see Sandra R. Joshel, "Nurturing the Master's Child: Slavery and the Roman Child-Nurse," *Signs* 12 (1986):6-10; Bradley, "Wet-Nursing at Rome: A Study in Social Relations," in idem, *Family in Ancient Rome*, pp. 201, 216; Balsdon, *Roman Women*, p. 201; Pomeroy, *Goddesses, Whores, Wives, and Slaves*, p. 212. See in general Dixon, *Roman Mother*, pp. 120-29, 145-46; Valerie Fildes, *Wet Nursing: A History from Antiquity to the Present* (Oxford: Basil Blackwell, 1988), pp. 4-25; Bradley, "Wet-Nursing at Rome," pp. 201-29; idem, "The Social Role of the Nurse in the Roman World," pp. 13-36; Gardner, *Women in Roman Law and Society*, pp. 242-45.

initial social role as daughter.[271] Although she was reared in a faithful Christian home, she did not attribute her discipline to the diligence of her mother but to an elderly maidservant who had carried her father on her back. For her age and customs she was in virtuous charge of the daughters of the household. Except during meals with their parents, she forbade them even to quench their thirst, moralizing: "Just now you drink water because you do not have the possibility of wine; but when you do homage to husbands as ladies of the storerooms and cellars, water will seem base; yet the custom of drinking it will prevail." By such method and authority she formed their thirst to an honest mode. It happened, however, that winebibbing stole upon Monica. When, as customary for a sober girl, she was ordered by her parents to draw wine from the cask, before filling the flask she would sip a little. She did so, not from any drunken desire for wine, but from the excesses of her age bubbling over. Those were usually checked in puerile spirits by their elders. Daily sipping a bit more, she fell into the habit of draining small cups that were nearly full. Where were father, mother, nurse? demanded Augustine. The remedy came from God alone, through the quarrelsome female slave who used to accompany her to the cask. One-to-one she upbraided Monica for the crime, calling her, with the taste of bitterest wine in her mouth, an "afternoon lush." Monica regarded her defilement, immediately sentenced herself, and departed from the scene. The rebuke was private; perhaps, Augustine speculated, the slave feared that she herself would be tried for having delayed it.[272] That slave was not merely quarrelsome but litigious, for her suit involved the crime about women and wine. Unlike Patricius and his winebibbing (*vinulentia*) joy at Augustine's puberty, Monica courted a drunken (*temulenta*) cupidity that jeopardized his very birth.

Females were forbidden by Roman law to drink wine (*temulentii*). In primitive law the penalty was death, as in the case of the husband who bludgeoned his wife with a rod. Matrons were even refused the right of the key to the storeroom for wine. Their male blood relations had the right to kiss them on the mouth, not as a gesture of affection, but for detection of alcohol on their breath. The literary rationale for such severity was that wine promoted wrath; wrath, desire; desire, adultery.[273] Satirists ridiculed the drunkenness of grand ladies whose independence degenerated into license, a

---

[271] For the role of daughters see Hallett, *Fathers and Daughters in Roman Society*, pp. 62-149, and for eulogy of females, pp. 41-43, 241-42.

[272] Augustine, *Confessiones* 9.8.18. The description of Monica as *puella* does not render her a child, since it was even used of married women. See, e. g., Hallett, *Fathers and Daughters in Roman Society*, p. 140.

[273] Cantarella, *Pandora's Daughters*, pp. 118-19; Pomeroy, *Goddesses, Whores, Wives, and Slaves*, pp. 153-54; Balsdon, *Roman Women*, pp. 21, 24, 213; Luciano Minieri, "Vini usus feminis ignotus," *Labeo* 28 (1982):150-63.

license in morals that loosened familial ties.[274] The charge of female drunkenness was eventually not retained in classical law as a just cause even for repudiation by divorce. Yet medical texts, especially on gynecology, considered wine both contraceptive and abortive. It was unfavorable to conception, even abortive, because the wrath it induced did not retain semen. Because it was a contraceptive drug, women in the first trimester of pregnancy were forbidden to drink it. After childbirth wine tainted the milk of nurses and deranged infants. Husbands were advised to forbid their wives wine on the pretext that female frailty would conduct them fatally from use to abuse.[275]

Augustine's legalistic language (*temulentus*, *litigo*, *obiecio*, *crimen*, *damno*, *periclito*) was anachronistic, since his prospective mother would not in the fourth century have been so charged with crime. Yet, just as he had blamed his father by republican morality for his "intoxicated" behavior at the baths, so he implicated her by ancient Roman custom in a grave social sin of the female sex. By her winebibbing Monica jeopardized her prospects for marriage and for progeny: him. Nursed by her milk, Augustine drank in the name of Christ the savior but also the proclivity to concupiscence that had once circulated in her veins as wine. When Augustine strained to recall the sin of his infancy, he first mentioned wailing for her breast.[276] By that memory he stereotyped himself as the son, for *filius* derived from *felo*, "to suck";[277] so that he was the suckled one. His boiling over in lust was unchecked by his mother; she refused him the boundary of marriage. Her bubbling over in drunkenness was checked, not by her parents or nurse, but by a female slave of the household. That alluded to the female slave who during the republic gave evidence to the authorities against the noble Roman women who were brewing poison alleged as medicine.[278] Augustine called her the divine source of his mother's cure, her tongue a surgical blade cutting off in one slash Monica's rottenness.[279] Female rottenness was harped on by moralists and satirists as symptomatic of a sick society, according to the established Roman principle associating the virtue of women with the welfare of the state. If the civic hearth, whose flame symbolized the continuity of the family and the community, was extinguished, the vestal

---

274 Richlin, "Invective against Women in Roman Satire," p. 68; Carcopino, *Daily Life in Ancient Rome*, p. 93.

275 Marcel Durry, "Les femmes et le vin," *Revue des études latines* 33 (1955):108-13. See in general Eyben, "Family Planning in Graceo-Roman Antiquity," *Ancient Society* 11-12 (1980-81):5-82.

276 Augustine, *Confessiones* 3.4.8; 1.7.11.

277 See Hallett, *Fathers and Daughters in Roman Society*, p. 212, without reference to Augustine.

278 For the history see Balsdon, *Roman Women*, pp. 30-31; Cantarella, *Pandora's Daughters*, p. 126.

279 Augustine, *Confessiones* 9.8.18.

virgins who tended it were scourged. If one of them violated chastity, she was buried alive. The tending of the familial hearth was the responsibility of the virtuous daughter.[280] Monica's filial drinking threatened familial stability.

Relative to the dining room, the bedroom was a private place; but it was still a room for the reception of intimate friends and for the conduct of confidential business, such as certain imperial trials. It participated in a social grading of the intimacy of guests: a promiscuous group in the atrium or the peristyle, a large group in the grandest room, a small group in the dining room, ones and twos in the bedroom.[281] Even the bedroom, among the most private of domestic spaces, was ambiguous. A Roman bedroom was of minimal size, furnished sparsely with couch, chest, chair, mat, pot. The bed was a mattress and bolster stuffed with straw or reeds for the poor, wool or down for the rich.[282] In north African homes it rested on a dais, its location marked by a simpler design of tiles than the rest of the room. Although bedrooms could be complex and opulent,[283] the mediocrity of private chambers contrasted with the luxury of reception rooms.[284] Bedrooms were juxtaposed with reception rooms in a commonplace arrangement of interspersing private and public spaces. Opening the bedroom door to strangers symbolized debauchery.[285]

The bedroom provided Augustine no social security. "In tribulation," he lamented, "a person can flee from the field to the city, from the public area to the house, from the house to the bedroom; yet tribulation will follow. For from the bedroom he has nowhere to flee, unless into his interior bedroom." Even that could be a perilous place: cluttered, smoky, flaming.[286] Augustine's conflict on the threshold of his conversion was "in my interior house," "in my heart," in anguish that moved him to cry out to his friend Alypius "in our bedroom." That was social, not private, space. Augustine berated both of them for their inability to quit its sexual activity. From the bedroom he rushed to the garden of the house, seated himself as far as possible from the apartments, then threw himself beneath a fig tree. That was another sexual symbol,[287] in the same class as the pear,[288] although also a so-

---

280 Pomeroy, *Goddesses, Whores, Wives, and Slaves*, pp. 210-11; and for the vestal fire as symbol of food for the state, Balsdon, *Roman Women*, pp. 231-34.

281 Wallace-Hadrill, "Social Structure of the Roman House," pp. 59, 94.

282 See Carcopino, *Daily Life in Ancient Rome*, pp. 152-53. See in general Mario Praz, *An Illustrated History of Interior Decoration* (London: Thames & Hudson, 1987), pp. 76-103.

283 Thébert, "Private Life and Domestic Architecture in Roman Africa," pp. 378-79.

284 Charles-Picard, *Civilisation de l'Afrique romaine*, p. 221.

285 Thébert, "Private Life and Domestic Architecture in Roman Africa," pp. 361, 378.

286 Augustine, *Enarrationes in psalmos* 45.3.

287 Augustine, *Confessiones* 8.8.19. See Vinzenz Bucheit, "Augustinus unter dem Feigenbaum (zu Conf. VIII)," *Vigiliae christianae* 22 (1968): 257-71; Adams, *Latin Sexual Vocabulary*, pp. 113-14; Boyle, "Augustine in the Garden of Zeus," pp. 121-22. For figs as fodder for pigs see Renfrew, *Palaeoethnobotany*, p. 136.

cial symbol.

The figs on the dinner table of the satirical Trimalchio were north African.[289] The very Punic war had been incited by Cato brandishing in the senate figs from north Africa and demanding, "Carthage must be destroyed."[290] A fig tree worshiped as sacred grew in the Roman forum on the spot where, when the foundations of the empire were collapsing, a virtuous and pious man Curtius had leaped into the chasm to his death. A sacred fig tree near the Lupercal marked the shrine of Rumina, numen of suckling and goddess of Rome, where the wolf had legendarily nursed the civic founders Romulus and Remus.[291] To shelter beneath a fig tree was to be concupiscent. Concupiscence defined Roman society at all times, beginning from the infantile sin of gaping for the breast, and in every place, beginning with the bedroom. After his conversion Augustine asked God to speak truthfully in his heart, while he dismissed all others and retired to his own bedroom. There he sang love songs to him, groaning inaudible groans. In his mental pilgrimage he recalled Jerusalem, elevating his heart to that city as his fatherland and his mother, over which God reigned in the comprehensive social roles of father, guardian, and husband. It was there, not in the orchard near the familial vineyard, that were produced the first fruits of his spirit.[292] God conferred good "not in my vineyard, not in my herd, not in my cask, not in my table, but in my heart."[293]

Augustine's conversion did not transpire in a house, even in the relative privacy of the bedroom, but in its garden. The garden recalled paradise.[294] The house was social space with impure associations. During that era there was such coincidence of architectural elements, like multiple apses or arches supported by columns, that certain buildings in Roman north Africa are not decisively identifiable as public or private. In official residences or guesthouses, and in centers of confraternities, the needs to be served architecturally were similar to those in a private home. Although all spaces belonged to private life, individuals could dwell in a house in various ways, ranging from sheer isolation to the reception of crowds of visitors with whom the owner was not socially intimate. Some areas were closed to outsiders, others not; yet labels of private and public were inaccurate. The arrangement of the public areas determined the very location of the more intimate rooms. The total design was shaped by the master's social requirements. The common areas bore the flow of the traffic. Public and private

---

288 Pliny, *Naturalis historia* 15.19.68.

289 Petronius, *Satyricon* 35.

290 Pliny, *Naturalis historia* 15.20.74-76; Plutarch, *Cato maior* 27.1.

291 Varro, *De agri cultura*, 15.20.77; 2.11.5.

292 Augustine, *Confessiones* 1.7.11; 12.16.23.

293 Augustine, *Enarrationes in psalmos* 53.8, cited by Getty, *Life of the North Africans*, p. 3.

294 See also Grimal, *Jardins romains*.

space was heterogeneous, with rooms interspersed. There were multiple doors, or hangings, to close off access; curtains barred and blocked passage. Compartmentalization facilitated independent access to individual rooms.[295] Yet domesticity was necessarily social, and society for Augustine was corrupt.

The house itself communicated with the street. There was no simple doorway in a façade. A main entrance, as a symbolic and particular transition from the outside to the inside, was emphasized by the construction of a porch, or a roof on two columns. The true division between the house and the street was the door, or the gate, or several hierarchical gates. The entrance as a symbol of social ambition was the focus of architectural attention by its opulence. Beyond it was the vestibule, another transitional area, in which the visitor was scrutinized. There were enclaves for business, such as the unloading of provisions for the household. Many houses had shops along the outside walls for the sale of household products or for rental to outsiders; there were apartments for tenants. The very right to a private life as a Roman citizen was owed to the city. As the architect Vitruvius declared, "A house came into being not in response to individual needs but as a consequence of social organization." The unity of domestic architecture depended on the social homogeneity and political cooperation of the regional elites, who built to live in the Roman manner. They so symbolized their participation in the imperial government and enhanced their prestige before the local clientele. Social theory gave domestic architecture an ideological cast.[296]

The origin of housing in classical architectural theory was social. Humans had universally lived in simple savagery until the accidental discovery of fire enabled the establishment of society. The sounds uttered around the fire created speech and language, later the deliberative assembly and social exchange. Those conditions favored the construction of shelters. The art of imitation and the application of intelligence and industry to shelters produced improvements; those promoted advances in carpentry, then in other trades and techniques. The transition from rusticity to civilization was explained by deriving the theory of cultural development from the theory of domestic development. Yet building, then architecture, were criticized precisely as invented from such necessity. God created humans needy in order to compel them to discover arts. Those arts were the products of persons disinterested in religion and philosophy, since prosperity at building insured the neglect of intellection. The construction of buildings as an unphilosophical task was moralized by observation of the state of Roman

---

295 Thébert, "Private Life and Domestic Architecture in Roman Africa," pp. 353, 333, 384-85, 387-88.

296 Ibid., pp. 331, 353-57, 319, 327, 329.

cities. Its multistory tenements, in which the majority of the populace lived, were forever collapsing. They were shoddily engineered with their base insubstantial to their height. Such were the products of ingenuity, not wisdom, the work of practical persons bent on the ordinary. Wisdom taught minds, not trained hands. The acerb disparagement of the tradesman suggested, nevertheless, his effectiveness in altering the very nature that preoccupied philosophers.[297]

Augustine catalogued and praised the arts that human genius had discovered and developed for necessity or for pleasure. He included architecture, the "wonderful, stupendous" achievements of the industry of building.[298] Yet he concurred with the moralists who personified building as a vice, Aedificatio. Its luxury was a social debility that squandered patrimony on show.[299] The flimsy apartments by unscrupulous and avaricious builders were a visible model of corruption from Thagaste to Hippo. For the lack of a regional history, evidence for urban development in Roman north Africa is sketchy, with many sites desolate since imperial rule and with few detailed archaeological excavations.[300] Yet hundreds of inscriptions disclosed the vitality, population, and prosperity of many of its cities and towns in the fourth century. Characteristic in the proconsular province was the large number of small towns, like Thagaste, with the entire apparatus of the Roman municipality. The abundant epigraphic evidence is that the peak of the construction and repair of public buildings and works in Proconsularis was A. D. 363-83.[301] Thus Augustine's formation, as the son of a decurion responsible for such projects, coincided with the boom in building. The architect in charge of public buildings for Carthage even played a cameo role in his *Confessions*, as the rescuer from the mob in the marketplace of a student falsely accused of theft. Yet he saved him not because he truthfully perceived his innocence but because he had noticed him socializing in the home of a senator.[302]

There was no epigraphic trace documenting Christianity, however. No

---

[297] Clarence J. Glacken, *Traces on the Rhodian Shore: Nature and Culture in Western Thought from Ancient Times to the End of the Eighteenth Century* (Berkeley: University of California Press, 1967), pp. 107-8, 297, 245, 118. For philosophy vs. architecture see, e. g., Seneca, *Epistulae morales* 90.7-11, 16, 24, 42-44.

[298] Augustine, *De civitate Dei* 22.24.

[299] See Wallace-Hadrill, "Social Structure of the Roman House," p. 44, without reference to Augustine.

[300] See Paul-Albert Février, "Notes sur le développement urbain en Afrique du nord: Les exemples comparés de Djemila et de Sétif," *Cahiers archéologiques* 14 (1964):1-47.

[301] Warmington, *North African Provinces*, pp. 27, 33; Lepelley, "Saint Augustin et la cité romano-africaine," pp. 14-15; idem, "La crise de l'Afrique romaine au début du Ve siècle, d'après les lettres nouvellement découvertes de saint Augustin," *Académie des inscriptions et belles-lettres, comptes rendus des séances de l'année 1981* (Paris: Boccard, 1981), p. 449; and for public works, idem, *Cités de l'Afrique romain*, 1:59-120.

[302] Augustine, *Confessiones* 6.9.15.

city constructed a church or a monument to the new official religion; those were built by local congregations from their own resources or from donations by the laity. Inscriptions on the dedication of Christian monuments mentioned bishops, priests, donors, but never public authorities, provincial or municipal. The donor of a mosaic to a basilica might be from a grand local family active in municipal affairs but in the church he was identified as a believer, not as a magistrate or dignitary. There was no conversion of municipal life: public buildings were not decorated with Christian symbols, and there was no clerical benediction on new appointees or at the opening of a curial session. The municipal and the ecclesiastical were separate domains with distinct roles.[303]

The ancient pagan city was a coherent unity politically, socially, and culturally. Christians had ruptured that unity by declaring themselves strangers in the city. That had been a fundamental reason for their persecution. Although after the edict of Constantine they coexisted with the pagan citizens peacefully, the two orders were profoundly distinct, even opposite. Christians did not live within a Christian system of a stable universe, perceived as coherent and having a collective order founded on moral and cultural values unanimously assented. Theirs was the official religion, but it was not the civic bonding. Law and institution, education and culture were pagan. There remained a profound division between the traditional civilization of north African cities and the Christian ideal of its citizen Augustine.[304] That was the urban reality establishing his theological dichotomy of the city of God and the city of man.[305] Ordinary urbanization, to the fact of the construction of buildings, undergirded his undomestic mentality. When Augustine did write of the divine indwelling, its human habitation was a consecrated temple, not a secular home like his own, with its necessary transaction of municipal business in the peristyle.

Augustine rarely mentioned the home, either as edifice or as household.[306] His silence coincided with the best documented aspect of ancient life: the male outside the home. About male domesticity, the law stated its substance; it was almost as if Roman men had no domestic life.[307] Augustine borrowed marginally from architecture, mentioning the use of stone and wood as building materials[308] or the examination by the carpenter of the pith

---

303 Lepelley, "Saint Augustin et la cité romano-africaine," pp. 34-35; idem, *Cités de l'Afrique romaine*, 1:331-69, 371-76.

304 Lepelley, *Cités de l'Afrique romaine*, pp. 402-3, 383.

305 For the theology see R. A. Markus, *Saeculum: History and Society in the Theology of St Augustine* (Cambridge: Cambridge University Press, 1970), pp. 45-71.

306 Hamman, *Vie quotidienne en Afrique du nord*, p. 101; Mary Emily Keenan, *The Life and Times of St. Augustine as Revealed in his Letters*, Catholic University of America Patristic Series, 45 (Washington, D. C.: Catholic University of America Press, 1935), p. 57.

307 See Rousselle, *Porneia*, p. 8.

308 Augustine, *Epistolae* 228.7, cited by Keenan, *Life and Times of St. Augustine*, p. 57.

of hewn wood for damage or rot.[309] The practice of erecting scaffolds during construction prompted a moral. The architect employed them to build a house that would last, while Augustine heard all about him the cries of the senescence of the world. If the world was indeed crumbling, he asked, then why did its inhabitants not flee it? An architect who warned that a house was about to collapse would be heeded without hesitation; yet, when the Architect of the world revealed that it was about to tumble into ruins, people disbelieved him. That sermon about collapsing tenements was realistic; his idealization about standard architectural practice was not. He preached that a builder established very solid foundations in the earth to erect the structure securely. In those foundations he set solid blocks capable of supporting the edifice, with the foundations always proportionate to the size of the building.[310] The remarkable characteristic of an apartment building was indeed its dizzying height, which suspended the Roman city in the air. But it was erected perilously, for its foundation was not usually calculated to bear its weight.[311] Augustine's analogy was unfactual. Yet he knew of failure in engineering, for he also preached on temples constructed of stone and marble, reinforced with iron and lead, that nevertheless crumbled. That was his moral on mortality.[312]

Just as a city consisted in its citizens rather than its walls,[313] so the Roman term "house" included its dwellers.[314] A marble edifice might be bad and a straw hut good. In his descriptions of the homes of the wealthy, Augustine inventoried marble walls, graceful pillars, fretted ceilings, spacious peristyles, golden hangings, beautiful art. Yet he disparaged the splendor as good; for the sky covered as a roof both rich and poor, and starry skies were more pleasing to the poor than gilded ceilings to the rich. About the houses of the poor he noted only that they were small and smoky.[315] The poor might even be homeless, lodging in the open air, or lurking among the porticoes and markets. He complained to his congregation about the Dives ignoring the pauper lying on his doorstep.[316] Housing he described as socially contentious. Litigations over the right of sunshine through windows unjustly sought the demolition of the obstructing house.[317]

---

309 Augustine, *Enarrationes in psalmos* 45.3, cited by Getty, *Life of the North Africans*, p. 9.

310 Augustine, *Sermones* 60.6.7; 362.8.8, cited by Getty, *Life of the North Africans*, p. 30.

311 Carcopino, *Daily Life in Ancient Rome*, pp. 24-26.

312 Augustine, *Sermones* 84.1, cited by Getty, *Life of the North Africans*, p. 60.

313 Augustine, *Sermo de urbis excido* 6, cited by Markus, *Saeculum*, pp. 61, 149.

314 Saller, "*Familia, domus* and the Roman Conception of the Family," pp. 349-55.

315 Augustine, *Sermones* 174.4, cited by Getty, *Life of the North Africans*, p. 60. *Enarrationes in psalmos* 72.13; 127.16, cited by Getty, *Life of the North Africans*, pp. 57-61, and van der Meer, *Augustine the Bishop*, p. 135. See also for ornamental ceilings vs. starry skies Ambrose, *Hexameron* 9.8.52.

316 Augustine, *Sermones* 345.1, cited by MacMullen, *Roman Social Relations*, p. 87.

317 Augustine, *Sermones* 50.5.7; *Enarrationes in psalmos* 128.5, cited by Getty, *Life of the*

An extensive epideictic topic of describing a man by his house had originated, as did pears for the harvest, with the palace of Alkinoös.[318] Augustine typified humanity by that of Pelops, situated in an ancient, haunted, nocturnal grove of melancholy boughs, and glowing eerily from within without a sign of fire.[319] Augustine could not provide a home for God because he judged himself, like all humans, profoundly disoriented. Siting was the primary consideration in the founding of cities and for the foundation of homes. Position had to be considered concerning the winds and the sunrise, for each aspect of the compass had its own characteristic. Cities oriented toward the sunrise were healthy cities, because the solar rays purified; and their inhabitants thrived in temperament, intelligence, and voice.[320] Pliny, the younger's, villa was enhanced by "the amenities of its situation," socially in relation to other homes and naturally to the atmosphere of sun and wind and changing seasons.[321] A tradition of meditation on the city influenced urban foundation and renovation; and it determined housing by dictating sites, dimensions, and orientations. Domestic location affected domestic design.[322] Christian churches were oriented east to salute Christ in eclipse of the imperial cult of a solar Apollo.[323] Augustine confessed that he had his back to the source of light and his face to its illuminated objects, so that it was unilluminated. He had his back to God.[324]

His mother had piously feared for his turning his back, and not his face, to God.[325] The fate of those who turned their backs on God was to flow like rivers into the bitterness of the sea, Augustine's cardinal metaphor for creation as corrupted. With it he disallowed humans even the security of walking on land, for they were condemned like fish to swim together in nets where they devoured one another. Their only rescue was aboard the plank of the cross piloted by Christ across the tempestuous waves of this world. Christians pilgrimaged in a flood that spurted bitter and briny from Adam's navel.[326] The bitterness of the sea was like the bitterness of the wine with

---

North Africans, p. 59.

318 Don Cameron Allen, *Image and Meaning: Metaphoric Traditions in Renaissance Poetry*, rev. ed. (Baltimore, Md.: Johns Hopkins University Press, 1968), pp. 191-96.

319 See Seneca, *Thyestes* 641-82.

320 Hippocrates, *De aeris, aquis, locis* 1, 5.

321 Pliny, the younger, *Epistulae* 2.17.1, 16-19, 27; trans. Radice, 1:133.

322 Thébert, "Private Life and Domestic Architecture in Roman Africa," pp. 327, 339.

323 See Franz Joseph Dölger, *Sol Salutis: Gebet und Gesang im christlichen Altertum*, Liturgiewissenschaftliche Quellen und Forschungen, 16-17 (1925; reprint ed., Münster: Aschendorff, 1972), pp. 1-20; idem, *Die Sonne der Gerechtigkeit und der Schwarze: Eine Religionsgeschichtliche Studie zum Taufgelobnis*, ibid., 14 (1918; reprint ed., Münster: Aschendorff, 1970), pp. 1-10.

324 Augustine, *Confessiones* 4.16.30; 2.3.6.

325 Ibid. 2.3.7.

326 Boyle, "Cusanus at Sea: The Topicality of Illuminative Discourse," *Journal of Religion* 71 (1991):183-90.

whose taste the slave accused his mother;[327] as if it were, as Homer poetized, "wine-dark."[328] At the climax of the memorial part of his *Confessions*, Augustine located himself socially at a seaport. That was a perilous place according to the belief that associated geography and virtue. Dangers to mortals were classically gravest at a maritime location, with its opportunities for foreign influences and the evils of cultural contact. Ports participated in the advantages of trade but they also imported alien ideas that could disturb a civilization, luring it from its ancient customs and traditions. The maritime location caused minds to wander in hopes, dreams, temptations, to a luxury incited by the commerce of the sea.[329] Cicero believed that Romulus upon his arrival on the coast had founded Rome in the interior because of the dangers of the Mediterranean sea.[330] The sea also stirred Augustine's mind to flight from its temptations of luxury and culture.

He was in a seaport with his mother, at Ostia, awaiting her departure for north Africa. Of all the Roman provinces, Augustine's native Proconsularis had the closest association with Ostia, whose facilities as a harbor were extensively developed for the import of its grain. The mosaics on the pavement of the sixty-one small rooms opening off the portico behind the theater are dominated by the names of traders from north African towns, who had representatives there to manage their business.[331] Hippo Regius, whose episcopacy Augustine would assume, was with its fortified walls and coastal guard such an export center for the Roman market.[332] Ostia was in his *Confessions* an ideal location indicating the social orientation of Augustine's family. The curia to which his father belonged was responsible for collecting the annual provincial payment of taxes by produce and for shipping it to Rome through the port of Ostia. North Africa was the single greatest granary of the Roman empire, providing durum wheat of the finest quality.[333] Cereals were grown in the northern strip, with the southern limit at Madauros, the demarcation of the necessary rainfall for grain.[334] The standard of living of the mass of its rural population was at the level of subsistence

327 Augustine, *Confessiones* 9.8.18.

328 Homer, *Odyssey* 2.420.

329 See Glacken, *Traces on the Rhodian Shore*, pp. 92, 102.

330 Raymond Chevallier, *Ostie antique: Ville et port* (Paris: Belles lettres, 1986), pp. 12-13.

331 See Russell Meiggs, *Roman Ostia*, 2d ed. (Oxford: Clarendon, 1973), pp. 214-15; Rickman, *Corn Supply of Ancient Rome*, pp. 69, 126, 226. For the Piazzale delle Corporazioni see Raissa Calza and Ernest Nash, *Ostia* (Florence: Sansoni, n.d.), pls. 59, 91.

332 See Rickman, *Corn Supply of Ancient Rome*, p. 110; van der Meer, *Augustine the Bishop*, p. 19.

333 See Rickman, *Corn Supply of Ancient Rome*, pp. 13, 112, 202-4, 67-71, 231-35; Charles-Picard, *Civilisation de l'Afrique romaine*, pp. 59-76 on agriculture; and Boudewijn Sirks, *Food for Rome: The Legal Structure of the Transportation and Processing of Supplies for the Imperial Distributions in Rome and Constantinople*, Studia amstelodamensia ad epigraphicam, ius antiquum et papyrologicam pertinentia, 31 (Amsterdam: J. C. Gieben, 1991).

334 Rickman, *Corn Supply of Ancient Rome*, pp. 109-10.

through taxation, rent, and expropriation; but it paid its taxation of grain, at the rate of eighths.[335] That taxation of grain was regulated by imperial constitutions, overseen in north Africa by a special official on site, and organized by the local shippers.[336] Augustine's father was involved as a curial landowner; he was both tax collector and taxed citizen. So important was the tax that the grain officials based in north Africa could be paraded before the populace in Rome and executed or freed according to their reception. When the fleet of grain shipped from north Africa was delayed in A. D. 359-61 because of poor weather, the urban prefect of Rome appeased the rioters who demanded his death by offering them as a sacrifice his small sons. Twin gods obligingly calmed the winds so that the ships might enter Ostia.[337]

Yet north African corn was in easy grasp of Rome by sea, usually a week away. The navigational season was from late May to early September, or from early March to early November. The direction of the prevailing winds over water in summer created the pattern for sea trading. Ships sailing southerly from Italy to north Africa could expect to make good time on an easy journey. A voyage from Ostia to north Africa is recorded as the fastest in antiquity: two-hundred-seventy nautical miles in two days.[338] Augustine's location of his mother's ultimate voyage, across the material sea to the celestial port, as departing from Ostia to north Africa bade her Godspeed. Their conversation at Ostia recalled the dialogue of Minucius Felix's *Octavius*, in which other north Africans, a pagan and a Christian, strolled its shore near the baths. That apology had argued against skepticism for the resurrection of persons as immanent in nature, in the erect posture and uplifted gaze of humans. Its argument from creation involved the well-kept house. By its refinement, arrangement, and furnishing, such a domicile signified a superior owner who cared for it. So did the providence, order, and law of the house of the world indicate a lord of the universe.[339] The dialogue testified to the favor of philosophy in Ostia after its decline in commercial prosperity. A marble head of a philosopher, probably Plotinus, has been found in an attractive building with furnishings suggestive of a cultural society or educational institution.[340]

Originally a military fortification, Ostia was entirely and magnificently rebuilt in the second and early third centuries. Scratches on the walls of houses, in contrast to those of Pompeii, had no literary quotations. Trade

---

335 Peter Garnsey, *Famine and Food Supply in the Graeco-Roman World: Responses to Risk and Crisis* (Cambridge: Cambridge University Press, 1988), pp. 182-83, 245.

336 Rickman, *Corn Supply of Ancient Rome*, pp. 112, 129-30.

337 Garnsey, *Famine and Food Supply in the Graeco-Roman World*, pp. 243, 182-83; Meiggs, *Roman Ostia*, p. 345.

338 Rickman, *Corn Supply of Ancient Rome*, pp. 129, 128; Meiggs, *Roman Ostia*, p. 56.

339 Minucius Felix, *Octavius* 2; 11-12; 13; 17-18; 40.

340 Meiggs, *Roman Ostia*, p. 393; Calza and Nash, *Ostia*, p. 78 and pl. 110.

was the city's dominant concern, as evident from the graffiti of numbers, accounts, and records of debts and dates, and from the many sketches of ships down to the details of their rigging.[341] Yet, when Constantine withdrew the municipal rights from Ostia and transferred them to Portus, the hub that had been in its diversity and utility the pulse of Rome declined. Although Ostia remained the seat of the annual taxation by produce from the provinces, by the arrival of Augustine and his family it was commercially decadent, its civic authority absent or indolent. As the last pagan poet proclaimed, only the glory of Aeneas remained. The shippers had likely moved; inscriptions were scavenged from their office building to repair the theater. Edifices destroyed by fire were not rebuilt, while those that toppled were left ruined. Numerous buildings were crumbling through neglect or abandon, collapsed above the second story. Temples were stripped of their marble decorations, statues were mutilated, and the loot carted off to repair pavements or floors. The bases of statues were clamped together for walling, heads of quality raised the level of the main street, and entire statues blocked the entrances of houses from raiders. The public latrine built in the forum had seats of marble slabs taken from sarcophagi, tombstones, and other architecture. The ruined edifices and the very streets were heaped with shards, rubble, and garbage. The dead could even be buried in the public baths.[342] When Augustine, in the cultural commonplace that bathing eased and cleansed bodily and mental pain,[343] sought relief there upon the death of his mother, he was hardly escaping mortality.[344]

By then the baths were more important than the warehouses. Ostia had been a city of brick, with lavish marble façades of temples and public buildings. Yet it was still a middle-class town, with a harbor for maintaining Rome's supplies, until even the brick industry collapsed under the failure of centralized powers. The decline of the apartment and the renewal of the house reflected the decline of trade; and, with the collapse of the mercantile class, a yawning gulf between the rich and the poor. In the fourth century Ostia was converted into an attractive residential town providing the wealthy with the amenities of leisure. Its independent houses of the late empire indicated rich residents, perhaps not active in civic management, although the prefect for the provincial taxation, who was directly in charge of the town, may have lived there temporarily. Traders and travelers whose principal business was in Portus may have preferred its escape from the bus-

---

[341] Meiggs, *Roman Ostia*, pp. 64-78, 230.

[342] G. Calza and G. Becatti, *Ostia*, trans. C. H. Penrock and Meiggs, 5th ed. (Rome: Istituto poligrafico dello stato, 1965), pp. 10-11, 13, 15; Gustav Hermansen, *Ostia: Aspects of Roman City Life* (Calgary: University of Alberta Press, 1981), p. 12; Chevallier, *Ostie antique*, p. 13; Meiggs, *Roman Ostia*, pp. 4, 94, 98, 309.

[343] See Yegul, *Baths and Bathing in Classical Antiquity*, p. 5.

[344] Augustine, *Confessiones* 9.12.32. For the public baths see Chevallier, *Ostie antique*, pp. 74-82; Meiggs, *Roman Ostia*, pp. 404-20, and for the cemeteries, pp. 455-70.

tle of that harbor. Perhaps a similar desire for quiet explained the lodging of Augustine and Monica in Ostia. Probably they stayed there with friends or acquaintances, senatorials with north African connections, such as Anicius Bassus, who would erect Monica's epitaph. Ostia was dominated socially by Roman senators. The region traditionally had the lure of leisure—the Laurentine villa of Pliny, the younger, was only about five miles distant. The new houses within the town were maintained handsomely in decorative style and architectural form. Novel architecture emerged, such as stylized and schematic capitals presaging the Byzantine fashion, and columns combined with the brick arch that was to become a common medieval pattern. The striking feature of housing in Ostia was the wealth of marble. A common feature was retirement from the street, a focus inward, with a display of water in a fountain or even a nymphaeum in a spacious garden.[345]

When Monica's departure for north Africa was imminent, she and Augustine were alone together, leaning on a window, from which they could observe the garden within the courtyard of the house where they lodged. There, far from the crowds, they rested after their long arduous journey. They conversed sweetly about the future: the eternal life of the saints. Meditating through creation by degrees, from the delights of carnal sensuality they achieved with rapid thought the wonders of the human mind, until with understanding they transcended it to approach slightly, although with a full "heartbeat," the boundary line (*regio*) of eternity. That was simply "to be."[346] As still carnal, they could not cross it; for, as Augustine postulated in *De Trinitate*, there was a common boundary (*confinium*) that humans shared with beasts. And, the will to see the window required one act, the will to see through that window the passersby, yet another.[347] With his vision of the boundary line of eternity Augustine nevertheless replaced the social horizon of his family, which was the basic boundary line of necessity. Houses in Ostia could be sacral, for they did have religious shrines;[348] but Augustine avoided that symbolic choice. Although he was situated with his mother in a house, they were focused outwardly on its axial garden as symbolic of paradise.[349] Their leaning out the window physically anticipated the spiritual straining of their minds and hearts. Their posture and gesture were quite the opposite of the metaphor in the Song of Songs, where the

---

345 Meiggs, *Roman Ostia*, pp. 90, 72-73, 77, 83, 97, 94-95, 213, 212, 69, 258-61. For Monica's epitaph see p. 400; and for mothers' epitaphs in general, Dixon, *Roman Mother*, pp. 199-200.

346 Augustine, *Confessiones* 9.10.23-24.

347 Augustine, *De Trinitate* 12.1.1; 11.6.10.

348 David G. Orr, "Roman Domestic Religion: The Evidence of the Household Shrines," in *Aufstieg und Niedergang der römischen Welt: Geschichte und Kultur Roms im Spiegel der neueren Forschung*, ed. Hildegard Temporini (Berlin: De Gruyter, 1972), 2.16.2:1587.

349 Augustine, *Confessiones* 9.10.23. For background see Jacqueline Amat, *Songes et visiones: L'au-delà dans la littérature latine tardive* (Paris: Études augustiniennes, 1985).

lover peers in through the lattices of the window at the soul.[350] Augustine and Monica were tending outwardly for God. They were in a house, but neither it, nor they, were the divine house: that was without.

Windows in antiquity were minor social centers for conversations with neighbors, especially those opposite across the narrow street.[351] Windows in Ostia lit the interior of houses through the exterior walls facing the street and the courtyard. They were usually rectangular and of normal size, with double or triple openings, occasionally loopholes. Those opening onto gardens and interiors were larger and made of selenite or mica, although not glass. There was frequently an interior courtyard, neither an atrium nor a peristyle, onto which the windows, stairways, and doors opened, as in modern apartment buildings. In Ostia the traditional Roman house was completely altered in plan and elevation, to the legal maximum of four stories, so that space was extended vertically, rather than horizontally.[352] Houses in that city were narrow, and their tenants leaned on their windowsills to gawk at the sites or chat from apartment to apartment. Below the window on the sidewalk the flayer stripped a carcass, the grammarian droned the alphabet, the notary drew up a contract, the barber shaved a customer, the cleaner hung garments, and the butcher cut meat. There were itinerant vendors and lounging gamblers, and, especially for the idlers in the porticoes, the street was their parlor. Ostia afforded scarce privacy; its life was public. By extension of social space people spent their daily labor or leisure in their neighbor's house.[353] Even wealthy homes were not segregated, for it was the Roman urban pattern to mingle the residential with the commercial and the industrial. Even the spacious independent houses of the aristocracy employed their frontage on the streets for shops. Social distinctions between different areas were not readily apparent in Ostia, as rich and poor rubbed housing together without a visible slum.[354]

Augustine and Monica had their backs to that street. They had their backs to the Roman empire, for it was at Ostia that Aeneas had landed from north Africa to sacrifice the prodigious sow and found the new city.[355] Their portrait at the window was social, archetypal: the Madonna, as the mother with son. Augustine's father was celestially removed from the scene by death. His sister was absent. His male siblings and his son were also

---

350 For the topic see Hans-Jürgen Horn, "Respiciens per fenestras, prospiciens per cancellos: Zur Typologie des Fensters in der Antike," *Jahrbuch für Antike und Christentum* 10 (1967):30-60.

351 Hermansen, "The Medianum and the Roman Apartment," *Phoenix* 24 (1970):344.

352 Calza and Becatti, *Ostia*, pp. 17-19. For housing in Ostia see also Meiggs, *Roman Ostia*, pp. 235-62; Chevallier, *Ostie antique*, pp. 86-99; Calza and Nash, *Ostia*, pp. 21-38.

353 Carcopino, *Daily Life in Ancient Rome*, pp. 64-65.

354 Meiggs, *Roman Ostia*, p. 142.

355 Vergil, *Aeneid* 8.43-44, 83.

absent, only entering the room at Monica's death for the expected rites.[356] Women in Ostia were commemorated on funeral monuments affectionately; one, Sergia Prisca, received a public funeral as tribute to her son. They owned houses and slaves, even a workshop, but they had no place in the trade guilds. They were prominent in religion, however, especially in the cults of the goddesses.[357] Ostia was a fitting location for Augustine's homage to his mother; for the cult of the Magna Mater had been among its most important, with her sacrifices of a bull and with her sacred colleges prominent in its colonial life. Ostia provided, of all cities outside of Rome, the most valuable epigraphic and archaeological evidence for the Phrygian cults under the empire. The ship that brought Cybele's sacred stone, credited with the salvation of the republic during the second Punic war, was greeted at Ostia. There it was grounded at the mouth of the river, unable to be dislodged, until a woman Claudia Quinta, who prayed to the goddess for vindication from false accusation, jumped in the water and miraculously towed the vessel up the Tiber.[358] Augustine loathed the cult of the Magna Mater, whose eunuchs he remembered from the streets of Carthage. In their debauchery they surpassed even the gods.[359] He displaced that impure cult with the memory of his chaste mother.

Women as models for admiration in Roman society were often widows, enhanced in status because of their command of property.[360] As a widow desolate in this world, Monica personified the entire city of God.[361] Her contemplation with her son was of the divine household in which the saints dwelled simply, abstracted from the diversity of ordinary life. That place in which Monica and Augustine lodged in Ostia may have been an inn, ordinarily a house with an atrium or interior courtyard, providing chambers upstairs for guests and stables for the poor. Because of the bad reputation of hotels, however, Christians preferred a hospitable home; and so presented letters of recommendation signed by their bishop that would admit them as

---

356 Augustine, *Confessiones* 9.11.27; 9.12.29. For the expectation that the children would perform the funeral rites see Dixon, *Roman Family*, p. 109; Wiedemann, *Adults and Children in the Roman Empire*, pp. 39-41.

357 Meiggs, *Roman Ostia*, p. 229.

358 Lily Ross Taylor, *The Cults of Ostia*, Bryn Mawr College Monograph Series, 11 (Bryn Mawr, Pa.: Bryn Mawr College Press, 1912), pp. 57-66; Chevallier, *Ostie antique*, pp. 232-39; Meiggs, *Roman Ostia*, pp. 52, 355-66; and for the temple of Cybele and the field of the Magna Mater see Calza and Nash, *Ostia*, pls. 132, 133. The miracle was frequently cited, as by Minucius Felix, *Octavius* 7. Balsdon, *Roman Women*, p. 32; Meiggs, *Roman Ostia*, p. 365. For Christianity at Ostia see Chevallier, *Ostie antique*, pp. 253-61; Meiggs, *Roman Ostia*, pp. 389-92, 518-26; Février, "Ostie et Porto à la fin de l'antiquité: Topographie religieuse et vie sociale," *Mélanges d'archéologie et d'histoire* 70 (1958):295-330.

359 Augustine, *De civitate Dei* 7.26.

360 Dixon, *Roman Mother*, pp. 31, 35.

361 Augustine, *Enarrationes in psalmos* 131.23. For the status of women married once see Marjorie Lightman and William Zeisel, "*Univira*: An Example of Continuity and Change in Roman Society," *Church History* 46 (1977):19-32.

brethren into households or hospices.[362] In Ostia the buildings of Christians were those of the poor: unimpressive, improvised, shoddily constructed. Only one extant wealthy home had a Christian design, a mosaic of a fish and chalice at its entry.[363] An apartment in Ostia could also be termed a house, however; and two sites matched Augustine's description of the architectural plan: the apartments of the Insula di Bacco Fanciullo and its neighboring Insula dei Dipinti. They were defined by a central hall from which there was access to rooms, with windows open to the street and to the courtyard.[364] The latter building seems to have been abandoned by the beginning of the century, however, although there is no evidence from the ruins of a fire.[365]

The silting of the Tiber, which rendered its delta unnavigable, created at Ostia what the eruption of Vesuvius had at Pompeii and Herculaneum: a treasury of the domestic architecture of ancient Rome. Only the very wealthy in Ostia afforded a house; the middle and lower classes lived in apartment buildings, of which certain garden houses were the most impressive examples. In one neighborhood of apartments, shops, and gardens there was a planned complex that was strikingly similar to modern development in its sense of order and design. The pattern was rich in philosophical suggestiveness. In those garden houses of Ostia, dating to its heyday in the second century, a rigorous geometry prevailed at every scale, from the total configuration of the buildings to the layout of the mosaic floors. It was a large, single project of the city's boom in building, likely a private investment rather than an imperial patronage. It was situated desirably by the sea, away from the busy river front, and probably intended for well-off merchants. Constructed of vaulted concrete faced with brick, only the ground floors survive of what probably towered to four stories and housed between four-and seven-hundred people in unusually large and well decorated apartments.[366]

The complex was oriented to the east and focused on the center, a hallmark of Roman design. All that remains of the original gardens are six

---

362 See Hamman, *Vie quotidienne en Afrique du nord*, pp. 86-87, citing Augustine, *Sermones* 356.10 on such a hospice at Hippo. For accommodations in Ostia see Tönnes Kleberg, *Hôtels, restaurants et cabarets dans l'antiquité romaine: Études historiques et philologiques*, Bibliotheca ekmaniana, 61 (Uppsala: Almquist & Wiksells, 1957), pp. 53-56. For a rest home for Christian pilgrims at Portus built by the Roman senator Pammachius, who was known to Augustine, see Meiggs, *Roman Ostia*, p. 403.

363 Meiggs, *Roman Ostia*, pp. 400, 523.

364 Hermansen, *Ostia*, pp. 27-31, 15 n. 26. For the Insula dei Dipinti see ibid., pp. 43, 47, 151-52; Calza and Nash, *Ostia*, pl. 32; Meiggs, *Roman Ostia*, p. 68.

365 Meiggs, *Roman Ostia*, p. 250.

366 Donald J. Watts and Carol Martin Watts, "A Roman Apartment Complex," *Scientific American* 255-6 (1986):132-34. Their analysis is repeated in Jay Kaproff, *Connections: The Geometric Bridge between Art and Science* (New York: McGraw-Hill, 1991), pp. 28-29. For the garden houses see also Meiggs, *Roman Ostia*, pp. 139, 242-43.

fountains near the eastern and western edges of the courtyards. The fountains and courtyards were key elements in the order, deliberately sized and positioned by an unknown architect. His geometry lent unity and harmony to the design by ensuring proportional relations. The pattern, based on the square and a certain method of its division, was the "sacred cut." Executed by a straightedge and compass, it was based on a referential square divided into a grid of nine parts. In the pattern there was near equality of the arc and the straight line, so that empirically it almost squared the circle. The circle represented the unknowable spiritual; the square, the comprehensible world. To square the circle was to express the unknowable by the knowable, the sacred by the familiar. The sacred cut, pervasive in those apartment buildings, just as in the design of the Pantheon in Rome, emphasized the center and axes of the complex. It prevailed in the design of the apartments to the very detail of the windows, which as a unit were significantly seven-feet wide. Those dimensions were precisely the numbers generated by the Pythagorean procedure for approximating the irrational square root of two. The architect was making a philosophical statement, like the squaring of the circle. He expressed the irrational and undefinable by the rational and definable. The sacred cut was a geometric pattern among many Roman designs insistently repeated that were centralized and axial.[367] The posture and focus of Augustine and Monica out the window onto the garden of the courtyard of the house replicated it.

Their reasoning on the windowsill from the sensible to the ontological replicated the philosophy of the sacred cut. Perhaps they were in Ostia in that famous architecture, in an apartment designed for divinity, leaning out its window measuring the significant seven feet toward the boundary line of sheer existence. Or perhaps Augustine imaginatively located himself and his mother in that philosophically significant space. It was a certainly a calculated place. The lodging of son and mother at Ostia, whether real or rhetorical, was but a step to God, who dwelled vertically beyond them. The house was not invested with sacral significance, only with utilitarian value as a location. It was merely a topic or place from which they could reason toward the mind itself. Only in intellectual transcendence of that mind to its creative source in God did they brush eternity, where the felicitous society dwelled in the divine house. Theirs was but a temporary location symbolic of the human condition.

Instability sprang, or rather blew, from their native soil, for the constrained factors of the geography of north Africa—a very partitioned relief, a climate marked by a long summer of aridity, and often sparse vegetation—created a natural environment inauspicious for a powerful sedentary civiliza-

---

367 Watts and Watts, "A Roman Apartment Complex," pp. 134-38.

tion.[368] Thagaste itself was situated at the crossroads of important routes.[369] The instability, even restlessness, of humanity Augustine developed into an allegory of pilgrimage, which prevailed in Christian culture.[370] Humans were aliens in their own homes, even in their very chairs.[371] Any delight of the will, like the "rest" of a foot while walking, was not the end for which it strove. There was no rest of a citizen in his native country (or house), only the refreshment of a traveler in a lodging.[372] As Lord Fairfax in the seventeenth century would still moralize "Upon the New-built House att Apleton":

Thinke not ô Man that dwells herein
This House's a stay but as an Inne
Which for Convenience fittly stands
In way to one nott made with hands
But if a time here thou take Rest
Yett thinke Eternity's the Best.[373]

Pilgrimage was not indigenous to the gospel, however. The word occurs but once, when the travelers on the road to Emmaus greet a visionary Jesus as *peregrinus* (Lk. 24:18 Vulg.). That term meant not pilgrim but "foreigner": that Jesus was not a local citizen. Imagination, impelled by Augustine's ideology of peregrination, converted him into a pilgrim, with Christians dogged in his footsteps. The earliest such document dated from the Spanish kingdoms, from the monastery at Ripoll.[374] The earliest depictions were also Spanish: a miniature in the Ripoll bible, and a sculpture in

---

368 Madeleine Rouvillois-Brigol, "Quelques remarques sur les variations de l'occupation du sol dans le sud-est," in *Commission d'Afrique du nord*, Actes du IIIe colloque international, Montpellier, 1-5 avril 1985 (Paris: C. T. H. S., 1986) p. 36. For background on movement of the population see also Jean Marie Lassère, *Ubique populus: Peuplement et mouvements de population dans l'Afrique romaine de la chute de Carthage à la fin de la dynastie des Sévrès (146 a. C.- 235 p. C.* (Paris: Centre national de la recherche scientifique, 1977).

369 Perler, *Voyages de saint Augustin*, p. 120.

370 See Victorino Capágna, "Augustín, guía de peregrinos: Hacia una teología augustiniana de la peregrinación," *Helmantica* 26 (1975):73-85; Georg Nicolaus Knauer, "Peregrinatio animae (Zur Frage der Einheit der augustinischen Konfessionen)," *Hermes* 85 (1957):216-48; and for the city of God as alien, Johannes van Oort, *Jerusalem and Babylon: A Study into Augustine's City of God and the Sources of his Doctrine of the Two Cities*, Supplements to *Vigiliae christianae*, 14 (Leiden: E. J. Brill, 1991), pp. 131-42; and for the homelessness of humans, Markus, *Saeculum*, p. 167.

371 Augustine, *De civitate Dei* 1.15.

372 Augustine, *De Trinitate* 11.6.10.

373 Bodlein MS. Fairfax 40, cited by *The Poems and Letters of Andrew Marvell*, 1:282 note at line 71; Allen, *Image and Meaning*, p. 190.

374 For the plays on the Emmaus pericope see F. C. Gardiner, *The Pilgrimage of Desire: A Study of Theme and Genre in Medieval Literature* (Leiden: E. J. Brill, 1971), pp. 86-156; Julia Bolton Holloway, *The Pilgrim and the Book: A Study of Dante, Langland and Chaucer*, American University Studies, series 4, 42 (New York: Peter Lang, 1987), pp. 19-43; and on Christ as a pilgrim, Juergen Hahn, *The Origins of the Baroque Concept of Peregrinatio* (Chapel Hill: University of North Carolina Press, 1973), pp. 22, 29, 131-33.

the cloister of Santo Domingo de Silos in which Christ is garbed as a pilgrim down to the emblematic detail of shells.[375] Augustine would himself be portrayed in religious garb washing the feet of a pilgrim Christ in a painting from an Augustinian convent.[376] Like the medieval pilgrims on route to the shrine at Santiago de Compostela, travelers in Roman north Africa were in a vulnerable, even hostile, position. Although officials were carried in litters, commoners walked. Off the highways all classes were subject to the heat, the precipices, the rivers, the beasts, and the cutthroats. Bandits and migrant laborers were a particular threat, since the accidents of the terrain provided hiding places. Augustine wrote of proceeding vainly over trackless country among ambushing deserters from the military. The circumcellions institutionalized robbery for sustenance, as armed with hatchets and slings they scoured the isolated countryside besieging rural farmhouses and villas with the war cry: Praise be to God! Even the churches were open for the rest of travelers. Monica spent the night before embarking for Rome in a chapel near the port of Carthage.[377]

Augustine preached that to receive another pilgrim in hospitality was to feed and shelter Christ. "Take in a guest, if you would know the Savior."[378] The inn was the necessary place in his allegory of pilgrimage. As he exhorted the human as traveler, "Let him know that he walks a path, and in these riches enters as if into an inn. Let him take refreshment; he is a traveler. Let him refresh himself and pass on, for one does not take with him

---

[375] Justo Pérez de Urbel, *El claustro de Silos* (Burgos: Aldecoa, 1930), pp. 131-38, pls. pp. 133, 135; Sixten Ringbom, "Some Pictorial Conventions for the Recounting of Thoughts and Experiences in Late Medieval Art," in *Medieval Iconography and Narrative: A Symposium* (Odense: Odense University Press, 1980), pp. 50-51.

[376] St. Augustine washing the feet of the pilgrim Christ, from an Augustinian convent, Musée de Moulins, Toulouse. Reproduced in Joan Evans, *Monastic Iconography in France: From the Renaissance to the Revolution* (Cambridge: Cambridge University Press, 1970), pl. 51.

[377] Hamman, *Vie quotidienne en Afrique du nord*, pp. 84-85, citing Augustine, *Confessiones* 7.21.27; 5.8.15. For churches as overnight lodgings for travelers see Davies, *Secular Use of Church Buildings*, pp. 21-22.

[378] Augustine, *Sermones* 236.3; 225.3; *In epistolam Joannis ad Parthos* 10.6; 40.10, cited by Hamman, *Vie quotidienne en Afrique du nord*, p. 87. For some background on ancient hospitality see Julian Pitt-Rivers, "The Law of Hospitality," in idem, *The Fate of Shechem or the Politics of Sex: Essays in the Anthropology of the Mediterranean* (Cambridge: Cambridge University Press, 1977), pp. 94-112; idem, "The Stranger, the Guest and the Hostile Host: An Introduction to the Study of Laws of Hospitality," in *Contributions to Mediterranean Sociology*, ed. J. G. Peristiany, Publications of the Social Sciences Centre, Athens, 4 (Athens: Social Sciences Centre, 1963), pp. 13-30; Cristiano Grottanelli, "Notes on Mediterranean Hospitality," *Dialoghi di Archeologia* 9-10 (1976-77):186-94; Philippe Gauthier, "Notes sur l'étranger et l'hospitalité en Grèce et à Rome," *Ancient Society* 4 (1973):1-21. For typical literary scenes see Steve Reece, *The Stranger's Welcome: Oral Theory and the Aesthetics of the Homeric Hospitality Scene* (Ann Arbor: University of Michigan Press, 1993). For citation of patristic texts on hospitality see Rowan A. Greer, *Broken Lights and Mended Lives: Theology and Common Life in the Early Church* (University Park: Pennsylvania State University Press, 1986), pp. 122-36.

what he finds in an inn." Of temporal goods: "Let us place ourselves in the inn of this life, as if pilgrims about to pass through, not as possessors about to remain." Against avarice he emphasized that goods were like the inn of the traveler, not the mansion of the owner; they were merely for refreshment and passage. A person should use them as the pilgrim did the utensils in an inn.[379] Even adult baptism did not confer a new beginning. The convert was not healed but wounded still, like the traveler of the parable who was abandoned by the roadside from Jerusalem to Jericho, saved from death by the unguent of baptism, but resigned to a life of convalescence in the "inn" of the Church.[380] Augustine confessed that his own soul sensed itself to be, whether reclining or standing, in that very inn to which the Samaritan had carried the wounded wayfarer.[381]

Augustine believed that humans as rational animals were superior to the bee that cleverly made a honeycomb or the swallow that skillfully built a nest.[382] Yet in singing hymns, which pastime he recommended for pilgrims to relieve their journey and banish fear,[383] he inhaled and exhaled the divine fragrance in a house of hay,[384] as if he were a fledgling. A nest was a home, as in Ulysses's seaborn longing for Ithaca, "lodged like a nest upon the roughest of small crags."[385] Yet it was merely temporary shelter. "A house is selected for perpetuity, a nest is assembled for time." To be in the nest was to exist in faith. "Here is the nest, here the pilgrimage, and here the sighing." Certain people were blessed with vast farms or civic rank; yet "if you have your own home you are a pauper, if you have the house of God you are a Dives. In your home you will be afraid of robbers; in the house of God the very wall is God."[386] Augustine desired to fly back from earth to God,[387] but incapably fell rather than flew. God mercifully picked him up and replaced him in the nest, lest he be trampled to death.[388] God then faithfully hovered at a distance above his head.[389] So he confessed. Augustine borrowed the metaphor from Basil of Caesarea's commentary on the Spirit

---

379 Augustine, *Sermones* 14.4.6; 80.7; 177.2; 178.8; *Tractatus in evangelium Iohannis* 40.10, cited by Gerhart B. Ladner, "*Homo viator.* Mediaeval Ideas of Alienation and Order," *Speculum* 42 (1967):236 n. 4.

380 Augustine, *Sermones* 131.6, cited by Brown, *Religion and Society in the Age of St. Augustine*, p. 203.

381 Augustine, *De Trinitate* 15.12.50.

382 Augustine, *De ordine* 2.19.49.

383 Augustine, *Enarrationes in psalmos* 66.6; 125.4; 137.10, cited by Hamman, *Vie quotidienne en Afrique du nord*, p. 85.

384 Augustine, *Confessiones* 9.6.16, and for the flesh as a house of grass also 9.7.16.

385 Cicero, *De oratore* 1.44.196; *De oratore*, trans. E. W. Sutton and H. Rackham, 2 vols. (Cambridge, Mass.: Harvard University Press, 1948), 1:137.

386 Augustine, *Enarrationes in psalmos* 83.7-8.

387 Augustine, *Confessiones* 3.4.8.

388 Augustine, *Sermones* 51.6.

389 Augustine, *Confessiones* 3.3.5; in contrast to his praise as a rhetorician of Medea, 3.6.11.

stirring above the primal waters of creation (Gen. 1:2b). Such was the activity of the Holy Spirit warming the inchoate mass with fostering care, like a hen brooding upon her nest of eggs to impart vitality from the heat of her body.[390] Since the activity was love,[391] Augustine imagined a dove, symbol of Venus,[392] the mother of Aeneas. The egg symbolized hope; for, although it was not alive yet, it would be.[393] The young remained in the nest of faith with God, safely growing feathers and nourishing their wings of charity with the food of sound faith.[394]

Humanity had fallen into that nest from "our home, thy eternity."[395] God himself was a luminous and beautiful house of lovely decor, a dwelling of glory. To it Augustine on pilgrimage sighed to be carried like a stray animal on the shoulders of Christ, the "homebuilder," the mason or carpenter (*structor*). Condescending to human weakness, Christ had already "built for himself a humble house from our mud."[396] But that muddy construction of his human nature was not truly an edifice but only a road. In the incarnation God "through his humility has become a temporal road for us, so that through his divinity he might be an eternal dwelling for us."[397] It was from the divine house (*divina domo*)[398] that Augustine heard the command "Take it, read it" that prompted his conversion from cupidity to charity.[399] The chant was not of children playing in the neighborhood. It derived from a psalm praising the grandeur of creation as culminating in the wonder of humans: "Thou whose glory above the heavens is chanted by the mouth of babes and infants" (Ps. 8:1-2). In the imperial cult of Rome its place was the sacred household of the emperor (*divina domo*).[400] In Augustine's ap-

---

390 Basil, *Hexameron* 2.6, which Augustine had in Eustathius's Latin translation.

391 Augustine, *De Genesi ad litteram* 7.13-8.14, which repeats Eustathius's verb *superfero*.

392 See Geoffrey Grigson, *The Goddess of Love: The Birth, Triumph, Death and Return of Aphrodite* (London: Constable, 1976), pp. 186-90; Paul Friedrich, *The Meaning of Aphrodite* (Chicago: University of Chicago Press, 1978), pp. 76-77.

393 Augustine, *Epistolae* 130.7.16.

394 Augustine, *Confessiones* 4.16.31.

395 Ibid. See also O'Connell, "The Fall of the Soul in the *Confessions*," in *Atti II Sezioni di studio II-IV*, Congresso internazionale su S. Agostino nel XVL centenario della conversione, Roma, 15-20 settembre 1986, Studia ephemeridis "Augustinianum" 25 (Rome: Institutum Patristicum "Augustinianum," 1987), pp. 48-49.

396 Augustine, *Confessiones* 12.15.21; 7.18.24.

397 Augustine, *De Trinitate* 7.3.5.

398 Courcelle, *Recherches sur les Confessions de saint Augustin*, rev. ed. (Paris: E. De Boccard, 1968), pp. 195-96. See also Henry Chadwick, "History and Symbolism in the Garden at Milan," in *From Augustine to Eriugena: Essays on Neoplatonism and Christianity in Honor of John O'Meara*, ed. F. X. Martin and J. A. Richmond (Washington, D. C.: Catholic University of America Press, 1991), pp. 42-55.

399 Augustine, *Confessiones* 8.12.29.

400 For the term see Duncan Fishwick, "Une dédicace a la *domus diuina* a Lambese," in *Histoire et archéologie de l'Afrique du nord* (Paris: C. T. H. S., 1986), pp. 367-71, and Vol. 3 of idem, *The Imperial Cult in the Latin West: Studies in the Ruler Cult of the Western Provinces of the Roman Empire*, Études préliminaires aux religions orientales dans l'empire

propriation of the term he designated the Church as the celestial house of God. It was from that Church, proclaiming scripture, that he heard the decisive command to take and read its text. As he preached, by their elegance and magnificence, buildings humanly designed and constructed delighted corporeal sight. So did the decor of the house of God, the place of the tabernacle of his splendor, delight when the hearts of the faithful as living stones were bonded in charity. Whoever delighted in the decor of the house of God delighted in the church—not its fabricated walls and roofs, not its polished marble and gilded ceiling, but its faithful persons, the saints who loved God with all their heart, soul, mind, and strength, and their neighbors as themselves.[401]

The house of God that believers formed with the angels was in heaven.[402] The city of God sojourning in this world was like Noah's ark,[403] a portable construction. By custom, Augustine noted, north African houses bore inscriptions on their lintels to identify the owner, lest a visitor enter rudely or refrain timidly.[404] The emperor did not scruple to have *divina domo* carved over his temple. Yet Augustine never inscribed the name of God above the entry to his soul, as if he were a holy house divinely possessed. He struggled with invoking God into himself as a place that could not encompass the Creator. He puzzled over inviting him within, since his very existence testified that God was already within him. Augustine decided conversely that his existence testified that he was rather in God as the source of all things. The Creator was uncontained in persons, as in vessels; he gathered persons into himself. Augustine confessed that the entry to his own interior place was "narrow," in need of divine enlargement. It was "ruinous," in need of divine reconstruction. It was furnished with offenses, which needed divine cleaning. In his dichotomy God was "more interior than my intimate place and more superior than my supreme place." Intimacy was compromised by transcendence in Augustine's polarity. He did not reason to a radical identity in God by which his transcendence of creation was his intimacy to it. Augustine's antithesis forced him to confess rather the principle of human existence as the scriptural phrase "in the image" of God (Gen. 1:26).[405] The divine indwelling was only by image in a temple, not by possession in a house.

When he developed human experience as an analogy for the divine Trin-

---

romain, 108 (Leiden: E. J. Brill, 1987-), forthcoming; Mason Hammond, *The Antonine Monarchy*, Papers and Monographs of the American Academy in Rome, 19 (Rome: American Academy in Rome, 1959), p. 234 n. 73. For the foundation of the imperial cult of Africa Proconsularis see Fishwick, *Imperial Cult in the Latin West*, 1-2:257-68.

401 Augustine, *Sermones* 15.1.

402 Augustine, *Enarrationes in psalmos* 126.3; *Confessiones* 12.11.12, 13.

403 Augustine, *De civitate Dei* 15.26.

404 Augustine, *Enarrationes in psalmos* 55.1, cited by Hamman, *Vie quotidienne en Afrique du nord*, p. 64, and Getty, *Life of the North Africans*, p. 58.

405 Augustine, *Confessiones* 1.2.2; 1.3.3; 1.5.6; 3.6.11; 3.7.12.

ity, humans were posited as created in the image of God, not in the corporeal body, but in the rational mind. In Augustine's dichotomy of matter and spirit, outer and inner, not the whole human but only the part superior to beasts reflected the divine exemplar. The relationship of Father and Son was not established socially on father and son, but psychologically on mind and knowledge. Intellection, rather than generation, the mind, rather than the body, provided the model. The human family Augustine repudiated as an improbable opinion, even an absurd falsehood, for any image of God as relational, personal. The proper analogy was the prudential triad of the faculties of the individual mind: memory, understanding, and will. It was not kinship or any other socialization. The marriage of male and female with their offspring could not be argued for the Father and Son as husband and child, with the Spirit as wife. The only allegation of truth in that error concerned the original creation of woman as an analogy: for the procession of the Spirit from Father and Son without being a child. Since woman was produced from man, Eve from Adam, without being his daughter, not every creature produced from a person was a child. Yet it was offensive in considering the Trinity, he concluded, to arouse any sensual images of conceptions and births.[406] Augustine argued for the simplicity of God against the pagan fragmentation of Jupiter into multiple deities for his roles in childcare: Diespater for generation, Mena for menstruation, Opis for the placement of the newborn on the ground, Vaticanus for the opening of its mouth to cry, Levana for the raising of the newborn from the ground, Cunina for the guarding of its cradle.[407]

There was no religious incorporation from Augustine's familial experience as the father of Adeodatus or as the son of Patricius. He had criticized his father for failing in piety by a lust he was taught to imitate. Augustine considered the true father of a family as acting not from the lust to dominate but from a sense of duty, not from regal pride but from parental concern. He cared for the entire household as for his own children toward the desire and propitiation of God, desiring and hoping for their arrival at the heavenly home. In that household there would be no necessary office of governing mortals, because there would be no necessary duty of caring for those in immortal bliss.[408]

The human house was disdained. A rich house was crowded with good objects, abundant furnishings, precious vessels, servants and beasts of burden, pictures, marbles, ceilings, columns, spaces, and bedchambers. All were objects of desire that the citizen of Jerusalem must banish, neither glancing back nor loitering on the road. Augustine exhorted, "Desire the house of

---

406 Augustine, *De Trinitate* 4.1.2; 12.7.12; 11.1.1; 11.5.9; and against a familial model 12.5.5.

407 Augustine, *De civitate Dei* 4.11.

408 Ibid. 19.14.16. See also Markus, *Saeculum*, pp. 93-94.

God, desire the goods of that house; but do not be wont to covet the things of your own house, or your neighbor's house, or your patron's house." And, he urged with a customary transfer from a domestic to an ecclesiastical model, "Love righteousness and you will be the temple (*templum*) of God." What was the divine house? "The house of God is the city itself. The household is God's, his people, because the house of God is the temple of God."[409]

Augustine's morals on housing derived from social disparity, as depicted in the Carthaginian mosaic of lord Julius, seated enrobed in his orchard at the harvest of pears, his splendid villa contrasting with the straw huts of his migrant pickers.[410] As in the country so in the town, the beautiful homes of the wealthy vied with the smoky hovels in which most of the lower class, which comprised the Christian community, barely survived.[411] Even modest homes were made of smallish rock with a mortar of mud; brick and tile were rare. Augustine praised the innocence of an average owner, whose repose was his house, his household, his wife, his children, his patch of farmland newly planted with vines by his own hands, his residence constructed by his own zeal.[412] Yet even the poor could appease their hunger better not on the land, not even on church property, but in the Lord's "living orchards" carefully cultivated.[413] God willed people to love eternity, for there was bitterness mingled even in the innocent delights of agriculture. The farmer experienced the death of his loved ones; the drought, hail, and aridity of the vineyard; soured casks; exhausted cattle; a position dishonored by the disobedience of his children and slaves; and disharmony with his wife. By such tribulations the farmer was disciplined to love the better by the bitterness of the worse, "lest as a traveler on route to the fatherland he prefer the inn to his proper home."[414] Augustine's sole repose was in the divine house, and that was not himself.

---

[409] Augustine, *Enarrationes in psalmos* 64.8; 126.3.

[410] Mosaic, late fourth to early fifth century, Musée National du Bardo, Inv. 1. Frequentlly reproduced, e.g., by Parrish, *Season Mosaics of Roman North Africa*, pl. 15, and catalogue no. 9, pp. 111-13; Ackerman, *Villa*, p. 58. See also Hamman, *Vie quotidienne en Afrique du nord*, p. 62.

[411] Augustine, *Sermones* 170.4.4, cited by Hamman, *Vie quotidienne en Afrique du nord*, pp. 62-63; Getty, *Life of the North Africans*, p. 58.

[412] Hamman, *Vie quotidienne en Afrique du nord*, p. 63, partially citing Augustine, *Enarrationes in psalmos* 40.5.

[413] Augustine, *Epistolae* 21, cited by Hamman, *Vie quotidienne en Afrique du nord*, p. 8.

[414] Augustine, *Enarrationes in psalmos* 40.5; 136.5.

CHAPTER TWO

SANCTUARY

The disappearance of the peristylar house marked the end of antiquity: none was built after A. D. 550. It had been as the choice of the aspiring aristocrat a Roman ideal. Classical culture did not vanish with invasion, earthquake, or plague, but waned in the socioeconomic changes of the fourth to fifth centuries. There was the formation of a class of principals who assumed control of municipal councils, then seized responsibility for appointing local magistrates and supervising tax collection. In north Africa that occurred before the Vandal invasion, when new houses ceased to be built. With the concentration of personal wealth and the increase of autocratic patronage, aristocrats conducted more business from home than from the assembly. The most important movement in Roman housing throughout the empire in the mid-fifth century was the absorption to their homes of a variety of public functions. Each house—the richer the more elaborate and extensive architecturally—became a separate city with reception rooms, baths, and chapels. Public buildings were converted into housing for the poor, and the earlier noble homes were subdivided into small, impoverished apartments. With the control of wealth and power by a few aristocrats and the change in the form of personal patronage, the culture was restricted to an elite, as reflected in domestic architecture.[1]

No Roman villas survived the fall of the empire. Cities were sacked and burned; the population clustered for defense around ecclesiastical and civil strongholds. No major European city today reveals a single stone of a street or secular building between the fifth and the tenth centuries, except in a few archaeological digs. The physical character of the settlements is as unknown as those of Paleolithic man.[2] In the early medieval home burned the most beneficial fire. A person threatened or injured there was accursed and impure no matter whether the fire was accident or arson. Homes were protected from fire by a cross, an image, or a relic. Fire was so important that among the Franks men would be buried with oval iron rings attached to their belts, used for lighting fires by striking against flint. In the older method, the "fire of necessity," a stick of dry hard wood was spun with a short cord in a piece of dry soft wood until the tip of the stick heated and flamed. The

---

[1] Simon P. Ellis, "The End of the Roman House," *American Journal of Archaeology* 92 (198 8):565-76.

[2] James S. Ackerman, *The Villa: Form and Ideology of Country Houses*, Bollingen Series, 35-34 (Princeton: Princeton University Press, 1990), p. 63.

technique was believed magical.[3]

Yet the fire on the hearth was not the center of religion in society. The hearth that the vestal virgins had guarded symbolized the Roman populace, especially the procreative power of its males. That was literally the social *focus*.[4] The cult of the flame of the domestic hearth was of the "seat" (*sedes*), the place of belonging by right of descent or occupation. It was by definition unmovable.[5] Christian society was in perpetual motion, like Augustine's heart restless until it should rest in God.[6] The temper was movement, even in physical stability, and the disquiet of a people on pilgrimage could be strained to a disturbance that was pathological. Security was scarce. Augustine's metaphor of the turbulent sea of the world in which big fish devoured little fish was echoed by bishops convened at Rheims in the tenth century. Surveying towns emptied, monasteries razed, and fields desolate, they lamented, "Everywhere the strong oppress the weak and men are like fish of the sea that blindly devour one another."[7] Ostia, his site of contemplating the divine home, had receded into a malarial marsh. Although the papacy dredged it for salt, only a handful of people lived there.[8]

There was continual movement of the ordinary populace—the peasant society—as individuals or groups: from a valley to a plateau, from a plain to a mountain. Beyond local moves were migrations, wanderings, and exiles, which unsettled people and impelled them by tyranny, hunger, or danger from one country to another. Even within a single landholding there was incessant movement, as minute parcels of ground changed hands almost every generation. Early medieval society seems to have been in permanent agitation. Although boundaries to fields were laid on ancient lines, the culture was vastly marching, with makeshift huts rather than dwellings. Materials for construction were of limited durability—raw dirt and such vegetation as thin trunks of trees, branches, and foliage—not squared-up timbers. Cemeteries were fixed sites. Indeed, the cemetery acquired the name that had defined the architecture of the Roman house: atrium.[9]

---

[3] Michel Rouche, "The Early Middle Ages in the West," in *A History of Private Life*, Vol. 1: *From Pagan Rome to Byzantium*, ed. Paul Veyne (Cambridge, Mass.: Harvard University Press, Belknap Press, 1987), pp. 495, 465.

[4] Judith P. Hallett, *Fathers and Daughters in Roman Society: Women and the Elite Family* (Princeton: Princeton University Press, 1984), p. 84, and for the association of the phallus and the hearth, pp. 84-85 n. 29.

[5] W. K. Lacey, "Patria potestas," in *The Family in Ancient Rome: New Perspectives*, ed. Beryl Rawson (London: Croom Helm, 1986), p. 125.

[6] Augustine, *Confessiones* 1.1.

[7] Cited by Marc Bloch, *Feudal Society*, trans. L. A. Manyon, Vol. 1: *The Growth of Ties of Dependence* (Chicago: University of Chicago Press, 1964), p. 3, without reference to Augustine. For the metaphor see also Irenaeus, *Adversus haereses* 5.24.2.

[8] Russell Meiggs, *Roman Ostia*, 2d ed. (Oxford: Clarendon, 1973), pp. 11, 101; M. I. Finley, *The Ancient Economy* (London: Chatto & Windus, 1973), pp. 31-32.

[9] Robert Fossier, *Peasant Life in the Medieval West*, trans. Juliet Vale (Oxford: Basil Blackwell, 1988), pp. 49-50; Jean Chapelot and idem, *The Village and House in the Middle*

Anchorites revived the primitive methods of food-gathering; but, although some collected thorns for firewood, most ate their meals raw. Their renunciation was not dire, however. Without a family to support, the ascetic in the desert could earn a better living than the fellahin in the valley.[10] The anchorites eschewed family. Their absolute religious value was homelessness. Augustine marveled that ascetics were populating the desert;[11] but they were not at home there. It was as if their fasting reflected a belief in the absence of the bridegroom, the period when Jesus said his disciples would mourn rather than celebrate (Matt. 9:14-15). Their voluntary disorientation of expatriation and exile as strangers was an ascetic ideal. Jerome proclaimed that a Christian could not succeed spiritually at home, for Christ had said that a prophet was not without honor in his own country. Their ascetic discipline was inherited from the Stoics: quitting the family to philosophize, as in Augustine's portrayal of his friend Nebridius, who relinquished a fine ancestral villa and familial home to join his experimental community of believers. The figurative type was the patriarch Abraham, ordered to abandon his country, kin, and house to depart to the place the Lord would indicate (Gen. 12:1). This asceticism involved not simply material displacement but also mental oblivion of everything left behind. In the solitude of the desert was cultivated a hidden and silent life.[12]

Some, discontent with wandering like the patriarch to a divinely designated place in the wilderness, adopted vagrancy as a permanent asceticism. There were two methods of such discipline: to voyage, as in the navigations of the Irish monks like Brendan, who designed a currach for a cell with the ocean for his desert; or to live as a stranger within a community.[13] Columban, who established a rule for Irish monks, was certain that, if his earthly tent were folded, God would provide a new habitation, a shelter in heaven made by no human hands. While humans were in the body they were traveling away from their destination. Some monks, reasoning that God was everywhere, took as their real destination anywhere, like the trio washed up on shore adrift in an oarless boat.[14] A medieval phenomenon

Ages, trans. Henry Cleere (London: B. T. Batsford, 1985), pp. 70, 127-28, 24, 134.

[10] Aline Rousselle, *Porneia: On Desire and the Body in Antiquity*, trans. Felicia Pheasant (Oxford: Basil Blackwell, 1988), pp. 146, 169.

[11] Augustine, *Confessiones* 8.6.15. For an introduction see Derwas Chitty, *The Desert a City* (Oxford: Basil Blackwell, 1966).

[12] Antoine Guillaumont, "Le dépaysement comme forme d'ascèse, dans le monachisme ancient," École practique des hautes études, Ve section, sciences religieuses, *Annuaire 1968-69* 76 (1968):31-58; rpt. in idem, *Aux origines du monachisme chrétien: Pour un phénoménologie du monachisme*, Spiritualité orientale, 30 (Bégrolles en Mauges: Abbaye de Bellefontaine, 1979), pp. 89-116. Augustine, *Confessiones* 6.10.17.

[13] Jean Leclercq, *Aux sources de la spiritualité occidentale: Étapes et constantes* (Paris: Cerf, 1964), pp. 45-48; Giles Constable, "Monachisme et pèlerinage au moyen âge," *Revue historique* 258 (1977):8.

[14] Jonathan Sumption, *Pilgrimage: An Image of Mediaeval Religion* (London: Faber & Faber, 1975), p. 96.

were the gyrovagues, spiritual vagabonds who were literally "monks" as solitaries. Their wandering was impelled by the decadence of monasteries or by hesychasm, a doctrine of deification through a solitary discipline of prayer. One gyrovague acquired the nickname "the hut burner," because, if his solitude was interrupted by a visitor or aspirant, he would set fire to his building and move on. These compulsive, antisocial travelers[15] were scorned by Benedict in his monastic rule. He disdained "gyrovagues, who spend their entire lives drifting from region to region, staying as guests for three or four days in different monasteries. Always on the move, they never settle down, and are slaves to their own wills and gross appetites." He would pass over these disgraceful men in silence and draft a plan for the cenobites.[16]

Explicating the tools of the spiritual craft, Benedict defined, "The workshop where we are to toil faithfully at all these tasks is the enclosure of the monastery and stability in the community." The novice was tested in this stability over a period of trial and perseverance in his promise. The prime vow of the monk was stability, and once professed he was by the rule no longer free to leave the monastery.[17] Benedict was the first to bind a monk to his monastery by a vow of stability, relating him to an enclosure where he would abide until death, never to depart or roam. There was legal permanence in the profession of the evangelical counsels and in aggregation to a local, determined community with a particular abbot. Stability comprised perseverance in decision and conduct, fidelity to routine and tradition, dispossession of property, and communal life in a particular place.[18] The socioeconomic crises of the late Roman empire and the barbarian invasions had formed a floating population of landless migrant workers that civil regimentation and ecclesiastical institutionalization confronted with stability.[19]

Stability had been a prominent feature of Neoplatonism and Gnosticism in the contemplative process of withdrawal to the condition of Existence as standstill. At the climax of its revelation was the human mental state of standing at rest. The contemplative of Plotinus's *Enneads* apprehended in stillness the One like the sun rising from the horizon of the sea. The contemplative retreat of the wise was in Philo of Alexandria's exegesis like Moses standing still before Yahweh, in receiving the Torah as an entry into

---

15 Donald M. Nichol, "*Instabilitas loci*: The Wanderlust of Late Byzantine Monks," in *Monks, Hermits and the Ascetic Tradition*, ed. W. J. Sheils, Studies in Church History, 22 (Oxford: Basil Blackwell for the Society for Ecclesiastical History, 1985), pp. 193, 195, 200.

16 Benedict, *Regula* 1.10-12; *Regula*, trans. Timothy Fry (Collegeville, Minn.: Liturgical Press, 1980), p. 171.

17 Ibid. 58.9; 58.17; 58.28; 60.9; 61.5.

18 Ambrose Wathen, "*Conversatio* and Stability in the Rule of Benedict," *Monastic Studies* 11 (1975):6-7, 43.

19 Ernest W. McDonnell, "Monastic Stability: Some Socioeconomic Considerations," in *Charanis Studies: Essays in Honor of Peter Charanis*, ed. Angeliki E. Laiou-Thomadakis (New Brunswick, N. J.: Rutgers University Press, 1980), pp. 116, 135.

the Platonic forms (Deut. 5:31; cf. Gen. 18:22). In contrast to divine stability was sensual instability. Instability or ignorance paced restlessly, or it was tossed in the fluctuations of the sea, like Augustine before philosophy. Stability was the virtue of abbot Antony, the archetypal ascetic, who not only remained in place physically but was morally unshakeable though the demons rattled his very cell. Immovability was the character of those who contemplated God.[20] Even in Roman culture, stability had been equated in Cicero and Seneca with law, marriage, residence in one's own home, peace, freedom, and by extension, with tranquillity of soul enjoyed in leisure in opposition to agitation in business.[21]

Yet the very permanence of the medieval monk was the ascetic state of pilgrimage. Pilgrimage in stability and stability in pilgrimage became an ambiguous conciliation of concepts.[22] Although the concepts were literally incompatible, many monasteries were centers of pilgrimage, around graves of saints or as stopovers on the long routes to shrines. Many monks abandoned the vow of stability to pilgrimage to holy sites, either to escape the routine and discipline of the cloister, or as sent in penitence by their superior to rid the monastery of their embarrassing presence.[23] Outside the cloister monks visited spiritual guides, acted as couriers, conducted routine business, converted heathen, and moved from monastery to monastery and even among orders.[24] Clerical life favored wandering. The church was an international community with a common language. Affiliations between monasteries—an abbey to its daughter churches—and the territorial dispersal of their patrimony required the visitation of property. On the road monks met refugees, adventurers, peasants, and most analogously pilgrims. Did not salvation require a journey?[25]

Augustine had compared the tribulations of the north African farmer on the land, so that he might know himself as but a pilgrim at an inn, to a classical education (*paideia*).[26] The metaphor for earth as a classroom was imitated in the prologue of Benedict's rule, which defined the monastery as a "school for the Lord's service." Yet this school, despite its vow of stability, was peripatetic. It was a school for and in motion, the road itself. Benedict

---

[20] Michael Allen Williams, *The Immovable Race: A Gnostic Designation and the Concept of Stability in Late Antiquity*, Nag Hammadi Studies, 29 (Leiden: E. J. Brill, 1985), pp. 8-33; idem, "Stability as a Soteriological Theme in Gnosticism," in *The Rediscovery of Gnosticism*, Vol. 2: *Sethian Gnosticism*, ed. Bentley Layton, 2 vols., Studies in the History of Religions, 41 (Leiden: E. J. Brill, 1981), pp. 819-29.

[21] Leclercq, "In Praise of Stability," trans. Jacques St. Laurent, *Monastic Studies* 13 (1982):90-92.

[22] Idem, "Monachisme et pérégrination du IXe au XIIe siècle," pp. 45-46, 87.

[23] Constable, "Monachisme et pèlerinage au moyen âge," p. 3. See also idem, "The Opposition to Pilgrimage in the Middle Ages," *Studia gratiana* 19 (1976):123-46.

[24] McDonnell, "Monastic Stability," pp. 119, 129.

[25] See Bloch, *Feudal Society*, 1:63.

[26] Augustine, *Enarrationes in psalmos* 119.17.2.

enjoined the monks not to "run away from the road that leads to salvation" but with progress to "run on the path," not swerving but persevering in stability.[27] The analogy was not promising. All medieval roads were bad, with a normal distance of between nineteen-and twenty-five miles a day for a caravan of merchants, a noble in retinue, or an army with baggage. A professional courier or a resolute traveler could manage twice the distance;[28] but the monk, forbidden to travel by horse or carriage, could not imaginatively have expected a swifter journey to perfection than the rest of humanity.

Contemplation as a "road," the royal highway on which the pilgrim advanced straight to his celestial country,[29] was the election of Bernard des Fontaines, who arrived with thirty kith and kin at the site of Cîteaux. That "new monastery" had been erected on a marsh by Benedictine monks from Molesmes, discontent with neglect of the rule and intent on its final chapter about the asceticism of the desert fathers.[30] Cîteaux was named from its site, *cisternae* for bogs, or perhaps from its position on the old Roman road "on this side of the third milestone" (*cis tertium*).[31] A bishop evangelizing in fifth-century France, who discovered rustics celebrating a festival on the edge of a marsh formed in a volcanic crater, announced, "There can be no religion in a swamp."[32] Yet the Cistercians were determined differently. Their site was, according to the prime source, "a place of horror and immense solitude" (Deut. 32:10) overgrown with brambles and thornbushes. There the monks cleared a space and constructed a wooden monastery from sections of roughly-squared trees.[33] The founder was usually responsible for the clearance of the site and the construction of the buildings, which were completed before the arrival of an abbot with a dozen monks and some lay brothers. Cistercian abbeys were all dedicated to the Virgin Mary. They usually derived their name from a natural characteristic of their site—ford, fountain, floral valley, lovely land, beautiful spot; or from a sigh for paradise—valley

---

[27] Benedict, *Regula* prol. 45, 48, 49, 50; trans. Fry, p. 165.

[28] See Bloch, *Feudal Society*, 1:62.

[29] Bernard of Clairvaux, *Sermones super Cantica canticorum* 43.4; *In quadragesima sermo* 6, cited by Constable, "Monachisme et pélerinage au moyen âge," p. 7.

[30] Adriaan H. Bredero, *Cluny et Cîteaux au douzième siècle: L'Histoire d'une controverse monastique* (Amsterdam: APA-Holland University Press, 1985), p. 351. For the issue of authentic observance see Constance B. Bouchard, "Merovingian, Carolingian and Cluniac Monasticism: Reform and Renewal in Burgundy," *Journal of Ecclesiastical History* 41 (1990):365-88; John Van Engen, "The 'Crisis of Cenobitism' Reconsidered: Benedictine Monasticism in the Years 1050-1150," *Speculum* 61 (1986): 269-304; W. E. Goodrich, "The Cistercian Founders and the Rule: Some Considerations," *Journal of Ecclesiastical History* 35 (1984):358-75.

[31] Peter Ferguson, *Architecture of Solitude: Cistercian Abbeys in Twelfth-Century England* (Princeton: Princeton University Press, 1984), p. 3 n. 2.

[32] Cited by Peter Brown, *The Cult of the Saints: Its Rise and Function in Latin Christianity* (London: S C M Press, 1981), p. 111.

[33] Jean Owens Schaefer, "The Earliest Churches of the Cistercian Order," in *Studies in Cistercian Art and Architecture*, ed. Meredith P. Lillich, 3 vols., Cistercian Studies, 66, 69, 89 (Kalamazoo, Mich.: Cistercian Publications, 1982-87), 1:2.

of God, valley of light, God's acres, dead to the world. Clairvaux, which Bernard would be commissioned to found, was the "clear valley".[34] The horror of Cîteaux was exaggerated by the polemics of Bernard, who was not even present at its foundation. The evidence from charters indicates that the land on which further Cistercian houses were founded was not so desolate and wild as the rhetoric evoked.[35]

Although the basilica of Hippo Regius where Augustine officiated still stands, the original wooden structures of Cîteaux and Clairvaux have disappeared, either rotted or burned. Their reconstruction is from literature, both hagiographical and documentary. Cistercian monasteries could be established only on isolated land at a minimum of twelve Burgundian leagues distance from the founding house. After the prospective site was examined, on the chosen spot were erected temporary shelters of wood or wattle and daub.[36] When Bernard was ordered to establish an abbey, the site was near the river Aube in the district of Langres, on which plateau the majority of Cistercian houses were in the twelfth century founded. It was in an ancient "den of thieves" called the valley of Absinth, either because of an abundance of that herb or because of the bitterness of falling into the hands of robbers. "There in that place of horror and immense solitude those virtuous men settled in the den of thieves a temple of God and a house of prayer."[37] The region, although of poor soil and hard climate, infertile except for vines, was disputed for its property among lords and landowners, often in bloody conflicts.[38] Laborers at Clairvaux cleared the thorns by hand and built a dwelling from trees, like Cîteaux at its inception. A humble chapel about twenty-feet long and fourteen-feet wide to accommodate thirteen men was erected in several days and served for the divine office. The first permanent oratory was a chapel built to the west of the present buildings. It seems to have been small and austere, square in plan, with an aisle on all four sides of the unified central space. A Cistercian visitor in the seventeenth century described it as a temple of poverty, the altar as bare as Bernard had left it, with a bad painting on wood of Christ crucified.[39]

According to the statutes, Cistercian monasteries were to be located not in cities, towns, or villages, but in sites remote from human conversation. The Cistercians chose valleys, harnessing the watercourses for their supply and working the fields. The foundation of the abbeys was an incentive for

---

[34] Ferguson, *Architecture of Solitude*, p. 8.

[35] Bouchard, *Holy Entrepreneurs: Cistercians, Knights, and Economic Exchange in Twelfth-Century Burgundy* (Ithaca, N. Y.: Cornell University Press, 1991).

[36] Ibid., pp. 7-8.

[37] William of St.-Thierry, *Vita prima* 1.5.25.

[38] For Langres see Bouchard, *Holy Entrepreneurs*, p. 183; Fossier, "Le plateau de Langres et la fondation de Clairvaux," in Commission d'histoire de l'ordre de Cîteaux, *Études et documents*, Vol. 3: *Bernard de Clairvaux* (Paris: Alsatia, 1953), pp. 67-75.

[39] Schaefer, "Earliest Churches of the Cistercian Order," pp. 4-5.

the development of an agrarian society.[40] In strict poverty the monks renounced cash revenues from seigniorial and ecclesiastical sources, and established a landed economy worked by and for the community on isolated terrain in isolated labor. The withdrawal of educated men from secular activity to supervision of rustic chores like clearance of land and animal husbandry revolutionized agricultural techniques. As a contemporary admired, "Give the Cistercian a wilderness or forest, and in a few years you will find a dignified abbey in the midst of smiling plenty."[41] In agricultural practice Cistercian monasteries were distinctive in their system of granges, employment of lay brothers or "converts," and aggregation of coherent and contiguous plots of land. They were not pioneers. The Cistercians did not acquire land for their granges by clearance and reclamation of uninhabited plots but through the purchase and reorganization of holdings often long cultivated. They collected pastural and forestal rights, such as for the autumnal grazing of pigs on acorns, and they raised profitable livestock in a time of accelerating demand for meat and its by-products. The revenue from their surplus sold in town was shrewdly invested in further acquisition of land.[42] The Cistercians were not exclusively farmers—cultivating the land traditionally, innovative only in methods of drainage. Their asceticism was compatible with developing economic practices, in an exchange that enabled the order's rapid growth and success on its sound agricultural basis. The monks acquired farmland through gifts, leases, pawns, and purchases; and their property was efficiently planned and managed.[43]

Burgundy was a crossroads politically and economically even before the Romans invaded Gaul. It was not by the twelfth century a wilderness, and what solitude the monks desired had to be found in patches of wood and field bounded by neighbors. In subsisting on remote farms the Cistercians were not excluded from social contact. Their houses were easily accessible on horseback by a short ride from a neighbor only a few miles distant.[44] The rule of siting monasteries in isolation was not always followed, and the earliest record demonstrated that a Cistercian monastery was not a primitive community either in material or organization.[45] Although the horror of the

---

[40] Bredero, *Cluny et Cîteaux au douzième siècle*, p. 354.

[41] Ferguson, *Architecture of Solitude*, p. 7.

[42] Constance Hoffman Berman, *Medieval Agriculture, the Southern French Countryside, and the Early Cistercians: A Study of Forty-Three Monasteries*, Transactions of the American Philosophical Society, 76-5 (Philadelphia, Pa.: American Philosophical Society, 1986); Bouchard, *Holy Entrepreneurs*, pp. 106-12. For the model as seignorial domination, not capitalist acquisition, see Isabel Alfonso, "Cistercians and Feudalism," *Past and Present* 133 (1991):3-30. See also Jacques Dubois, "L'Institution des convers au XIIe siècle: Forme de vie monastique propre aux laïcs," in *I laici nella "societas christiana" dei secoli XIe e XIIe*, Università del Sacro Cuore, Miscellanea del Centro di studi medioevali, 5 (Milan: Vita e pensiero, 1968), pp. 183-261.

[43] Bouchard, *Holy Entrepreneurs*, pp. 185, 187, 188.

[44] Ibid., pp. 189, 103, 192-93.

[45] Bredero, *Cluny et Cîteau au douzième siècle*, p. 352.

place was frequently cited, the physical plant with its diverse localities and quarters evidenced a rich and vibrant monastic life. There was a chapel and adjoining sacristy for the divine office and liturgy; a chapter room for prayer, instruction, and communal affairs such as profession or discipline; a parlor for necessary speech; a kitchen, cellar, and two refectories—for the community and for the abbot; a dormitory, and an infirmary. A special heated room invited warming oneself; it was also the spot for greasing shoes and being bled. The cloister, the wide corridor connecting most of the areas, was the place for reading and studying, the weekly maundy, and the occasional haircut and shave. Novices and guests were separately housed, with their own refectory, dormitory, and infirmary. The society was ordered by seniority in the choir and other places and it discharged at least ten different regular offices. The monastery included the "family": domestics, visitors and guests, neighbors, and passersby.[46]

The principal characteristic of Cistercian churches was the chevet, simpler in form, easier to construct, and more economical than other plans. It was also influenced by local architecture, conforming to the design of rural churches. There was a great diversity in plans, so that there was no Cistercian style.[47] There was Cistercian policy. In construction their churches were not to be majestic. The only statute specifically on architecture prescribed wooden, but not stone, towers, limited to two bells weighing not more than five hundred pounds, so that a single man could ring them. Doors could be painted white. No more than two colors of stained glass could be used in the windows, which were forbidden painted images. The artistic legislation of the founders proscribed altar cloths and vestments of silk, except for the stole and maniple; ornaments, vessels, and utensils of gold, silver, or jewels, except for the chalice and fistula. Statues and paintings were forbidden in the church or in any room of the monastery, except for painted crosses of wood above the altar. Forbidden also were ornate floors of mosaic or colored stone, and murals, except in churches converted from Benedictine establishments. Only five lamps burned at strategic locations, and in the sanctuary there was a single candle in a wrought-iron holder. The monks chanted in unison unaccompanied by organ. When Pope Innocent II visited Clairvaux in 1131 he saw nothing in the church except its four bare walls. Such austerity criticized the social involvement of other monasteries, like the holding of court there by the nobility. It rejected

---

[46] Bede K. Lackner, "Early Cistercian Life as Described by the *Ecclesiastica officia*," in *Cistercian Ideals and Reality*, ed. John R. Sommerfeldt, Cistercian Studies Series, 60 (Kalamazoo, Mich.: Cistercian Publications, 1978), pp. 62-65.

[47] Anselme Dimier, "Églises cisterciennes sur plan bernardin et sur plan bénédictin," in *Mélanges offerts à René Crozet*, ed. Pierre Gallais and Yves-Jean Riou, 2 vols. (Poitiers: Société d'études médiévales, 1966), 2:697. See also idem, *Recueil de plans d'églises cisterciennes*, 2 vols., Commission d'histoire de l'ordre de Cîteaux, 1 (Grignan, Drôme: Abbaye Notre Dame d'Aiguebelle, 1949).

Benedictine luxury, which was centered on the cult of the dead through transactions of cash and gifts, and on the cult of the saints through the reception of pilgrims as a lucrative source of income, as reflected in the monastic acquisition of art. Cistercian policy was social disengagement.[48]

Lavish ornaments were renounced so that money could be given to the indigent. The avoidance of costly procedures in building was a frugality in solidarity with the poor of the countryside where the Cistercians settled. Certain types of building were also rejected as impeding the quest of the soul for the beauty that is God with a curiosity distracting from self-knowledge.[49] Bernard criticized in an *Apologia* oratories of immense height, immoderate length, unnecessary width, with sumptuous decorations and curious depictions that deflected prayer and hindered devotion. He deplored as absurd and expensive the depravity of the capitals in certain cloisters.[50] Those iconographical types were spiritually distracting: animals; hybrids and monsters, as contradictory to nature; men in worldly pursuits, both soldiers in combat and hunters blowing horns, as an invasion of the secular imagery of the aristocracy, to which the vast majority of monks whom his *Apologia* addressed belonged. Such forms were denounced as irrational.[51]

Architecture and art were to provide a setting conducive to contemplation by pure line, harmonious structure, and tranquil luminosity. Simplicity, a quality of the soul, was imitated in the removal of the superfluous to reveal the beautiful material, the proportionate harmony, and the fine craftsmanship of the building. The foundations from Clairvaux, of which as abbot Bernard directed twenty two, all had rectilinear chevets and flat-ended transepts with two or three chapels separated from each other by a wall. The design was cheap to build and to expand, without complex curves or necessary calculations of the thrust of the vault in the foundation of the chevet. It also interjected no sensual stimulants to interfere with contemplation. Bernard's monastic friend William of St.-Thierry articulated the principle that the hu-

---

[48] Conrad Rudolph, "The 'Principal Founders' and the Early Artistic Legislation of Cîteaux," in *Studies in Cistercian Art and Architecture*, ed. Lillich, 3:4-21; H. d'Arbois de Jouvainville, *Études sur l'état interieur des abbayes cisterciennes et principalement de Clairvaux au XIIe et au XIIIe siècle* (Paris, 1858), pp. 28-34; Ferguson, *Architecture of Solitude*, pp. 9-11; Christopher Holdsworth, "The Chronology and Character of Early Cistercian Legislation on Art and Architecture," in *Cistercian Art and Architecture in the British Isles*, ed. Christopher Norton and David Park (Cambridge: Cambridge University Press, 1986), p. 55.

[49] Emero Stiegman, "Saint Bernard: The Aesthetics of Authenticity," in *Studies in Cistercian Art and Architecture*, ed. Lillich, 2:1-2, 3-4, 7-8.

[50] Bernard of Clairvaux, *Apologia ad Guillelmum abbatem* 12.28-29.

[51] Rudolph, "Bernard of Clairvaux's *Apologia* as a Description of Cluny, and the Controversy over Monastic Art," *Gesta* 27 (1988):127-28. See also idem, *The "Things of Greater Importance": Bernard of Clairvaux's Apologia and the Medieval Attitude Toward Art* (Philadelphia: University of Pennsylvania Press, 1990), pp. 133-57. For the historical background see David Summers, *Michelangelo and the Language of Art* (Princeton: Princeton University Press, 1981), pp. 48-50. Hybrids were also taboo in scripture as mixed creatures. See Mary Douglas, *Purity and Danger: An Analysis of the Concepts of Pollution and Taboo* (London: Ark, 1984), p. 53.

man interior was benefitted by surroundings arranged in accordance with the mind and its ideals. A spirit inwardly intent was better served by an absence of decoration. Although Cistercian interiors were colorless, they were luminous. The sunshine flooding the sanctuary symbolized the divine light illumining the intellect. The very fenestration had a sense of order with geometric and foliated patterns accompanying the luminosity.[52]

Bernard never anticipated the change of sensibility and style that would in the seventeenth century carve him into a statue flanking the retable of main altars—at Avignon of gilt wood, or paint him flanking the Last Supper and in cycles of his own life: receiving illumination from heaven, meditating before a crucifix, enjoying a vision of the Madonna, even arriving with his companions at Cîteaux in portraiture of contemporary members of the house; or, in the ultimate irony, pointing to heaven and dictating to a monk the rule, which forbade the very picture.[53] In his initial biography Bernard seemed not to notice his surroundings. It depicted him as after a year in the novitiate oblivious of whether or not its ceiling was vaulted, and as reporting only one window in the apse of the abbey, whereas there were three. Yet that was the hagiographical topic of the suppression of the senses, as related about an abbot who lived twenty years in his cell without ever raising his eyes to the ceiling.[54]

Like Augustine, Bernard exclaimed how wonderful it was for men to live in accord in the same house like brothers.[55] Yet those quasi brothers dwelling in the house were not homes, not to themselves or to God. Here was not our permanent city, Bernard wrote in his exposition on the Song of Songs. Men warred in their bodies like soldiers in tents storming the kingdom of heaven by violence. "This habitation of our body is neither the abode of a citizen nor the home of a native, but either the tent of a soldier or the inn of a traveler."[56] The flesh entertained as its noble guest the soul, which was a pilgrim. If a peasant were asked by a very powerful nobleman for hospitality, he would gladly creep to bed into some corner, or under the stairs, or even among the ashes of the hearth, yielding him his own place. So should the monk tolerate all injuries and vexations of the body for the

---

52 Elisabeth Melczer and Eileen Soldwedel, "Monastic Goals in the Aesthetics of Saint Bernard," in *Studies in Cistercian Art and Architecture*, ed. Lillich, 1:34-35, 40. For an introduction see also Wolfgang Bickel, "Die Kunst der Cistercienser," in *Die Cistercienser: Geschichte, Geist, Kunst*, ed. Ambrosius Schneider et al. (Cologne: Wienand, 1974), pp. 193-340.

53 See Joan Evans, *Monastic Iconography in France: From the Renaissance to the Revolution* (Cambridge: Cambridge University Press, 1970), pp. 90-91, pls. 40-42.

54 Rudolph, "Bernard of Clairvaux's *Apologia*," pp. 126-27. The anecdote from *Vita prima* 1.4.20 is frequently cited, e. g., Otto van Simson, "The Cistercian Contribution," in *Monasticism and the Arts*, ed. Timothy Gregory Verdon with John Dally (Syracuse, N. Y.: Syracuse University Press, 1984), p. 116; Brooke, "St Bernard, the Patrons and Monastic Planning," p. 19.

55 Bernard of Clairvaux, *Sermones de diversis* 42.4.

56 Bernard of Clairvaux, *Sermones super Cantica canticorum* 26.1.1.

sake of its spiritual guest.[57] Bernard pronounced the misery and distress of exile in a eulogy for his brother Gérard, for whom he restrained his tears in public, like Augustine at the death of Monica, enduring her wake and burial dry-eyed.[58] "He was brother by birth, but brother more by religion," he preached, "brother in the flesh, but neighbor in the spirit, companion in the project." Of their relationship he elaborated, "My soul clung to his soul; and one was made from two: not consanguinity but unanimity. Carnal necessity was not lacking; but there was more a society of joined spirit, a consensus of minds, a conformity of habits." A sword cleaved the brothers, placing one in heaven, leaving the other in the dirt. "I, I am that miserable portion thrown in the mud," Bernard lamented. Gérard was "by blood a brother, by profession a son, by solicitude a father, by spirit a consort." He died sighing "Father, Father" and proclaiming the goodness of God in becoming a father to humans, whose glory was in being sons and heirs.[59]

That affective fraternal-filial piety of the monastery transcended the austere asceticism of the desert. The ascetic there was dead to familial relationships. A model anecdotally threw into the fire a parcel of letters from family and friends, unopened and even untied, lest remembering their faces he be deflected from his path.[60] A certain Pior, who was persuaded against his better judgment to visit his sister, kept his eyes closed through their entire interview to minimize contact with her. The same principal of separation was observed even among those members of a family who embraced asceticism—and very many ascetics were related by blood. Their best hope was a resumption of familial ties in heaven. On earth they altered the basis of their relationships to an ideal of cooperation in a spiritual task. Anoub of the desert repeatedly pelted the statues in the temple, repeatedly begged their forgiveness, then explained his strange behavior to his brothers as a moral example of how they should forbear with one another in community.[61]

Cistercian origins were in the lesser nobility, who did not quit their families and milieu as did the hermits of fourth-century Egypt seeking solitude in the desert. Nor were they like their inheritors, the Irish monks, who by the rule of Columban minimized contacts with relatives and friends by discouraging the recruitment of kin to the same monastery. Even Irish buildings, reconstructed archaeologically in models, show that communal living never dominated there. The individual cells were grouped in a common area,

---

57 Bernard of Clairvaux, "In adventu" 6.3.

58 Bernard of Clairvaux, *Sermones super Cantica canticorum* 26.1.1-26.2.3. Augustine, *Confessiones* 9.12.19.

59 Bernard of Clairvaux, *Sermones super Cantica canticorum* 26.3.5; 26.5.7; 26.6.8; 26.6.9.

60 John Cassian, *De institutis coenobiorum* 5.32, cited by Rousselle, *Porneia*, p. 183.

61 Philip Rousseau, "Blood-Relationships among Early Eastern Ascetics," *Journal of Theological Studies* 23 (1972):135-36, 141. For development see Laurent Theiss, "Saints sans famille? Quelques remarques sur la famille dans le monde franc à travers les sources hagiographiques," *Revue historique* 255 (1976):3-20.

but the monk could have easily maintained an eremitical existence within that space. Bernard altered a natural family into a monastic one with his dramatic arrival at the gate of Cîteaux. He brought or cajoled all the males of his family into the religious life with him and even provided care for his sister, although the Cistercians in the first decade avoided the organized care of women. After their monastic profession, the bonds of kinship still mattered, and friendship flourished among the Cistercians from the mid-eleventh to the thirteenth centuries. Its practice obviated traditional fear that exclusive ties would form cliques and conspiracies undermining the community in its uniformity of love, and perhaps ascetic fear of homosexuality. Classical and patristic traditions, the feudal background of recruits, and the emphasis on personal experience all `contributed to the toleration of friendship.[62]

The roots of spiritual kinship were in the Christian communities of the Roman empire. Although the sponsor for infant baptism was ordinarily one of the parents, in early medieval practice some parents invited an outsider to sponsor. As the custom became common, a voluntary kinship was formed in a relationship so holy as to supersede bonds of kinship by blood and marriage. Spiritual birth implied spiritual parentage and it extended to a spiritual family with traits of sexual purity and altruism foreign to the natural family, which was created by sexual relations and based on economics. The behavioral code of spiritual kinship was one of respect and honor, with sexual relations between parties forbidden. In its complexity the sponsor and sponsored were related as parent to child; the baptizer, as also a spiritual parent but not a godparent; the sponsor and natural parents, as coparents to each other through the baptized; and the baptized, as a spiritual sibling of the children of the sponsor. Even the spouses of the spiritual kin tended to be assimilated into the spiritual family.[63] Similar was the concept of illicit sexual relations among the religiously professed as "incest" rather than fornication.[64] When the hagiographical *Vita prima* described Bernard as "like a spiritual father of his brothers reborn in Christ, and understanding the hand of the Lord to be working,"[65] it applied the spiritual kinship of baptism to monasticism as a second baptism. The hand (*manus*) of the Lord at

62 Brian Patrick McGuire, "Monastic Friendship and Toleration in Twelfth-Century Cistercian Life," in *Monks, Hermits and the Ascetic Tradition*, ed. Sheils, pp. 147-49, 151-54; and on the Irish monks, idem, *Friendship and Community: The Monastic Experience 350-1250*, Cistercian Studies, 95 (Kalamazoo, Mich.: Cistercian Publications, 1988), pp. 102-3.

63 Joseph H. Lynch, "*Spiritale vinculum*: The Vocabulary of Spiritual Kinship in Early Medieval Europe," in *Religion, Culture, and Society in the Early Middle Ages: Studies in Honor of Richard E. Sullivan*, ed. Thomas F. X. Noble and John J. Contreni, Studies in Medieval Culture, 23 (Kalamazoo, Mich.: Western Michigan University Press, 1987), pp. 181-83.

64 See Graciela S. Daichman, *Wayward Nuns in Medieval Literature* (Syracuse, N. Y.: Syracuse University Press, 1986), p. 41 and pp. 168-69 n. 14.

65 William of St.-Thierry, *Vita prima* 1.3.13.

work among the family was not a vague activity but a precise exercise of legal authority over a household, as in Roman society.

In Bernard's eulogy for Gérard he was a brother by birth but more so by religion. By his profession before Bernard as the father abbot he was a son; yet by his solicitude he was a father himself; and by his spirit, a consort. Their relationship was not ultimately consanguinity but unanimity,[66] the unanimity of brothers dwelling in a house, which had established the monastic experience for Augustine.[67] Yet, when Bernard persuaded his brothers into the monastery, he effectively terminated the propagation of the line of the lord of Fontaines-lès-Dijon.[68] The family intensified in spiritual relationships but by its multiple vows of chastity it ended as a natural family. "They departed from the paternal home, Bernard as father of his brothers, with his brothers as his spiritual sons whom in Christ, the word of life, he had begotten." They left behind with their father their only sister and their youngest brother, Nivard, telling him, "To you alone belong all of our earthly possessions." The boy retorted: "Therefore, for you heaven and for me earth?! This is not done by an equal share." Soon he joined them, as did eventually their father, while their sister Humbeline separated from her husband and child to enter a convent.[69] The lordship of the family seems to have passed to a daughter of the eldest brother, Gui, who had separated from the family. She married a man named Bartholomew, who became lord of Fontaines as well as of Sombernon, his own family.[70] So effective was Bernard at breaking up families that reputedly mothers hid their sons, wives detained their husbands, and kin averted their kinsmen.[71]

Bernard's father, Tesclin Sorus, appeared frequently in the charters of the duke of Burgundy at the beginning of the twelfth century identified as a knight of the lord of Châtillon. He himself was lord of Fontaines-lès-Dijon, not a powerful position, but one that only exercised influence through the Church. It did not even merit a castle.[72] Cistercian hagiography described him as a man (*vir*) of the old and lawful military service. The title "brilliant" (*clarus*) designated both of Bernard's parents by dignity in this world; but they were more dignified and noble according to the piety of Christian religion.[73] Thus was asserted the primacy of sacral over secular status. The appellation "man" (*vir*) was exchangeable indiscriminately in Latin charters from the end of the eleventh century with "vassal" (*miles*), an

---

66 Bernard of Clairvaux, *Sermones super cantica canticorum*.

67 Augustine, *Praeceptum* 1.1.

68 Bloch, *Feudal Society*, 1:86; Bouchard, *Sword, Miter, and Cloister: Nobility and the Church in Burgundy, 980-1198* (Ithaca, N. Y.: Cornell University Press, 1987), p. 61.

69 William of St.-Thierry, *Vita prima* 1.3.13; 1.3.17; 1.6.30. For a minor as heir see Bloch, *Feu-dal Society*, 1:201-2.

70 Bouchard, *Sword, Miter, and Cloister*, p. 331.

71 William of St.-Thierry, *Vita prima* 1.3.15.

72 Bouchard, *Sword, Miter, and Cloister*, pp. 329, 78.

73 William of St.-Thierry, *Vita prima* 1.1.1.

occupation rendered in the French texts not as "soldier" but as "knight".[74] A knight owned land, which he did not work, and he was situated between the nobles and the free peasants and townspeople. He held land and even his own house, rather than being an armed household retainer of the castellans. He did not have his own castle, however, or even a little wealth.[75]

The title *clarus* had been a favorite Roman epithet for distinguished public characters from consuls to senators. In medieval documents and chronicles a *vir illuster*, or its synonym, might have been a noble.[76] Reference to that title, or even *nobilis*, insufficiently denoted aristocracy, however, because the scribes were sporadic in their application of the terms, even omitting their usage when legitimate; so that charters did not qualify all who merited the title. The origin of *miles* or "knight" is unclear: whether it descended from the old families of counts and barons as younger sons; or whether it derived from the general population of peasants, as from local administrative families on the great estates. From the mid-twelfth century on the term *miles* transcended occupational description to acquire tenurial and social connotation. In the final two decades of the century the titles *domini* and *milites* were so indiscriminate in the charters that great and modest families could not be distinguished by title alone.[77] Bernard's father Tesclin was identified as a knight worshipful of God and steadfast in justice.[78] As a knight he mingled with and may have attained the lower rank of nobility. He was not an aristocrat, however. Although he spent his adult life principally at the castle of the lords of Châtillon, he was a dependent knight not a blood relative.[79]

Bernard's mother Aleth was classically commended as submissive to her husband in an honest and just marriage as a lawful and faithful wife. She was suggestively like the Virgin Mary in bearing her children less by her husband than by God. The first mention in her eulogy was that she raised her children faithfully educated and on their way in the world.[80] The female domestic task went unmentioned, although since late barbarian antiquity women were involved in all phases of cloth making—spinning, weaving, dying, and sewing—and since the early medieval period the great estates had a women's workshop for their labors.[81] The important fact demonstrating her civic duty and portending Bernard's public morality was not suppressed: she suckled her own infants, refusing the services of a wet nurse. When

---

74 Bloch, *Feudal Society*, 1:161, 162.

75 Bouchard, *Holy Entrepreneurs*, pp. 167-68.

76 Bouchard, *Sword, Miter, and Cloister*, p. 27.

77 Theodore Evergates, *Feudal Society in the Baillage of Troyes under the Counts of Champagne 1152-1284* (Baltimore, Md.: Johns Hopkins University Press, 1975), pp. 97, 114.

78 William of St.-Thierry, *Vita prima* 1.1.1; 1.2.5.

79 Bouchard, *Sword, Miter, and Cloister*, pp. 237-38.

80 William of St.-Thierry, *Vita prima* 1.1.1.

81 See David Herlihy, *Medieval Households* (Cambridge, Mass.: Harvard University Press, 1985), pp. 39, 52-53, 67.

they were weaned, she fed them an eremitical diet of crude and common fare in prescient preparation for their monastic life. In her household, marriage, and business, she herself emulated an eremitical or monastic vocation. With scant food and mean dress she abdicated the delights and pomps of the world—intent on fasts, vigils, and prayers. She compensated for her lack of religious profession as a nun by tireless dedication to alms and charity.[82]

Aleth's place of origin as sister of the lord of Montbard was a fort (*castrum*).[83] A fort is what Bernard termed Clairvaux, so that he was prolonging the military status and occupation of his parentage in an ideology of monastic warfare. The battlefield and the home were ideologically distinct places, just as French epic separated male and female spheres of action by alternating scenes at battle and at home. The soldier who thought of the home front, his wife and his property, would not fight valiantly. The emphatic female role in those epics, where the women served the men shoulder of boar with mazer of wine, was as the nurturer, provider of food.[84] Aleth's maternal role, as Bernard's nourisher at the breast and at the table, contrasted and competed with the usual nourishment for the sons of knights. That was education at or for court, termed *aulica nutritura*. It was instruction in the necessary customs and courtesy of the knightly station, an elegance of manners as a "nursemaid" of moral instruction.[85] Bernard studied at Notre-Dame at Châtillon, a house of secular canons.[86] A lord maintained his vassal either in his own household or provided him an estate or income, a method called "housing." It was the lord's obligation to raise his vassal's son, a participation in his domestic life that created strong ties of respect and gratitude. A boy remembered all his life that he had been the *nourri* of his lord. The lord was even called the giver of loaves, and the men, his bread eaters.[87]

Aleth had dreamed in pregnancy that Bernard was a barking dog with white fur and a tawny back, the "future guard of the house of God." Bernard as a boy once at the feast of the Nativity dozed off during a delay for the solemn office and was introduced to the mysteries of contemplation. The infant Jesus appeared to him like a bridegroom issuing from his wedding chamber, as if Bernard saw before his very eyes the Word being born from the Virgin's womb, more beautiful than the sons of men.[88] Portents were

---

[82] William of St.-Thierry, *Vita prima* 1.1.1; 1.2.5.

[83] Ibid. 1.1.1. For Aleth's family see Bouchard, *Sword, Miter, and Cloister*, pp. 334-38. For wet nursing in the twelfth century see Fossier, *Peasant Life*, p. 22.

[84] See Penny Schine Gold, *The Lady and the Virgin: Image, Attitude, and Experience in Twelfth-Century France* (Chicago: University of Chicago Press, 1985), pp. 5-8, 15-16, without reference to Bernard's family.

[85] See C. Stephen Jaeger, *The Origins of Courtliness: Civilizing Trends and the Formation of Courtly Ideals 939-1210* (Philadelphia: University of Pennsylvania Press, 1985), pp. 215-26, without reference to Bernard.

[86] William of St.-Thierry, *Vita prima* 1.1.3.

[87] Bloch, *Feudal Society*, 1:163, 226, 236.

[88] William of St.-Thierry, *Vita prima* 1.1.2; 1.2.4.

common in hagiography—the mother of Dominic had also dreamed during pregnancy of her son as a dog; and the saints were heralded in childhood by prodigies.[89] Yet the social status that Bernard renounced in entering the monastery was not exalted, as if his gesture were heroic. He desired escape from concupiscence—the naked girls who slipped seductively into his bed—and also from the false vanities of the world. He wanted to hide in the secrecy of the divine face from human disturbance; but more so from vanity, whether that of being well-born, or keenly talented, or reputed for sanctity.[90] Yet his good birth was only from a father who was a landowner with tenants, and not a lord. The status of Bernard's family was not even stable. It was the monastery that offered him what the manor denied him: stability. "I am staying quietly and obediently where I was put," wrote Bernard from Clairvaux.[91]

Aristocrats were defined by family; knights like Tesclin, by job. Their status was not owing to noble birth or even to linkage to the great families. Knights began only in the late twelfth-and early thirteenth centuries to acquire aristocratic status by fusing with the old families for titles, attributes, and privileges. In the twelfth century knights were armed retainers without the social status, military importance, or economic resources of the aristocrats, who were endogamous and whose bloodlines alone preserved their stability. The prestige and privilege of knights only increased well after Bernard's death, through intermarriage and alliance with the aristocrats in checking the encroachment of the townspeople on tenure of fief by marriage and by purchase.[92] The nobility that the knights of the twelfth century like Tesclin Sorus were ambitious to join had high potential in position and purpose. Yet it had high instability, ever threatened with loss through heredity or by war. Knights were further threatened by their neighbors—other nobles with greater power, by townspeople, and even by the king.[93]

The termination of Bernard's family through enclosure was not rare, only perhaps unusual in its method. The rate of infant mortality approached thirty percent.[94] The disintegration of even the great families of counts and lords from lack of male heirs was in the eleventh and twelfth centuries a regular occurrance.[95] In the Roman empire the problem had been legally solved by adoption, which prolonged the lineage. In the Middle Ages adop-

---

[89] See Donald Weinstein and Rudolph M. Bell, *Saints and Society: The Two Worlds of Western Christendom, 1000-1700* (Chicago: University of Chicago Press, 1982), pp. 19-47.

[90] William of St.-Thierry, *Vita prima* 1.3.7-8.

[91] Bernard of Clairvaux, *Epistolae* 76, cited by Gillian Evans, *The Mind of St. Bernard of Clairvaux* (Oxford: Clarendon, 1983), p. 19, and for Bernard against instability see pp. 18-21.

[92] Evergates, *Feudal Society in the Baillage of Troyes*, p. 145-46.

[93] See Bouchard, *Sword, Miter, and Cloister*, p. 28, without reference to Bernard.

[94] See Norman J. G. Pounds, *Hearth and Home: A History of Material Culture* (Bloomington: Indiana University Press, 1989), p. 217.

[95] Evergates, *Feudal Society in the Baillage of Troyes*, pp. 106-7.

tion as a strategy for heir virtually vanished. The estates of heirless couples devolved to the church, in an acquisition of property from the laity that was more usually solicited by voluntary bequests.[96] There was already within clerical government a ruthless indifference to the termination of a family, whose sorry condition was exploited rather than alleviated. The preference for spiritual affinity to carnal kinship had been established by Augustine. When he considered that the consequence of his moral standard of total restraint from sexual intercourse was the end of the human race, he pronounced that good. More rapidly would the city of God, rather than man, be populated and the end of the world hastened.[97]

The entire progeny of a clan could also be decimated accidentally during military exercise or violently during military warfare. The rules of the management of patrimony, which as in Roman law the father tenaciously held even when his children were adults, encouraged the sons to leave home. Although the right of primogeniture was not established among the lesser nobility until the end of the twelfth century, the best hope of the younger members was a lucrative ecclesiastical position. Marriage, negotiated by the father and elders, was primarily for the eldest son, who would inherit. There was caution to disallow many of the younger sons to marry, lest the lateral branches of the family multiply to overwhelm the main line, and lest the patrimony, which supplied the matrimonial settlement, be depleted. Eligible women were scarce, because previous alliances had made cousins of the entire knightly class and there were ecclesiastical sanctions against marriages of incest and consanguinity. Death in childbirth further reduced the female population, while for remarriage widowers had the advantage over youths. Youths were at an unstable margin, until as head of a household and father of a family they might belong to the body of settled men.[98]

Youth was the age of hiatus between households: between the household of the father during childhood and a personal household as a father

---

[96] Jack Goody, *The Development of the Family and Marriage in Europe* (Cambridge: Cambridge University Press, 1983), pp. 98-102. For background see Mireille Corbier, "Divorce and Adoption as Roman Familial Strategies (Le divorce et l'adoption 'en plus')," in *Marriage, Divorce, and Children in Ancient Rome*, ed. Beryl Rawson (Oxford: Clarendon Press for the Humanities Research Centre, Australian National University, Canberra, 1991), pp. 63-76; Suzanne Dixon, *The Roman Family* (Baltimore, Md.: Johns Hopkins University Press, 1991), pp. 112-13. Some evidence for adoption in medieval France is stated by Natalie Zemon Davis in her review of Goody's book, *American Ethnologist* 12 (1985):150. For an alternative to Goody's economic analysis see, e. g., Michel Verdon, "Virgins and Widows: European Kinship and Early Christianity," *Man* 23 (1988):488-505.

[97] Augustine, *De sancta virginitate* 3, *De bono coniugali* 10; the latter also mentioned by Herlihy, *Medieval Households*, p. 25, without documentation. See also David G. Hunter, "Resistance to the Virginal Ideal in Late-Fourth-Century Rome: The Case of Jovinian," *Theological Studies* 48 (1987):45-67.

[98] Georges Duby, "Youth in Aristocratic Society: Northwestern France in the Twelfth Century," in idem, *The Chivalrous Society*, trans. Cynthia Postan (London: Edward Arnold, 1977), pp. 116-120.

during manhood. It defined the adult sons of well-born men who were armed and dubbed as knights. It was epic in a protracted period of impatience, turbulence, and instability, its vagabondage a necessary stage of male development. All descriptions fundamentally characterized it by the refusal of place. Youth was in departure or on route.[99] Monasticism as a pilgrimage anthropologically enshrined liminality, the ritual insurance of safe passage from one state of life to the next.[100] Yet the entire human race was defined religiously as marginal, bordering between angels and beasts. Although the concept was developed notably in Giovanni Pico della Mirandola's *Oratio de dignitate hominis*, Thomas Aquinas entertained the idea.[101] It had been commonplace among the ancients, as in Sallust's moral on the Cataline conspiracy.[102] Historically medieval monasticism was a state of perpetual youth. It was not socially a threshold to anywhere, more like a no-man's land in which the monks spiritually roamed and sighed for a security unattainable on earth. Stability was not absolutely unobtainable to youths: ignoble class might be overcome by military honor. Monks rendered it unattainable by their triply vowed rejection of ordinary society but especially by their celibacy. They sought to create an artificial stability in a social regrouping that was incapable even of perpetuation. To this monastic society were transferred the values of kinship, spiritualized.

The majority of the youths who joined the Cistercian order as choir monks were of the lesser nobility or of the rank of knight, as was the tendency in twelfth-century monasticism. The Burgundian nobility no longer dominated politics as it had in the previous century—partly from the resurgence of the French king and the growth of the lesser nobility, partly from the Gregorian reform, which blunted secular control over local churches. Bernard urged conversion even against the objections of parents, citing Jesus' demand of absolute love over parental affection (Matt. 10:37). He averted to the harsh counsel of Jerome that a person should tread on the body of his father prostrate over the threshold, spurn his mother displaying the breasts that nursed him, or a small nephew clinging to his neck. To step on one's father's back was an advancement toward salvation, which required the denial of the familial and the domestic.[103] When Bernard arrived with his companions at Cîteaux, the monks there had been desolate for lack of new members. With his infusion they rejoiced to bear more children than a

---

[99] Ibid., pp. 112-14. See also for context Phyllis Gaffney, "The Ages of Man in Old French Verse and Epic Romance," *Modern Language Review* 85 (1990):570-82.

[100] Victor Turner, *The Ritual Process: Structure and Anti-Structure* (Chicago: Aldine, 1969), pp. 102-8.

[101] Gerard Verbeke, "Man as a 'Frontier' according to Aquinas," in *Aquinas and Problems of his Time*, ed. idem and D. Verhelst, Mediaevalia lovaniensia, 1-5 (Louvain: University Press, 1976), pp. 195-223.

[102] Sallust, *Bellum civile* 1.1.

[103] Bouchard, *Sword, Miter, and Cloister*, p. 55.

woman from her husband (Is. 61:1) and to see grandsons into many generations. Some of his companions, like his eldest brother, were married; so a convent called Jully was erected nearby Langres for their wives. Bernard himself lived an "angelic life in the presence of God, inebriated with the abundance of God's house."[104]

Yet it was Bernard's eldest brother who, in becoming a Cistercian, singularly renounced social status. As the third son of a knight, Bernard could not have expected more than a similar, probably lesser, dependency than his father. Prospects of marriage, affording him some status as an established man rather than a perpetual youth, would have been poor or none. Prospects of survival in the livelihood of combat were uncertain. Although he and his brothers did not select a comfortable position in a lax order, where they might have prolonged or even bettered the amenities of military service, they did join the "new monastery," as Cîteaux was called. The austerity of its discipline must have attracted men dedicated to the ethical ideals of their courtly education. But its newness also allowed for social mobility within its ranks. As abbot of Clairvaux in the service of the Lord, Bernard exercised more social responsibility than he probably could have attained as a knight at Châtillon in the service of its lord.

Beyond the charitable reality of social responsibility, there was inherent in asceticism the vicious attraction of social status. The nobles of Burgundy regularly donated and bequeathed property and rights to the Cistercians in exchange for prayers for their deceased members of family. Clairvaux during Bernard's tenure as abbot was unique in recording no gift that would generate revenue.[105] It had a just reputation for integrity. There was a medieval concept of a division of labor among those who prayed, those who fought, and those who worked.[106] The concept was the invention of but one of those divisions, however, the clergy. There was little enthusiasm for it among the workers, who were struggling to emerge from their category.[107] The division was not strict between the upper echelons either, since the monks applied military ideology to their role, while the nobles adopted religious ideology for theirs, notably in the crusades. Why, then, did a knight endow a monk with land in exchange for prayer? Why did he not value his own prayer as efficacious for the soul of his dead parent? Why was the prayer of an outsider to the family, who had even renounced parent-

---

[104] William of St.-Thierry, *Vita prima* 1.3.18-4.19. See Bernard of Clairvaux, *Sermones super Cantica canticorum* 52.2.5. See also Suso Frank, *Angelikos bios: Begriffsanalytische und begriffsgeschichtliche Untersuchung zum "engelgleichen Leben" in frühen Mönchtum*, Beiträge zur Geschichte des alten Mönchtums und des Benediktinerordens, 26 (Münster: Aschendorff, 1964).

[105] Bouchard, *Holy Entrepreneurs*, p. 97.

[106] Constable, "The Orders of Society," in idem, *Three Studies in Medieval Religious and Social Thought* (Cambridge: Cambridge University Press, 1995), pp. 251-341.

[107] Alexander Murray, *Reason and Society in the Middle Ages* (Oxford: Clarendon, 1978), pp. 96-98, and for the deprecation of peasants, pp. 237-42.

age, judged holier than that of an insider? Because it was the person of anomalous behavior, like the celibate monk, to whom adhered the reputation for holiness and with it social status.

Christian ascetics were not ignorant of the phenomenon. Evagrius Ponticus, the desert father who formulated the concept of the seven capital vices, named vainglory as the most difficult temptation, because effort to escape it might occasion it. Vainglory was, as a species of pride, the desire to be socially observed and praised. It tempted the monk with fantasies of people flocking to his cell for counsel and cure that would resound with his praise.[108] Augustine warned that it practiced a "crafty semblance of holiness," deceiving a person under the pretence of service to God.[109] Bernard himself considered it the wile of demons lying in ambush to deceive monks through simulated good. He advised those who had attained to the grace of devotion to guard against an injurious attraction to asceticism—to spiritual loss. Prudence taught the avoidance of its excesses.[110]

Although the Cistercians were antisocial in their celibacy, they were not in their economy. For survival they required substantial holdings of property, which their very austerity prompted nobles to give generously. Their reformed monasteries were still dependent on the benevolence of their neighbors for gifts and for members, indeed for their very foundations. A conflict of interests developed between vowed poverty and the economic wealth ironically necessary to sustain it. The Cistercians were given land, churches, rights of pasturage and of forest, even town houses they could not possibly use. Yet such gifts minimized their distinction from other powerful landholders, thus juxtaposed the monastery and the manor.[111] When the prior and brethren of Clairvaux insisted that the narrow site of the abbey was inadequate, and so recommended its relocation in a suitable clearing down river, Bernard balked at the proposal to rebuild. He protested that the laity would judge the monks flighty and fickle, quite mad, since they lacked the funds to duplicate the project.[112] Cistercian building projects were criticized even within the order for arousing envy rather than respect among the laity. As one strict observant complained, "What you are building are palaces rather than guest-houses, fortifications rather than walls, towers rather than refectories, castles rather than dormitories, temples rather than chapter-

---

108 Evagrius Ponticus, *Logos praktikos*, prol., 3, 13, 30-32.

109 Augustine, *In Epistolam Joannis ad Parthos tractatus* 8.9; *Homilies on the Gospel according to St. John, and His First Epistles*, trans. H. Browne, 2 vols. (Oxford, 1848), 2:1198; *De sermone Domini in monte* 2.12.41.

110 Bernard of Clairvaux, *Sermones super Cantica canticorum* 33.6.13; "In Circumcisione Domini, Sermo" 3.1. For the cultural dissemination of his exegesis see Kathleen M. Ashley, "The Specter of Bernard's Noonday Demon in Medieval Drama," *American Benedictine Review* 30 (1979):205-21.

111 Bouchard, *Sword, Miter, and Cloister*, pp. 171-246, 253; *Holy Entrepreneurs*, p. 254; and for gifts to monasteries by the laity, pp. 66-87; for conflicts over property, pp. 128-59.

112 Arnald of Bonneval, *Vita prima* 2.5.30.

houses, strongholds rather than chapels, villas rather than granges."[113] To Bernard's hesitations and objections, the prior responded that God would provide. Bernard relented; and God did provide, in the person of count Thibault of Champagne, who supplied everything necessary and more; local bishops and nobles also made donations. The enclosure was quickly constructed, the abbey erected, and the church developed as if it had a living soul.[114]

Cistercian houses in the first two generations were founded by monks desiring a place to settle but also by laymen willing to grant them such a place. Transactions between the Cistercians and their neighbors, originally by oral agreement but later recorded in episcopal charters of confirmation, could be a layman's gift of a meadow, the monks' burial of a patron, or a mutual exchange of cropland. Pawning, leasing, and purchasing secured their earliest records in Burgundy, not in the transactions of burgeoning cities, but in the archives of rural monasteries. The laity regarded the monks as a source of ready credit, because, as corporate, the monasteries had more liquid capital for long-term investments than did individuals. Cistercian agriculture was economically successful because of such integral exchange. Socially those transactions created and strengthened bonds of mutuality and friendship between the monks and the seculars. Knights, who were the principal donors and geographical neighbors, especially formed a social relationship with Cistercian houses in a network of ties by blood and friendship.[115]

The experience of social solidarity, transformed in the monastery from natural consanguinity to spiritual unanimity, provided a slight yet delighted theology of divine indwelling that varied Augustine's inn with Bernard's sanctuary. In his series of sermons on the dedication of churches Bernard exhorted the brethren to the observance of that festivity particular to them, unlike all other ecclesiastical feasts, which were common to the faithful. "It is ours because it is about our church; but is is more ours because it is about our very selves." To anticipated disbelief about a festival to monks, he explained that the walls of the church at Clairvaux were holy, but only because of the bodies that inhabited them: monastic bodies were truly holy because they were the "temples" of the Holy Spirit. That Spirit within the monks sanctified their bodies because of their souls and the house of God because of their bodies.[116] The architectural church as an enclosure was thus the foundation for a spiritual ascent to the body, to the soul, to the Spirit.

---

113 C. H. Talbot, "The Cistercian Attitude towards Art: The Literary Evidence," in *Cistercian Art and Architecture in the British Isles*, ed. Norton and Park, p. 63.

114 Arnald of Bonneval, *Vita prima* 2.5.31.

115 Bouchard, *Holy Entrepreneurs*, pp. 21-22, 31-33, 35-36, 43, 165-70, 183. For pawning property as the predominant form of credit see pp. 35-43; for gifts to monasteries by the laity, pp. 66-87; for donations of land, 97-106; for monks and society in conflict over property, 128-59.

116 Bernard of Clairvaux, *Sermones in dedicatione ecclesiae* 1.1.

Bernard praised the miracle of so many noble youths confined there as in an "open prison" without any fetters save the fear of God. The wonders of their perseverance in an affliction of penitence beyond human virtue, above nature, and against custom was proof of the indwelling of the Spirit. Just as the indwelling of the soul in the body was manifest by the senses, so was the indwelling of the Spirit in the soul revealed by the exercise of the monastic virtues. The festival the monks celebrated was their own dedication to the Lord and his election and assumption of them as his own. Renunciation of secular possessions allowed them to become "possessions" of the author of the secular and to have him as their proper possession as lot and inheritance. It was not those with full barns and fat oxen who were blessed but those who had the Lord for God.[117]

The aspersion, inscription, unction, illumination, and benediction of the ecclesiastical house performed visibly by pontiffs were accomplished invisibly in souls daily by Christ the high priest. He cleansed sins, inscribed the law, anointed with grace, illumined with works—in all these operations constituting monastic merits; but he reserved as the monastic reward his blessing at the end. On that day the monk would enter a house not humanly constructed but built with living stones, the angels and saints. Its dedication would coincide with the completion of the structure. Wood and stones did not make a house unless they were cemented in conjunction. The perfect unity of celestial spirits would render God a habitation whole and fitting, which the indwelling glory of his majesty would ineffably beatify. Those living stones would be privy to the divine secrets just as palatial stones witnessed to the counsels of a king. The juncture and connection of that house would be a glue of double mixture, full knowledge and perfect love. The desire for that felicitous house was to covet the atriums of God and to swear entry into his tabernacle.[118]

Just as David designed on earth a house for God, which Solomon built, so God fabricated, joined, furnished, and decorated for the human soul a sublime house in the body, in which it might gloriously and delectably dwell. And for the body he created a noble, accommodated, and elegant house in the sensible inhabited world. Just as he built humans a house, so should they build him a temple. On earth humans had a certain house, but for certain it was shortly about to collapse, exposing them to the harsh elements. Yet the monk believed that, if his earthly home fell, he still had a building in heaven. Where would he find a site or architect for that edifice? The material and visible temple of the church at Clairvaux had been built for the monks and their habitation, because almighty God did not dwell in manufactured places. What temple could be built for him who filled the universe? Bernard said he would be anguished to reply to that question if he had not

[117] Ibid. 1.2-3.
[118] Ibid. 1.4-7.

heard the Lord Jesus addressing his disciples, "I and the Father will come to him, and we will make our abode (*mansio*) with him" (John 14:23).[119]

This verse instructed Bernard, who then instructed the brethren, about where the house was to be readied, for nothing took possession of God unless it was in his image. "The soul is capable of him because doubtless it has been created to his image." He exhorted the monks to ready the nuptial couch, because the Lord would inhabit the land, and to rejoice, because the Lord would inhabit them. They should repeat the consent of Mary and the praise of Elizabeth for that benignity and dignity rendering dignified and glorious the human soul. In it the Lord of the universe, who had no need, ordered a temple to be made for him. Bernard instructed the monks to build a spiritual temple, solicitous for the divine dwelling in the individual, then in the community. The soul was to be simplified, because divisive walls would totter and collapse; and intact in its faculties from delusion, perversion, and defilement. Communal indwelling would occur by the cement of perfect charity. Yet the second cement of full knowledge was impossible, even undesirable, on earth. It was reserved for the heavenly home, whose parts would be more firmly fastened, since it was destined to stand for eternity.[120]

At Clairvaux the monks had "the tent of warriors," which less perfectly cohered. If they were victorious in virtue, they would exchange military armament for celestial reward. That house, the monastic church, was the stronghold of the celestial king, besieged by enemies and defended by virtues, with angelic guards supporting human defenses.[121] Bernard emphasized that the house of the church of Clairvaux was holy by the bodies of the monks who frequented it; their bodies holy by the souls that animated them; their souls sanctified by the indwelling Spirit. Blessed were they who dwelled in it but more blessed still, those who dwelled in the eternal house! While the monks lived here below in the tents they were to perform military service in a manly fashion; so that after death they might rest pleasantly in the atriums, then glory sublimely in the house. Bernard took his watch in the tower to seek the house of God, the temple, the city, and the spouse. With fear and reverence he affirmed the identity of that divine house: "We are! We are, I say, but in the heart of God; we are, but in his conferral of status, not in our own dignity."[122]

Bernard's sermonizing from ecclesiastical architecture, the very church dedicated at Clairvaux in which he stood, developed Augustine's distinction. The divine indwelling on earth was only by image in a spiritual

---

[119] Ibid. 2.1-2.

[120] Ibid. 2.2-4. For a recent study of Bernard on charity and contemplation see Bernard McGinn, "Freedom, Formation and Reformation: The Anthropological Roots of Saint Bernard's Spiritual Teaching," *Analecta cisterciensia* 46 (1990):91-114.

[121] Bernard of Clairvaux, *Sermones in dedicatione ecclesiae* 2.4; 3; 4.1-3.

[122] Ibid. 4.4-6; 5.8.

"temple." In heaven the image was in a spiritual "house," or better, "household," since the company of angels and saints comprised its living stones cemented by their charity. The model was again sacral, not secular; ecclesiastical, not domestic; imitative, not possessive. The monastic church was not even for Bernard ultimately sacral, for God disdained to dwell in any fabricated place. There was clear medieval preference in expressing the sacred for natural, rather than cultural, models. The monastery as a paradise, the cloistral garden on which the buildings centered, was more pleasing than the monastery as an edifice. The land as divinely created, not the artifice as humanly constructed on it, was fundamental. When Dante arrived in paradise, he traveled through the celestial spheres to discover Bernard the contemplative not in a mansion but in a flower, the mystical rose.[123]

The power of the monks and their helpers by discipline and association to alter a landscape, especially by deforestation, surpassed in magnitude and fervor the modest efforts of the laity. In converting wastelands into pleasant abodes, new creations, the monastic image of paradise included the elegance of the buildings; but it centered on the trees, the grasses, the vines. For a poet considering the Benedictine foundation of Monte Cassino, it was the gardens, vineyards, and crop that provided his moral on barren deeds, converted to fruitful works by the rain of grace on arid hearts and the uprooting of thorns from the tough breast. There was the monk who traversed the ground of a potential monastic site, viewing all of it advantages of proper soil and water supply. They more he surveyed it from every angle, the more pleased he became. He was so charmed with the beauty of the place that he spent almost an entire day wandering over it to explore its possibilities. Then he blessed it and turned his face to home.[124] Bernard claimed to discover the meaning of revelation in the wood and field, with stones and trees for masters. Once when at harvest he was ordered to rest, because he lacked the skill and strength for reaping, he was saddened. Withdrawing in prayer, he asked God to grant him the grace to crop. God so granted it, and from that day harvesting was the work in which he most excelled. He enjoyed it with the more devotion because its ability was from grace alone.[125]

The cultivation of the soil was, as in Roman morality, a model for the culture of the soul. The church was a building for monastic, not divine, society, as if God still yearned to stroll with humans on the primeval earth. Yet by a gradation of reasoning the monk could ascend mentally from the

---

[123] Dante, *Paradiso* 31-32. For the gardens see Paul Meyvaert, "The Medieval Monastic Garden," in *Medieval Gardens*, ed. Elisabeth B. MacDougall, Dumbarton Oaks Colloquium on the History of Landscape Architecture, 9 (Washington, D. C.: Dumbarton Oaks, 1986), pp. 23-53.

[124] For the descriptions see Clarence J. Glacken, *Traces on the Rhodian Shore: Nature and Culture in Western Thought from Ancient Times to the End of the Eighteenth Century* (Berkeley: University of California Press, 1967), pp. 311-13, 303-4, 306-7.

[125] Bernard of Clairvaux, *Epistolae* 106; William of St.-Thierry, *Vita prima* 1.4.23.

ecclesiastical structure of the abbey in which he worshipped, to his body, to his soul, to the Spirit indwelling. Yet the "abode" of the Vulgate translation of the topical verse John 14:23 was *mansio*, which philology emphasized its transitory status: crumbling, tottering walls, just as Bernard preached. A *mansio* was an "abode", "dwelling", "habitation"; but only temporarily, as "nocturnal quarters", "lodging-place", "inn". It was, like the monk as pilgrim, a movable shelter. It was a *tabernaculum*, the box for the repose of the Eucharist on the altar; or simply a "tent", in which and from which the monk conducted his warfare against the world. In preaching on "the cloistral paradise" Bernard mixed metaphors to identify it as a military or seigniorial fortress. "Truly the cloister is paradise," he said, "an area with a fortified wall of discipline in which there is a fecund fertility of precious wares. A glorious thing that men by one custom should live in a house; good and agreeable that brothers should dwell as one." Observing the various activities of the monks from repentance to contemplation, he exclaimed like Jacob awaking from his dream of the ladder: "The forts of the Lord are these. How terrible is this place! This is none other than the house of God and the gate of heaven" (Gen. 32:2, 28:17).[126]

The *castrum* that he identified as Clairvaux was a late Roman fortification, like Langres in whose diocese it was situated. That city of Roman status was an impressive site atop a prominent hill, an important point for the crossing of main imperial roads. Only one Roman monument survives: an ornamental, possibly triumphal, arch incorporated into the later thick circuit of walls composed from former monuments. The sole literary reference to those walls was to Constantius Chlorus, who, when chased by Alemannic tribesmen, scaled them with ropes in a narrow escape.[127] The bishop of Langres, like others, had appropriated the *castrum* and perched the diocesan cathedral on a hill in the center of the city.[128] Cistercian houses in the twelfth century were closely integrated with the diocesan hierarchy. Unlike the Cluniacs, they sought no exemption from episcopal authority. Canonically the monks at Clairvaux were obedient and subject to the bishop of Langres. It was he, rather than the abbot Bernard, who confirmed a gift or transaction to the monastery and sealed the charter.[129] Yet in designating

[126] Bernard of Clairvaux, *Sermones de diversis* 42.4. For the fortune of the idea see Friedrich Wilhelm Wodtke, "Die Allegorie des 'Inneren Paradieses' bei Bernhard von Clairvaux, Honorius Augustodunensis, Gottfried von Strassburg und in der deutschen Mystik," in *Festschrift für Josef Quint anlässlich seines 65. Geburtstages überreicht* (Bonn: Emil Semmel, 1964), pp. 277-90.

[127] See Stephen Johnson, *Late Roman Fortifications* (London: B. T. Batsford, 1983), pp. 82, 84.

[128] Bouchard, *Sword, Miter, and Cloister*, p. 32. See also Wilhelm Schlink, *Zwischen Cluny und Clairvaux: Die Kathedrale von Langres und die burgundische Architektur des 12. Jahrhunderts*, Beiträge zur Kuntsgeschichte, 4 (Berlin: Walter de Gruyter, 1970).

[129] Bouchard, *Holy Entrepreneurs*, pp. 20, 21, 18. For Cistercian relations with dioceses see Bernard Bligny, *L'Église et les ordres religieux dans le royaume de Bourgogne au XIe et*

Clairvaux as the numinous *castra* where Jacob had wrestled with the angel to secure the patrimony of Israel (Gen. 28:17), Bernard implied that the monastery, and not the see, was the defense of the Church. Cistercian values were rural not urban.[130]

Bernard was not utterly negative about housing. The wine cellar that Augustine had typified as an occasion for social depravity he reinterpreted as a necessary condition for the brethren. It was a place of zeal for charity, its wine inspirational for government; indeed, because of its plenitude it was "the storeroom (*cella*) of grace."[131] In founding Clairvaux he relocated the monastery to a site better for viniculture and he permitted the use of wine, although only from necessity and preferably just a sip. The cellarer had charge of the financial administration of the abbey. He ordered the meals and saw that they were served on time and he dished out each monk's portion into his bowl. He received the account of the convert in charge of the agriculture, the laborers, and the domestics. His duty was the inspection of the abbey. The original cellarers at Clairvaux were Bernard's own brothers, Gérard and Gui.[132] In his eulogy for Gérard he observed that while he, Bernard, was addressed as abbot, Gérard excelled in care: in the buildings, the fields, the gardens, the water supply, all the skills of the rustics. He was easily the master of masons, blacksmiths, farmers, gardeners, cobblers, and weavers.[133]

What in that monastic complex of the secrets of the bedroom? A letter by a queen of Sicily who visited Clairvaux in 1517 described its establishment as enclosed by a wall, with a small garden in front in which was located a wooden reception room, tiny and low. Beyond the gate was a refectory with a dormitory above. At the top of the stairs was Bernard's chamber, very small, with a wooden bed and stone headboard. The room was located close to the roof, where there was a window with a view into the old wooden chapel. A Cistercian monk who visited it in the next century considered Bernard's chamber "quite small, more like a dungeon than a room."[134] Augustine had retired to his interior bedroom to moan love songs to God afar in the celestial city. Bernard commented on the Song of Songs concerning the bedroom, where God was perceived at rest, not as judge or teacher, but as bridegroom. In his rare and brief stays in the soul God was likened to a king after a long day of litigation, who unburdened his responsibility and went home at night to his own place. There he welcomed a few friends

---

XIIe siècles, Collection des cahiers d'histoire publiées par les Universités de Clermont, Lyon, Grenoble, 4 (Paris: Presses Universitaires de France, 1960), pp. 370-94.

130 For rural values see Bouchard, *Holy Entrepreneurs*, pp. 193-94.

131 Bernard of Clairvaux, *Sermones super Cantica canticorum* 23.3.7.

132 D'Arbois de Jouvainville, *Études sur l'état interieur des abbayes cisterciennes*, pp. 120-21, 227-28.

133 Bernard of Clairvaux, *Sermones super Cantica canticorum* 26.5.7.

134 Schaefer, "Earliest Churches of the Cistercian Order," p. 5.

into the intimacy of his private suite. Yet even that bedroom was for Bernard not located in a house. It was a "sanctuary" (*arcanum*) and a "shrine" (*sanctuarium*). The divine bedroom was to be sought "in the sanctuary of philosophically speculative contemplation (*in theoricae contemplationis arcano*)."[135]

Asking forbearance for his foolishness, Bernard admitted the frequent advent of the Word into himself. As often as it entered him, he was not sensible of when it would enter. He sensed its presence, remembered it; sometimes he had presentiment of its entry, but he never sensed its coming or going, whence it came or whither it went. Of this advent imperceptible to the senses, Bernard wondered whether it indeed entered, since it did not exist outside the soul. Yet it did not come from within, since he confessed nothing good within him. By ascent in his soul he comprehended the Word as more eminent than his pinnacle and by descent, more profound than his basement. Bernard explored outside: it extended beyond his horizon. He scrutinized inside: it was yet deeper within. And he knew by his examinations the truth of Paul's citation of the philosophers in the midst of the Areopagus: "In him we live and move and having our being" (Acts 17:28). Blessed is he, Bernard wrote, who experiences this living and efficacious Word.[136]

That was not phenomenology but characterization of a divine-human relationship. Bernard's soul had no porter. The divine Word visited it mysteriously, yet freely, as its own property. It was a guest there but not a stranger. In Cistercian monasteries there was the office of porter, a monk lodged in a cell next to the gate. He was at his post from sunrise to sunset, except during meals and Mass, when he was replaced by the sub-porter. If a stranger knocked at the door, he responded "Thanks be to God," then opened it to him, asked his blessing and his business. If the stranger wished to enter and could by the rule be admitted, the porter received him on his knees. The visitor was seated in the cell and told: "Wait a minute. I am going to announce your arrival to the abbot, and then I shall come for you." The porter searched throughout the monastery for the abbot until he found him or assured himself of his absence, in which case he addressed the prior. The abbot would then send with the porter a monk charged with receiving the stranger on his behalf, if he did not see need to receive him personally. The monk representing the abbot and the porter, upon arrival at the gate, knelt before the stranger. They conducted him to the church, prayed with him, read him a lesson with an explanation if necessary, then brought him to the hostelry.[137]

---

[135] Bernard of Clairvaux, *Sermones super Cantica canticorum* 23.6.15-16; 23.4.9.

[136] Ibid. 74.5-6.

[137] D'Arbois de Jouvainville, *Études sur l'état interieur des abbayes cisterciennes*, pp. 202-3.

There were few medieval inns outside of villages, so that hospitality was an obligation. In Burgundian law a fine of three solidi was levied for refusal to offer a visitor shelter and warmth; and in winter, hay or barley for his horse.[138] The romances always related how the knight errant was accorded hospitality at a chateau: a cordial greeting, fresh garments, a feast, bathing and medicine, and lodging for the night.[139] It was important to his adventure; and his behavior as a guest was, like combat and love, a measure or test of his chivalry.[140] Hospitality was a religious act in the charity of houses of God that provided free hospitals and hospices in remote localities. Abbeys also had to receive travelers and the sick. The rule of Benedict prescribed that the monk should receive the poor and the pilgrim in the certainty that he welcomed Christ. The guest was offered water to wash his hands, and the abbot and the monks themselves washed his feet. He was fed from the abbot's own table. The hostel was to be supervised by a God-fearing monk and furnished sufficiently with beds and bedding. "It is the house of God, which should be administrated wisely and by sages," the rule declared. These principles were obeyed by the Cistercians, who reversed the abuse of their charitable purpose. Barons gathering to celebrate the great liturgical feasts would hold in Benedictine monasteries their courts of justice, like Hugues the count of Champagne at Molesmes. The Cistercians resumed the reception of the poor and the sick. One night when Bernard was at prayer there arrived at Clairvaux an evangelically poor man who died in the hostelry. Bernard heard the angels who bore his soul to heaven chanting. The hostelry was also open to well-off persons, but from social necessity or for pious retreat. "The stones of your church," remarked one noble, "are softer than all the mattresses of my chateau."[141]

Visitors were frequent: monks, canons, seculars, ecclesiastical dignitaries, and lay lords. All could participate in the Mass and receive the Eucharist with the kiss of peace. The local ordinary, the pope or his representative, and prospective lay benefactors were received in the chapter room. Some visitors freely entered the monastery without announcement to the abbot, because it was unseemly to keep them waiting at the gate. At that gate passersby and women with infants were given bread, and leprous women, free food. In famine any woman could be donated food at the abbot's orders.[142] At Clairvaux a brother of Bernard's, André, was the porter. He

---

[138] Rouche, "Early Middle Ages in the West," p. 440.

[139] Edoardo Esposito, "Les formes d'hospitalité dans le roman courtois (Du *Roman de Thèbes* à Chrétien de Troyes)," *Romania* 103 (1982):197-234.

[140] Matilda Tomaryn Bruckner, *Narrative Invention in Twelfth-Century French Romance: The Convention of Hospitality (1160-1200)*, French Forum Monographs, 17 (Lexington, Ky.: French Forum, 1980).

[141] D'Arbois de Jouvainville, *Études sur l'état interieur des abbayes cisterciennes*, pp. 219-22; and see for background Denys Gorce, "Die Gastfreudlichkeit der altchristlichen Einsiedler und Mönche," *Jahrbuch für Antike und Christentum* 15 (1972):66-91.

[142] Ferguson, *Architecture of Solitude*, p. 72.

guarded the abbey against even the visitation of Bernard's sister Humbeline, whom he piteously refused to greet. She was not yet converted to asceticism and she scandalized him by the glamour of her retinue and clothing.[143] No brother by blood or religion guarded Bernard's soul from Jesus as brother. According to the rule, guests were to be welcomed at the monastery as Christ himself, from his saying "I was a stranger and you welcomed me" (Matt. 25:35). Fitting honor was to be exhibited to the faithful and to foreigners, with a prayer before the kiss of peace. The guest was to be addressed on arrival and departure with complete humility, bowing the head or prostrating the body as in adoring Christ, for he was welcomed in them. Christ was even more particularly received in the poor and the pilgrim, who were especially respected in denial of social awe of the rich and the landed. No one might converse or associate with a guest unless ordered by his superior, however. If a brother met or saw a guest, he was to greet him humbly, ask his blessing, and continue on his way, explaining that he was not allowed to converse with him.[144] There was no such monastic regulation or social ceremony between Bernard the abbot and Christ the guest as Word in his soul. Divine visitation was at divine will; and, although it indwelled rarely and briefly as in a sanctuary not a home, Bernard's theological imagination extended beyond Augustine's alone in his bedroom.

Bernard had preached in his final sermon on the dedication of churches about the modes of divine presence. God was present everywhere since he was confined nowhere, containing and disposing everything, although very differently. That distinction of presence related to the morality of the person. To the wicked the divine presence was surpassing and concealing; to the elect, effecting and saving; to the celestial, feeding and reclining; to the infernal, accusing and damning. Bernard applied to the blessed in heaven the divine activity of "reclining" (*cubans*), the very word Augustine had used of his relationship (*cubo*) with his concubine, whose status (*concubinium*) was derived from the verb, as was the bedroom (*cubiculum*) they shared. "Where he sleeps (*cubo*)," Bernard preached of God, "he is the spouse, and blessed the soul whom he has introduced into his bedroom!" In the church at Clairvaux, where God was only effecting and saving, the monks were enjoined to be penitent and expectant. They were located there only to be repentant of past sins and expectative of future rewards.[145] The divine house, certainly its bedroom, was remote in the common monastic imagination; probably it was only celestial for the majority of Bernard's congregation.

Yet Bernard had also preached that, just as the indwelling of the soul in the body was manifest by the senses, so was the indwelling of the Spirit in

143 D'Arbois de Jouvainville, *Études sur l'état interieur des abbayes cisterciennes*, p. 206.
144 Benedict, *Regula* 53.
145 Bernard of Clairvaux, "In dedicatione ecclesiae" 6.2-3.

the soul revealed by the exercise of virtues.[146] In a sermon for advent he considered three distinct comings of God: "to people, into people, and against people." The first was universal, the last common. There was also the advent into people, which was spiritual and secret. Concerning this Bernard cited the topical verse, "If someone loves me, he will keep my conversation, and my father will love him, and we will come to him and make our dwelling at his house" (John 14:23 Vulg.). Blessed, he exclaimed, is the one whom wisdom builds as its house, erecting seven pillars! Blessed the soul that is the seat (*sedes*) of wisdom! What is it? he inquired. The soul thoroughly just. Bernard applied the example of a piece of furniture, although hardly an ordinary domestic chair. Such a just soul was a *pulvinar*, the cushioned couch or marriage bed spread with a splendid covering of silk, reserved for the gods or emperor, or for persons receiving divine honors. This seat that the monks were to ready in their souls was "the virtue of justice," which rendered God his due. They prepared it by exercising justice at all levels of relationship: to superiors, inferiors, and equals. To superiors they owed reverence and obedience; to the brethren, among whom by the law of fraternity and human society the monks lived, they were to offer human counsel and assistance.[147]

"Justice in the heart is bread in the house," preached Bernard, and in considering Bethlehem as the "house of bread" he suggested an alternative to the tradition of divine indwelling by the created image. The monks should study the Nativity to become Bethlehem, so that Christ might deign to receive (*suscipere*) them.[148] The verb meant particularly to take up a newborn babe from the ground, to acknowledge it legally by Roman *patria potestas* as one's own.[149] At Bethlehem the monk could fill his soul faithfully with the pabulum of the divine word. Concerning that place Bernard discoursed more faithfully on scripture than he had in his reversion to Augustine's doctrine of the image. In his own imagination Bernard visited that town to see the Word made and manifested. Bethlehem was the house of bread, since where the word of God was there must be the bread that confirmed the heart (Ps. 103:15); for in the word that proceeded from the mouth of God people lived (Matt. 4:4). "He lives in Christ and Christ lives in him."[150]

There Christ was born, there he appeared. He loved not the faltering and vacillating heart, but the stable and strengthened one. Bernard immediately moralized about the vow of monastic stability, perhaps impelled by the reality of the winter solstice, when energies ebbed with the waning of light.

---

146 Ibid. 1.2.

147 "In adventu" 3.4.

148 Bernard, "In vigilia nativitatis Domini" 1.6.

149 For *suscipere* as the poetic version of *tollere* regarding infant rearing see Carl Sittl, *Die Gebärden der Griechen und Römer* (1890; rpt. edition, Hildesheim: Georg Olms, 1970), p. 130 and n. 2.

150 Bernard, "In vigilia nativitatis Domini" 1.6; 6.10.

Stability meant not to murmur, hesitate, or waver; not to wallow in the mire, or to return to the vomit, or to desert the vow, or to change purpose. Of a faltering monk he pronounced, "He is not Bethlehem, he is not a house of bread." Only a severe famine would compel descent into Egypt to feed the swine with husks, so remote from the house of bread, the house of the father, where even the hired hands had plenty. Christ would refuse to be born in such an unstable heart. It lacked "the fortitude of faith that is the bread of life; as scripture testifies, 'the just man lives by faith'" (Rom. 1:16). It was evident that "the true life of the soul, which he himself is, lives for the while only by faith in our hearts." Although Bernard proceeded to exhort constancy against mutability,[151] his brief exposition adhered scripturally to the topical verse of divine indwelling by fidelity to Jesus' words (John 14:23).

With the institutionalization of the monastery, the cultivation of individual friendships that had provided Bernard some analogy for divine familiarity was replaced by the concerns of government, the administration of property, and connections with other social organizations. From the mid-thirteenth century on, the most enlightened monks turned from friendship to the internal reform of the order and to external involvement in the university. Among the best and brightest men scholastic learning was challenging monastic experience.[152] A master at Paris from the newer orders of friars applied philosophical method to the matter of divine indwelling. It was Thomas Aquinas's argument rigorously to reduce the divine habitat to a human habit. He expounded Augustine's doctrine of humans created to the divine image as an approximation of an essentially distinct object. A human being was to that image by his intelligent nature, in his natural capacity for knowing and loving God. Scholastically just men were not like Bernard's monks plumping up the cushions of their matrimonial beds. They were to the divine image by their actual knowledge and love of God, although imperfectly; while blessed men, whose knowledge and love of God were perfect, were to the image of a divine likeness by glory. Aquinas's reference was solely to the mind; the image was like a penny stamped with the effigy of a ruler. A human being was to the divine image in the mental activity of knowledge and love, and in the source of those activities and powers.[153] But a virtue was the ultimate of a power,[154] and a virtue was a habit.[155] The the human mind was impressed to the divine image as ultimately a habit. Q.E.D.

Aquinas's theology was of man created to the divine image. Woman did

---

[151] Ibid.
[152] See McGuire, "Monastic Friendship and Toleration," pp. 158-59.
[153] Thomas Aquinas, *Summa theologiae* 1a, q. 93.1; 93.4; 93.6; 93.7.
[154] Ibid. 1a-2ae, q. 56.
[155] Ibid. q. 55.

not participate equally in that dignity, he reasoned, because man was her beginning and end, as was God of all creation. Woman was but a human image of the divine image in man, a copy inferior to his status. In Aquinas's numismatic simile the male mind was impressed to the divine image like the effigy of a ruler on a coin.[156] His analogy was faulty; for in medieval numismatics it was not the face of the temporal authority on the coin that made it money, but rather its intrinsic value of precious metal and its nominal value of fixed rate that made it a measure of values and an item of exchange.[157] Nor was one coin pressed from another, as in his analogy of the female image from the male image; all issued from a common die. The female mind, as a coin pressed from the male coin, he likely imagined as a brain of wax. Aristotle considered woman soft.[158] Mechtild of Hackenborn envisioned herself receiving through incorporation into Christ the imprint of divine resemblance "like a seal in wax."[159] The female mind was not freshly minted from the face of God.

Aquinas's precise analogy for female inferiority was economic. The spiritual inferiority of woman replicated her social inferiority even in domestic affairs. In marriage, Aquinas taught, the male and female partners were equal in the conjugal act. Yet they were unequal in the management of the household, although each played a role in it. The husband was superior to the wife in economics; he ruled while she was ruled.[160] Although Aquinas did not explicate his reason for her domestic subordination, it was derived from economics. Economics was the quality of prudence that regulated a household. That he defined as a speculative habit that was "maturely reflective" (*considerativus*), a word denoting contemplation and meditation, as practically and actively applied to the household.[161] Women, according to Aristotle whom he probably followed, possessed the deliberative part of the soul, but unlike men not sovereignly so. Deliberation was politically annulled or cancelled in females; it was lacking in rights and powers.[162] Since the men-

---

156 Ibid. 1a, q. 93.4.

157 See Françoise Dumas, "Monnayage et monnayeurs," in *Artistes, artisans et production artistique au moyen âge*, Colloque international, Centre national de recherche scientifique, Université de Rennes II— Haute-Bretagne, 2-6 mai 1983, ed. Xavier Barral i Altet, 3 vols., Vol. 1: *Les hommes* (Paris: Picard, 1986-90), p. 483.

158 For female softness as a defect or vice see Aristotle, *Ethica nichomachea* 1128b10, 1150a. See also Maryanne Cline Horowitz, "Aristotle and Woman," *Journal of the History of Biology* 9 (1976):210.

159 See Mechtild of Hackenborn, *Liber specialis gratiae* 1.1, cited without reference to Aquinas's argument by Caroline Walker Bynum, *Jesus as Mother: Studies in the Spirituality of the High Middle Ages* (Berkeley: University of California Press, 1982), p. 210.

160 Aquinas, In 4 *Sententiae* 15.2.5; *Summa theologiae* 2-2ae 32.8; In 4 *Sententiae* 32.1.2; 36.1; *Super 1 ad Corinthianos* 3.3.

161 Aquinas, In 3 *Sententiae* 33.3.1.

162 See Nicholas D. Smith, "Plato and Aristotle on the Nature of Women," *Journal of the History of Philosophy* 21 (1983):475, without reference to Aquinas. For women in Aristotle's politics and ethics see also Susan Moller Okin, *Women in Western Political Thought* (Princeton: Princeton University Press, 1979), pp. 73-96; W. W. Fortenbaugh, "Aristotle on

tal activity of females was but an image of the mental activity of males, who alone were immediately created to the divine image, the capacity of a wife to manage the home virtuously was necessarily subordinate to that of her husband's ability. The cardinal virtues including prudence were like the four corners of a house,[163] but woman was created inferior to man in the prudence to manage that house.

House was a frequent metaphor in Aquinas's teaching; yet it had scant authority from experience. While lecturing at the university of Paris he was not living in a house but in the Dominican convent of St. Jacques.[164] There the friars observed the rule of St. Augustine as adopted by canons. Its injunction to "live in the house unanimously as brothers" (Ps. 67:7 Vulg.) mistranslated scripture. The verse means "God gives the lonely a home." The error established households of religious men and women on a false foundation, for the scriptural revelation was not human sociability but divine graciousness. Grace in scripture did not expel people from their homes into monasteries but rather built them homes, even for the loners who had no families. Although Aquinas left no familiar correspondence, his domestic relationships were legendarily hostile. His birth portended him as a child of exceptional sanctity. A friar Bonus arrived at the family castle at Roccasecca and announced to his mother Theodora, "Rejoice, lady, because you are pregnant and you will bear a son whom you will call Thomas." The friar also prophesied that Thomas would join the Dominicans, rather than the Benedictines, as his family wanted. Theodora replied, "I am not worthy to bear such a son; let God do the good pleasure of his will." As an infant in the bath, Thomas would not yield his nurses a scroll on which was written "Ave, Maria"; so he swallowed it. Later his family abducted him and tried to seduce him with a harlot, but he drove the woman out with a burning brand. Praying that he would never again be sexually assaulted, he slept on that wish. Two angels in a dream assured him that God heard his prayer. They pressed his loins and said, "Behold, on the part of God we bind you with the cincture of chastity, which no woman will be able to break by temptation." Aquinas cried aloud in pain and awoke.[165] A few months be-

---

Slaves and Women" in *Articles on Aristotle*, ed. Jonathan Barnes, Malcolm Schofield, and Richard Sorabji, 4 vols., Vol. 2: *Ethics and Politics* (London: Duckworth, 1975-79), pp. 137-39.

163 Aquinas, *Summa theologiae* 1-2ae, q. 68.1.

164 For the Dominicans in Paris and for the church and cloister of St. Jacques, see Wolfgang Schenkluhn, *Ordines studentes: Aspekte zur Kirchenarchitektur der Dominkaner und Franziskaner im 13. Jahrhundert* (Berlin: Gebr. Mann, 1988), pp. 46-84, especially pp. 51-71. See also G. Meersseman, "L'Architecture dominicaine au XIIe siècle: Législation et pratique," *Archivum fratrum praedicatorum* 16 (1946):136-90.

165 Edmund Colledge, "The Legend of St. Thomas Aquinas," in *St. Thomas Aquinas 1274-1974 Commemorative Studies*, 2 vols. (Toronto: Pontifical Institute of Mediaeval Studies, 1974), 1:19-20, 21-22. For the cincture see François Garnier, *Le language de l'image au moyen âge: Signification et symbolique*, 2 vols. (Paris: Léopard d'or, 1982-89), 2:169-74.

fore his death, after a religious experience arrested his work, he visited a sister but remained withdrawn and taciturn,[166] like an ascetic of the desert avoiding eye contact with a relative.

Aquinas's legendary resort to the hearth, symbolic of male procreation, was an attack on a lewd woman with a burning brand siezed from it. The construction of a home was for him secular activity, which people could undertake voluntarily without the virtue of faith.[167] A house was built by artifice.[168] Aquinas employed architectural materials and elements as philosophical, not theological, similes even in explicating scripture. "Just as the column in the midst of a house sustains it, and the oil lamp in the midst of a house illumines it, so the heart in the midst of the body vivifies it."[169] Or, in considering the beginning of a product: an animal was from the heart, a house was from the foundation, and a line was from a point.[170] Just as in houses the species was walls and roof, so in humans the species was animal and rational.[171] A favorite comparison was the likeness of the house pre-existing in the mind of the architect or builder like intelligible being.[172] A house was by material cause a shelter constituted by stones, cement, and wood; by final cause, a shelter for humans from rain, cold, and heat.[173]

The form of a house was accident; its matter, substance.[174] In an argument about the soul as the substantial, not accidental, form of the body, since it perfected the whole and each part, Aquinas compared housing as inferior. "For since a whole consists of parts, if the form of the whole were not given to each part of the body its being, it would be a form in the sense of arrangement or order (*compositio et ordo*), like the design of a house (*forma domus*), and such form is of the accidental order." But the soul informed the body substantially, he reasoned.[175] Thus a house was implicitly a bad analogy for spiritual indwelling. In the Aristotelian philosophy of matter and form, which Aquinas appropriated for theology, the form of a house was merely accidental, not substantial. The construction and decor of a house had nothing important to suggest about the divine indwelling in human souls analogous to their souls dwelling in their bodies. The supporting column of a house was a simile for the vivifying presence of the heart in humans, but that was a corporeal presence. The heart was a physical

166 *Processus canonizationis S. Thomae, Neapoli* 79.

167 Aquinas, In 1 *Sententiae* 42.1.2; *Summa contra gentiles* 4.83; *In Boethii deTrinitate* 1.1.1; *Summa theologiae* 1-2ae 109.2.

168 Aquinas, *Super 1 ad Corinthianos* 1.2.

169 Aquinas, *Super ad Hebraeos* 2.3.

170 Aquinas, In 2 *Sententiae* 1.1.6.

171 Aquinas, *Summa theologiae* 1a, q. 12.10.

172 Ibid. 1a, q. 15.1; and see *domus* and its variants in *Index thomisticus*, s.v.

173 Aquinas, *In posterior analytica* 1.16; *In physicorum* 2.15; In 4 *Sententiae* 3.1.1.

174 Aquinas, *In metaphysicorum* 12.3.

175 Aquinas, *Summa theologiae* 1a, q. 76.8; *Summa theologiae*, Vol. 11: *Man (1a. 75-83)*, trans. Timothy Suttor (New York: Blackfriars with McGraw Hill, 1970), p. 85.

organ in the body; the soul was a spiritual substance in the body. For the soul, housing was an erroneous example because it was accidental, not substantial, and because its very edification was an activity indifferent to faith.

Aquinas's scholastic argument from the categories of philosophy demolished Bernard's monastic argument from the places of rhetoric. Although the friar did not criticize the monk for it, by scholastic reasoning the presence of the monks in the church at Clairvaux could not have established a theological ascent to the indwelling of the Spirit in their souls. Bernard was confusing categories that Aquinas distinguished. The soul did dwell substantially in the Cistercian's body; but his body did not dwell substantially in that church, only accidentally. More grievously, the Spirit did not dwell substantially in the Cistercian's soul, only accidentally. God alone was substantially present to himself. Thus, although Aquinas methodically construed analogies of the human with the divine, his categorical argument about architecture effectively displaced persons from their basic orientation and experience: place as social focus, whether the domestic hearth or the monastic sanctuary.

Aquinas was not ignorant of the household as the foundation of community. A human was part of a household; a house, part of a city; and a city was a community.[176] He remarked that some considered a house undistinguishable from a city except for its size.[177] And, although Bernard's use of sacral architecture—a monastic church rather than a lay house—did not mitigate his error scholastically, Aquinas also preferred ecclesiastical models for the holy. In the sacrament of confirmation the "quasi house" built in the soul at baptism was dedicated as a "temple" to the Holy Spirit.[178] A church was congruently called "a house of prayer."[179] Aquinas could not have denied the very designation of Jesus in driving the money lenders from the temple (Mark 11:17). Yet a house was not the fitting place for worship, he thought. Aquinas instructed that Mass should not be celebrated in homes, which were unconsecrated and even violated, except from necessity and with episcopal consent. The building in which Christ had instituted the Eucharist was unconsecrated, he conceded, an ordinary dining room in the upper story of a home prepared by the head of the household. Yet the church was a more appropriate place for the sacrament, he argued. Its altars and vessels were consecrated, not because they were susceptive of grace, but so that they might have a spiritual force for worship. A church was cleansed and exorcised before it was dedicated. Aquinas opined the probability that forgiveness of venial sins might be gained just by entering such a consecrated

---

[176] Aquinas, *Summa theologiae* 1-2ae, q. 90.3. For the biological evidence see Stephen J. Pope, "Familial Love and Human Nature: Thomas Aquinas and neo-Darwinsism," *American Catholic Philosophical Quarterly* 69 (1995):447-69.

[177] Aquinas, *Sententia libri politicorum* 1.1.

[178] Aquinas, *Summa theologiae* 3a, q. 72.11.

[179] Aquinas, In 2 *Sententiae* 10.1.4.

building. In reiterating canon law on the violation of ecclesiastical consecration, Aquinas exposed the profound scholastic division between the holy and the house. What defiled a church? Blasphemy? No, "the shedding of semen."[180] The hearth, the traditional location of the male procreative force in Graeco-Roman civilization, became canonically unholy. The home was the antithesis, rather than the analogy, of sacred presence in the clerical culture that regulated organized medieval religion. The church was best reserved for celibate males, who would not defile it with their semen.

In practice the church was not wholly sacral but served multiple secular purposes. Since the maintenance of the nave was the responsibility of the parishioners, they appropriated its ample space for social gatherings called "ales"; for the sale of goods at fairs on feast days; and for the recreation of dances, games, and plays. It was their place for civic meetings, legal proceedings, and publication of notices. Peasants who had no security entrusted their few valuables, their deeds and documents, to the parish chest kept there. The weights and measures for the village and its firefighting tools were also stored in the church, as were curios such as meteors and crocodiles (stuffed). It was the church that sheltered the perpetual lamp for kindling fire in the home.[181] Impoverished persons could seek shelter in any cathedral, church, or chapel merely by registering in a symbolic group of twelve companions. The parvis, the triple colonnaded gallery adjoining the western façade, belonged to the patron saint and so was inviolable. It became the place of the fugitive slave, the hardened criminal, the abandoned woman. Its right of asylum sheltered even families.[182] But the division of the home and the sanctuary was virtually absolute, because the home was the procreative place. Ultimately Aquinas, like Augustine, projected the location of the sacred off the earth. As he argued, just as the house of some lord stands more handsomely in the city than in the country, so is the tabernacle of God seen more beautifully in heaven.[183] The house of God into which his adopted sons were inducted was finally not the empyrean but the divine beatitude itself.[184]

Even the privileged human sexual place that could have been argued for divine indwelling, the womb of the Virgin Mary, was poorly considered. When Aquinas deliberated whether Mary played an active role in the con-

---

180 Aquinas, *Summa theologiae* 3a, q. 83.3.

181 See J. G. Davies, *The Secular Use of Church Buildings* (London: S C M, 1969), pp. 46-76, 81-92; Pound, *Hearth and Home*, pp. 185-86.

182 Rouche, "Private Life Conquers State and Society," in *History of Private Life*, ed. Veyne, 1:437; for sanctuary, Davies, *Secular Use of Church Buildings*, pp. 41-44. For an example of late medieval practice see Kathryn L. Reyerson, "Flight from Prosecution: The Search for Religious Asylum in Medieval Montpellier," *French Historical Studies* 17 (1992):603-26; for background, Moshe Greenberg, "The Biblical Conception of Asylum," *Journal of Biblical Literature* 78 (1959):125-32.

183 Aquinas, *1 Ps.* 18.

184 Aquinas, In 3 *Sententiae* 10.2.2.

ception of Christ's body, he decided no. Since she was the mother, not the father, her role was passive. A female's power of generation was imperfect: just as in the arts the inferior art disposed the matter and the superior art induced the form, so the female prepared the matter for the male to fashion it. Mary merely ministered the matter for conception. By the Aristotelian physiology Aquinas adopted, that was menstrual blood, which was considered malignant.[185] The menstruation of woman was active potency, he thought, just as the form of the house in the mind of the builder was the potency of the house.[186] Mary provided quasi matter for a potential house; but her womb was not by analogy an actual house.

Neither was it the construction Bernard of Clairvaux supposed, an aqueduct. Aquinas condemned that metaphor as the great error of Valentinius, who argued that the Virgin was no place for the incarnate Son, that he merely passed through her like water flowing through an aqueduct. Aquinas insisted that Christ's body was not immaterial, receiving nothing from his mother; he used her menstrual blood for his conception.[187] Neither had Augustine considered the incarnation an aqueduct, although one of the most impressive examples outside of Italy was at Carthage, where the main road south from Tunis passed under the arcade.[188] Nor did Augustine in his climactic meditation with his mother from sensible matter to sheer existence mention anything so mundane as household plumbing, although the domestic architecture at Ostia provided the necessity of good drainage. In its apartment buildings ample pipes transported waste down from the upper stories; then small drains flowed from the blocks to the main drains below the streets, which sloped to the Tiber whose current swiftly carried away the refuse. Bad housing with poor sanitation usually accompanied and largely accounted for short expectancy of life in the Roman empire. Augustine could not have blamed Monica's death on that, for conditions at Ostia favorably compared with those of any other society before the middle of the nineteenth century.[189] Drainage was among the remarkable civic works of Roman engineering, which his father had supervised as a decurion.

Its impressive feat, which Bernard did appropriate, was the system of

---

[185] Aquinas, *Summa theologiae* 3a, 32.4; In 3 *Sententiae* 3.5. For Aristotle see Prudence Allen, *The Concept of Woman: The Aristotelian Revolution, 750 BC-AD 1250* (Montreal: Eden, 1985), pp. 83-126. For the *menses* as malignant see Aristotle, *Historia animalium* 521a22-27; Pliny, *Naturalis historia* 28.23.77-86. See also Vern L. Bulloch, "Medieval Medical and Scientific Views of Women," *Viator* 4 (1973):487-49; Charles T. Wood, "The Doctors' Dilemma: Sin, Salvation and the Menstrual Cycle in Medieval Thought," *Speculum* 56 (1981):710-27; Jane Fair Bestor, "Ideas about Procreation and their Influence on Ancient and Medieval Views of Kinship," in *The Family in Italy from Antiquity to the Present*, ed. David I. Kertzer and Richard P. Saller (New Haven, Conn.: Yale University Press, 1991), pp. 150-67.

[186] Aquinas, In 2 *Sententiae* 18.2.3.

[187] Aquinas, *In symbolorum apostolorum* 5; *Summa contra gentiles* 4.30.

[188] See K. D. White, *Greek and Roman Technology* (London: Thames & Hudson, 1984), p. 163, without reference to Augustine.

[189] See Meiggs, *Roman Ostia*, pp. 143, 234, without reference to Augustine.

aqueducts. They were so renowned for the purity of their waters that the physician Galen voiced popular opinion when he commented, "None emits water that is foul, mineralized, turbid, hard, or cold," although he conceded that the water from the stone aqueducts above the Tiber was "certainly a little cold." General knowledge of them was from *De aquis urbis Romae* by the civil servant Frontinus, a twelfth-century manuscript of which at Monte Cassino was the exemplar. Rome invented the system of hydraulics still in use to the middle of the last century, as for the distribution to Paris of water from the reservoirs in the towns.[190] In Gaul there were four aqueducts at Lyon that used inverted siphons, a costly procedure.[191] The famous architecture was the storied Pont du Gard that transported waters of the source d'Eure near Ucetia (Uzès) to the colony of Nemausus (Nîmes). It was bold in conception and design, reasonably stressed, and remarkably efficient. Calculations for it were in Roman numerals aided by an abacus, with wax tablets as sheets for drawing; but its formulas remain a mystery. An enormously large structure of three tiers bridging three kilometers over the deep valley of the river Gardon, the utilitarian design was an artistic work.[192]

Construction was predominantly subterranean, however, across rugged and rocky countryside. In the trenches, walls of ashlar stonework were built along edges of concrete pavement, on which a semicircular vault was built, with air shafts at intervals. The arcades of the Pont du Gard were exceptional in having stone plates, rather than vaulting, as a cover. The dressed masonry walls of the conduit, and in some areas the concrete floor, were covered with a stucco tinged pink from minute shards of pottery and tile. That liner was painted with olive oil, then covered with maltha, a recipe of slaked lime, pork grease, and the viscous juice of unripe figs. Although the surface that resulted was smooth and durable, from the lack of proper maintenance the aqueduct suffered severe incrustation. It was due to the chemical composition of the water—low in magnesium, high in calcium—and to the very low gradients of the conduit, so that velocities were quite low. Despite the incrustation, the efficient and generous design of the channel allowed the aqueduct to accommodate the available flow for about four centuries after cessation of maintenance.[193] That cessation was caused by successive invasions of Franks, Visigoths, Arabs, and Normans that destroyed portions of

---

[190] Thomas Ashby, *The Aqueducts of Ancient Rome* (Oxford: Clarendon, 1935), pp. 10, 27-29. For a brief, but more recent, treatment see White, *Greek and Roman Technology*, pp. 162-68.

[191] A. Trevor Hodge, "Siphons in Roman Aqueducts," *Scientific American* 259-6 (1985): 114-19; White, *Greek and Roman Technology*, pp. 163-64.

[192] George F. W. Hauck, "Structural Design of the Pont du Gard," *Journal of Structural Engineering* 112 (1986):105-20. For a survey of his research with color photographs see "The Roman Aqueduct of Nîmes," *Scientific American* 260-3 (1989):98-104; and idem, *The Aqueduct of Nemausus* (Jefferson, N. C.: McFarland, 1988).

[193] Hauck and Richard A. Novak, "Interaction of Flow and Incrustation of the Roman Aqueduct at Nîmes," *Journal of Hydraulic Engineering* 113 (1987):144, 155-56.

the conduit and reduced the population at Nîmes from a thriving colony of perhaps fifty-thousand citizens eager for the amenities of Roman civilization like baths.[194] Maintenance and repairs ended after the fourth century; by the ninth century the populace was removing stones from it for use in local buildings.[195] To Bernard of Clairvaux the aqueduct, not the house, suggested the incarnation.

When architectural metaphors were applied to the pregnant Virgin Mary, the tradition was the gate. She was sexually the closed gate, from the prophetic vision prefiguring her perpetual virginity (Ezek. 44:2). She was spiritually the open gate as the mediatrix of heaven (Gen. 28:17).[196] That was the verse Bernard cited about Clairvaux: "How awesome is this place! This is none other than the house of God and this is the gate of heaven."[197] Such was the exclamation of Jacob upon dreaming of the ladder to heaven, with which image the gate of heaven merged. Marian conceits were popular. She from whom was born the door opened the door. As the gate of God she became the gate to God. That version was especially popular because it allowed an antithesis with Eve, who had shut the gate of heaven. Yet Mary was not an ordinary gate to a residence but a royal gate, identified as the eastern gate to the palace, since she produced light for the world.[198] The concept of the gate was analogous to the door of the house: it was its outer limit as the hearth was its inner focus. Through it the bride processed from being an outsider to becoming a member of the family.[199]

Bernard wrote typically that the antidote to the venom of the serpent that had poisoned the human race entered it by the same gate of salvation, a woman.[200] His concept of Mary the gate encompassed more than the image of the one his brother André, the porter, tended at Clairvaux. She was the gate at the end of a lengthy aqueduct, as at Nîmes. There the channel emptied into the castellum, a circular distributive basin at the foot of a steep hill about ten meters above the mean elevation of the town. The pipes for distribution and the channel of the aqueduct were designed for optimal effectiveness at the probable rates of flow. The openings of the drain were rationally proportioned. An adjustable gate mechanism measured the flow of water and facilitated drainage. As a water meter, the gate functioned by measuring the flow through a submerged orifice, with the size of the orifice as the

---

[194] Hauck, "Structural Design of the Pont du Gard," p. 117.

[195] Josef W. Konvitz, *The Urban Millennium: The City-Building Process from the Early Middle Ages to the Present* (Carbondale: Southern Illinois University Press, 1985), p. 2.

[196] See Richard Hillier, "Joseph the Hymnographer and Mary the Gate," *Journal of Theological Studies* 36 (1985):311.

[197] Bernard of Clairvaux, *Sermones de diversis* 42.4.

[198] See Hillier, "Joseph the Hymnographer and Mary the Gate," pp. 313, 314, 316, 317-18.

[199] Lacey, "Patria potestas," pp. 129, 130.

[200] Bernard of Clairvaux, "In annunciatione" 2.1.

parameter. It was a device of excellent engineering with superior properties.[201]

As abbot Bernard was knowledgeable about the function of aqueducts, since efficient plumbing by conduits and drains was as much a Cistercian mark as was plain austerity. Although the monks selected for their monasteries remote sites, they were commodious valleys where rivers afforded excellent drainage and where streams supplied sufficient water to the lavatory and kitchen.[202] A contemporaneous drawing describes the water system of the priory of Christ Church, Canterbury, which may have been representative. Water was piped beneath the city walls from an outside source into the monasterial grounds, where it was conveyed beneath a corner of the infirmary to a series of tanks on successively lower levels. In the great cloister it emerged to supply the laver in which the monks washed their hands in individual jets of water before eating. There the pipes divided, with one branch serving the kitchen, brewhouse, and bakery, and the hall of the almonry; while a subbranch headed for the bathhouse and the prior's bathtub. Another branch from the cloister surfaced in the laver of the infirmary. Used water, supplemented with rainwater from gutters in the roof of the cloister, flushed the lavatories of the dormitory and infirmary.[203] Bernard objected to the relocation of Clairvaux down river precisely because ducts for water had been fitted through its offices at great labor and expense. Their abandonment he considered frivolous, although he finally relented. In the rebuilding lay brothers collaborated with hired hands, dividing the river Aube, setting it in new channels, and engineering it to the mill wheels. Artisans applied their skills "that the river might flow fast and do good wherever it was needed in every building, flowing freely in underground conduits; the streams performed suitable tasks in every office and cleansed the abbey and at length returned to the main course and restored to the river what had been lost."[204]

Bernard imagined Clairvaux as a basin, like the castellum at Nîmes, into which the grace of the incarnation poured for distribution to the monks. Its overflow was channeled outside to the local region, which lay at a lesser spiritual elevation than its own steep incline toward God. He preached Christ as a fountain of many spouts: issuing pardon from mercy to lave sin, prudence from wisdom to quench thirst, devotion from grace to irrigate works, zeal from charity to cook food and warm affection, and life from the

---

201 See Hauck and Novak, "Water Flow in the Castellum at Nîmes," *American Journal of Archaeology* 92 (1988):393, 395, 404, without reference to Bernard of Clairvaux.

202 See Brooke, "St Bernard, the Patrons and Monastic Planning," p. 15.

203 John D. Thompson and Grace Goldin, *The Hospital: A Social and Architectural History* (New Haven, Conn.: Yale University Press, 1975), p. 19 and p. 20 fig. 17. See also Lawrence Wright, *Clean and Decent: The History of the Bath and Loo* (London: Routledge & Kegan Paul, 1980), pp. 18-24.

204 Arnald of Bonneval, *Vita prima* 2.5.30-31. Cited also in translation by Brooke, "St. Bernard, the Patrons and Monastic Planning," p. 17, without reference to the castellum at Nîmes.

wound in his side.[205] He understood the incarnation as a downpour. It was not a spring erupting from within creation but a celestial flow toward it. The advent of Christ was a descent from the height of the heavens, the heart of God the father, to the depths of the earth, the womb of the Virgin Mother. Bernard did employ the conventional agricultural metaphor for sexuality, which had informed Augustine's theft of pears. Mary as the stem from which flowered Jesus (Is. 11:1-2) was a field that flourished without an human implements of farming: not sown by any hand, not deeply dug with a hoe, not enriched with manure. Her flesh flowered inviolate, integral, and chaste into a celestial plant, the tree of life bearing the fruit of salvation.[206] Bernard elaborated, however, a chthonian metaphor for her womb, the aqueduct. Its subterranean construction recalled apocryphal associations of the Nativity with the cave.[207]

The prime consideration in the creation of an aqueduct was the selection by practical observations and tests of a suitable source. The spring had to emit water visibly pure and clear, inaccessible to pollution, with an outflow free of moss and reeds. Its local consumers were examined by the architects for general health, especially a good complexion, strong bones, and clear eyes. At a new source, samples of water were tested in a bronze vessel for corrosion, sparkle, pour, foreign bodies, and rapid boiling. For the conveyance of the water, bridges and tunnels were in question. Aqueducts supplied the general public before the private household, serving primarily the fountains in the streets from which water was drawn and secondarily, the baths. Those institutions required a continuous flow, with overflow for continuous flushing of the drains to ensure public health. Roman hydraulic theory used gravitational flow assisted by a slight fall in the conduit. Siphons skillfully employed the principle that water rises to its own level. The architects carefully surveyed the projected course to determine the levels.[208]

The next procedure was the acquisition of the necessary land, purchased by the state or municipality. A proprietor could not legally be forced to sell property, however. There were no rights of expropriation in this or other public works, so that the refusal of right of way caused the abandonment of

---

205 Bernard of Clairvaux, "Sermo in nativitate domini 1.6. For fountains see also Naomi Miller, "Paradise Regained: Medieval Garden Fountains," in *Medieval Gardens*, ed. MacDougall, pp. 135-53.

206 Bernard of Clairvaux, "In adventu" 1.6; 2.4. For the poetic popularity of Mary as a rod flowering into Jesus as fruit see Patrick S. Diehl, *The Medieval European Religious Lyric: An ars poetica* (Berkeley: University of California Press, 1985), pp. 124-26.

207 See Michael Gervers, "The Iconography of the Cave in Christian and Mithraic Traditions," in *Mysteria Mithrae*, Proceedings of the International Seminar on the "Religio-Historical Character of Roman Mithraism, with Particular Reference to Roman and Ostian Sources," Rome and Ostia, 28-31 March 1978, ed. Ugo Bianchi (Leiden: E. J. Brill, 1979), pp. 579-96, without reference to Bernard.

208 Ashby, *Aqueducts of Ancient Rome*, pp. 34, 36, 37.

the project. The republican aqueducts were built by the treasury from the booty of war. There was a policy of spoils or gifts paying for public works, with a gradual obligation of successful officials to pay for them. Although the Roman method for the catchment of springs is unknown, on leaving the spring or the basin the water entered into the channel of the aqueduct proper. Pipes of stone, lead, earthenware, leather, masonry, and wood were used. Above ground the channels were constructed of stone slabs, keyed with slots filled with cement, or of concrete faced in block work or rubble, or in the empire of reticulate and brick. The lining was of fine cement. Below ground the work depended on the depth and nature of the soil. A trench could be dug with the conduit at its bottom, or a tunnel could be bored through rock. There was regular maintenance for cleaning of encrusted channels and for repair of leaks from great variations in heat and frost.[209]

The aqueduct was suggestive theologically. It conveyed to the populace from an unpolluted, cold source necessary water for drinking and bathing that was pure and refreshing. It was skillfully designed. It was constructed through personal property by consent; as Mary said, "Behold, I am the handmaid of the Lord; let it be to me according to your word" (Luke 1:38). The association of women with the water supply was a commonplace, for at the fountains or wells of a town they gathered to draw water for households. Or they took the laundry for scrubbing to the banks just outside the town, in whose stream they also washed their hair.[210] As a supremely female place of meeting, riverbanks acquired the connotation of the lovers' tryst. In the Hispano-Arabic love poetry that decisively influenced that of the medieval troubadours and minnesingers, the river and the fountain were dramatic places of amorous encounter.[211] A Marian aqueduct for the conception and birth of Christ was an intelligible cultural concept.

The Roman aqueduct was not a very moral comparison, however, for it was grievously abused. The supervisors of the waterworks winked at the slaves executing jobs on the side. There was deliberate tapping into the system by fraudulent methods such as punctures; supplementary water in brooks and streams was stolen; overflows from the reservoirs were illegally sold. There was neglect and embezzlement of rentals. All offenses were tolerated with the connivance of the staff, the workers, and the landowners. Yet a particular aqueduct would have appealed to Bernard, the Aqua Virgo. It was named "virgin" because a little girl indicated the springs to some soldiers seeking water. The diggers discovered an enormous volume. A shrine was erected on its site, which was tested by military engineers peerless in

---

209 Ibid., pp. 39-44.

210 See Fossier, *Peasant Life*, p. 65.

211 For the poetry see Jeanne Battesti-Pelegrin, "Eaux douces, eaux amères dans la lyrique hispanique médiévale traditionelle," in *L'Eau au moyen âge* (Marseille: Jeanne Laffitte, 1985), pp. 48-51.

practical experience at selecting water. From its head in the marshy basin, it proceeded to Rome above and beneath ground, with arches beginning below the gardens of Lucullus the epicure on the Pincian hill and ending in the Campus Martius. Aqua Virgo was reported as pleasant for bathing, its exceptionally cold waters especially invigorating for a plunge after a hot steam bath. Cassiodorus praised it as superlative. "The Aqua Virgo flows with a most pure delight. . . for while others during excessive rain are polluted by earthly matter, this glides with a purest current like a sky never clouded."[212]

By the tenth century it was merely trickling. Wells in the area of the forum, or even the Tiber river, had succeeded the aqueducts[213] when Bernard visited Rome. The concept of the Aqua Virgo would have appealed greatly to his monastic congregation, however. A piped supply of water, such as the monks enjoyed at Clairvaux, was a privilege. The local rural community relied on springs and wells whose discharge was inadequate sometimes and irregular always. Certain villages, especially in regions where the subsoil was dry, were founded solely because of an abundant spring. Names of places throughout Europe, like Bernard's natal Fontaines-lès-Dijon, incorporated "fountain" or "spring" as an unusual quality of the site. In mountainous and sparsely populated areas water from springs may have been virtuous. In villages, from which the monks were recruited, the water that surfaced would have been vicious. There was but slight protection of their sources of water from the drainage of stables with their heaps of manure. Infection spread by contaminated water among animals and humans in a range of diseases of the digestive tract like dysentery. Not only was the quality of the water polluted, but the amount available was at times desperately short everywhere. A drought in summer could be a disaster. People were very sparing in their use of water for bathing, laundering, and cleaning. The rivers and streams, from which much of the water for domestic use and consumption was taken, received the effluent of the urban cesspits, slaughterhouses, and tannage yards, and the seepage of rural stables and dung heaps.[214] Even baptismal water was unclean, since directives cautioned the clergy against changing it frequently: if an infant defecated in the font, the water should be thrown out; if it only urinated, the water should be reused.[215]

The medieval populace resorted, as had the Romans, to public baths in the towns. The king of England only later in the twelfth century had a bath at Westminster, furnished with a piped supply of water when a lavatory was constructed.[216] The Cistercians had in the aqueduct a model of their special

---

212 See Ashby, *Aqueducts of Ancient Rome*, pp. 31-32, 34, 167-69, without reference to Bernard.

213 Ibid., p. 16.

214 See Pounds, *Hearth and Home*, pp. 188-89, without reference to Bernard.

215 Barbara A. Hanawalt, *The Ties that Bound: Peasant Families in Medieval England* (New York: Oxford University Press, 1986), p. 173.

216 See Pounds, *Hearth and Home*, p. 191.

clean society with its piped supply of water. Bernard appropriated for the Virgin Mary the civic project of the aqueduct because it coincided with his typology of the relationship of the Cistercians to her as a client-patron relationship. They were on pilgrimage. She was the royal road by which the Savior came, proceeding from her womb like a bridegroom from his chamber. The monks were to walk that way to ascend to him by whom Christ had descended. Mary had access to Christ, through her integrity, humility, charity, and fecundity. By these powers she could excuse, amend, hide, and supply the monks. She was their lady, mediatrix, and advocate, reconciling the Cistercians to her Son, commending them, representing them as her clients.[217] Not only were all their churches dedicated to her, but the official seals of their abbeys had her image as mediatrix and protectress of their business.[218]

In his sermon on Mary's nativity Bernard preached about the font of life as Christ, distributed to humans just as water was supplied in the streets. The heavenly watercourse descended through an aqueduct, not delivering the abundance of the fountain but pouring the rainwater of grace into arid hearts. The aqueduct was full throughout, so that others might accept its fullness, but it was not plenitude itself. That aqueduct was she whom the angel saluted as "full of grace" (Luke 2:28). The construction of such an aqueduct gave Bernard pause for wonder; for its top, like the ladder Jacob dreamed as touching heaven, was to transcend even the heavens to tap the most vivifying fountain of water above the heavens. That valiant woman attained its height by the vehemence of desire, the fervor of devotion, and the purity of prayer. In her uncorruption she was the sealed fountain (Song 4:12), as traditionally interpreted. She was also the "temple" of God and the "sacristy" of the Holy Spirit. The monks should commend their offerings to Mary, so that they might return to the giver of grace by the same trough by which grace streamed. God had the power to pour forth grace without an aqueduct but he wished to provide a conveyance.[219]

Like the mediator as God-man, Mary united the sublime and the lowly, "so venerable that she is saluted by an angel, so humble that she is espoused to a worker."[220] Her moral status elevated her; her social status debased her.

---

217 Bernard of Clairvaux, "In adventu" 2.5. For an introduction across centuries and cultures see Gianfranco Poggi, "Clientelism," *Political Studies* 31 (1983):662-67; S. N. Eisenstadt and Louis Ronger, "Patron-Client Relationships as a Model of Structuring Social Exchange," *Comparative Studies in Society and History* 22 (1980): 42-77.

218 Pierre Bony, "An Introduction to the Study of Cistercian Seals: The Virgin as Mediatrix, then Protectrix on the Seals of Cistercian Abbeys," trans. Soldwedel, in *Studies in Cistercian Art and Architecture*, ed. Lillich, 3:201-40.

219 Bernard of Clairvaux, "In nativitate beatae Mariae: De aquaeductu" 3, 4, 5, 9, 18. For the exegesis of the sealed fountain see Friedrich Muthmann, *Mutter und Quelle: Studien zur Quellenverehrung im Altertum und im Mittelalter* (Mainz: Philipp von Zabern, 1975), pp. 376-78, 393-96, 365-66.

220 Bernard of Clairvaux, "In laudibus Virginis Matris" 1.5.

She was espoused to a worker: by tradition Joseph the artisan (Matt. 13:55), who was virtually invisible in medieval literature until very late, when he was introduced as a feeble elder.[221] Although he may have been a carpenter, there was as little respect among the monks for the builders of houses as there was for their houses. Manual work was intrinsic to the vow of poverty, in solidarity with all humanity as descended from a cursed but penitent Adam (Gen. 3:17-19). The monastic rule and monastic experience valued the alteration of work and prayer. But the labor of the monks was not in agriculture or in crafts but rather in studies. The converts, or lay brothers, performed the crude manual labor.[222] The Cistercians did not all build with their own hands, laying each stone, although their sites and constructions presupposed expert knowledge of design and crafts within the order. The manuscript illuminations from Cîteaux under abbot Stephen Harding, who dispatched Bernard to Clairvaux, depicted monks felling trees and hewing logs; but those were caricatures of inept religious at manual labor. The professional skill of Cistercian architecture owed to the lay brothers, not to the choir monks, who were strictly separated. Recruits to the monastery must have included many skilled craftsmen.[223]

Yet they seem to have been disdained, as in the classical topic derived from leisure and necessity that opposed the philosopher and the artisan. Virtually all medieval professions were contemptible, with variation by document, region, or era. First on the nefarious list were innkeepers, those proprietors of the temporary lodging allowed by Augustine to the Christian as pilgrim. Lust was the reason for their condemnation, in a survival of primitive taboos against blood and impurity that had Aquinas rank dishwashers at the bottom of society. With urban development there was some revision of attitudes concerning tradespeople, who became assimilated into Christ's family, although condemnation persisted against vagabonds and vagrants as the devil's family.[224] Yet monks devoted to the ideas of the mind remained traditionally hostile to the works of the hands. Bernard's correspondent and convert to asceticism Abbot Suger preciously detailed his personal supervision of the construction of the abbey of St. Denis. His artisans, even his master mason, remained anonymous, however.[225] Peter Cantor, who was in-

---

221 For the cult of Joseph see Herlihy, *Medieval Households*, pp. 127-30.

222 See Holdsworth, "The Blessings of Work: The Cistercian View," in *Sanctity and Secularity: The Church and the World*, ed. Derek Baker, Studies in Church History, 10 (Oxford: Basil Blackwell for the Ecclesiastical History Society, 1973), pp. 59-76.

223 See Brooke, "St Bernard, the Patrons and Monastic Planning," pp. 17, 18.

224 Jacques Le Goff, "Licit and Illicit Trades in the Medieval West," in *Time, Work, and Culture in the Middle Ages*, trans. Goldhammer (Chicago: University of Chicago Press, 1980), pp. 59, 60, citing Aquinas, *Sententia libri politicorum* 1.9; 62-63. See also idem, "Trades and Professions as Represented in Medieval Confessors' Manuals," ibid., pp. 107-21.

225 Brooke, "St Bernard, the Patrons and Monastic Planning," pp. 18-19. For the architect see Pierre Du Colombier, *Les chantiers des cathédrales: Ouvriers—architectes—sculpteurs*, rev. ed. (Paris: A. & J. Picard, 1973), pp. 61-71.

fluential in establishing the theological commonplace, stated that the only useful arts were agriculture, skinning and tanning, carpentry, weaving, and cobbling. Building was a useless art, especially the construction of sumptuous labyrinthine palaces. Beautiful and spacious dwellings only beckoned haughty guests. Construction of them shared dishonor with the enamelling and gilding of harness, the tailoring of expensive garments, and the making of dice for gambling. Such craftsmen and sculptors should not receive sacramental absolution from sin unless they renounced their idle arts. He added that when Bernard of Clairvaux saw the thatched huts of peasants he wept with nostalgia for the Cistercian origins of poverty and simplicity.[226]

Bernard may have recalled the simple cottage in which he lived for a year, when as abbot he fell ill to exhaustion during the planning and construction of a daughter monastery at Trois-Fontaines. By episcopal orders he was moved to a small house beyond the precincts, where he was holed like a hermit in an infirmary. It was described as a wooden cottage like the hovels erected at the crossroads for lepers.[227] Privileged lepers could by permission live in the countryside in a small wooden cottage on four props surrounded by a fence.[228] Lodgings for lepers were usually located beyond the moat, walls, and gate of the city, yet on the main road so that alms might be solicited from passersby. The model was social isolation. There were then in France no less than two thousand hospitals for lepers, separated from the community by order of the Third Lateran Council and frequently by clerical ritual. At Amiens a leper was required to stand in a grave while the priest threw three spadefuls of dirt on his head.[229] Bernard did not comprehend the social significance of the peasant hut in which he briefly dwelled, however, for he failed to center religion on the hearth. The need of the populace to live settled and productive had returned women under the roof. Open fires for communal cooking were extinguished. The fire was reinstated within the house or moved close to it in a separate or adjacent structure. Fire became the property of the new, smaller domestic group that gathered about it. Hearth meant "family".[230] When the great landlords issued fran-

---

226 Talbot, "Cistercian Attitude towards Art," p. 63. The multistoried house of Arnold, count of Boulogne, designed c. 1120 with a labyrinthine entrance earned its architect Louis de Bourbourg praise as a virtual Daedalus. Spiro Kostoff, "The Architect in the Middle Ages, East and West," in *The Architect: Chapters in the History of the Profession*, ed. idem (New York: Oxford, 1977), p. 76.

227 William of St.-Thierry, *Vita prima* 1.7.32-33. For a twelfth-century leprosarium surviving in Périgueux see Thompson and Goldin, *Hospital*, pp. 46, 48.

228 Saul Nathaniel Brody, *The Disease of the Soul: Leprosy in Medieval Literature* (Ithaca, N. Y.: Cornell University Press, 1974), pp. 70, 74.

229 Richard Palmer, "The Church, Leprosy and Plague in Medieval and Early Modern Europe," in *The Church and Healing*, ed. Shiels, Studies in Church History, 19 (Oxford: Basil Blackwell for the Ecclesiastical History Society, 1982), p. 81.

230 Fossier, *Peasant Life*, pp. 68-69, without reference to Bernard of Clairvaux. His statement of the great increase of female influence in the twelfth and thirteenth centuries is contradicted by Herlihy's research on the terms of marriage in *Medieval Households*, pp. 98-

chises abolishing tenurial obligation for a fixed tax comprising all taxation, it was levied on hearths.[231]

Augustine had typified the huts of the poor as smoky[232] from the braziers for cooking, such a perennial fire hazard that Roman law required tenants to keep water in their apartments at all times.[233] In the mid-twelfth century the hearth entered the living area of the house as its only comfortable feature. In its simplest initial form it consisted of flat stones set in the middle of a floor of beaten dirt. Although it was centered away from flammable walls, smoke only escaped through whatever opening was available or it lingered to foul the air. The significant development was the location of the hearth against an outer wall. A stone or brick fireplace, with a masonry chimney well mortared with lime, funneled smoke to the outside. The earliest example in France dated to the late tenth century but it was in a palatial building of stone. The amenity was available to peasants only by the mid-fourteenth century since its proper construction was expensive; insubstantial masonry burned right through, igniting entire villages on fire. A transitional method among peasants was a hood mounted on four uprights over the central hearth, as in the Cistercian abbey at Longpont and various rural settlements. The movement of the fire from the center to the wall of the room significantly improved diet, for bread could be baked in a recess and meat roasted on a spit.[234]

The hearth in the house altered peasant attitudes toward familial structure and social arrangement. Women, who tended it, drew power and influence. There they sat on rough chairs to spin, as they had in classical antiquity, or there they prepared food for the family to eat at a trestle table with benches. Elders, who warmed themselves at the hearth, recounted the history of family and village. Although no cradles have survived, grooves close to extant fireplaces evidence the rocking of infants. Those babes placed by the fire for warmth had improved chance of survival.[235] The communal character of rural life declined. Although there were still open fires, enclosures for animals, and collective silos, the individual hearth became the basis for taxation. The "hearth" of a married couple would have required at least three children to

103. The image of women in secular literature has been argued as varied and ambivalent, rather than central and exalted, by Gold, *Lady and Virgin*, pp. 1-42.

[231] Evergates, *Feudal Society in the Baillage of Troyes*, pp. 138-44.

[232] Augustine, *Sermones* 170.4.4, cited by A.-G. Hamman, *La vie quotidienne en Afrique du nord au temps de saint Augustin*, new ed. (Paris: Hachette, 1985), pp. 62-63; Marie Madeleine Getty, *The Life of the North Africans as Revealed in the Sermons of St. Augustine*, Catholic University of America Patristic Studies, 28 (Washington, D. C.: Catholic University of America Press, 1931), p. 58.

[233] Gustav Hermansen, *Ostia: Aspects of Roman City Life* (Calgary: University of Alberta Press, 1981), pp. 43-44, without reference to Augustine.

[234] Pounds, *Hearth and Home*, pp. 194-95; Fossier, *Peasant Life*, p. 69; Chapelot and Fossier, *Village and House*, pp. 193, 217-19.

[235] Fossier, *Peasant Life*, pp. 69, 24; Pounds, *Hearth and Home*, p. 196.

maintain the level of population.[236]

Not only social patterns but also domestic architecture changed with the hearth. Its entry into the house dispelled the livestock whose warmth had been indispensable for heating the human inhabitants. Although humans and animals might continue to share a common entrance, eating and sleeping quarters for the species became separated. The basic dwelling was established: a living room where the fire burned and a separate bedroom that doubled for storage. Where land was available, rooms were joined to that initial block, radiating from it or aligned with it on a nave or corridor. Another story might be built where local stone enabled the construction of sturdy walls. The fragmentation of the extended family into small households, centered on a married couple, promoted independence: the hope of living from the fruits of one's own labor. It also fostered marital intimacy. The bed had been familial, a straw mattress on a wooden framework where parents and children slept together naked under coarse wool covers. The separation of a master bedroom established the premise for a more intimate relationship between husband and wife and, with that, a higher status for women within the home.[237]

In the Cistercian monastery the men slept in common in a dormitory; only the abbot had the privacy of a cell. The monks had no immediate personal analogy for comprehending Bernard's sermons on the Word's secret entry into and possession of the soul in a sumptuous matrimonial bedchamber. Although by Bernard's death the amenities of the hearth and the bedroom were only becoming available to the peasantry, they were already popular with the nobility, from whom the choir monks were drawn. To profess at Clairvaux was to regress socially. Beyond its dormitory the characteristic bed of the nobility was four posts, bobbin-turned or faceted and surmounted by knobs, heightened about fifteen inches above the mattress contained by a low railing. Curtains as part of the chamber, rather than the bed, were either hung between columns or slung to form a cubicle. They served to ward off drafts, not to create privacy, although modesty may have originated with them. Beds of seigniorial and ecclesiastical lords were an important piece of furniture, elaborately built of wood and metal inlaid with enamels, carved, or painted. Expense was lavished on the textiles with which they were hung as an index of power. Persons versed in courtly manners deduced from the furnishings of the chambers the degree of honor due the occupant.[238]

---

236 Fossier, *Peasant Life*, pp. 75, 18.

237 Ibid., pp. 69-70, 21, 73. See in general Gwyn I. Merion-Jones, "Vernacular Architecture and the Peasant House," in *Themes in the Historical Geography of France*, ed. Hugh D. Clout (London: Academic, 1977), pp. 343-406; Chapelot and Fossier, *Village and House*, pp. 72-110; Hanawalt, *Ties that Bound*, pp. 38-40, 48-51.

238 Penelope Eames, *Furniture in England, France and the Netherlands from the Twelfth to the Fifteenth Century* (London: The Furniture History Society, 1977), pp. 73-74, 77. For curtains as the possible origins of modesty see Fossier, *Peasant Life*, p. 76.

Bernard's designation of the monastic marital bed as silken was consistent with that culture of honor denoted by cloth. Yet even the celebrants of Mass at Clairvaux were forbidden silk chasubles. The vivid imagery of his rhetoric was at odds with the forbidden imagery of his abbey. The monks vested their bodies in white wool but were to furnish their souls in colorful silk. Bernard used to tell novices to leave their bodies outside the cloister; the flesh was useless, since only spirits could enter.[239] The body was "only a crumbling wall." While it stood, the intensely bright ray of God could not pour in through open doors, but only filter in through chinks and crevices.[240] The impediment of the body to the spirit was not a universal monastic concept, however. Abbot Suger recorded at St. Denis textiles of very fine quality and he urged their display on his anniversary to propitiate the divine majesty, to enhance the devotion of the brethren, and to provide an example for his successors in office.[241] He countered Cistercian austerity with Benedictine anagogy. Since the monks were being built into a temple by the Spirit spiritually, he argued that they should build their church in a lofty and fitting manner materially. In the adornment of that church as a chosen bride he spared no elegance or expense.[242] Its splendor was justified as anagogic, the sense that conducted to higher truths whoever desired to behold the decorous house of the celestial fatherland, not constructed by hands but eternal in heaven.[243] There was no intimation that a domestic house, rather than an ecclesiastical "house," was anagogic, however—even though Suger compared his abbey to a mother who "cherished and exalted him" and "most tenderly fostered him from mother's milk." An oblate as a boy, born in an unknown place to poor and lowly parents, the abbey "with maternal affection had suckled him as a child, had held him upright as a stumbling youth, had mightily strengthened him as a mature man and had solemnly settled him among the princes of the Church and the realm."[244] Church replaced home; the monastic community, his natural family.

There was in asceticism a factual denial yet spiritualized revival of sensuality and sociability. A neat example was the monastic rule of silence. It had been obviated since cenobitism by the creation of a sign language, so

---

[239] William of St.-Thierry, *Vita prima* 1.4.20.

[240] Bernard of Clairvaux, *Sermones super Cantica canticorum* 57.8.

[241] See Abbot Suger, *De rebus in administratione sua gestis* 1.

[242] Ibid. 30; *Libellus alter de consecratione ecclesiae sancti Dionysi* 5.

[243] Bede, *Hexameron* 4 (*Patrologia latina*, 91:168). This definition, or a similar one, is more probably Suger's source than Panofsky's argument for a Neoplatonist program based in the writings of Pseudo-Dionysius the Areopagite. For further criticism see Peter Kidson, "Panofsky, Suger and St Denis," *Journal of the Warburg and Courtauld Institutes* 50 (1987):1-17. The influence of Pseudo-Dionysius is still argued, however, by Rudolph, *Artistic Change at St-Denis: Abbot Suger's Program and the Early Twelfth-Century Controversy over Art* (Princeton: Princeton University Press, 1990), pp. 48-57, 70-75.

[244] See Suger, *De rebus in administratione sua gestis* 1, 28; *Abbot Suger on the Abbey Church of St.-Denis and its Art Treasures*, trans. Erwin Panofsky (Princeton: Princeton University Press, 1946), pp. 41, 51; and ibid., pp. 30-31.

complete for diet, clothing, choir, refectory, and dormitory that a monk could distinguish his choice for dinner between salmon and trout.[245] The egregious ascetic contradiction was a celibacy that rejected human marriage, yet resumed "marriage" as the relational ideal with God. Scripture compared the relationship of the Church to Christ as the marriage of a bride to a spouse (2 Cor. 11:2; Eph. 5:22-32). Yet the primitive Church was communal, and its social basis in human marriage was respected as an analogy. No reproduction, no population, no congregation. It was Bernard of Clairvaux who in his exposition of the Song of Songs transposed the Pauline ecclesiastical metaphor into one of the individual soul. A canonical decision fortified that misuse of marriage in celibate piety. There was the vexing theological problem of reconciling belief in Mary's perpetual virginity with her historical espousal to Joseph as a real marriage. If procreation was the purpose of marriage, could marriage without sex be legitimate? Since it was decided that consent alone contracted a legal marriage, it was concluded that asexual marriage was canonically valid.[246] The oxymoron of the celibate marriage between Mary and Joseph—a theological anomaly—established the contradiction of the celibate marriage of the monk to Christ as an ordinary concept. The relegation of that marriage to the monk's disembodied soul further alienated ordinary marriage from spiritual legitimacy. By Bernard's allegorisation, celibacy could be marriage, spiritually speaking. Could marriage therefore be celibacy,[247] spiritually speaking? Certainly not. Bernard fumed against the diocesan institution of a feast of Mary's immaculate conception as forcing the consort of the Holy Spirit in the sin of lust. Mary could not have been conceived sinlessly, he argued, because sexual intercourse was necessarily unchaste.[248]

The monastic arrogation of marriage to its own spirituality altered the state for those actually, rather than metaphorically, married. The spiritual marriage of the Cistercians to Christ was more than rhetorical oxymoron.

---

245 *Signa loquendi: Die cluniacensischen Signa-Listen*, p. 253 for Fleury on salmon and trout, pp. 123-24 for Cluny. See also Gerard van Rijnberk, *Le langage par signes chez les moines* (Amsterdam: North Holland, 1954); Robert A. Barakat, *The Cistercian Sign-Language: A Study in Non-Verbal Communication*, Cistercian Studies, 11 (Kalamazoo, Mich.: Cistercian Publications, 1975).

246 See Gold, "The Marriage of Mary and Joseph in the Medieval Ideology of Marriage," in *Sexual Practices and the Medieval Church*, ed. James Brundage and Bulloch (Buffalo, N. Y.: Prometheus, 1982), pp. 102-17; Brooke, *The Medieval Idea of Marriage* (Oxford: Clarendon, 1989), pp. 278-80; Herlihy, *Medieval Households*, pp. 80-81; Steven Ozment, *When Fathers Ruled: Family Life in Reformation Europe* (Cambridge, Mass.: Harvard University Press, 1983), p. 26, all without reference to Bernard of Clairvaux. The decision for consent, as advocated by the theologian Peter Lombard, against that of consummation by the canonist Gratian, follows a Roman opinion, for which see Treggiari, *Roman Marriage*, pp. 54-57, 170-80.

247 For the practice of celibacy within marriage, although usually after sexual experience, see Dyan Elliott, *Spiritual Marriage: Sexual Abstinence in Medieval Wedlock* (Princeton: Princeton University Press, 1993).

248 Bernard of Clairvaux, *Epistolae* 174.7.

Bernard and his brothers collaborated in the breakup of the marriage of their eldest sibling and the relegation of his wife to a convent.[249] Women were forbidden at the door of Clairvaux from all places inhabited by the monks and even from the enclosure of the granges. They could not enter the church of an abbey except at its dedication and octave. A Cistercian monk could never speak alone with a woman.[250] Even a widow negotiating with the monastery to donate a gift was required to stand outside the gate and hope that some monks would issue to speak with her; or she could send a male representative within the enclosure.[251] Bernard's married sister Humbeline with a retinue once visited the abbey. He despised and cursed her as a diabolical snare for souls in her sumptuous dress.[252] Clothing was an exemplary topic: for chastity, against cosmetics.[253] Moralists allowed wives to adorn themselves but only toward rendering the marriage debt, lest their husband's eyes rove into adultery.[254] Yet Bernard strictly refused to meet Humbeline, as did her other brothers. André, the porter, even informed her that she looked like "a dung clod."[255] All sensual enjoyment was rejected as "dung" in Bernard's catalogue of the material decoration of churches so necessary to excite carnal souls to devotion: beauteous glitter, melodious sound, delightful fragrance, sweet taste, pleasant touch.[256] At the epithet of "dung" Humbeline burst into tears, acknowledged her sin, and begged counsel of her brothers; so they condescended to come out to meet her at the gate. Although she renounced her costume and jewelry, she declined to terminate her marriage immediately but returned home completely changed to abide as a hermit in the world. She lived with her husband, who dared not touch her as a temple of the Holy Spirit. He finally conceded that she might join the nunnery at Jully. There she proved "a sister of those men of God no less in the spirit than in the flesh."[257] The opinion of her brothers was more important to her than that of her husband, even though she was vowed

---

[249] William of St.-Thierry, *Vita prima* 1.3.18-19.

[250] D'Arbois de Jouvainville, *Études sur l'etat interieur des abbayes cisterciennes*, pp. 7-9.

[251] Bouchard, *Holy Entrepreneurs*, pp. 161-63.

[252] William of St.-Thierry, *Vita prima* 1.6.30.

[253] See *Le livre du Chevalier de La Tour Landry pour l'enseignement de ses filles* 27.

[254] Elliott, "Dress as Mediator between Inner and Outer Self: The Pious Matron of the High and Later Middle Ages," *Mediaeval Studies* 53 (1991): 288-89.

[255] William of St.-Thierry, *Vita prima* 1.6.30.

[256] Bernard of Clairvaux, *Apologia ad Guillelmum abbatem* 13.28.

[257] William of St.-Thierry, *Vita prima* 1.6.30. For female norms see Jane Tibbetts Schulenburg, "Sexism and the Celestial Gynaeceum—from 500 to 1200," *Journal of Medieval History* 4 (1978):117-33. French manuals for females dating from the thirteenth century categorized women by chastity, failed to address the responsibilities of married women, and judged marriage incompatible with a spiritual life. See Geneviève Hasenohr, "La vie quotidienne de la femme vue par l'église: L'enseignement des 'journées chrétiennes' de la fin du moyen âge," in *Frau und spätmittlelaterlicher Alltage*, Internationaler Kongress, Krems an der Donau, 2. bis 5. Oktober 1984, Österreichische Akademie der Wissenschaften, Philosophisch-historische Klasse, *Sitzungsberichte* 473 (1986):19-101.

to him, with the moral responsibility of rearing their child.

Although the abbey had the warming room, despite Bernard's piety of spiritual kinship there was no Cistercian hearth as "family". Bernard, when he was ill, used to be visited at the cottage by his friend William of St.-Thierry, who conversed with him about the Song of Songs. Yet Bernard's exegesis of that erotic poetry was remote from the domesticity of the cottage, as if he were indeed oblivious of his architectural surroundings, just as the hagiography claimed. He explicated that the Virgin Mary, reminiscent of folklore about the opening of the womb, conceived by a polished arrow. It pierced her through with love "that she might become the mother of charity, whose father is God as charity." Yet, when the child Jesus was born of that charity, he did not dwell among people (John 1:14). He pitched his tent in the sun (Ps. 18:6 Vulg.) to fulfill the prophecy of being a light to the nations.[258] Bernard's exegesis substituted a celestial domain for a terrestrial place, the cosmic for the domestic. Since Augustine, the situation of Christ had been a seat, the professorial chair (*cathedra*).[259] Bernard of Clairvaux relocated even that chair securely in heaven. The monastic chapter was a school of Christ, a spiritual classroom; yet Christ as wisdom taught from the august rostrum of the angelic thrones as the seat of God.[260] The focus of the monk was celestial and eschatological.[261] Bernard's exegesis also preferred, as did much monastic exegesis, the sapiential literature of the Old Testament to the kerygmatic literature of the New Testament. The psalm chanted in the choir drowned out the gospel proclaimed in the pulpit.

The announcement of Emmanuel, "God among us," was not unheard merely because Cistercian ears were male. The medieval home may have been the place of the female but it was, as in Roman society, the preserve of the male. Women as professed or pretend religious also capitulated to asceticism. When Peter the Venerable wrote Héloïse upon the death of Abélard that "crossing through the desert of this pilgrimage you have erected in your heart a precious tabernacle for God,"[262] she did not protest that her heart was not a portable ark but a permanent home. Augustine wrote that Wisdom built its house (Prov. 9:13) in the womb of the Virgin Mary.[263] So did Bernard of Clairvaux, who exclaimed blessed the soul in whom wisdom also built its house.[264] Hildegard of Bingen, a Benedictine

---

258 Bernard of Clairvaux, *Sermones in cantica canticorum* 29.4.8. Childbirth was aided in folk customs by symbolic openings of the womb such as opening doors and windows of the room, unlocking chests, or shooting arrows. Hanawalt, *Ties that Bound*, p. 217, without reference to Bernard.

259 Augustine, *Sermones* 234; *In epistolam Iohannis ad Parthos* 119.2.

260 Bernard of Clairvaux, *Sermones super cantica canticorum* 19.2.4.

261 Leclercq, *The Love of Learning and the Desire for God: A Study of Monastic Culture*, trans. Catharine Misrahi (New York: Fordham University Press, 1961), pp. 65-86.

262 Peter the Venerable, *Epistolae* 115.

263 Augustine, *De civitate Dei* 17.20.

264 Bernard of Clairvaux, *Sermones de diversis* 52.

abbess and principal author among medieval women, described the human heart as a house within whose gates personifications of the virtues and vices dwelled. Any fearful woman could be a house of wisdom by childbearing or by charity, she thought; but a married woman should stay out of church until the wound of her defloration was healed. Hildegard was a tenth child, dedicated to the Church by her parents as a tithe. In her dualistic rejection of sexuality only virginal persons were sacral. God eternal and triune she imagined as an active fire. The flesh of the Virgin Mary blazed from the warmth of God yet it was like a "tabernacle," not a home. It bore Jesus miraculously through her side, not her vagina. Hildegard in *Scivias* claimed that the divine fire also came upon her, not burning, but warming like sunlight; and the manuscript illustrated her inscribing its inspiration on wax tablets. It was not the fire of a domestic hearth, however, which she likened to a woman in passion (a man was a blazing volcano). In her melancholy she envisioned the hearth as the month of November.[265] Just as winter had been depicted in the seasonal mosaics of Roman north Africa by the wild boar, so in the medieval calendars November was illustrated by the slaughter and curing of swine.[266] For Hildegard, however, that month was a figure before the hearth, a decrepit old man, fearful of the chill, folding his limbs to warm himself.[267]

Not only a monk like Bernard of Clairvaux received the Word as a guest in his bedchamber. The anchoress Julian of Norwich experienced divine "showings" on a sickbed in her room. Yet she envisioned her soul as a citadel, a city, a kingdom. When Christ reigned "in his own house" that was in heaven.[268] So did Margery Kempe envision him on her very bed but in response she performed the typical medieval piety: she went on pilgrimage. The daughter of John Burnham of Lynn in Norfolk, a principal English town of which he was mayor for several terms, she was of a prosperous family. Adolescent daughters enjoyed more legal and economic autonomy than wives, however, so that at marriage she passed to a position of depen-

---

[265] See Barbara C. Newman, *Sister of Wisdom: St. Hildegard's Theology of the Feminine* (Berkeley: University of California Press, 1987), pp. 81-82, 202, 214, 252-53, 182, 18, 67, 175-77, 47 and frontispiece, 130, 20. See also Elisabeth Gössmann, "'Ipsa enim quasi domus sapientiae': Die Frau ist gleichsam das Haus der Weisheit: Zur frauenbezogenen Spiritualität Hildegards von Bingen," in *"Eine Höhe, über die nichtsgeht": Spezielle Glaubenserfahrung in der Frauenmystik?*, ed. Margot Schmidt and Dieter R. Bauer, Christliche Mystik, 4 (Stuttgart: Günther Holzborg, 1986), pp. 1-18.

[266] Marie Collins and Virginia Davis, *A Medieval Book of Seasons* (London: Sidgwick & Jackson, 1991), pp. 109, 114; Chapelot and Fossier, *Village and House*, p. 153 and fig. 50e; Hanawalt, *Ties that Bound*, pp. 53, 125. See also Perrine Mane, *Calendriers et techniques agricoles (France—Italie, XIIe-XIIIe siècles)* (Paris: Sycomore for Centre national de recherches scientifiques, 1983), pp. 222-30.

[267] Hildegard of Bingen, *De operatione Dei* 1.4.98, cited by Newman, *Sister of Wisdom*, p. 20.

[268] Julian of Norwich, *A Book of Showings to the Anchoress Julian of Norwich* 2-10; or 68, 14 (long text).

dency.[269] Married to a burgess at twenty or later, she quickly conceived. A difficult pregnancy and labor left her fearful for survival. She summoned a priest but, because of his severe attitude, she was unable to confess a concealed sin of the past. Between dread of reproof and damnation she lost her wits for more than half a year. Devils tempted her to slander herself and others. She flayed her breast with her fingernails and bit her hand so violently that the marks of her teeth left permanent scars.[270] Clawing one's flesh and biting the back of one's hand were cultural gestures of despair, as in late medieval paintings of expulsion from paradise, lamentation at the cross, and damnation in hell.[271]

Once in that puerperal illness, when Kempe was unattended, Christ appeared to her "in the likeness of a man, most seemly, most beauteous and most amiable that ever be seen with man's eye, clad in a mantle of purple silk, sitting upon her bedside, looking upon her with so blessed a face that she was strengthened in all her spirit, and said to her these words: — 'Daughter, why hast thou forsaken Me, and I forsook never thee?'" He then ascended into heaven. Calmed in her senses and reason, she asked her husband for the keys to the buttery, resuming her matronal role.[272] Her description of Christ coincided with the conventional criteria for a marriageable male : manliness, family, looks, and speech. Since the nuptial couch was classically decked in purple,[273] his purple cloak on her bed was quite suggestive. His regal garb and celestial Ascension identified him as the triumphant Lord, of better social status than her husband. Christ was soon to oust him from the marital bed. Religion with its festivals provided medieval married couples the occasion for leisure together.[274] Religion with its fantasies provided Margery Kempe the excuse to separate.

After her cure she was reputedly vainglorious, dressing in fashionable clothing and jewelry for the respect of her kin and to the envy of her neighbors. From avarice she became a brewer, one of the most successful in town

---

269 See Judith M. Bennett, *Women in the Medieval English Countryside: Gender and Household in Brigstock before the Plague* (Oxford: Oxford University Press, 1987), pp. 110-14.

270 *The Book of Margery Kempe* 1.1. Citations follow the modern version, which places several chapters in an appendix, rather than the literal copy of the manuscript in Middle English. For its literary composition see recently Diana R. Uhlman, "The Comfort of Voice: The Solace of Script: Orality and Literacy in *The Book of Margery Kempe*," *Studies in Philology* 91 (1994):50-69; and for its authorship as fictional in social criticism, Lynn Staley, *Margery Kempe's Dissenting Fictions* (University Park, Pa.: Pennsylvania State University Press, 1994).

271 Moshe Barasch, *Gestures of Despair in Medieval and Early Renaissance Art* (New York: New York University Press, 1976), p. 17. Although Barasch was unable to locate the source of the concept, it was a declamatory exercise in the Roman schools. See Seneca, the elder, *Controversiae* 3.7, and allusion to it in Quintilian, *Institutiones oratoriae* 8.2.20; 8.5.23. Cf. Ovid, *Metamorphoses* 8.877-78.

272 *Book of Margery Kempe* 1.1.

273 See Treggiari, *Roman Marriage*, pp. 85-89, 146, without reference to Kempe.

274 For married leisure see Hanawalt, *Ties that Bound*, p. 218.

for several years, until she lost a considerable sum. She undertook a new housewifery, a horse mill, until the horses balked at the work and her man quit. Kempe interpreted these economic failures as signs of divine punishment.[275] For males commercial brewing was associated with public power, as an access to holding office, but not for alewives, who had to accommodate their commercial activities to their husband's work. Their profits were submerged in the conjugal fund, which the husband legally controlled. Milling and brewing were ill reputed. There was animosity toward the purveyors from the poor, in a tension between their need for food and their inability to produce it.[276] Yet brewing provided the opportunity to practice charity, since in a mixture of conviviality and almsgiving "ales" as village events raised funds for parochial expenses, endowed brides, and assisted the needy on hard times. Women were very active in these social events as brewers, organizers, hosts, and guests.[277] Kempe failed at both businesses, however, her only domestic activities mentioned other than sexual duties. Once in bed with her husband she heard a sweet melody, as if she were in paradise, so that she bolted exclaiming: "Alas that ever I did sin! It is full merry in Heaven." She lost desire for sexual relations with her husband. Although she paid the matrimonial debt in obedience, it became so abominable to her that it would have been preferable to eat the ooze and muck in the gutter, she said. She informed her husband, "I may not deny you my body, but the love of my heart and my affections are withdrawn from all earthly creatures and set only in God."[278]

Although little is known about private aspects of married life, medieval English villagers expected emotional and sexual satisfaction. The medical literature indicated that women did experience sexual satisfaction; indeed, females were considered more sexual than males. In town a companionable love, if not the ideal romance of the court, was valued. Augustine's teaching that good faith was the first element of a vital marriage ensured its esteem. Personal incompatibility was a common reason for the dissolution of marriages, and flexibility of customs allowed ecclesiastical courts to adjudicate in a partner's displeasure with a spouse.[279] Few cases of separation—for

---

275 *Book of Margery Kempe* 1.2. For Kempe's fancy clothing see Elliott, "Dress as Mediator between Inner and Outer Self," pp. 294-95; and see in general Ann Eljenholm Nichols, "Costume in the Moralities: The Evidence of East Anglian Art," *Comparative Drama* 20 (1986-87):305-14.

276 Bennett, *Women in the Medieval English Countryside*, pp. 126-28; idem, "The Village Ale-Wife: Women and Brewing in Fourteenth-Century England," in *Women and Work in Preindustrial Europe*, ed. Hanawalt (Bloomington: Indiana University Press, 1986), pp. 20, 29.

277 Bennett, "Conviviality and Charity in Medieval and Early Modern England," *Past and Present* 134 (1992):19-41.

278 *Book of Margery Kempe* 1.3.

279 Bennett, *Women in the Medieval English Countryside*, pp. 101-4. For Kempe's sexual attitudes as atypical see also Brundage, *Law, Sex, and Christian Society in Medieval Europe* (Chicago: University of Chicago Press, 1987), pp. 503-4, 507; for marriage and for marital

adultery, cruelty, or heresy—appeared in those courts, however. Kempe could not sue for divorce because she had no legal grounds, such as consanguinity or precontract. Consent validated marriage, and hers was ratified by consummation.[280] It was a dictum of canonical, theological, and pastoral texts that the husband who loved his wife too ardently was an adulterer.[281] Yet the penitentials required legitimate sexual compliance. Payment of the marriage debt was such a serious obligation that it could even be rendered in church, although the building would have to be reconsecrated.[282] Kempe obeyed her husband's desires but bewailed her unchastity with fasting and vigilance, some days being shriven several times. She wore a haircloth from a kiln of the type malt was dried on. And she continued to bear children, although she felt "no lust," only "very painful and horrible" sexual intercourse. Temptations to lechery—and despair for them—contrarily tormented her. Kempe then replaced the haircloth on her back with one on her heart, exchanged eating flesh for receiving communion every Sunday, and relinquished the rosary for meditation.[283] Meditation introduced her to an alternative society. Her factual relations of kin[284] and her ordinary obligations of household became supplanted by imaginary ones.

In her meditations Kempe imagined St. Anne pregnant and asked to be her maid and servant. When the Virgin Mary was born, Kempe arranged to keep the girl until twelve years of age with good food and fair white clothing. She then became the servant of Mary and went forth with her and Joseph, bearing a pottle of wine and honey and also spices. They visited cousin Elizabeth—all greeting each other and dwelling together. After John the Baptist was born, Kempe took leave of his mother, begging her prayers that she might become a good servant of Mary. Assured that she did her duty well, she returned with the holy couple to Bethlehem. There Kempe was in charge of purchasing the nightly lodging, begging the cloths for swaddling the infant, providing bedding for mother and son, and also begging meat for them. Kempe herself swaddled Jesus, assuring him that she

---

relations see also Ralph A. Houlbrooke, *The English Family, 1450-1700* (London: Longman, 1984), pp. 63-126.

280 For separation and divorce see Hanawalt, *Ties that Bound*, pp. 209-14. See also Frederik Pedersen, "Did the Medieval Laity Know the Canon Law Rules on Marriage?: Some Evidence from Fourteenth-Century York Cause Papers," *Mediaeval Studies* 56 (1994):111-52.

281 See Henry Ansgar Kelly, *Love and Marriage in the Age of Chaucer* (Ithaca, N. Y.: Cornell University Press, 1975), p. 245, and for marriage without intercourse in an English context, pp. 290-302.

282 For the conjugal debt see Thomas N. Tentler, *Sin and Confession on the Eve of the Reformation* (Princeton: Princeton University Press, 1977), pp. 162-232; Pierre J. Payer, *Sex and the Penitentials: The Development of a Sexual Code 550-1150* (Toronto: University of Toronto Press, 1984), pp. 19-36; Elliott, *Spiritual Marriage*, pp. 132-94.

283 *Book of Margery Kempe* 1.3-5.

284 For an introduction to the subject see David Cressy, "Kinship and Kin Interaction in Early Modern England," *Past and Present* 113 (1986):38-69.

would not bind him tightly. She envisioned Mary swaddling him with a white kerchief as symbolic of how she herself must live "chaste and clean."[285]

Swaddling was not an uncriticized practice. Physicians in the Roman empire had blamed it for indoor confinement, inadequate diet, and lack of exposure to sunlight causing rickets.[286] It was thought to protect and anchor the soft limbs of an infant, just as Girolamo Savonarola likened his reforms for Florence.[287] Yet Savonarola scolded nuns for playing with baby dolls as if those were Jesus, a devotional practice that became a commercial business. The dolls were idols, he said. They were but the realistic conclusion, however, of the imaginative prayer proposed by such popular books as the meditations ascribed to Bonaventure or Ludolf von Sachsen's life of Christ. Receive and hold the infant in your arms, they urged; kiss him, then return him to his mother. Observe how Mary nurses, cares for, and serves Jesus; imitate her.[288] Such pious authors were but extending to the imagination what had been a common actual ritual in pagan antiquity, the dressing and bathing of religious statues.[289] Yet the swaddling cloths of her imagination bound Kempe tightly, as they became confused with the fair white cloths she provided prayerfully for Mary the girl, then demanded actually from her husband and the bishop for herself.

When in her meditations Christ asked Kempe whom she would have in heaven with her, she preferred her confessor to her father and her husband. For her charity Christ ensured her the salvation of her entire household. Kempe then made Christ the executor of her will to parcel out her merits on others, for which deed she was promised double reward. Not only did she make Christ a broker of merits: she made him a breaker of marriage. Together they connived to end her husband's "lust." With bargaining Kempe's husband agreed to a vow of chastity, if she would continue to share his bed, pay his debts before pilgrimage to Jerusalem (as legally required), and break

---

285 *Book of Margery Kempe* 1.6; 1.85. The simplicity of Mary's kerchief was contrasted polemically with the fashionable horned headdresses in a ballad by John Lydgate, p. 47, cited by Aileen Ribeiro, *Dress and Morality* (London: B. T. Batsford, 1986), p. 52.

286 Peter Garnsey, "Child Rearing in Ancient Italy," in *The Family in Italy from Antiquity to the Present*, ed. Kertzer and Saller, p. 57. For late medieval practice see Danièle Alexandre-Bidon and Monique Classon, *L'Enfant à l'ombre des cathédrales* (Lyon: Presses Universitaires de Lyon, 1985), pp. 94-102.

287 See Richard C. Trexler, *Public Life in Renaissance Florence* (New York: Academic, 1980), p. 462. For swaddling see also Houlbrooke, *English Family*, p. 132; Georges Vigarello, *Concepts of Cleanliness: Changing Attitudes in France since the Middle Ages*, trans. Jean Birrell (Cambridge: Cambridge University Press, 1988), pp. 15-16.

288 Christiane Klapisch-Zuber, "Holy Dolls: Play and Piety in Florence in the Quattrocento," in idem, *Women, Family, and Ritual in Renaissance Italy*, trans. Lydia Cochrane (Chicago: University of Chicago Press, 1985), p. 324, citing Girolamo Savonarola, Predica 14 in *Prediche sopra Amos e Zaccaria*; p. 323, citing Pseudo-Bonaventure, *Meditationes* 60 and Ludolf von Sachsen, *Vita Jesu Christi*, 1:77-78.

289 See for the ancient practice Barasch, *Icon: Studies in the History of an Idea* (New York: New York University Press, 1991), pp. 34-36.

her Friday fast and abstinence at his table. Faithful when all others failed her, he asked the bishop for a mantle and ring for her and for the all white clothing she coveted. Since his consent was canonically required, he placed his hands between those of the bishop and promised that the couple would vow chastity. It was her husband who was pained at the japes and rebukes to her, which were many. Kempe persisted in supposing that "every good thought and every good desire that thou hast in thy soul is the speech of God." She sought religious validation never from other married women, only from celibate women like the anchoress Julian or nuns in a convent, and from a hierarchy of celibate men: bishops, abbots, friars, and priests. When commoners ridiculed her, she took refuge in her image of Christ, who confirmed her celibacy, consoling her even in bed for her tribulations. He insisted that she had him to thank for giving her a husband who would permit her vow of chastity.[290]

God was in her soul as grace, she believed, and so he accompanied her to church, to table, to bed, to town.[291] Yet, except for church, those places were secular to Kempe; and even the church had nothing in common with marriage. Medieval marriages were not solemnized in church, at best only at its door. In the more common practice ecclesiastics simply recognized private arrangements between families or partners.[292] And in her imagination Kempe displaced all of her female roles of kinship onto God. As he consoled her, "Thou art a very daughter to me, and a mother also, a sister, and wife and spouse." She was a daughter in her zeal to please, a mother in her lament of his passion, a sister in her weeping for others' sins, and a spouse and wife in her longing for heaven. "For it belongeth to the wife to be with her husband, and to have no very joy until she cometh into his presence."[293] That wifely definition had no application to Kempe's real marriage, which she considered an obstacle to divine acceptance. Yet in her imagination Christ did assure her that he loved wives, especially those who would be chaste. Virginity was better than widowhood, and that better than marriage, he reiterated. He affirmed that he loved Kempe as well as any virgin, for his love quenched sin. Although she rued the loss of her maidenhood, he told her that she was a maiden in her soul and that he would dance with her in heaven among all the other virgins as his "dearworthy darling."[294]

Divine love of married persons depended for Kempe not on creation as good but as forgiven. Sex was sin, as in the rigorist penitentials. Divine preference among the married, already the most inferior class, was for those

---

290 *Book of Margery Kempe* 1.15-17; 1.54 and passim; 1.84; 1.65.

291 Ibid. 1.14.

292 See Hanawalt, *Ties that Bound*, p. 203; and on the issue of the church door, Brooke, *Medieval Idea of Marriage*, pp. 248-57.

293 *Book of Margery Kempe* 1.14.

294 Ibid. 1.21-22.

spouses who renounced sexual expression. Since sex was necessary for propagation, Kempe's imagination projected on Christ the belief of Augustine or Bernard of Clairvaux, who were indifferent about the future of the human population. Christ the spouse of "this creature" Margery was cavalier about the generation of other creatures. He commanded Kempe to have a ring made and engraved "Jesus Cryst est amor meus" and he informed her that the Godhead willed to wed her. When she shied from the announcement, since her previous experience was with the humanity of Christ only, he excused her as too young and inexperienced. Yet in her fantasy the Father took her hand spiritually before the Son and the Holy Ghost, before Mary, the twelve apostles, saints Katherine and Margaret among many others, and a multitude of angels, and pronounced: "I take thee, Margery, for my wedded wife, for fairer, for fouler, for richer, for poorer, so that thou be kindly and gentle to do as I bid thee. For, daughter, there was never a child so gracious to its mother as I shall be to thee, both in weel and in woe, to help thee and comfort thee. And thereto I make thee surety."[295]

The celestial company at her marriage included the virginal saints Margaret and Katherine, whose grace she was promised. Patrons of childbirth and chastity, they were invoked as exemplary in *Hali Meidenhad* against sex as filthy. They were popularly paired in female piety,[296] most famously as the commanding voices of Joan of Arc.[297] St. Margaret was an obvious choice to witness Kempe's marriage, for she was the patron of Lynn's oldest and most important church, a gift of the bishop of Norwich dating from the eleventh century. Kempe was likely baptized there; she was named Margery after Margaret. The church, with its twin western towers defining the skyline, stood next to the Saturday market, where it was in constant use by traders and also by citizens for the religious solemnization of civic ceremony. The guild hall of the Holy Trinity, for which Kempe's father presided as alderman, was adjacent to St. Margaret's church, so that it had familiar, filial associations.[298] But St. Katherine, her other witness, never existed. She was not even a vague historical figure to whom martyrly legends accrued.[299] That imaginary woman was artistically celebrated as married to

---

295 Ibid. 1.35.

296 For their cult see Eamon Duffy, "Holy Maydens, Holy Wyfes: The Cult of Women Saints in Fifteenth- and Sixteenth-Century England," in *Women in the Church*, ed. Sheils and Diana Wood, Studies in Church History, 27 (London: Basil Blackwell for the Ecclesiastical History Society, 1990), pp. 184-85, 187, 190; Rozsika Parker, *The Subversive Stitch: Embroidery and the Making of the Feminine* (London: Women's Press, 1984), p. 56.

297 See Pierre Tisset, *Procès de condemnation de Jeanne d'Arc*, 3 vols. (Paris: Klincksieck, 1960-71), 1:74-75, 3:94.

298 Vanessa Parker, *The Making of Kings Lynn: Secular Buildings from the 11th to the 17th century*, Kings Lynn Archaeological Society, 1 (London: Phillimore, 1971), pp. 136, 141, 142, 143.

299 See René Coursault, *Sainte Catherine d'Alexandria: Le mythe et la tradition* (Paris: Maisonneuve & Larose, 1984).

Christ, however, so that female desires of divine union gathered around her figure.

Kempe's imagination again conflated her religious roles toward God as wife, daughter, and mother. It also displaced her real roles toward humans as wife, daughter, and mother. Her relationship with her father was mentioned only as a source of social status provoking the vice of vainglory; that with her mother or siblings was ignored. Her relationships with her husband and children were supplanted with fantasies. She supposed it fitting for a wife to be "homely" with her husband, to lie together and rest in joy and peace. In her imagination Christ declared: "Right so must it be between thee and Me. . . . I must needs be homely with thee, and lie in thy bed with thee." Addressing her as daughter, he asked her to be his wife and mother. "Take Me to thee as thy wedded husband, as thy dearworthy darling, and as thy sweet son, for I will be loved as a son should be loved by the mother, and I will that thou lovest Me, daughter, as a good wife ought to love her husband." He bade her boldly to take him into the arms of her soul and sweetly to kiss his mouth, head, and feet.[300]

Kempe affirmed in one of many hearings of her case, this before the abbot of Leicester and his assessors, that she loved no man as much as God. Her renunciation of sex was associated with her reception of the Eucharist. The penitentials judged sexual intercourse before or after holy communion sinful, or incompatible with the sacrament.[301] Thomas Aquinas taught that, because sex corrupted wisdom, communion could not be received the day after such carnal activity.[302] It was during questioning on the Eucharist that she testified having no part in any man's body in sinful deed, except her husband's by the law of marriage. She had compared sexual relations to eating the muck and ooze of the gutter.[303] Kempe may have meant the domestic gutter for catching rainwater and drippings from the house; or, the town gutter, an open sewer into which emptied latrines and privies and into which people dumped dung and rubbish from the stables.[304] Among the civic orders for maintenance passed in Lynn during her lifetime were the restriction to Wednesdays and Saturdays of the passage of manure carts through town and a penalty for throwing refuse on the muckhills or in fleets and ditches.[305] Yet filth blocking the streets and watercourses of Lynn remained its worst problem for health. Rubbish was thrown from habit into convenient open

---

300 *Book of Margery Kempe* 1.36.

301 See Tentler, *Sin and Confession*, pp. 215-18.

302 John Giles Milhaven, "Thomas Aquinas on Sexual Pleasure," *Journal of Religious Ethics* 5 (1977):158.

303 *Book of Margery Kempe* 1.48; 1.3.

304 See Ernest L. Sabine, "Latrines and Cesspools of Mediaeval London," *Speculum* 9 (1934):303-21; Lynn Thorndike, "Sanitation, Baths, and Street-Cleaning in the Middle Ages and Renaissance," ibid. 3 (1928): 192-203; and for privies in homes, Margaret Wood, *The English Mediaeval House* (London: Phoenix House, 1965), pp. 377-88.

305 *The Making of King's Lynn: A Documentary Survey* #274.

space, while pigs ran loose in the town. There were the necessary muckhills, especially near the marketplaces and thus Kempe's church. The public privies, timber structures built beside or over the fleets, were only flushed out by the tide.[306] Sex was such filth.

It was only in consuming the Eucharist, the white host clean and chaste, that Kempe could assume familial roles, although only in fantasy. She imagined in receiving the sacrament that her soul had three cushions, of cloth of gold, red velvet, and white silk, for the repose of the three persons of the Trinity. "And by the great homeliness that I shew thee at that time," spoke God in her imagination, "thou art much the bolder to ask Me grace for thyself, for thy husband, and for thy children, and thou makest every Christian man and woman thy child in thy soul for the time, and wouldst have as much grace for them, as for thine own children." In asking mercy for her husband, who allowed her chastity despite his good health, she imagined, "Daughter, if thou knewest how many wives there are in this world, that would love Me and serve Me right well and duly, if they might be as free from their husbands as thou art from thine. . . ." She received communion each Sunday like a wife receiving her husband come home after a trip.[307] The service of God "right well and duly" required freedom from a human husband, so that as a spiritual wife Kempe might welcome him. Kempe's actual husband, like Augustine's concubine, was never named.

Nameless also were her children. She testified during the hearing that she had borne fourteen.[308] Childlessness was considered a worse plight than overbearing, so that she would not have elicited easy sympathy.[309] Medieval women spent most of their adult years either pregnant or nursing, although their fertility was probably low through contraception and abortion. In ideal circumstances in the early modern period, with its improved circumstances over Kempe's century, a mother who nursed likely produced during a marriage of twenty years eight children. In the fourteenth century stress and famine causing amenorrhea would have produced fewer conceptions and births. After the Black Death, although food and wages increased, the mean size of families decreased.[310] The declared fertility of Margery Kempe was

---

306 Parker, *Making of Kings Lynn*, pp. 160-61.

307 *Book of Margery Kempe* 1.86. For the salutations "hail" and "welcome" in English devotion to the Eucharist see Miri Rubin, *Corpus Christi: The Eucharist in Late Medieval Culture* (Cambridge: Cambridge University Press, 1990), pp. 159-60.

308 *Book of Margery Kempe* 1.48. See also Laura L. Howes, "On the Birth of Margery Kempe's Last Child," *Modern Philology* 90 (1992):220-25.

309 See Houlbrooke, *English Family*, p. 126; and for parent-child relations, pp. 126-201.

310 Bennett, *Women in the Medieval English Countryside*, pp. 115-6. See also P. P. A. Biller, "Birth-Control in the West in the Thirteenth and Early Fourteenth Centuries," *Past and Present* 94 (1982):3-26; Hanawalt, *Ties that Bound*, pp. 100-1, and for the age of marriage, pp. 95-100; Jean-Louis Flandrin, "Contraception, Marriage and Sexual Relations in the Christian West," trans. Patricia M. Ranum, in *Biology of Man in History: Selections from the Annales économies, sociétés, civilisations*, ed. Robert Forster and Orest Ranum (Baltimore, Md.: Johns Hopkins University Press, 1975), pp. 23-47; rpt. from *Annales* 24 (1969):1370-90; Alan

far in excess of the probability. Yet her book was not a statistical record of births but epideictic rhetoric. She spoke before the ecclesiastical hearing to confirm herself as a legally irreproachable wife in rendering the conjugal debt. The biblical generations to Christ were all fourteen (Matt. 1:7). Fourteen was also twice the perfect number of seven; perhaps she meant she had fulfilled her matrimonial duty to double perfection. Seven was symbolic of the forgiveness of injury, which she considered her husband's sexual "meddling" with her to be. The disciples were commanded in the gospel to forgive seven times daily (Luke 17:4), even seventy times seven (Matt. 18:22).

Kempe interpreted the command to "increase and multiply" (Gen. 1:28), not only of bodily children but also of virtues as spiritual fruit.[311] Medieval theologians did not advocate the propagation of large families as an ideal. Her interpretation was consistent with their valuation of spiritual goods, especially those issuing from celibacy, as primary.[312] Although her children passed anonymously, without a detail of her nurturing, Kempe indulged the infant Jesus. On the Purification, a major feast for married women,[313] and on the many occasions when women were being churched after childbirth, Kempe pictured its gospel vividly with weeping, sobbing, crying. At nuptials she imagined the wedding of Mary and Joseph or that of the soul to Christ; her meditation was punctuated with the boisterous shouts that marked her for attention. Once she was tested for deceit by priests who removed her to a rural chapel, with themselves and children as witnesses of her tears and shouts. On route home they met women with babes in arms,[314] for the infants of peasants were taken swaddled to the fields where their parents worked and placed in trees or on the ground.[315] Kempe inquired of them whether there was any male child. Told no, she was mentally ravished into the childhood of Christ with such desire to see him that she collapsed and cried marvelously. The priests then trusted her, because she wept in private as well as in public, in a field as in the town. Others were dubious about, even derisive of, her screams and seizures, which began during her pilgrimage to Jerusalem when she meditated on Calvary about the passion.[316]

MacFarlane, *Marriage and Love in England: Modes of Reproduction 1300-1840* (Oxford: Basil Blackwell, 1986); in general, John M. Riddle, *Contraception and Abortion from the Ancient World to the Renaissance* (Cambridge, Mass.: Harvard University Press, 1992).

311 *Book of Margery Kempe* 1.51.

312 See John T. Noonan, Jr., *Contraception: A History of its Treatment by the Catholic Theologians and Canonists*, enlarged ed. (Cambridge, Mass.: Harvard University Press, Belknap Press, 1986), p. 279.

313 See Hanawalt, *Ties that Bound*, p. 217; Kate Mertes, *The English Noble Household 1250-1600: Good Governance and Politic Rule* (Oxford: Basil Blackwell, 1988), p. 153.

314 *Book of Margery Kempe* 1.82; 1.83.

315 Hanawalt, *Ties that Bound*, p. 176.

316 *Book of Margery Kempe* 1.83; 1.28. For fainting and tears in meditations on the passion see James H. Marrow, *Passion Iconography in Northern European Art of the Late Middle Ages and Early Renaissance: A Study of the Transformation of Sacred Metaphor into De-*

Her devotion to the infancy of Christ was characteristic of her spirituality.[317] There was no scripture of the infancy, only two gospels of his birth, so that the imagination was free to explore. At the reception of communion Kempe invited the Madonna into the chamber of her soul, decorated with flowers and spices, to nurse the infant Jesus there.[318] Yet the Eucharist was physically bread received not into the soul but into the body. The lack of the spiritual integrity of body and soul was accompanied in Kempe by the distintegration of reality into fantasy. In her imagination Christ thanked her for bathing him "in thy soul, at home in thy chamber, as if I had been there present in my Manhood." He thanked her for the times she "harboured Me and My blessed mother in thy bed." He thanked her for tending him as Mary's maiden. Whatever she did in service to herself, husband, confessors, or guests, would be rewarded in heaven as if it were done to him.[319] There was no inclusion in her fantasies of tending the infant Jesus about nurturing her own children, even for heavenly reward, with which she was much occupied.

Kempe was once asked by a worried husband to visit his wife, just delivered of a child and out of her mind, as she herself had been after her initial parturition. The new mother failed to recognize her husband or neighbors, but only roared and cried, imagining demons about the room. Because she would smite and bite, she was manacled on her wrists. Comforted by Kempe's presence, after some confinement in shackles in a chamber at the edge of town, the woman was miraculously cured.[320] Christ thanked Kempe for tending the sick in his name and promised her a reward as if she had done it to him. As a penance on pilgrimage she once served a poor old woman just as she would have served the Virgin. Kempe slept without a coverlet, so that she became full of vermin; she fetched water and kindling, and she begged meat and wine.[321] Margery Kempe performed ordinary charity within that context of heavenly reward and punishment; and by the imaginative device of elevating its recipient to a higher, even sacral, social status than herself. The celebrity at such acting was Catherine of Siena, who managed her household chores by pretending that her father was Jesus,

---

scriptive Narrative, Ars neerlandica, 1 (Kortrijk: Van Ghemmert, 1979), pp. 10-28.

317 For other recent interpretations of her spirituality see, e. g., John C. Hirsh, *The Revelations of Margery Kempe: Paramystical Practices in Late Medieval England*, Medieval and Renaissance Authors, 10 (Leiden: E. J. Brill, 1989); Clarissa W. Atkinson, *Mystic and Pilgrim: The Book and the World of Margery Kempe* (Ithaca, N. Y.: Cornell University Press, 1983); Nona Fienberg, "Thematics of Value in The Book of Margery Kempe," *Modern Philology* 87 (1989):132-41.

318 *Book of Margery Kempe* 1.86. For Marian associations with Eucharistic piety see Rubin, *Corpus Christi*, pp. 142-47.

319 *Book of Margery Kempe* 1.86; 1.84.

320 Ibid. 1.75. For childbirth see Hanawalt, *Ties that Bound*, p. 216.

321 *Book of Margery Kempe* 1.86; 1.34.

her mother was Mary, and her siblings were apostles.[322] Kempe similarly condescended to tend the old woman by pretending that she was the Virgin.

Another poor woman once beckoned Kempe into her house and made her sit by the small fire. She offered her wine in a stone cup, while she nursed her son there. The boy later toddled to Kempe, as his mother sat sorrowing. Kempe burst into tears, as if the two were Mary and Jesus during the passion. Christ told her, "'This place is holy.'"[323] Yet she disbelieved any domestic spot holy unless it was an epiphany of the Madonna. Whether the scene at the hearth was an incident or a meditation, it evoked a sooty hearth as an ambiguous, even deadly, place. As the wife of a burgess of Lynn, Kempe would not have nursed her own children. Unlike Monica and Aleth, who reserved that moral prerogative, women of her station hired wet nurses.[324] At Mass she invited the Madonna into her soul to nurse the infant Jesus—the apparition of the Child in the host was an extensive medieval topic, especially in female piety.[325] There was even a heterodox but popular devotion to the sacrament as the body of Christ *and* Mary, her flesh in his flesh.[326] Kempe in her meditations bathed and swaddled Jesus, although a servant probably performed those chores for her own children.

She took him imaginatively into her own bed, but she did not nurse him, unlike the female saints who enlarged their affections with their breasts. One virgin envisioned the swelling of her breasts and those of all celestial virgins on Christmas day at the thought of nursing Jesus. Another so joyfully meditated on the infancy that her breasts overflowed with milk seasonally from Christmas to the Purification. For the consolation of a dejected saint the infant appeared in a cradle, then sat up in the Virgin's lap to nurse. In another vision a weary Mary handed a virgin the infant to hold; in experiencing his littleness she surrendered herself to his majesty. To the saint who imagined her breasts engorged the devil frequently appeared as a crying child to distract and preoccupy her. To another saint a delightful family appeared but diabolically, to tempt the abandoned and lonely girl to jealousy and despair for lack of human affection.[327] Such virginal meditations contradicted maternal reality. For a celibate woman to nurture the infant Jesus in fantasy was considered saintly; to desire her own infant in reality, devil-

322 Raymond of Capua, *Vita S. Catharinae* 1.4.50.

323 *Book of Margery Kempe* 1.39.

324 See Hanawalt, *Ties that Bound*, p. 178.

325 See Leah Sinanoglou, "The Christ Child as Sacrifice: A Medieval Tradition and the Corpus Christi Plays," *Speculum* 48 (1973):491-509; in general Peter Browe, *Die Eucharistischen Wunder des Mittelalters*, Breslauer Studien zur historischen Theologie, n. f. 4, 1 (Breslau: Müller & Seiffert, 1938). See also Rubin, *Corpus Christi*, pp. 113, 114, 116, 118-19, 135-39, and on women p. 120.

326 Richard of St.-Laurent, *De laudibus beatae Mariae virginis* 12.1; 12.7.

327 For the hagiography see Herlihy, *Medieval Households*, pp. 120, 126, 125. See also Shulamith Shahar, "Infants, Infant Care, and Attitudes toward Infancy in the Medieval Lives of Saints," *Journal of Psychohistory* 10 (1982-83):283-91.

ish. For a married woman actually to raise a child was ambiguous.

The sorrowful poor mother at the hearth whom Kempe visited reflected both reality and religion. It was peasant women who nursed their infants, for two to three years, in devout and deliberate imitation of the Madonna.[328] Yet the hearth was their perilous position. In an English peasant home it was located in the center of the main room, with a clay canopy but not before the sixteenth century with a chimney. The first task of the housewife upon rising was to light its fire. The open hearth was covered during the night with a perforated ceramic lid, shaped like a large inverted bowl, with a strap for handling. The cover preserved the glowing coals but prevented sparks from igniting the straw on the floor. At dawn the housewife removed the cover and ignited the embers, with kindling gathered in the close or with straw from the stack. English homes were heated by wood, peat, and coal, and the collection of the fuel was difficult. A woman gathering deadwood by hook and by crook could fall from the tree she had climbed. In digging a bit of peat from the turbaries she might be buried by the collapse of their unstable walls. The load carried home on her back, with a strap across her forehead, was a chore. If the fuel was damp, the household was hoarse and bleary from the smoldering of the fire. In winter, when the doors and windows were closed against the draft, the cottages were full of soot. The final female task at night was to hang the precious candle on the hook on the wall by the bed and to blow it out—lest as it burned down, the house burned down.[329] That precaution was the mark of a good housewife.[330]

The hearth on which the housewife stirred the porridge for breakfast was raised from the floor, perhaps on a clay platform, to deter such a house fire. Yet cooking in the central room was hazardous to her offspring. Liquids—water, milk, wort—and the eponymous pot-au-feu were always heating in earthenware pots, whose trivets could break, spilling the contents to scald children at play. Or infants, unswaddled so they could practice walking, could be burned when in their creeping they knocked over the simmering vessels. The majority of accidental deaths of babies among the English peasants was from fires about the house, especially in the cradle. Fires to cradles claimed one third of infants dead under a year of age. Infants were commonly swaddled and left tied in cradles by the hearth when no adult was minding them. Swaddled they could not creep into mischief; but neither

---

[328] See Hanawalt, *Ties that Bound*, pp. 178-79. See also Valerie Fildes, *Wet Nursing: A History from Antiquity to the Present* (Oxford: Basil Blackwell, 1988), pp. 32-48; Houlbrooke, *English Family*, pp. 128, 132-34.

[329] See Hanawalt, *Ties that Bound*, pp. 39-40, 147, 40, 147, 49-51, 152. See also Anthony Quiney, *House and Home: A History of the Small English House* (London: British Broadcasting Company, 1986), pp. 37-55; Wood, *English Medieval House*, pp. 257-73; Nicholas Hills, *The English Fireplace: Its Architecture and the Working Fire* (London: Quiller, 1985), pp. 20-35.

[330] *Le menagier de Paris* 2.3; Christine de Pisan, *Le livre de trois vertus* 2.24.

could they escape flames. Unattended they were victims of fires frequently blamed on chickens pecking for food on the hearth: either the bird dropped a burning straw or twig into the cradle; or its feathers caught fire, and in flapping them it set the cradle alight.[331]

More vicious were the pigs, a staple of the peasant diet as bacon. Although in the charge of the housewife, they were a common nuisance in the streets and fields. They might get into the house, maul the baby, and tussle and overturn its cradle into the fire. But also a nursing mother might suffer a seizure and let her child slip into the flames. Penitential manuals, detailing the problems of raising children, warned of these fireside dangers. Swaddling cloth was linen, linsey-woolsey, or wool, so that cradle fires smoldered, alerting the family; but often the adults were too far from home, gone to the field, at the well, or even in church. Marian carols and maternal lullabies vented the woes of nurturing. Sadder was the frustration of raising children who might die before maturity, as one-fourth to one-third in the preindustrial era did. As a Middle English lullaby rued, "Child, thou nart a pilgrim byt and uncouth gest."[332]

Kempe said that she was given a wondrous flame of fire, hot and enjoyable, that was love. It was the heat of the Holy Ghost burning away her sins as a token of his inner trinitarian presence. Yet, although its fire warmed her in cold weather,[333] it did not warm others. A fire in Lynn was social and domestic, the focus for most household activities. The common element of housing in that town, from a fisherman's cottage to a merchant's house, was the hall, since it was the only room in which a fire could be lit.[334] English town houses were unfortified, constructed in the simple idiom of tie-beam and crown-post. In Lynn the majority of late medieval homes were of timber, although merchants constructed facing the river Ouse two-storied houses of stone, featuring imported bricks and in some rooms imported tiles.[335] Such social stability did not inspire Margery Kempe to abide with her family, however. Housing afforded little privacy, which she required for meditation. The simple interior layout and insubstantial con-

---

331 Hanawalt, *Ties that Bound*, pp. 48, 40, 178, 175-76. See also the crucified Christ saving a boy fallen into the fire when a huge cauldron tips over. Votive image, Italian, 15th century. Reproduced in Arnoldo Cearrocchi and Ermanno Mori, *Italian Votive Tablets* (Udine: Doretti, 1960), VIb.

332 Hanawalt, *Ties that Bound*, pp. 52, 147, 176-79. For pigs killing unattended infants see also Esther Cohen, "Law, Folklore, and Animal Lore," *Past and Present* 110 (1986):11; in general, Fossier, *Peasant Life*, p. 118; Collins and Davis, *A Medieval Book of Seasons*, pp. 53-55, 108-9.

333 *Book of Margery Kempe* 1.35.

334 Parker, *Making of Kings Lynn*, p. 66.

335 See Maurice Barley, *Houses and History* (London: Faber & Faber, 1986), pp. 72, 33 and fig. 10, 36, 37; also Parker, *Making of Kings Lynn*, pp. 53-78. See in general Douglas Knoop and G. P. Jones, *The Medieval Mason: An Economic History of English Stone Building in the Later Middle Ages and Early Modern Times*, 3d ed. (Manchester: Manchester University Press, 1967).

struction of English dwellings, the high density of housing along the streets of towns, and the employment of servants all made privacy difficult. Although law and convention discouraged snooping and prying among neighbors, well-governed towns such as Lynn had the closest supervision of its populace, as the interaction of its citizens for her praise and blame evidenced.[336] Kempe was in the ascetic tradition of Bede's *Historia ecclesiastica gentis anglorum*. He had compared human life to a sparrow flying swiftly through a royal hall on a wintry day: in through one door, past the comforting fire, and out the other door into the cold again.[337] Her inner fire was purgative, not charitable; ecclesiastical, not domestic. There was once a great fire in Lynn, burning the Guild Hall of the Trinity which her father served as alderman, and spreading about the town. Its flames threatened the church, which she entered shouting and weeping, only to see sparks igniting the choir. Hollering for help, she prayed for weather to extinguish the flames. Three men approached and informed her of good news: they had snow on their clothing. Her boisterous behavior was tolerated in town that day, for hope of mercy from her prayers. She was bid by the citizens to be cheerful and give thanks.[338]

Moralists cited scripture to advise household charity.[339] Kempe emphasized how God was "homely" with her,[340] meaning "familiar, intimate". Yet she refused being homey with others, except for the celestial characters of her imagination. The word *home* developed from the Anglo-Saxon and Middle-English terms for the village with its cluster of cottages, so that its initial meaning denoted the importance of the community as the context of the family. By the fourteenth century *home* acquired its modern sense of a fixed family residence, the seat of domestic life. As with the Latin *domus*, the term still most common in medieval records, a house was both the physical structure and its affective inhabitants, the household.[341] Typical was the nuclear, conjugal family as the focus of an individual's primary loyalties.[342] A household could compose a religious community; for the laity owned statuary, relics, and even portable altars, while the nobility boasted of chapels and chaplains.[343] Kempe expended her religiosity unstably in pilgrimages: locally with her husband in tow, then about the continent, di-

---

336 See Houlbrooke, *English Family*, p. 23, without reference to Kempe.

337 Bede, *Historia ecclesiastica gentis anglorum*, 2.13.127, cited by Houlbrooke, *English Family*, p. 16, without reference to Kempe.

338 *Book of Margery Kempe* 1.67.

339 Felicity Heal, "The Idea of Hospitality in Early Modern England," *Past and Present* 102 (1984):72; see also idem, *Hospitality in Early Modern England* (Oxford: Clarendon, 1990).

340 *Book of Margery Kempe* proem, 1.17; 1.31; 1.86.

341 For the philology see Hanawalt, *Ties that Bound*, p. 31, and the *Oxford English Dictionary*, s. v.

342 Houlbrooke, *English Family*, pp. 18-20.

343 Mertes, *English Noble Household*, pp. 139-60, 24-25, 47-48.

vulging her divine dalliances or "chats" to whomever would listen, or screaming them at an affronted crowd. There was "a flame of fire about her breast, full hot and delectable,"[344] but it chilled her family.

After their vow of chastity, Kempe and her spouse separated their households to avoid gossip that they were indulging in sex covertly. Her husband barefoot and barelegged once slipped on the stairs, fell, and so broke his head that five linen plugs were needed to drain the suppurating wounds. The citizens of Lynn blamed her sorely for neglect. Christ promised Kempe the same reward as if she were at prayer in church for caring for her husband in her home. Christ bid her keep her husband as she would keep him, for her husband had allowed her to serve him by living "chaste and clean." So Kempe kept him for his lifetime, with much labor, she said, since he became senile. The cleanliness of her imaginary marriage with Christ contrasted with the foulness of her actual marriage to anonymous. His linens head to bottom were not white like hers. Kempe portrayed her ailing and aged husband by the hearth, voiding his excrement into diapers. She had so much labor in laundering them, she complained, that it kept her from "contemplation."[345] Laundry was thought ignoble; numerous books of courtesy and household management, in warning against the temptations of women, singled out as a sinner the laundress.[346] That household task was punishment, Kempe believed, for her youthful lust with her husband. Although she served him as she would have served Christ, domesticity was penance for the sin of sex that invented it. Kempe would have her reward, Christ promised, "when thou comest home into Heaven."[347]

---

344 *Book of Margery Kempe* 1.10; 1.26; passim; 1.89.

345 Ibid. 1.76. A frequently cited summary of the physical aspects of aging included "smelly excrement." Michael Goodich, "The Virtues and Vices of Old People in the Late Middle Ages," *International Journal of Aging and Human Development* 30 (1990):121, citing Halys, *Liber regialis* 2.1.24. See for general background *Aging and the Aged in Medieval Europe*, Selected Papers from the Annual Conference of the Center for Medieval Studies, Univesity of Toronto, held 25-26 February and 11-12 November 1983, ed. Michael M. Sheehan, Papers in Mediaeval Studies, 11 (Toronto: Pontifical Institute of Mediaeval Studies, 1990). For the English and bathing see Wright, *Clean and Decent*, pp. 25-40.

346 See Mertes, *English Noble Household*, p. 57.

347 *Book of Margery Kempe* 1.76; 1.64. The second brief book, composed by a different scribe, concerns her conversion of her son from lechery. See Karen A. Winstead, "The Conversion of Margery Kempe's Son," *English Language Notes* 32 (1994):9-12.

CHAPTER THREE

VILLA

In the terminology of charters at Bernard of Clairvaux's birth *villa* meant "domain", a lord's direct and unlimited control over a large landed estate with buildings and personnel. In the first two decades of the twelfth century the term suggested built-up areas that were precisely located, like the churches in a *villa*; or even a place for inhabitants in a sense closer to "village" than to "domain". By the year of his death the original meaning of *villa* as the lord's managed lands became *dominium*; a *villa* became the buildings and plots in a specific locality. *Villa* was the accepted term for a center of population: a hamlet of a few families, a castellany town of several hundred persons, or even Troyes with its population of about ten thousand—all reckoned by the number of hearths.[1] The opposite in twelfth-century charters to a *villa* as a bounded area with a settled population was a *desertum*, not as a wild untillable region, but simply as one without a permanent population. The designation was not agricultural or architectural but social.[2]

An inhabitant of such a deserted place in the fourteenth century wrote a Dominican friar about the possibility of visiting him, of seeing his convent in Tivoli, of touring Horace's classical villa.[3] He was Francesco Petrarca, who inquired of his own status, "Pilgrim or exile—which ought I to say?"[4] He was indeed an exile, not a metaphorical one like Augustine or Bernard, but a political one. His father Ser Petracco was an exiled Florentine notary, who had settled his family when Petrarch was eight in Carpentras, a town about fifteen miles from Avignon, where the papacy held court, also in exile.[5]

Exiled from Italy, where civic strife
Kept me from living what to me is life,

---

[1] Theodore Evergates, *Feudal Society in the Baillage of Troyes under the Counts of Champagne 1152-1284* (Baltimore, Md.: Johns Hopkins University Press, 1975), pp. 30-31.

[2] Constance Brittain Bouchard, *Holy Entrepreneurs: Cistercians, Knights, and Economic Exchange in Twelfth-Century Burgundy* (Ithaca, N. Y.: Cornell University Press, 1991), p. 102.

[3] Petrarch, *Epistolae familiares* 6.3.

[4] Petrarch, "Exul ab Italia"; *Petrarch at Vaucluse: Letters in Verse and Prose*, trans. Ernest Hatch Wilkins (Chicago: University of Chicago Press, 1958), p. 181.

[5] Wilkins, *Life of Petrarch* (Chicago: University of Chicago Press, 1963), p. 106. For the condition see Randolph Starn, *Contrary Commonwealth: The Theme of Exile in Medieval and Renaissance Italy* (Berkeley: University of California Press, 1982).

Regretfully, yet willingly, I came
Hither, to pleasant field and wood and stream.[6]

That place was Vaucluse, also fifteen miles from Avignon yet a country farther, he declared, from that city than east was from west.[7] "I have one great comfort in this or any other place of exile," he wrote, "for I have learned in whatsoever place I am, therewith to be content—provided only that it is not Avignon."[8] Reviving the classical antithesis of the country and the city, Petrarch reserved his contempt for that particular locale. His poetic vocation aspired to the removal of the papacy from Avignon to the see of Rome for the restoration of imperial and Italian peace.[9] The papal court, "the noble mansion of Jesus Christ, once the citadel of divine worship," had become "a den of ravening thieves," as in Bernard's metaphor for the rescue of the horrid spot the monks had renamed Clairvaux. "May almighty God rescue his House!" exclaimed Petrarch.[10]

His literature composed a symbolic landscape dominated by the poetic laurel; but he also wrote of the real landscape of his property, planted in two gardens by his own hands, and of its rustic and rugged environs at the mouth of the river Sorgue. He had visited Vaucluse in his youth and there he hoped to die, "content with modest but shady gardens and a very small house."[11] He did not die there but in his native Italy, after dedicated service in diplomatic missions, ecclesiastical charges, and humanist studies. His will instructed that his house in Vaucluse be donated to the local hospice for Christ's poor.[12]

Petrarch did not live there as indigent, although his urban friends complained of his austere conditions as a pitiable prison from which to escape.[13] Unlike the Cistercians he did not define virtue by asceticism but by moderation. It was more noble, he argued, to scoff at than to shun wealth, so that it became neither frightening nor alluring but merely indifferent. He sought a poverty toward contemplation that was not squalid and sad but honorable and tranquil.[14] Against avarice, epitomized by the papal court, he declared: "I have ground of my own—if anything on earth can be called one's own—in which I may be buried; I have a place to live in for a little while and a place to live in for a longer time; I have enough to eat and drink; I have shoes for my feet and clothes for my body; I have servants; I have a dog to keep me company and a horse to carry me; I have a

[6] Petrarch, "Exul ab Italia"; trans. Wilkins, p. 179.
[7] Petrarch, *Epistolae variae* 42.
[8] Petrarch, *Epistolae familiares* 15.3; trans. Wilkins, p. 177.
[9] Marjorie O'Rourke Boyle, *Petrarch's Genius: Pentimento and Prophecy* (Berkeley: University of California Press, 1991).
[10] Petrarch, *Liber sine nomine* 13.
[11] Epigram to *Epistolae familiares* 11.12; 11.4; 11.2; 6.3; trans. Wilkins, p. 34.
[12] Petrarch, *Testamentum* 27.
[13] Petrarch, *Epistolae metricae* 1.16.
[14] Boyle, *Petrarch's Genius*, pp. 125-26.

roof over my head and a room to sleep in; and I have places in which I may wander as I please: what Roman emperor has more?"[15] No tapestries decked the walls of his home. No couch at the top of a steep flight of stairs beckoned for sleep at night amid gleaming marble and purple hangings.[16] A marble house was superficial pleasure in comparison with his humble cottage.[17]

He counted its visible household as his faithful dog, his servants, and himself. The dog was a gift from his patron Giovanni Cardinal Colonna, an animal he praised poetically for its good qualities—not failing to mention that the mange it had contracted in the torpid city was now cleansed in the local stream and healed by the rural air. Dog guarded the house against intrusions by the peasants come to ask Petrarch legal questions about their rights, their households, and their marriages.[18] Petrarch had two servants and a very solicitous overseer, who lived in an adjoining cottage that would, he thought, benefit by a small gate. The man's wife was the sole female of the place, although Petrarch had conceived an illegitimate son by an unknown woman. He described his female servant's burned and withered countenance as an ugly face, although her just soul was quite unselfconscious about that. After toiling all day in the fields, she devoted herself to the household tasks as if she were a fresh young girl, without grumbling, whining, or impatience. She took the most scrupulous care of her husband and sons, and of Petrarch's household and its guests, with an astonishing lack of concern for herself. "And this woman of iron has for bed a bit of flooring covered with a little straw."[19]

Her coarse brown bread Petrarch himself ate; but his urban friends disdained his light supper seasoned with the daily toil and fast.[20] It was a poet's repast from Vergil's pastorals: "Apples ripe, / Soft chestnuts, and a jug of fresh-drawn milk." The main dish was hard and simple bread. There might be a stray rabbit caught by the dog, a crane sent as a gift, or the pungent flesh of a wild boar.[21] His friends absented themselves from Vaucluse, dreading the hard diet and deterred by the brambles and snows of the region. Except for tourists to the famous limpid fountain of the Sorgue, visitors were few.

'Tis much if once or twice within the year
Old friends of mine enter this Vale Enclosed:

---

[15] Petrarch, *Epistolae familiares* 16.3; trans. Wilkins, pp. 187-88. For a detail see Patrick Reuterswärd, "The Dog in the Humanist's Study," in idem, *The Visible and Invisible in Art: Essays in the History of Art* (Vienna: IRSA, 1991), pp. 207-9.

[16] Petrarch, "Exul ab Italia."

[17] Petrarch, *Epistolae familiares* 3.18.

[18] Petrarch, *Epistolae metricae* 1.6; 3.5.

[19] Petrarch, *Epistolae familiares* 13.8; trans. Wilkins, p. 120; ibid. 13.8.

[20] Ibid.; *Epistolae metricae* 1.6.

[21] Petrarch, *Epistolae familiares* 11.11; trans. Wilkins, p. 45.

Distance o'ercomes affection. But their letters
Visit me constantly, and breathe my name
In winter evenings by the glowing hearth
Or in the coolness of the summer shade:
Ever by day and night they speak of me.[22]

Petrarch's house was also frequented by the Muses, he claimed, and by his "company of secret friends" from every century and nation.

Only a corner of my house they ask;
They heed my every summons: at my call
They are ever with me, ever welcome while they stay,
Ready to go, if I wish, and to return.

These were the authors of the books he avidly collected.

So much they give: they ask but for a home.
They too have known adversity; and few
And hesitant are those that give them refuge.
The humblest shelter is to them a mansion
Where, trembling, they may linger, till the clouds
Are gone, and till the Muses rule again.[23]

The house in which Petrarch puttered in literary leisure revived a classical ideal. Illustrations of Petrarch in a study with handsome furnishings and valuable objects gave learned persons impetus to design in the recesses of their own homes a similar place. Such a private retreat, as derived from the monastic cell, had been an amenity of prominent ecclesiastics; or, as derived from the secular treasury, of eminent men for the display of their riches and curiosities. Merchants also coveted such a place. The study behind the bedchamber was to become a distinctive feature of renaissance domestic architecture. And many studies were located in the corner of a bedchamber, as paintings of the annunciation depict the Virgin Mary reading.[24]

Significant was Petrarch's inclusion of himself in the household as a companion rather than an adversary to himself.[25] Petrarch was experienced in asceticism, "the uncertain battle for the control of my two selves," carnal and spiritual, until he rejected it as discipline but not wisdom. Since humans were in transcendental movement, he elected the vertical path of poetry as more direct, more enlightened, more sublime. Petrarch countered a monk's vision of divine judgment against his literature with a poet's vision of Christ as the very source of his inspiration. He had, he believed, a genius divinely endowed and deeply within. A genius was the tutelary spirit that in Roman antiquity animated nature, residing in every peasant, plot, and

---

22 Petrarch, *Epistolae metricae* 1.6; trans. Wilkins, p. 9.

23 Ibid.; trans. Wilkins, p. 10.

24 See Peter Thornton, *The Italian Renaissance Interior: 1400-1600* (London: Weidenfeld and Nicolson, 1991), pp. 296, 298.

25 Petrarch, *Epistolae metricae* 1.6.

plough. The genius of the family, whose generative power symbolized semen, was the particular embodiment of that animism. The concept extended beyond the paterfamilias to other paternal figures such as the founders of cities and institutions, the gods, the senate and the plebs, the emperor, and the state.[26] The cult of the genius had been widespread in the Roman empire, as at Ostia in dedications to the genius of the trade guilds, of the decurions, of the colony, of the populace, and of "the place."[27]

Despite the late antique belief in such divinities, who were associated with all persons at their birth as guides of conduct, very few humans had claimed to see them. Those who did were revered as extraordinarily close to their invisible guardians. Mani, whose teachings enthralled the young Augustine, so contacted his protector that his subjective identity was fused with his celestial twin. That spirit came to him and chose him, judged him fit, and separated him from the sect in which he was raised. As for Mani, "I made him mine, as my very own." The emperor Constantine prepared for his conquests with a vision of an Apollo of youthful beauty and salvational gift. Ordinary Christians had guardian angels as "kinsfolk and friends," who were present to those who prayed. In the crisic and in the ordinary, sensibilities were fashioned by dialogue with invisible companions.[28]

A poet who transferred the language of the daimon, the genius, and the guardian to a human figure was Paulinus of Nola, considering Felix, the martyr over whose grave he was given episcopal charge. When he observed the dust sifting from the sarcophagus, Paulinus feared that an animal had disturbed the remains but he lifted the lid; and there they lay still. Although Felix was physically dead, spiritually he was vital to Paulinus. In him the bishop had not just a distant intercessor but a guardian of identity. Felix was virtually a personification of Paulinus, as if he were a layer of the self, so that the saint's feast was honored as the man's own birthday. From Christ's guardianship of Felix, to Felix's guardianship of Paulinus, extended a chain of patronage, and even friendship. Paulinus poetized that Christ had handed him to Felix, his dear friend, to be his very own. With that patronage Paulinus emerged from serving as the saint's lowly doorkeeper to acting as imperial arbiter in a disputed papal election.[29] Patronage, as always, conferred power.

Paulinus lucidly delineated between classical and Christian modes of being a poet.[30] Conversion required the renunciation of leisure, fiction, and

---

[26] Boyle, *Petrarch's Genius*, pp. 11-43, 156. For the natal Genius and the patronage of poetry see Kathryn Argetsinger, "Birthday Rituals: Friends and Patrons in Roman Poetry and Cult," *Classical Antiquity* 11 (1992):175-93.

[27] Russell Meiggs, *Roman Ostia*, 2d ed. (Oxford: Clarendon, 1973), p. 383.

[28] Peter Brown, *The Cult of the Saints: Its Rise and Function in Latin Christianity* (London: S C M, 1981), pp. 52-53.

[29] Ibid., pp. 76, 56-57, 64.

[30] Charles Witke, *Numen litterarum: The Old and the New in Latin Poetry from Constan-*

ambition for the laurel. Petrarch resolutely differed. He not only rejected a dichotomy of the sacred and the secular; he integrated them by eliminating a middle. There was no Felix for him as a patron before the deity, but rather Christ immediately indwelling. Christ was present to him as a witness of thought and action, surpassing notions of any guardian angel or intercessory saint. "There is absolutely no Christian who doubts that Christ himself is always present in the most secret recesses of the soul, examines what goes on there and sees everything as though it were openly exposed," he wrote. Yet a multitude of Christians did doubt and even disbelieve that. They projected the presence of Christ externally: to reside in heaven, in church, in scripture and sacrament; but in humans, only in privileged persons like the Virgin Mary, and that temporarily. Their religion was exteriorized, not merely in a superficiality of works, as reformers would complain, but in its very focus. Petrarch was egregiously focused within: on "Christ alive and real and always present to us." That presence he conflated with the figure of the genius as the justification and inspiration for his poetic vocation.[31]

Although Petrarch's genius was rare and elite, defended staunchly against the crowd of poetasters who would usurp its privilege,[32] he summoned all to interiority. If the entire world offers no spot of tranquillity and solace, he counseled, "enter into your own room and into yourself." That room was not a sanctuary, as in Bernard's exegesis, nor was its personal space the ambiguous bedroom of Augustine's preaching, cluttered and hazardous. It was an inviting place of varied leisure. "Keep vigil with yourself, hold converse with yourself, hold silence with yourself, walk with yourself, stand still with yourself." The prospect of self-encounter was not lonely. A person with himself was not alone; a person not with himself *was* alone, even in a crowd. Petrarch advised, "Make for yourself in the midst of your soul a place where you may hide, where you may rejoice, where you may rest undisturbed, where Christ may abide with you." The accomplishment of this construction was the task of virtue, which taught "that things external to yourself cannot be possessed; that all things that are your own are within you; that nothing that is not your own can be given you, and nothing that is your own can be taken away; that your choice of a way of life is your own."[33]

Petrarch's own choice was not basically autonomous. He was forced by the dishonesty of his father's executors to choose a career in religion, although there is no evidence that he took even minor orders.[34] Within that profession, however, he pursued poetry at odds with asceticism, even ventur-

---

tine to Gregory the Great (Leiden: E. J. Brill, 1971), pp. 42-65.

31 Boyle, *Petrarch's Genius*, pp. 27-34.

32 Ibid., p. 154.

33 Petrarch, *Epistolae familiares* 15.7; trans. Wilkins, pp. 101, 102.

34 Wilkins, "Petrarch's Ecclesiastical Career," in idem, *Studies in The Life and Works of Petrarch* (Cambridge, Mass.: Mediaeval Academy of America, 1955), pp. 3-32.

ing the assertion that poetry was contemplative. "For Rachel have I served, and not for Leah."[35] There was precedent for a spiritualization of the secular within his family. He wrote about his great-grandfather Garzo as "a man of saintly life. . . so endowed with righteousness and piety that the only thing that prevented him from being denoted as blessed was the lack of a sponsor." Petrarch's evidence for his potential beatitude, except for some pious conversation on his deathbed, was not of the sort an ecclesiastical inquiry would have recognized. Garzo's virtues were utterly secular. Although he was not literarily gifted, he had such a remarkably keen mind that "his neighbors came to consult him about household affairs, business activities, contracts, and the marriages of their children, and magistrates came to consult with him on official matters—as was the case, we are told, with the blind Appius—and what is more, men of letters came to see him or wrote to him with regard to lofty and philosophic problems, and they all marveled at the soundness of judgement and keenness of mind that appeared in his responses."[36] Solomon revived he was; but those prudential matters of household, business, contract, and marriage were not respected by the clergy as holy. Even his philosophical acuity would not have merited Garzo beatification.[37]

Sanctity among the laity was reserved for those who renounced their very secularity with its necessary domesticity. Angela of Foligno stripped naked beside a crucifix and fearfully but compulsively offered each of her bodily members to Christ. In her meditation on his passion she had so recognized her sins that she felt she had personally crucified him. She offered not to offend him with any bodily part and accused each, one by one. She was frightened of her vow, but "the fire" of meditation forced her to promise it; she could not otherwise act. Yet Angela could not feel the way of the cross because she was still living with her husband. Since her family was a great impediment to her religious devotion, she prayed for their deaths. And one by one, she said, God willed that those obstacles did die: her mother, her husband, and all of her children. "I had great solace from their deaths," she affirmed. The sentiment was as ancient as that of the ascetic Melania, who at the deaths of her husband and two sons smiled rather than wept, since she could serve God more readily for relief from their burden. It was when Angela tried to sell her choice country property, to distribute its profits to the poor, that her screaming began. The fire in her heart became so burning that if anyone spoke to her of God she screamed. "It was the best land I had,"

---

35 Boyle, *Petrarch's Genius*, pp. 41-43, 156-57, 121.

36 Petrarch, *Epistolae familiares* 6.3; trans. Wilkins, p. 31.

37 For the norms see André Vauchez, *La sainteté en occident aux derniers siècles du moyen âge: D'après les procès de canonisation et les documents hagiographiques*, Bibliothèque des Écoles françaises d'Athènes et de Rome, 241 (Rome: École française de Rome, 1981); Pierre Delooz, *Sociologie et canonisations*, Collection scientifique de la Faculté de droit de l'Université de Liège, 30 (Liège: Faculté de droit, 1969).

she explained, wondering if others were right in thinking her demonically possessed.[38] The feast of Angela of Foligno was celebrated on 4 January. As Petrarch astutely observed, a sponsor was necessary for beatification: the Franciscans established her cult.

Then there was Francesca Bussa dei Ponziani, obediently married young to a wealthy landowner in the Trastevere district of Rome. According to the process for her canonization, she preferred virginity but accepted "the marriage yoke." The first instance of her austerity was that she never drank wine. She transformed her noble house into a hospice for the poor and during a drought ladled them the best vintage from the cellar, refilling its empty vats miraculously with a murmured prayer. She disdained the dress and jewelry worthy of a woman of her estate. She wore on her bare thighs tight metal bands with spikes that punctured her flesh and she flagellated herself until blood ran. Tears in meditation on the passion inundated her like mountainous torrents. At home she had visions of devils; in church, of saints.[39]

Her notable asceticism concerned chastity. Ponziani had to be ordered by her confessor to render the marriage debt. As a child she refused to allow any male to see her naked or to touch her. As an adult she would not permit anyone even to take her hand, unless she first covered it with a cloth she carried about for that purpose. Males polluted with vice smelled fetid to her. She suffered her only experience of sexual intercourse with "violent stupor, out of her mind, and loathing." Upon that consummation of her marriage, she vomited hugely until she vomited blood. Her husband "liberated" her from the duty of sex and attended to mundane affairs, while she became absorbed in prayer; they slept separately. Once after Mass in adoring the Eucharist, Ponziani had a vision of Mary's parturition of Jesus and she worshiped the Son as a bridegroom issuing from his chamber. Next to him was a sort of fount emanating a liquid not water, from which the mother of God received a little and placed it into the side of Ponziani's spirit. In a high voice Ponziani cried, "I am healed."[40] Her feast was celebrated on 9 March. She founded a female community of Benedictine oblates of the Olivetan branch, living in a convent in Tor de'Specchi and performing charity. At the process of canonization the women testified to her sanctity.

Ponziani had let someone touch her, if only in her imagination, if only the most holy Mother placing the classical female substance of liquid into her spirit. The Madonna placed it asexually into her side, in imitation of

---

[38] Angela of Foligno, *Librum de vere fidelium experientia* 11, 12, 21. Cited also in Peter Dronke, *Women Writers of the Middle Ages: A Critical Study of Texts from Perpetua (†203) to Marguerite Porete (†1310)* (Cambridge: Cambridge University Press, 1984), pp. 215-16. For the prototype Melania, the elder, see Jerome, *Epistolae* 39.5.

[39] *I processi inediti per Francesca Bussa dei Ponziani (Santa Francesca Romana) 1440-1453* 2, 4, 5, 6, 7-8, 12, 23-26, 30-34.

[40] Ibid. 15, 6.

the pious parturition of Jesus from her own side. Mary was, if not an aqueduct, ever a conveyor of fluid from the fount. Yet more of the laity in meditating on the gospel were discovering the integrity of their state as Christian. Ascetic and charismatic practices were prevalent and popular in late medieval society, indicators of an immature religiosity that contradictorily repudiated sensuality or wallowed in sensationalism. The more significant phenomenon was that so many persons rejected those options, certainly in their extreme versions. Margery Kempe was ridiculed as annoying, embarrassing, or outrageous; except in her own imagination, by certain celibates, and, ironically, by the husband she rejected. Her very appearance in all white clothing aroused suspicion in the mayor of Leicester that she was in town to steal away the wives.[41] The struggle toward religious maturity was socially complex. It was not the case that women versus men established a respect for the domestic, nor that the laity versus the clergy elevated the secular to the sacral.

Leon Battista Alberti was not a family man, head of household, but he wrote appreciatively on kinship in *Il libro della famiglia.* He was a humanist of very catholic tastes, producing volumes in prose and poetry, Latin and vernacular, on law, codes, horses, hagiography, romance, history, and surveying. He compiled the first Italian dictionary and he composed a mock eulogy of his dog as a paragon of learning and virtue. Alberti was revolutionary for his science of artistic perspective, in which the two-dimensional plane of a picture became treated as if it were a window in which a three-dimensional scene appeared. His important architectural treatise was prompted by Giovanni Francesco Poggio Bracciolini's discovery in the monastery of St. Gall of Vitruvius's work.[42] Poggio also discovered in the monastery of Monte Cassino a twelfth-century manuscript of Frontinus's treatise on aqueducts.[43] Finds of classical texts complemented the appreciation of classical buildings. Literature and architecture collaborated to make history in Petrarch's peripatetic epistle amid the Roman arts and ruins.[44] History was

---

41 *The Book of Margery Kempe* 1.48; and for interrogations and defamation 1.51; 1.54; 1.58; 1.61; 1.62; 1.67; 1.83; 1.86; passim. For the significance of her dress see Mary C. Erler, "Margery Kempe's White Clothes," *Medium Aevum* 62 (1993):78-83; for dissent and Lollardy, Ruth Shklar, "Cobham's Daughter: The Book of Margery Kempe and the Power of Heterodox Thinking," *Modern Language Quarterly* 56 (1995):277-304.

42 For a survey see Joan Gadol, *Leon Battista Alberti: Universal Man of the Early Renaissance* (Chicago: University of Chicago Press, 1969), pp. 4-10; for the manuscript, p. 98; and for the science of perspective, pp. 21-54. For a biography see Girolamo Mancini, *Vita di Leon Battista Alberti*, 2d ed. (Rome: Bardi, 1967). See also John Oppel, "Alberti on the Social Position of the Intellectual," *Journal of Medieval and Renaissance Studies* 19 (1989):123-58; Franklin Toker, "Alberti's Ideal Architect: Renaissance or Gothic?" in *Renaissance Studies in Honor of Craig Hugh Smyth*, ed. Andrew Morragh et al., 2 vols. (Florence: Villa I Tatti, 1985), 2:667-74. For the influence of Vitrivius on domestic architecture see Thornton, *Italian Renaissance Interior*, p. 338.

43 Thomas Ashby, *The Aqueducts of Ancient Rome* (Oxford: Clarendon, 1935), p. 27.

44 Petrarch, *Epistolae familiares* 6.2. See Giuseppe Mazzotta, "Antiquity and the New

challenging philosophy for the hegemony among the disciplines. The revival of classical culture rendered Ostia, the place of Augustine's contemplation, a valuable hunting ground for the new connoisseur, as men of wealth and knowledge collected and preserved its inscriptions. Poggio visited the ruins; so did Cosimo di Medici, although with disappointment in finding in the Capitolium no further inscriptions. The catalogue of Lorenzo the Magnificent's antiques included artifacts from Ostia, and the site was methodically exploited for Roman buildings.[45] After the cessation of the aqueducts, their first commentator was Flavio Biondo describing a fifteenth-century expedition of Pope Pius II and his court to the summit of Mount Affliano. Descending on the short but steep western flank, they noted aqueducts in Valle d'Empiglione and along Via di Carciano. The pope commented on the expenditure of the massive remains and expressed interest in their repair. At the end of the sixteenth century under Sixtus V the Aqua Felice did transport to Rome the springs of Aqua Alexandriana, so that once again the populace could reside on the hills.[46] The aqueducts in renaissance mentality did not occasion Marian preaching but civic practicality.

Architecture was Alberti's fame, but his last word was *De iciarchia*, on the social responsibilities of the head of household. His occupation with the family was inspired by a revival of a classical morality emphasizing civic responsibility, but it was also prompted by his own circumstances. He was born in 1404 in Genoa as the second natural son of Lorenzo Alberti, an exiled Florentine banker, and Bianca di Carlo Fieschi, a widow of the urban patriciate. He had an elder brother Carlo and he acquired as a boy a Florentine stepmother. His father recognized both of his illegitimate sons; he educated Leon Battista in a humanist gymnasium at Padua, then at the university of Bologna where he earned a doctorate in canon law. At the death of their father, then of their guardian, the Alberti brothers were deprived of their inheritance by certain kin. Their malice was pilloried in *Il libro della famiglia* with the considerable literary skills Alberti had acquired and published. He was then in the service of the head of the papal chancery in Rome, which secretarial post he maintained for much of his lifetime. Alberti took holy orders by an annulment of his illegitimacy and he held as

---

Arts in Petrarch," *Romanic Review* 79 (1988):27-32; Thomas M. Greene, *The Light in Troy: Imitation and Discovery in Renaissance Poetry* (New Haven, Conn.: Yale University Press, 1982), pp. 88-93, and on his peripatetics, "Petrarch *Viator*," in idem, *The Vulnerable Text: Essays on Renaissance Literature* (New York: Columbia University Press, 1986), pp. 18-45, rpt. from *Yearbook of English Studies* 12 (1982):35-57; Angelo Mazzocco, "Petrarca, Poggio, and Biondo: Humanism's Foremost Interpreters of Roman Ruins," in *Francis Petrarch, Six Centuries Later: A Symposium*, ed. Aldo Scaglione (Chapel Hill: Department of Romance Languages, University of North Carolina; Chicago: Newberry Library, 1975), pp. 353-63; Roberto Weiss, *The Renaissance Discovery of Classical Antiquity* (Oxford: Basil Blackwell, 1969), pp. 31-35.

[45] Meiggs, *Roman Ostia*, p. 103.

[46] Ashby, *Aqueducts of Ancient Rome*, p. 1.

benefices the priory of Gangalandi in the diocese of Florence and the rectory of Borgo San Lorenzo in Mugello.[47] But his personal commitment was civic not clerical.

His book on the family was not a formal philosophical treatise but a vernacular dialogue in classical fashion,[48] "just a domestic talk among ourselves" on the topic of fortune and virtue. Extolling nobility of soul, it promoted a concatenation of the will: to power, to ability, to achievement. "I have undertaken," Alberti stated, "to investigate with all seriousness and diligence what might be the wisdom, applicable to the conduct and education of fathers and of the whole family, by which a family may rise at last to supreme happiness." Appealing in its varied arguments to classical authors and family elders, it intended to "seek the well-being, increase the honor, magnify the fame of our house." The dialogue was situated in Padua in the house of his father, who was quite ill. It was not Christ who appeared at his bedside, however, but his family, "good and faithful kinsmen." Instability was defined not monastically as wandering but morally as wickedness, while the interlocutors debated the means to the stability of virtue. The household topics were traditional: the medical and ethical debate about the milk of the mother versus that of the nurse. So were the civic topics traditional: big fish were still devouring little fish. The large spiny oyster opened its shell to a quantity of small fish, then with the stimulation of the shrimp closed the walls to consume its prey.[49] So did Florentines imitate nature.

Yet although nature conserved secret forces, like milk and mouths as productive of hate and love, it also incorporated in creatures manifest signs of character. The head of household was to observe even in its children the indications of sociability. He was to imitate the architect who intends to dig a well or fountain, and so locates a clean and rapid stream, then examines the ground for tender shoots and pliable grasses as signs of moisture.

---

47 Gadol, *Leon Battista Alberti*, pp. 3-6.

48 See David Marsh, *The Quattrocento Dialogue: Classical Tradition and Humanist Innovation*, Harvard Studies in Comparative Literature, 35 (Cambridge, Mass.: Harvard University Press, 1980), pp. 78-99. See also Angelo Cicchetti and Raul Mordenti, *Il libri de famiglia in Italia: Filologia e storiografia letteraria* (Rome: Di Storia e letteratura, 1985-), 1.

49 Alberti, *Il libro della famiglia* 2, p. 84; *The Family in Renaissance Florence*, trans. Renée Neu Watkins (Columbia: University of South Carolina Press, 1969), p. 93. Prol., pp. 7, 10 trans. p. 30; pp. 10-11, 12 trans. p. 32; 1, pp. 13, 14 trans. p. 34; 1, pp. 66, 34-38; 4, p. 268. The symbiotic relationship of the shell and the shrimp was applied to criticize male dominance of women by Moderata Fonte in *Il merito delle donne*, p. 82, cited by Patricia H. Labalme, "Venetian Women on Women: Three Early Modern Feminists," *Archivio Veneto* 117 (1981):89. See for nursing Christiane Klapisch-Zuber, "Blood Parents and Milk Parents: Wet Nursing in Florence, 1300-1530," in idem, *Women, Family, and Ritual in Renaissance Florence*, trans. Lydia Cochrane (Chicago: University of Chicago Press, 1985), pp. 132-64; J. B. Ross, "The Middle-Class Child in Urban Italy, Fourteenth to Early Sixteenth Century," in *The History of Childhood*, ed. Lloyd De Mause (London: Psychoanalytic Press, 1976), pp. 183-228.

Structure was established on clues. Building suited conditions; so did a family. Or the father was like an industrious spider who resided at the center of his web, alert to any tension on its finest and furthest filaments. His proper place was at the hearth, enjoying the satisfaction of being the paterfamilias, loved and revered in the midst of all. "I would want all my family to live under one roof, to warm themselves at one hearth, and to seat themselves at one table," declared the conversant Giannozzo.[50] That solidarity of the extended family was an ideal rarely realized. The average size of a Florentine household in Alberti's lifetime was only 3.8 persons, in Tuscany 4.4 persons.[51] Yet Alberti considered a central hearth not only sociable but economical. If the weather was bitter cold and many logs burned on the hearth, it would be less warming if each person took a portion of the fire to his own spot: the father with his share in one room, the boys with theirs in another nook. The fire was sufficient burning on the hearth unbroken but insufficient broken.[52]

A veiled saying in his *Intercenales*, or conversational tidbits, glossed a distinct moral. "Don't place an entire bundle in the fire" advised one not to risk an entire fortune on a single venture.[53] Fire could conventionally flame as passion or classically burn as love, divinely endowed to the human heart and inescapable by it. Fire could arbitrate life.[54] Alberti also rekindled the Roman civic hearth in a suppertime moral for its descendants. While the vestal virgins tended its flame, the stalk of a hardy plant sprouted from the hearth and grew a cubit high, shooting large speckled leaves in all directions. Some of the virgins considered uprooting the wonder, others consulted augurs; the populace was awed and frightened. The plant began to cover the fire, smothering the flames with its enormous growth. If its leaves were picked, it only produced more, soon overwhelming and entangling the vestal Reason. The vestal Truth stabbed the plant with a sacrificial knife, but it resisted wounding. Janus arrived *deus ex machina* to save the situation by ordering Truth to untangle Reason from the leafy coils and to seize the trunk of the plant near the flame and pull hard. The monster collapsed. Despite its size and strength, it had no roots, tendrils, or runners. When taken outside it vanished in the sunlight. The plant was Suspicion.[55]

Although Alberti so associated the hearth with religion, that was a classical tale for renaissance citizens. Fire was not in good hands with the

---

50 Alberti, *Libro della famiglia* 1, pp. 44-45; 3, pp. 215-16, 191 trans. Watkins p. 185.

51 David Herlihy, *Medieval Households* (Cambridge, Mass.: Harvard University Press, 1985), pp. 134-35.

52 Alberti, *Libro della famiglia* 3, p. 191.

53 For lack of a complete edition of Alberti's *Intercenales* reference is to *Dinner Pieces*, trans. Marsh, Medieval and Renaissance Texts and Studies, 45 (Binghamton, N. Y.: Medieval & Renaissance Texts & Studies with the Renaissance Society of America, 1987), p. 156.

54 Alberti, *Libro della famiglia* 1, pp. 35-36, 48; 2, pp. 91, 98; 1, p. 40.

55 Alberti, *Intercenales*, trans. Marsh, pp. 62-64.

Christian clergy, he thought. Alberti criticized them severely as vicious men[56] of "much leisure and little character." From his experience as a secretary at the papal chancery, he exposed in *Il libro della famiglia* the prime ecclesiastical household as exploding with strife and intrigue: with prelates demanding obsequious gestures of near adoration, and clergy vying in concupiscence and criminality. Their flames opposed the virtuous domestic hearth. "These priests," he wrote, "are like a lantern, when you put it on the ground it gives light to all, and, when you lift it high, the higher it goes, the more it casts useless shadows." The religion of the virtuous Alberti family of his dialogue was theistic. Humans were created to please, praise, thank, fear, honor, and reward God by good works.[57] Prayer was not devotional but propitiatory. As in his tidbit "Religio," worship at the sacrifice in the temple hoped for the favor of the gods.[58] In the household a citizen prayed with full piety as the good husband told Socrates to ask: that his bride would be fertile and that peace and honor would always abide in the house.[59]

A wife of irreproachable character was a special favor from God, he wrote; a husband should always pray that God keep her faithful, tranquil, and amiable. In a domestic scene Giannozzo, after traditional instructions to his bride on household management, escorted her to their locked room where in privacy they knelt and prayed.[60] In the *Ricordi* for another family Giovanni di Pagolo di Bartolomeo Morelli related how he prayed alone in his bedroom before a triptych for the repose of his son's soul. Such propitiatory ritual was rarely recorded in renaissance Florence, although there were recommendations for the incorporation into homes of altars, paintings, images, and candles. That severe friar Girolamo Savonarola required the separation of the sexes during prayer and the avoidance of the bedroom as polluted.[61] The Alberti couple flaunted such asceticism by praying together in their bedroom. Solitude could be the spouse of self-will, Giannozzo argued, and in talking to oneself a wife might be conversing with a bad woman. The couple prayed for the power to use well the possessions they had just reviewed. They prayed for the grace to live in peace and harmony for full years, with many male children. The husband requested wealth, friendship,

---

56 Ibid., pp. 19, 62, 75-76, and see also pp. 50-51.

57 Alberti, *Libro della famiglia* 4, pp. 281-83, trans. Watkins, p. 264; 2, pp. 132-33. For architecture and the papacy see Carroll William Westfall, *In This Most Perfect Paradise: Alberti, Nicholas V, and the Invention of Conscious Urban Planning* (University Park: Pennsylvania State University Press, 1974).

58 *Intercenales*, trans. Marsh, p. 19.

59 Alberti, *Libro della famiglia* 2, pp. 115-16.

60 Ibid. 2, p. 116; 3, p. 223.

61 Richard C. Trexler, *Public Life in Renaissance Florence* (New York: Academic, 1980), p. 160. For Morelli's experience, although erroneously identified as "contemplative procedure," see pp. 174-80; see also George W. McClure, *Sorrow and Consolation in Italian Humanism* (Princeton: Princeton University Press, 1991), pp. 113-14.

honor; and for his wife, integrity, purity, and the character to be perfect mistress of the household. He exhorted striving with all their joint will and ability to gain by their actions their prayers.[62]

In then lecturing his wife to appear respectable against any dishonor to God, himself, their children, and (last) herself, Giannozzo was clear that respectability meant chastity. Developing the traditional cosmetic topic of modesty, he taught the lesson of a lovely statue set gleaming in the center of an altar in their bedroom.[63] Statues in bedrooms were common since Roman antiquity, as that of Amor and Psyche in a house in Ostia.[64] Nothing was more fashionable in quattrocento Florence than an image of the Madonna for private devotion in the bedchamber.[65] Yet Giannozzo, not identifying the statue, only describing its composition of silver with head and hands of ivory, converted its artistic value to a domestic moral. Suppose, he suggested to his nameless wife, she were to smear its face each morning with chalk and calcium and ointments to whiten and color it; then, after the dust of the day had dirtied it, to wash it each evening. If she proposed to sell it, how much would it be worth? Would its value appreciate or depreciate? Giannozzo explained that its excellence by artisan skill determined its worth, so that the cost of the labor and materials to decorate it was a loss. The image would be further spoiled by scrubbing its ivory finish, roughening and discoloring it. Cosmetics were thus moralized as a ruinous application to the natural beauty of a woman's skin. Religious devotion became the premise for domestic duty. Giannozzo's wife was to be no contemplative, no idler with her elbows on a windowsill (like Monica), while her needlework slackened in her lap. She was to inspect the house from top to bottom. "Always keep busy," he ordered her.[66]

The Albertis were "practical householders"; yet their piety introduced momentous theological concepts. The practical Giannozzo mentioned his religious habit of leaving home each midmorning for the church, to praise God and adore the sacrament. Adovardo commended his excellent habit, for a man who would win the friendship and favor of his fellows should always

---

[62] Alberti, *Libro della famiglia* 1, pp. 47-48; 3, p. 223.

[63] Ibid., pp. 223-24.

[64] Gustav Hermansen, *Ostia: Aspects of Roman City Life* (Calgary: University of Alberta Press, 1981), p. 23; Raissa Calza and Ernest Nash, *Ostia* (Florence: Sansoni, n. d.), pl. 44.

[65] Ronald G. Kecks, *Madonna und Kind: Das häusliche Andachtsbild im Florence des 15. Jahrhunderts*, Frankfurter Forschungen zur Kunst, 15 (Berlin: Gebr. Mann, 1988); and for their renaissance location in bedrooms, see Thornton, *Italian Renaissance Interior*, p. 268.

[66] Alberti, *Libro della famiglia* 3, pp. 225-26; p. 235, trans. Watkins, p. 223. For needlework at home and for the home see Thornton, *Italian Renaissance Interior*, pp. 77-84. For windows as dangerous to chastity see the medieval examples of *Ancrene Riwle* 2; Philippe de Navarre, *Quatre âges de l'homme* 1.27; and for renaissance examples, Ruth Kelso, *Doctrine for the Lady of the Renaissance*, 2d ed. (Urbana: University of Illinois Press, 1978), p. 182; Lynne Lawner, *Lives of the Courtesans: Portraits of the Renaissance* (New York: Rizzoli, 1987), pp. 10, 19, passim.

seek first the favor of God. Giannozzo elaborated that it was proper to render thanks to God for his merciful gifts. He said that he also prayed for tranquillity and enlightenment in heart and mind, for continued enjoyment of health, for life, prosperity, a fine family, an honorable estate, good reputation, and even renown. Yet on that particular morning he had been detained from church by the familial dialogue. Lionardo interjected: "Remember, Giannozzo, that this was an act of parental piety which you performed here, and no less pleasing to God than your presence at the sacrifice would be. What you have been teaching us also is good and is sacred." Indeed, he affirmed, it was "the noblest of subjects. . . and the most practical."[67] The liturgy and the household were not quite antithetical in renaissance experience. A prayer in the canon of the Mass commemorated the living: blood relations and affines, household members and companions, and friends.[68] Alberti's elevation of home economics to the pinnacle of nobility and practicality was compatible with a classical piety that established the household as the basis of the state. It was also allowable in some Christian opinion to consider domestic matters "good"; but their designation as "sacred" was novel or rare. The equation of a family discussion about household management with worship at holy Mass was a stunning upset of the ascetic values by which the clergy ordered society in subordination of the laity. And it came from the pen of a priest, who was not even a pastor.

Although the dialogue quoted not a single verse of scripture among its copious classical references, it did declare a Christian revelation. "The man who does not love his family does not know how to love."[69] That was Lionardo fictionally speaking in Leon Battista Alberti's own voice. He echoed the scriptural admonition, "He who does not love his brother whom he has seen, cannot love God whom he has not seen" (1 John 4:20). Alberti defined the origin of the family as love. It was then bonded by piety and charity and by a certain duty required by nature toward one's own.[70] At issue was the analogy of the divine from the human, an analogy that the abnegation of family by asceticism ruptured. Alberti's aesthetics grounded his piety. The idea of beauty in painting and the law of congruity in architecture were unascetic. They embraced the sensible and the intelligible, the eye and the mind. Architecture enfolded the transcendent structures of the cosmos through the function of buildings, integrating them with the human moral sphere.[71] Alberti could well appreciate a home.

---

[67] Alberti, *Libro della famiglia* 3, p. 250; trans. Watkins, p. 235; ibid. 3, pp. 243-44; trans. Watkins, p. 230.

[68] See John Bossy, "The Mass as a Social Institution, 1200-1700," *Past and Present* 100 (1983):38-39.

[69] Alberti, *Libro della famiglia* 3, p. 209; trans. Watkins, p. 201.

[70] Alberti, *De ichiarchia* 3, p. 266.

[71] See David Kipp, "Alberti's 'Hidden' Theory of Visual Art," *British Journal of Aesthetics* 24 (1984):232-33, 237, without reference to piety.

It was the renaissance Italians who significantly contributed to civilization by establishing a standard of domestic comfort foundational for modern living. Good domestic architecture incorporated comfort, with considerable ingenuity exerted in securing the ultimate comfort for those who could afford its expense: privacy. In planning the distribution of rooms the renaissance architect considered the requirements of the client, as in Roman design, and perhaps splendor, but also comfort. As Alberti directed, the plan should serve "for the greatest convenience of the inhabitants." In quite the reverse of the Roman house, however, which had centered on the public atrium, the renaissance house centered on the private bedchamber. By day it was relatively private, by night, absolutely so. Yet the shutting of its doors was considered very bad manners, for the same implication of lust it had in the Roman empire. The bedroom could still be used as a reception room for honored guests, or as a drawing room for close friends, or as a reception room on special occasions such as the birth of a child. But the demand for privacy, so central to renaissance domestic architecture, proliferated rooms in the inner reaches of the great houses. There were various small rooms behind the bedchambers for servants, storage, and most important, study. The tendency was to locate the more private spaces the furthest from the main entrance to the house. Public functions transpired in the sala, a generous room for entertaining and dining and for more mundane activities, such as warming by the fire, observing passersby out the window, or—for women—taking advantage of sunlight or firelight for needlework. The rationalization of the ground plan from public to private space was introduced in the mid-fifteenth century in several buildings of progressive character. Alberti defined a linear progression into privacy from the kitchen and offices near the main entrance, to the master's lodgings, to the women's quarters at the rear, where only the nearest of kin could set foot. The principal contribution of renaissance architecture to indoor civilization was the invention of the apartment, a group of rooms designed for an individual.[72]

Alberti designed an important palazzo for the Rucellai family. A renaissance house was a framework for social life and ceremony, but it also afforded privacy by regulating architecturally the access inward by rank and honor. In the palazzo Rucellai the principal bedchamber had an antechamber, and there was a study halfway up the stairs.[73] The Rucellai family originated in the thirteenth century as active against magnates and from that popular movement they composed the oligarchy of the fifteenth century. Faithfully they accommodated the Medici regimes, and so did not suffer exile or dispersal; its most wealthy and extended households were its most political. The Rucellai combined in Florentine manner financial investment in land

---

[72] Thornton, *Italian Renaissance Interior*, pp. 13, 15, 284; 338 citing Alberti, *De architectura* 5.2; 285, 314, 290, 296, 294, 285, 301, 300.

[73] Thornton, *Italian Renaissance Interior*, pp. 300, 294, 296-98.

with mercantile and banking activities. Theirs was a large, fertile family with disparities of wealth and prestige. They lived in their ancestral district of Lion Rosso in the quarter of S. Maria Novella, clustered about their parish church of S. Pancrazio. The Rucellai were among its major benefactors and, because of the formal meetings there of the gonfalone, they were the most successful house in the scrutinies of the district. Giovanni Rucellai, who commissioned Alberti for his home and his tomb, composed *Zibaldone quaresimale* as a familial chronicle. He styled it a "mixed salad" to impart to his sons a useful knowledge of traditions and facts in a domestic perspective. One of the most extensive and accurate genealogies of Florentine lineage, it provided a short general history of Rucellai unity in politics and ritual; and also instructions on the art of living, including relations with kin. Its conversational tone echoed oral tradition; the text was continued to the end of the sixteenth century by descendents. Although Giovanni concentrated on his own domestic group, it was located within the lineage, since household and lineage in renaissance Florence were complementary rather than exclusive.[74]

A town house was usually the most expensive asset of a household, worth several hundred florins, and only in need did a Rucellai rent out his home temporarily. A house was strongly felt as the mainstay and refuge of the family, valuable not only because it was expensive but also because it was the symbol of the unity of a particular household. The houses of a Florentine family were physically close, typically grouped around a tower, piazza, or loggia. The Rucellai lived compactly along the Via della Vigna Nuova or adjoining streets, where the family had lived since the youth of Dante and where Giovanni would be buried. Their houses were centered on small piazzas in front of S. Pancrazio and the palazzo Giovanni would construct, while their villas were grouped in the Campi and Brozzi districts. In a cooperative venture the family erected a loggia for formal ceremonies such as weddings and for informal talk, an edifice that contributed to its reputation as a wealthy and powerful house.[75]

Patronage of the arts, especially architecture and sculpture, focused family pride of lineage in commemorating and proclaiming its piety, wealth, and

[74] Francis William Kent, *Household and Lineage in Renaissance Florence: The Family Life of the Capponi, Ginori, and Rucellai* (Princeton: Princeton University Press, 1977), pp. 16, 89-91, 26-27, 179-81, 114, 274, 273-78, 13-14. See also D. V. Kent and idem, *Neighbours and Neighbourhood in Renaissance Florence: The District of the Red Lion in the Fifteenth Century*, Villa I Tatti, the Harvard Center for Italian Renaissance Studies, 6 (Locust Valley, N. Y.: J. J. Augustin, 1982). For commentary on the text see Alessandro Perosso, "Lo Zibaldone di Giovanni Rucellai," in F. W. Kent et al., *Giovanni Rucellai ed il suo Zibaldone*, Vol. 2: *A Florentine Patrician and His Palace*, Studies of the Warburg Institute, 24-2 (London: University of London, 1981), pp. 97-152.

[75] Kent, *Household and Lineage*, pp. 76-77, 227, 232, 130, 234-36, 242-44. See also idem, "The Rucellai Family and its Loggia," *Journal of the Warburg and Courtauld Institutes* 35 (1972):397-401.

achievement. The Rucellai patronized ecclesiastical building, such as the façade for S. Maria Novella, which incorporated their coat of arms. Yet the commissioning of secular edifices was also rendered virtuous by Alberti and others who justified building a fine portico as an achievement of honor. Alberti was the architect for Giovanni Rucellai, who near his death wrote that his buildings reflected the honor of God and Florence and the memory of himself. Patronage expressed identity in an intense individualism within a domestic context. Construction was self-assertion yet familial devotion: Giovanni requested the badge of the house of Rucellai around his funereal bed.[76] In renaissance Florence the boom in building surpassed that of any medieval European city. Although the cathedral was impressive, and churches, monasteries, hospitals, convents, and guilds multiplied, its major sector was private construction, with perhaps a hundred palaces erected in the fifteenth century. Those palaces, which were large private town houses, coincided with stylistic innovation to elevate domestic architecture to fine art.[77]

Although most structures were anonymous, they represented a change in habits of investment. The artisan class most increased between the middle of the fourteenth and sixteenth centuries in construction and woodworking. There was a concentration of households in the same vicinity to confer identity, with its structures representing the public status of collective families and their involvement in communal affairs. Enlarged residential space identified the private home aesthetically. Building on a grand scale publicly displayed private status, and expenditure was justified on moral grounds. Alberti argued that the grandeur of buildings should be adapted to the status of owners and that it conferred a reputation for power and wisdom. Giovanni Rucellai was more satisfied in his soul for having spent money than having owned it. Palaces were not artistic creations but monuments to their patrons; the name of the architect was still scarcely mentioned. Giovanni insisted that his palace was to remain in the family, never alienated, or even rented. If the family were extinguished, the palace was to pass to the Florentine commune as a residence for an ambassador or foreign prince.[78]

Florence was among the first cities where individual private residences became a distinctive feature of the urban scene. The most original was Alberti's design for Giovanni Rucellai, although it was without imitators. As

---

[76] Kent, *Household and Lineage*, pp. 278-79, 100-4, 267-70, 280-88. Richard A. Goldwaithe, "The Florentine Palace as Domestic Architecture," *American Historical Review* 77 (1972):980-81, 989. See also F. W. Kent, "The Making of a Renaissance Patron of the Arts," in *Patrician and Palace*, pp. 7-95.

[77] Goldwaithe, "Florentine Palace," pp. 977-78. See also idem, "The Economy of Renaissance Italy: The Preconditions for Luxury Consumption," *I Tatti Studies: Essays in the Renaissance* 2 (1987):15-39.

[78] Goldwaithe, "Florentine Palace," pp. 978, 984-85, 989-91, citing Alberti, *De architectura* 9.1.

a public monument the façade of a palace manifested the civic implications of a morality that was individualistic. The interior with its living quarters expressed the altered social conditions beneath that morality: familial withdrawal into a private sphere. So excluded was the city from the palace that to look out a window a person had to climb up steps in the bays and peer over the sills—so high were the windows placed. Yet, although the interior was for the enjoyment of the family, only a small area was designed for residential use. A quarter or third was open as a courtyard, with arcades on the ground level and open loggia on the uppermost level, whose elevation could rival a six-or seven-story modern office building. There were only about a dozen rooms, principally on the middle floor. Documentation is scant on arrangements for living and relations of household, even in Alberti's book on the family; but the demand for possessions to furnish the palace fed the Florentine artistic tradition.[79] An inventory by Giovanni Rucellai included paintings by Domenico Veneziano, Filippo Lippi, Andrea del Castagno, and Paolo Ucello; drawing or design by Antonio Pollaiuolo, sculpture by Andrea del Verocchio, goldwork by Tommaso Finiguerra, inlaid woodwork by Giuliano da Maiano, and wood carving by Disiderio da Settignano and Giovanni di Bertino.[80]

The Rucellai palazzo was erected on the site of eight smaller dwellings, most of them ancestral property, but not easily or cheaply acquired. They included Giovanni's own house, which he had once shared with his three brothers. He was the sole builder of a renaissance palazzo in the lineage, although not from the desire to segregate himself from the family. He was a notable leader and benefactor and he built his home in the center of the traditional district. It housed an extended family soon after completion. Giovanni's desire was to accrue honor to himself and his posterity by a magnificent liberality and to provide for the large patrilineal family he idealized in his *Zibaldone quaresimale*.[81] Alberti applied the classical orders to the façade—an innovation, since columnar architecture had not been adapted in antiquity to private dwellings. He civilized the harsher genre of the Florentine fortress, like the Strozzi palace, by smoothing its rugged rustication

[79] Goldwaithe, "Florentine Palace," 996, 997, 104-6, 1108. The palace as the residence of a single conjugal family, pp. 997, 1003, has been corrected by Kent, *Household and Lineage*, whose research on the Rucellai is followed here. See also Anthony Molho, "Visions of the Florentine Family in the Renaissance," *Journal of Modern History* 50 (1978):304-11. For the dowry fund as a source for the patterns of intermarriage in the Florentine ruling class see idem, *Marriage Alliance in Late Medieval Florence*, Harvard Historical Studies, 114 (Cambridge, Mass.: Harvard University Press, 1994).

[80] Giovanni Rucellai, *Zibaldone*, pp. 23-24, cited by Thornton, *Italian Renaissance Interior*, p. 342. For paintings for the home see John Kent Lydecker, "Il patriziato fiorentino e la committenza artistica per la casa," in *I ceti dirigenti nella Toscana del quattrocento*, Atti del Ve VI convegno, Firenze, 10-11 diciembre, 1982, 2-3 diciembre, 1983 (Florence: Francesco Papafava, 1987), pp. 209-21.

[81] Kent, *Household and Lineage*, pp. 131, 228-29, 52, 37.

with flat masonry planes with bevelled edges. The architect treated the façade as a classical harmony of proportions, with orders compositional, rather than structural, in purpose. There were Doric pilasters on the ground floor, Ionic on the first, and Corinthian on the upper. The façade was divided into seven bays, its stories demarcated by entablatures with Rucellai emblems in their frieze. Congruity of element and form rendered it Alberti's most graceful architecture.[82]

In his dialogue on the family Giannozzo desired to buy a house, airy, spacious, and suitable. It would be a house in a good neighborhood on a well-known street, where he could settle among honorable citizens for the companionship of husband and wife. The entire household would dwell under one roof around its hearth. The house would be a thrifty purchase, and Giannozzo would endeavor to provide it from his own estates, rather than by purchases from the markets. He would not rent acreage to farm, but buy his own land with his own money and lovingly manage and cultivate it for himself and his posterity. He would want contiguous plots yielding different products: the Mediterranean triad of grain, wine, and oil; but also straw and wood. Suitable estates abounded in Florence, well situated for pure air, pleasing terrain, a beautiful view in all directions, temperate climate, good water—all aspects healthful and clean. The Alberti family possessed such estates gloriously, castles rather than villas.[83]

Giannozzo considered the ideal property to be so self-sufficient that only a quarter peck of salt needed to be purchased to feed the family for a year. A coherent arrangement would ease the inspection of the land and the supervision of the peasants, a wicked lot bent on cheating their masters. Yet in agriculture even adversity was moral: dealing with peasant villainy taught toleration of fellow citizens. Giannozzo would locate his property to avoid flooding by river or rain and plundering by bandits. Good air was as important as good soil for delicious fruits and healthy bodies. He preferred an estate near the city, for the easy transport of its crops to the house and for the pleasure of a morning stroll among its fig trees. He would attempt to grow every delectable and exotic fruit, arranged personally in orderly rows for admiration and practicality. The history of each fruit would be learned to recount it to friends; and, should their crop fail, the trees could be pruned for

---

82 Gadol, *Leon Battista Alberti*, pp. 126-28. Rucellai palace, ca. 1450-70, Florence. Reproduced p. 127 pl. 37; Spiro Kostoff, *A History of Arhcitecture: Settings and Rituals* (Oxford: Oxford University Press, 1985), p. 409 fig. 17.9. For the best photographs of Alberti's work see Franco Borsi, *Leon Battista Alberti* (Milan: Electa, 1977). See also Robert Tavernor, "Giovanni Rucellai e il suo complesso architettonico in Firenze," in *Leon Battista Alberti*, ed. Joseph Rykwert and Anne Engel (Milan: Olivetti/Electa, 1994), pp. 368-77, with the façade reproduced p. 369 pl. 1; Howard Saalman, "Giovanni Rucellai ed il suo Zibaldone, a Florentine Patrician and his Palace," *Journal of the Society of Architectural Historians* 47 (1988):82-90; Brenda Preyer, "The Rucellai Palace," in *Patrician and Palace*, pp. 153-225; Piero Sanpaolesi, "L'Architettura del palazzo Rucellai," ibid., pp. 227-237.

83 Alberti, *Libro della famiglia* 3, pp. 190-91, 194-95.

firewood or replaced by better experiments.[84]

Lionardo concurred about those unfailing pleasures. "The villa is of great, honorable, and reliable value. Any other occupation is fraught with a thousand risks, carries with it a mass of suspicions and of trouble, and brings numerous losses and regrets." Worry vexed every other economic transaction. "The villa alone seems reliable, generous, trustworthy and truthful," he affirmed. In a chain of reward upon reward, the months courteously yielded their bounty, so that "your house is never empty of some gift." The autumn produced its crop of fragrant pears; even the winter provided "wood and oil and juniper and laurel, so that when you enter your house out of snow and wind you can make a joyful and aromatic fire." The labors of the farm filled the house with goods and dispelled melancholy from the spirit.[85] The villa engaged good persons, prudent householders, in profit, pleasure, and honor. It was a peaceful retirement for nurturing the family, tending to personal affairs, and on holiday conversing agreeably about the farm. There was useful exchange of information about agricultural practice, free from the malevolence of urban commerce. "Yes, by God, a true paradise," exclaimed Giannozzo. Contrasting the blessed country with the vile city, he concluded that he would nevertheless raise his children in the city, so that by dwelling among corrupt people they might learn to deal with them. Lionardo added that in the city a child also learned citizenship and was prompted by esteem to the pursuit of excellence. The advantages of honor, fame, and glory resided there among people, rather than among rural logs and clods.[86]

Although Alberti composed a supper conversation about marriage in retirement at a villa, the place was not an entirely moral dwelling; it was also the place of a scheming procuress, who interrupted a harvest to hide a pregnant widow there for secretive childbirth.[87] A villa was not a particularly female place. Ancient writings excluded women, while renaissance versions included them as only marginal contributors to its recreations, such as the performance of music. At the villa distaste and distrust were more commonly devoted to women than companionship and affection. The social role of women there was familial management. They were not allowed to engage in the prized activities of reading and hunting, lest those occasion unchastity.[88]

Yet the classical topic of the villa continued in renaissance favor. Giuseppe Falcone in *La nuova, vaga, et dilettevole villa* revived the Roman agronomy of the proprietor on his estate. The city was reviled as a miser-

---

84 Ibid., pp. 196-98.

85 Ibid., pp. 198, 199 trans. Watkins, pp. 191, 192 with alteration of *villa* from "farm" to "villa".

86 Ibid., p. 200, trans. Watkins, p. 193; ibid., p. 201.

87 Alberti, *Intercenàles*, trans. Marsh, pp. 134-48, 192, 197.

88 James S. Ackerman, *The Villa: Form and Ideology of Country Houses*, Bollingen Series, 35-34 (Princton: Princeton University Press, 1990), pp. 120-21, 102-3.

able place where leisure brought "destruction, great damage, ruin, scorn, and infamy." Its hearth was cold. In his catalogue of urban decay, "the element fire, which is so active, is extinguished, the air becomes infected, the water is poisoned, the earth made sterile, gold is blackened, iron rusts, every room and lodging is ruined, the mind fattens, the human body sickens, the horse becomes defective, the ship is wrecked, the soldier becomes as a rabbit, the voice becomes raucous, the wine turns, the ruby discolors, the wood becomes worm-eaten and the cloth stained."[89]

Before the revival of the city from the tenth to the thirteenth centuries, power was based on land and the agrarian economy. Traders, artisans, and manufacturers founded cities and established communal government. They were the bourgeois or burghers of the new citadel and fortress. With surplus from their monetary economy they also revived the classical villa for relaxation, exercise, and investment. In late medieval Italy aristocrats had a dwelling in town with a defensive tower, but their principal seat was a fortified castle on rural property. Those castles were the symbolic and functional centers of their power and influence. Their architecture was rarely altered to conform to contemporary fashion, because their very age was preeminently valuable. Age signified the antiquity of the lineage, the precedence of the nobility to the bourgeoisie, the stability of tradition. The fortified castle, or *rocca*, like the estate of the Aquinas family at Roccaseca, was the seat of its proprietor's political and economic power. The villa, in contrast, was a place for relaxation from power and management. Petrarch's literature about Vaucluse was most influential for the revival of the villa. It incited a craze for building villas, centered in Florence and dotting its suburban hills. The villas were constructed as the modified castle of medieval forms, since the countryside was still not safe from bandits and marauders. Castellation with its towers, battlements, and crenellations was also adopted to express the aspirations of the class to power.[90]

Powerful families exploited religion. The monarchy conferred sacred rites with political functions as a means of propaganda to seek power, to obtain the approbation of subjects, and to exalt institutions. In Florence, where the nascent genius of a repatriated Alberti flourished in the artistic company of Filippo Brunelleschi, Lorenzo Ghiberti, Donatello, and Luca della Robbia,[91] the celebration of the Marian feast of the annunciation punctuated the key moments of the lengthy and difficult ascent of the Medici family. During their tenure as chiefs of the republic, then dukes and grand dukes of Tuscany, there was celebrated a "Rapprezentazione

89 Ibid., pp. 110, 113-14, citing pref. fol. i from the edition of Venice, 1628.

90 Ibid., pp. 63, 64, 65, 32, without reference to Aquinas. See also Joanna Woods-Marsden, "Images of Castles in the Renaissance: Symbols of 'Signoria'/Symbols of Tyranny," *Art Journal* 48 (1989):130-37.

91 Gadol, *Leon Battista Alberti*, p. 6.

dell'annunciazione." It derived from the progressive dramatization by theatrical troupes of Marian praises, poems in the recitation of which lay companies specialized. The Virgin was the particular advocate of the Florentine republic, and her feast initiated its calendar year. The portrayal of her annunciation was performed at weddings of the Medici family; its strongly militaristic prophecies included the terms vendetta, enemy, victory, and glory.[92] The annunciation was a Florentine civic symbol. When Antonio di Giuseppe Rinaldeschi, a noble but a reprobate, in a drunken stupor threw a dung clod at its image over a church door he was hung from a window of the Bargello.[93] Yet the citizens were not exercised about the accuracy of the image, only about its import, whose fouling was judged equal to a man's life.

Even a humanist chancellor of the Florentine republic did not promote the dignity of the populace as did Alberti the family. Coluccio Salutati in *De seculo et religione* ventilated contempt for the secular life. His ascetic treatise was composed at the request of a monk of the strict Camaldulensan observance, cloistered in the monastery of S. Maria degli Angeli in the center of Florence. Salutati obliged with a conventional condemnation of the disorientation of values that elected worldly achievement rather than heavenly retirement. "What is filthier? What is dirtier? What is more obscene than the world?" Regarding the impropriety of a secular man even writing the work, he posed, "What is more nauseous than to live sinfully and to offer oneself as a teacher of the good life to others?" He compared himself to a person trapped in a pit who could holler to others its dangers, so that they might choose a better course. The world was a terrible place: field of the devil, palestra of temptation, workshop of evil, factory of vice, theater of dishonor, den of misery. Its only mitigation derived from Augustine's metaphor of pilgrimage: highway for mortals, inn for travelers.[94]

In Florence after repatriation Alberti used to frequent for religion and for exercise the church of S. Miniato. He had adopted patterns and motifs from its baptistry and façade—rectangular panels of marble and serpentine, the smaller and larger arcades, the horizontal striping of the piers—for his

---

[92] Françoise Decroisette, "Fêtes religieuses, fêtes princières au XVIe siècle: Les Médicis et la fête de l'Annonciation à Florence," in *Culture et religion en Espagne et en Italie au XVe et XVIe siècles*, Université de Paris VIII-Vincennes, Documents et travaux de l'équipe de recherche culture et société au XVIe siècle, 4 (Abbeville: F. Paillart with Centre national de recherche scientifique, 1980), pp. 11-41. See also for some background Mary Bergstein, "Marian Politics in Quattrocento Florence: The Renewed Dedication of Santa Maria del Fiore in 1412," *Renaissance Quarterly* 44 (1991):673-719.

[93] See Samuel Y. Edgerton, Jr., *Pictures and Punishment: Art and Criminal Prosecution during the Florentine Renaissance* (Ithaca, N. Y.: Cornell University Press, 1985), pp. 47-58.

[94] See Ronald G. Witt, *Hercules at the Crossroads: The Life, Works, and Thought of Coluccio Salutati*, Duke Monographs in Medieval and Renaissance Studies, 6 (Durham, N. C.: Duke University Press, 1983), pp. 195, 198-99, 200, without reference to Alberti. See also Charles Trinkaus, *In Our Image and Likeness: Humanity and Divinity in Italian Humanist Thought*, 2 vols. (London: Constable, 1970), 2:662-73.

façade of S. Maria Novella.[95] From his favorite church elevated there on the left bank he proceeded customarily in his *De iciarchia*: not to a monastery but home. On the bridge over the Arno he met a pair of prudent citizens, one of their sons, and two of his own nephews. All retired to Alberti's place where "in the house we three sat near the fire, and around us the youths stood."[96] The hearth as a focus for serious conversation had been revived by Nicolas of Cusa in *Trialogus de possest*, which began with the interlocutors drawing near to the fire where the cardinal occupied a magisterial chair. Although the severe seasonal cold excused their closeness about the hearth, the fire also provided an example for their inquiry about the revelation of invisible things from visible (Rom. 1:20). The source of worldly heat, the sun, was a metaphor for God, who had solar being in a divine, perfect manner. If those philosophers considered the being of the sun, removing negation to regard the sun's being, they would comprehend eternal being prior to not-being, argued Cusanus. The warmth of the fire suggested the difference between sensible and cognitive heat. "In the senses, where heat is sensed, heat-which-is-not-devoid of heat is present; but in the imagination or in the intellect heat-without-heat is touched upon." The element of fire persuaded him that "all things which are present mundanely in the world are present non-mundanely in God (for in God they are present divinely and *are* God)." Yet in his dichotomy of human and divine methods truth was revealed to believers by God, who expelled their rational and intellectual darkness by his divine light.[97] Cusanus at the hearth remained a human homeless in the universe.[98]

Alberti in *Dell'architettura* did not consider fire or water, but rather roofs and walls, as the principal occasion for society. Construction in a cold climate necessitated the use of fire, preferably an open hearth in a room of sun-dried brick. "The very sight of the flame and light of a brick fire is a cheerful companion to the old men that are chatting together in the chimney corner."[99] The positioning of the hearth against the wall required a project-

---

95 See Phyllis Williams Lehmann, "Alberti and Antiquity: Additional Observations," *Art Bulletin* 70 (1988):389-90.

96 Alberti, *De ichiarchia* 1, pp. 187-88; 2, p. 219.

97 Nicolaus Cusanus, *Trialogus de possest* 1, 12, 68, 71, 75; trans. in Jasper Hopkins, *A Concise Introduction to the Philosophy of Nicholas of Cusa* (Minneapolis: University of Minnesota Press, 1978), pp. 147, 149. For a recent general interpretation of the work see F. Edward Cranz, "The Late Works of Nicholas of Cusa," in *Nicholas of Cusa in Search of God and Wisdom: Essays in Honor of Morimichi Watanabe by the American Cusanus Society*, ed. Gerald Christianson and Thomas M. Isbichi, Studies in the History of Christian Thought, 45 (Leiden: E. J. Brill, 1991), pp. 151-54.

98 Boyle, "Cusanus at Sea: The Topicality of Illuminative Discourse," *Journal of Religion* 71 (1991):199-200. See in general Pauline Moffit Watts, *Nicolaus Cusanus: A Fifteenth-Cneutry Vision of Man*, Studies in the History of Christian Thought, 30 (Leiden: E. J. Brill, 1982).

99 Alberti, *Dell'architettura* praef., 10.14; *Ten Books on Architecture*, trans. James Leoni (London: Alec Tiranti, 1955), p. 235.

ing hood to trap the smoke, and it became a talent for renaissance designers to convert the protrusion into the principal decorative accent of the home. As a Tuscan proverb reasoned, a beautiful doorway corrected an ugly façade, a beautiful nose made a man handsome; so "a fine chimneypiece makes a splendid room." Great architects like Alberti considered its proportion, with the hood wedged like a tent most fashionable. For its embellishment a coat of arms, either painted or carved, was prominent at the center.[100] A Tuscan hearth was familial. Bernardino of Siena distinguished a bachelor's place from a married household by the lack of a fire to heat the dwelling, or even oil to light a lamp.[101] A Florentine hearth was particularly marked as familial. From the workshop of Verrochio and others issued a vast quantity of inexpensive death masks of ancestors, which vivid votive offerings were commonly displayed in homes above the hearth.[102] The ancient Roman lares may have been deified ancestors worshipped at the hearth, for they were described as blackened and grimy with smoke.[103]

There at the hearth among family and friends Alberti, unlike Cusanus, discussed not philosophical concepts but civic virtues. The fire had not only abstract potentialities but real consequences: if a person blew on a hearth his complexion reddened.[104] Nothing was more contrary to human nature than to strive for no honest good, Alberti said. Nature did not confer on humans such aspects of talent, intellect, and reason so that they could spoil in leisure. A person was born to be useful to oneself and to others. The first utility was to exercise the strength of one's spirit in virtue, to recognize the reason and order of things, and to fear God. The integrity of the family and the embellishment of the fatherland was provided by those who extended charity to others; for God loved those who strove to imitate and participate in his divine goodness by sharing the gifts he had bestowed on them.[105]

Alberti reiterated the delights of the villa as worthwhile, unenvied work, full of marvelous delight and practical for well-being. Like Augustine faulting the theft of pears, he criticized youthful otiosity as a detestable vice. Not to care for or to work at any worthy, useful, and necessary task harmed

---

100 Thornton, *Italian Renaissance Interior*, p. 20, citation p. 369 n. 1.

101 Bernardino of Siena, *De honestate coniugatarum*, in *Opera omnia* 2:107-8, cited by Herlihy and Klapisch-Zuber, *Les Toscans et leurs familles: Une étude du catasto florentin de 1427* (Paris: Presses de la Fondation nationale des sciences politiques, 1978), p. 600.

102 See Kent, *Household and Lineage*, p. 111; Trexler, *Public Life*, p. 61. For the death masks see also David Freedberg, *The Power of Images: Studies in the History and Theory of Response* (Chicago: University of Chicago Press, 1989), pp. 218-20.

103 David G. Orr, "Roman Domestic Religion: The Evidence of the Household Shrines," in *Aufstieg und Niedergang der römischen Welt: Geschichte und Kultur Roms im Spiegel der neueren Forschung*, ed. Hildegard Temporini (Berlin: De Gruyter, 1972), 2.16.2:1564, 1566, 1567.

104 Alberti, *Intercenales*, trans. Marsh, p. 42.

105 Alberti, *De ichiarchia* 1, pp. 198-99; 2, p. 252.

the family—to the great detriment of the republic. On the analogy of the architect commanding his workers, Alberti played the *iciarco*, the supreme male and chief prince of the family. His duty was its health, calm, and integrity; indeed, its "familiarity": *domestichezza*.[106] Alberti acknowledged that many Florentine families had survived adversity because "their paternal habitations preserved and cherished them, as it were, in the bosom of their forefathers."[107] Like Petrarch, Alberti had been an actual, rather than metaphorical, exile. Of the injustice and hardship of his family's exile from Florence he wrote, "Fortunate those who do not know our sufferings, have not gone wandering through the lands of others without dignity, without authority. . . scattered far from relatives, friends, and dear ones."[108] The Alberti family did not fare poorly, however, since as international merchant bankers they moved to the other locations where their business was established.[109] Despite his misfortune, exile did not dominate Leon Battista's consciousness.

Even a church did not excite him to eschatological yearning. When in his consolatory dialogue *Profugiorum ab aerumna* Alberti strolled with friends under the cupola of the Florentine cathedral, they discussed tranquillity. Their emphasis was not on intellectualism, however, but on industry: the energy and effort to accomplish worthy and glorious tasks on earth.[110] The architecture of that church was graceful and majestic, both slender and solid,[111] designed to illustrate spiritual harmony. Just as a column could sustain any weight if it were upright, so the soul withstood adversity with the rectitude of virtue.[112] Alberti's moral departed from Aquinas's metaphysics of the column as an analogy for the presence of the soul in the body.[113] The temperate climate of spring and the sweet voices of the cathedral choir[114] were suggestive of a pleasance. The cathedral was a paradisiacal place; but it was an inspiration for new virtues of work, rather than leisure, that were civically, not ecclesiastically, oriented. To be civic was to be Christian.

Salutati, also surveying the city from the vantage of S. Miniato, observed differently. He saw the impermanence of Florentine architecture, not the

---

106 Ibid. 1, p. 200; 3, pp. 279, 273, 275.

107 Alberti, *Dell'architettura* praef.; trans. Leoni, p. ix; cited by Kent, *Household and Lineage*, p. 77 (modernized).

108 Alberti, *Libro della famiglia* 1, p. 39, trans. Watkins, p. 55. See also *Intercenales*, trans. Marsh, pp. 82-90.

109 See Susannah Foster Baxendale, "Exile in Practice: The Alberti Family In and Out of Florence 1401-1428," *Renaissance Quarterly* 44 (1991):720-56.

110 Gadol, *Leon Battista Alberti*, pp. 223-25.

111 Alberti, *Profugiorum ab aerumna* 1.

112 Christine Smith, "Della tranquillità dell'animo: Architectural Allegories of Virtue in a Dialogue by Leon Battista Alberti," *Journal of Medieval and Renaissance Studies* 19 (1989):106, 108 citing ibid., p. 113.

113 Thomas Aquinas, *Super ad Hebraeos* 2.3.

114 Alberti, *Profugiorum ab aerumna* 1.

grace and majesty of its human design as imitating divine creation. Its colossal structures threatened to crumble: the starry towers, enormous churches, and vast places, erected not by private wealth but at public expense. The Palazzo della Signoria had settled on its foundations and fissures were visible in its walls, announcing its ruin. The wondrous cathedral was cracking. Private houses decayed; many were already destroyed during the civic revolution. Salutati lived in a house in the Piazza dei Peruzzi, albeit rented, but convenient to the chancery. To its commodious cabinet he retreated for privacy from his municipal duties as chancellor. It was there amid his ample library that he successfully importuned the executors of Petrarch's estate for the manuscript of *Africa* they threatened to burn, and there that he invented his own literature. The full household comprised his second wife Piera, ten children by both marriages, a nephew, and servants including a female slave. His virility inspired an admiring notary to compose a poem to his penis. Yet Salutati reckoned that the laity for their labor merited only thirty-fold; the monks, one-hundred fold.[115] The world was a mirror of vanity, a more fragile and murky glass than a defective eye. It represented images not realities. God alone was true. Salutati's only domestic architectural metaphor for life was "domicile of hardships." The only embers of a hearth were womanly words, which like fire put to straw flared irrationally in human minds to create a conflagration.[116]

In the next generation Cristoforo Landino, a Florentine professor of rhetoric, who like Petrarch considered the poet divinely inspired,[117] situated his disputation not on the estate of a villa but of a monastery. Its characters climbed the Apennines from their domain in the valley to the hermitage of ancient religion at Camoldi, in the mountainous forest more than six thousand feet in elevation, well beyond the hospitality of the cenobitic monastery. There he cast Alberti as the spokesman, with Lorenzo de Medici and others as interlocutors. They did ultimately descend from that peak to activity; however, not before exploring the philosophical significance of Vergil's *Aeneid* for the Christian pilgrim[118] and debating the contemplative versus active life. The fictional Alberti compared the monastic site to the Socratic pleasance of the plane tree and babbling brook with only natural benches for philosophical discussion. Blessed are the cultured men, he proclaimed, who sometimes relinquished their public and private cares for soli-

---

[115] Coluccio Salutati, *De seculo et religione* 1.27.6-10. Witt, *Hercules at the Crossroads*, pp. 181-89, 202.

[116] Salutati, *De seculo et religione* 1.27; 1.26; 2.8.

[117] Trinkaus, *In Our Image and Likeness*, 2:712-21; Mario A. Di Cesare, "Cristoforo Landino on the Name and Nature of Poetry: The Critic as Hero," *Chaucer Review* 21 (1986):155-81.

[118] See Craig Kallendorf, "Philology, the Reader, and the Nachleben of Classical Texts," *Modern Philology* 92 (1994):137-56; idem, "Cristoforo Landino's Aeneid and the Humanist Critical Tradition," *Renaissance Quarterly* 36 (1983):519-46; Clemens Zintzen, "Zur 'Aeneis'-Interpretation des Cristoforo Landino," *Mittellateinisches Jahrbuch* 20 (1985):193-215.

tude, as in the theological exemplar of the sister Mary. "Abandoning Martha amid those waves in which she ever fluctuates, they repose with the complete tranquillity of Mary in port," safe from the perilous rocks and tempestuous winds of the world.[119]

That opinion introduced the biblical topic of Martha and Mary, into whose home Christ had entered as a guest (Luke 10:38-42). Alberti the interlocutor explained that in scripture, under the Jewish figure of Rachel and the Christian figure of Mary, was expressed "contemplation." In Leah and Martha was demonstrated "action." While Martha was troubled and distracted, bustling about in preparation of the household, Mary sat still in leisure, steadfastly entertaining the Lord. Martha did not quit the chaos, in which everything was greatly confused and tossed about on the varied waves of emotion. Mary with a singular mind, immortal and submissive to no pollution, performed her own service. As Jesus divinely judged, Mary had chosen the better part, which would not be taken from her (Luke 10:42). Yet that judgment was relative, argued the fictional Alberti, who taught action as good, although greatly superseded by contemplation. Humans were to investigate truths, mastering the supreme good; but also to act, so that self and family might escape misfortune. "For they are sisters, dwelling under the same roof, Mary and Martha. Both are pleasing to God: Martha that she may feed, Mary that she may be fed. Both are good, but the one is laborious, the other leisurely." Citizens must "cling" to Martha (like Augustine embracing his concubine) lest they desert the office of humanity. But they were to "marry" Mary, so that their minds might feed on ambrosia and nectar and so ascend to the knowledge of God.[120]

The historical Alberti thought it natural that the wife, "locked up in the house," should protect her husband's provisions by maintaining herself in a tension of tranquillity and vigilance. Her duties were the management of the household goods, good manners and amity in relations, and the children. The role imitated classical topics; but it also agreed with Florentine practice in the domestic literature, such as ledgers and familial records and chronicles. The wife was responsible but dependent on her husband's supervision. She in turn supervised the servants, who performed the tasks too mean for her: stoking the fire and drawing water; cooking, cleaning, laundry; tending the coops and stables; bathing, nursing, and minding the children. Theirs was transient work, sometimes with rapid turnover, when the local Tuscan

---

119 Cristoforo Landino, *Disputationes camaldulenses* 1, pp. 8-10. For the text see also Bruce G. McNair, "Cristoforo Landino and Coluccio Salutati on the Best Life," *Renaissance Quarterly* 47 (1994):747-69; Ursula Rombach, *Vita activa und vita contemplativa bei Cristoforo Landino*, Beiträge zur Altertumskunde, 17 (Stuttgart: B. G. Teubner, 1991).

120 Landino, *Disputationes camaldulenses* 1, pp. 36, 37, 41, 42, 47. For the comparison of Rachel and Leah see also his commentary on Dante, *Inferno* 2 and 3, and *Purgatorio* 27, cited by Jane Chance, "The Medieval Sources of Cristoforo Landino's Allegorization of the Judgment of Paris," *Studies in Philology* 81 (1984):153-45 nn. 15, 17, 18.

women, who formed the majority in service, quit without notice. They lived at the expense of their masters with secure lodging and donated clothing. Payment was rarely regular, however; and, despite the city statutes requiring nine or ten florins as an annual wage, they could be paid less or more. With a favorable economic and demographical conjuncture came better salaries and mitigated conditions, like ability to negotiate about the laundry. Women intent on gaining profit from the scarcity of labor, predominantly adult or elderly wives and widows, performed household tasks for others, to accumulate earnings for themselves. The situation for girls, who entered employment in exchange for only a dowry at the end of eight years of labor, was somber. Below them in status were the slaves, registered fiscally with the livestock and exploited sexually by their masters, with the illegitimate children abandoned at foundling hospitals. The servants of a household collectively were outsiders to the family, tainted and untrusted. They were scrutinized as thieves usurping the domestic role that Florentine men denied their wives, who were reserved for government and procreation.[121]

Handmaiden, which signified in religious literature the humble but pious female, especially the Virgin annunciate (Luke 1:38), acquired in secular life low and impious connotations of immorality, loquacity, treachery, and even whorishness. The servant girl, exploited by her master as concubine or by her mistress as go-between, became the competitor of the public prostitute. In one respect—the violation of the Florentine sumptuary laws on dress—her punishment was severer than that of a prostitute. If she failed to pay the fine, she was stripped naked, flogged in the marketplace, paraded through the streets, then flogged again. No other class of woman was subjected to such public shame. Of low repute sexually, her social status was reflected in the fine for her rape: the minimum. Her moral corruption was visible in her dirty work, castoff clothes, and bad diet. A hagiographical genre of the saintly servant was developed by the thirteenth century to bond the allegiance of those workers and to combat the abusive relationship with their employers. Domestic servants composed a large proportion of the marginal population gravitating to the city from the country. Their employment was a solution to female overpopulation and shortage of dowries: women of means entered a convent or beguinage, others sought a position in service. The phenomenon was paralleled by a rise in the number of domestic saints, of rural origin and often related to their employer. The elements of the ha-

---

[121] Klapisch-Zuber, "Women Servants in Florence during the Fourteenth and Fifteenth Centuries," trans. Nancy Elizabeth Mitchell, in *Women and Work in Preindustrial Europe*, ed. Barbara A. Hanawalt (Bloomington: Indiana University Press, 1986), pp. 56-80, citing at pp. 57-58 Alberti, *Libro della famiglia* 3, p. 265. For developments into the sixteenth century see Judith C. Brown, "A Woman's Place Was in the Home: Work in Renaissance Tuscany," in *Rewriting the Renaissance: The Discourses of Sexual Difference in Early Modern Europe*, ed. Margaret W. Ferguson, Maureen Quilligen, and Nancy J. Vickers (Chicago: University of Chicago Press, 1986), pp. 206-24.

giography were her cruel master, her charity to the indigent, and her resistance to sexual temptation. In one tale a cook revenged an upbraiding for her charity in giving leftovers to the poor. Since her mistress had ordered her to feed the scraps to the pigs, after death she returned nocturnally to grunt at her like a sow in a sty. Such saints, of solace and example to women of their class, were truly popular. To achieve canonization, however, they needed the patronage of a powerful family or order; they tended to be associated with the mendicant tertiaries, whose values of humility, poverty, and charity were compatible. In reality female servants were often unable to receive religious instruction or even to attend church.[122]

By contemporary practice the role of Mary the contemplative wife was restricted; that of Martha the dutiful servant, demeaning. On the model of the actual Florentine household, Landino's commendation of Martha as civic virtue was not much of a promotion from her status in monastic exegesis. The necessity of domestic life was considered well inferior to the liberty of philosophical speculation. With the metaphor of life as maritime turbulence Landino compared the difficulty of attaining the tranquil port of true knowledge to the voyage of Aeneas. The allusion correctly located the topic of the active versus contemplative life in classical thought. Contemplation he defined as "a penetrating and firm consideration of the spirit in true cognition." Landino identified the origin of the term in the early Latin designation of "temple" as the space in the heavens that the augurs marked for divination with their wands and that the birds then entered as omens. Because of that ancient practice, people said that those with a resolute eye on the temple "contemplated," intent on the investigation of an idea. Allied concepts were admiration and stupor; and also speculation, following Augustine, from the word for mirror (*speculum*). Landino then erred in medieval fashion by applying the classical topic to scripture. Contemplation, he argued, had the opinion of all the theologians and the authority of the psalm, "One thing I seek from the Lord, this I require" (Ps. 26:4 Vulg.). Explaining that contemplation transpired in leisure and quiet, he adduced the verse, "Be still and know that I am God" (Ps. 45:11 Vulg.).[123]

That initial verse continued by defining the single good sought and required as "to live in the house of the Lord all the days of my life" (Ps. 26:4 Vulg.). Dwelling in God's house was not associated in Hebrew wisdom with contemplation, however. Contemplation was not a scriptural word or concept, although medieval authors asserted it to be so, translating revela-

[122] Michael Goodich, "*Ancilla Dei*: The Servant as Saint in the Late Middle Ages," in *Women of the Medieval World*, ed. Julius Kirshner and Suzanne F. Wemple (Oxford: Basil Blackwell, 1985), pp. 119-36. For her treatment for violation of the sumptuary laws see Ronald Rainey, "Dressing Down the Dressed-Up: Reproving Feminine Attire in Renaissance Florence," in *Renaissance Society and Culture: Essays in Honor of Eugene F. Rice, Jr.*, ed. John Monfasani and Ronald G. Musto (New York: Italica, 1991), pp. 227-28.

[123] Landino, *Disputationes camaldulenses* 1, pp. 47, 20-21, 37.

tion into philosophy. The pericope of Martha and Mary was not scripturally a moral about the superiority of the contemplative life to the active life, nor about their collaboration. The reverberating arguments, monastic and humanist, were speculative exercises. The historical situation of the biblical sisters may have been unique. It was questionable behavior for a man to be alone with women not of his kin, and unprecedented for a rabbi to enter a woman's house specifically to teach her. The phrase "to sit at the feet of," which is used in the gospel of Mary, meant discipleship, not contemplation. Martha's behavior may also have been unusual, since women were forbidden to serve males at meals unless there were no servants. She was desirous, then, of assuming even a servant's role toward Jesus. The primary task in the judgment of Jesus was discipleship; and only in that context, hospitality. Jesus did not come to be served but to serve.[124]

Martha busied herself in serving, while Mary allowed herself to be served. The pericope perhaps dramatized the saying, "The Son of Man did not come to be served, but to serve" (Matt. 20:28). A parallel dispute arose at the Last Supper about which of the disciples was greatest. Jesus proclaimed, "I am among you as one who serves" (Luke 22:27). In John's gospel, when Peter refused to permit Jesus to wash his feet, he responded, "If I do not wash you, you have no part in me." His action was demonstrative and prescriptive. "If I then, your lord and teacher, have washed your feet, you also ought to wash one another's feet. For I have given you an example, that you also should do as I have done to you" (John 13:5-15). At issue in the biblical home of Martha and Mary was not contemplation but discipleship, then hospitality. A disciple was one who was served by the Lord, then in imitation served others.

That scripture of service could be misconstrued in Christian culture, as in a late medieval portrayal of Christ in the fine domestic setting of the sisters' house, seated on a throne canopied with cloth of gold.[125] There was some recognition of hospitality in the interpretation of that gospel, however. The knight of La Tour Landry instructed his daughters that Jesus lodged with Martha because she customarily harbored prophets and teachers. Every woman, he moralized, might take good example from her about harboring the servants of God, both preachers and teachers, and also pilgrims and needy persons.[126] Yet women in reflecting on that female task of hospitality did

---

[124] Although my interpretation rejecting the traditional active-contemplative dichotomy for the issues of service and hospitality was arrived at independently, it is similarly expressed in Ben Witherington III, *Women in the Ministry of Jesus: A Study of Jesus' Attitudes Toward Women and Their Roles*, Society for New Testament Studies Monograph Series, 51 (Cambridge: Cambridge University Press, 1984), pp. 100-1. For the ideal of female hospitality in renaissance courtesy books see Kelso, *Doctrine for the Lady of the Renaissance*, p. 115.

[125] Pietro Paolo da Santa Croce, Christ in the house of Martha and Mary, 1490s, Museo Vetrario, Murano. Reproduced in Thornton, *Italian Renaissance Interior*, p. 197 pl. 223.

[126] Geoffrey de La Tour Landry, *Le livre pour l'enseignement de ses filles* 102.

not challenge the ideology of contemplation versus action. Christine de Pisan, the first female professional writer and credited as the first feminist, was typically conservative. "Here is what you must do if you want to be saved," she counseled women. "The Scriptures tell of the two ways which lead to Heaven: the contemplative life and the active life. Without following these paths it is impossible to enter there." On the subject of the sisters, she continued, "Our Lord excused Mary, saying: Martha, you are very diligent, and your work is of great excellence and necessary for the aid and succor of others. Nevertheless, the contemplative life represents the abandonment of the whole world and all its demands only to meditate on Him. That is of greater dignity and more perfect." That was why, she explained, holy men established for women religious orders as the nearest estate to God.[127]

Yet the sisters might collaborate, and it was Bernard of Clairvaux who popularized Augustine's concept of that cooperation. Martha and Mary represented practical and speculative persons. They were unalike, just as people served God in different roles.[128] In his sermons for the Marian feast of the assumption Bernard developed the verse, "A woman named Martha received him into her house. And she had a sister called Mary" (Luke 10:38). As he explained their relationship, "They are sisters and they ought to be comrades." His word was *contubernales*, which in Roman military usage meant "tent-companion". The metaphor complied well with Bernard's understanding of monasticism as knightly service, and of the monastery as a fortress for defense or a tent pitched in the wilderness for warfare. Yet in Roman domestic usage, applying to a household such as that of the biblical sisters, *contubernales* were mated slaves, denied lawful marriage (*conubium*) because of their social status.

The arrangement of *contubernium* involved the willful consent to have the sexual partner as a spouse, although the legal ability to contract marriage was lacking because of the servile status of one or both. Slaves could not contract marriage under Roman law. A quasi dowry might be offered, however. The children issuing from such a union were illegitimate. They followed the status of the mothe: if she was a slave, so were they—by right, property belonging to her owner not to herself. Like concubinage, contubernium could develop into a valid marriage, if the slaves were freed by their masters, if they then became Roman citizens, and if they continued to cohabit with marital affection. The relationship implied the tacit consent of the slaveholders, just as marriage depended on the formal consent of the

---

[127] Christine de Pisan, *Livre de trois vertus* 1.6; *A Medieval Woman's Mirror of Honor: The Treasury of the City of Ladies*, trans. Charity Cannon Willard (New York: Persea, 1989), pp. 79, 80.

[128] Bernard of Clairvaux, *Apologia ad Guilelmum abbatem* 3.5. For a survey of medieval interpretations, but without analysis of Bernard, see Giles Constable, "The Interpretation of Mary and Martha," in idem, *Three Studies in Medieval Religious and Social Thought* (Cambridge: Cambridge University Press, 1995), pp. 3-120.

heads of household. The mated slaves probably continued to live in quarters in the household to which they belonged; if they belonged to separate masters, they may have only visited. Although evidence of the motivation for such unions is scant, owners must have encouraged mating for the breeding of children and for the morale of the slaves. Those who were meritorious were awarded mates. If slaves were allowed to choose their own mates, they would have been concerned with social standing within that class; prospects for a career, especially manumission; the amount of pocket money and private property; and physical health and attractiveness. They commemorated one another on tombstones far more frequently than free men did their concubines, and they emphasized their mutual affection. In imitation of a just marriage, between themselves they spoke as "spouses."[129]

Bernard's designation of the sisters as *contubernales* meant that their company was socially inferior to lawful marriage. Either both were slaves, or one was; probably he implied Martha as servile, Mary as free. Nor was the condition of the sisters as tent-companions much improved if marriage was the model. The unofficial wives of soldiers living in settlements outside the camps could not have spent much time with them in the barracks or tents. Yet the women's title of *focariae*, "housekeepers" from *focus* for "hearth", suggested that they did share meals and other comforts of home.[130] Bernard's interpretation was not very domestic in either the servile or military meanings, however, although it pertained to the monastic community. In the gospel Martha was occupied with personal service; her sister, intent on the Lord's conversation. Provision concerned Martha; but fulfillment, Mary, for she idled with the Lord so that the house might not be vacant. But to whom should be assigned the housework? inquired the practical abbot. A house that received the Savior had to be clean, furnished, and full. Bernard awarded the broom to Lazarus, who as their brother had a right to live in the common household. As raised from the dead, four days decayed, he typified penitence. The Savior frequently visited the house that Lazarus cleaned, Martha furnished, and Mary completed with her dedication to interior contemplation. If the soul neglected to ready the house, by cleaning and decorating only its exterior, the Savior would retract his footstep on its very threshold, as if he were stuck in mud. Superficiality allowed him no entrance, because he penetrated everything and his habitation was in innermost hearts.[131]

Of the two sisters, it was Martha the inferior one who received Jesus, ev-

---

[129] Susan Treggiari, *Roman Marriage: Iusti coniuges from the Time of Cicero to the Time of Ulpian* (Oxford: Clarendon, 1991), pp. 52-53, 410-11, 123-24, 53, 124. See also idem, "Contubernales in *CIL* 6," *Phoenix* 35 (1981):42-69.

[130] See Treggiari, *Roman Marriage*, p. 410; and for soldiers' families, also Suzanne Dixon, *The Roman Family* (Baltimore, Md.: Johns Hopkins University Press, 1991), pp. 55-58, 92.

[131] Bernard of Clairvaux, *Sermo in assumptione* 2.7, 5.

idently because she was older and because the beginning of salvation appropriated action more than contemplation. Although the Lord praised Mary, he was received by Martha. Although Jacob loved Rachel, her sister Leah was substituted in his bed, with the explanation that the custom was to give the elder daughter in marriage first. Since the house of the sisters in the gospel was a house of clay, it was easily understandable to Bernard why Martha, rather than Mary, welcomed the Lord into it. When scripture said, "Glorify and bear God in your body" (1 Cor. 6:20 Vulg.), it referred to Martha not to Mary; since Martha used the body as an instrument, while for Mary it was an impediment. A favorite verse of Bernard's was, "The perishable body weighs down the soul, and the earthly habitation presses the senses cogitating many things" (Wis. 9:15 Vulg.). It did not apply to a worker. Martha received the Savior into her house on earth; Mary considered how to be received by him in the house not built by human hands but eternal in heaven. If she received him into her house, it was in a spiritual sense. So the Word was welcomed by both sisters: the one in flesh, the other in speech.[132]

Martha's murmuring against her sister's idleness Bernard dismissed as inappropriate in a house that received Christ. "Happy the house and ever blessed its company where Martha complains of Mary!" he preached. It would be unworthy, even illicit, for Mary to emulate Martha by complaining that her sister had abandoned her to solitary leisure. God forbid that the person who dallied with God should aspire to the turbulent life of his officious brothers! As Jesus responded, "Martha, Martha, you are anxious and troubled about many things." The prerogative was Mary's, who had him as an advocate in every litigation. "Mary has chosen the better portion, which shall not be taken away from her" (Luke 10:42 Vulg.). Yet what consolation was there for toiling Martha in that reproof, which praised the role of her sister? Bernard considered two possible interpretations. Either the choice of Mary, which was the vocation of the monks, was praised as one to be elected by all persons; or she was praised as lacking nothing because she rashly favored neither role, obedient in which ever role she might acquire. Scripture praised the willingness of people to be at leisure or in ministry. So Bernard declared, "This is plainly the better part, which will not be taken away: this the better mind, which is not mutable, whatever its calling." Perhaps the leisured were better than the laborers, but the best person was perfect in both states.[133]

By the regulation of charity Bernard distributed the three characters in the house: the administration to Martha, the contemplation to Mary, the penitence to Lazarus. The soul that possessed those figures simultaneously was perfect. Yet individuals were intended for different tasks, so that Mary

[132] Ibid. 3.1-2.
[133] Ibid. 3.2-3.

might piously and sublimely perceive God, Martha benignly and mercifully the neighbor, and Lazarus miserably and humbly himself. Each person should consider his own level. Those unburdened with the construction of the ark—the task of Bernard as abbot—were free to be men of desire glowing with the fire of charity or men of sorrow frigid with the tears of compunction. All three roles admitted of divine espousal. The soul was friendly that interrupted its spiritual zeal to tend to the least of the brethren. The soul was lovely that contemplated toward its transformation into an image of glory. And the soul was columbine that wept and sighed as if buried in a sepulcher. Monastic characters were the officials as Martha, with the monks distributed as Mary or Lazarus.[134] Yet spiritual marriage did not extend in Bernard's exegesis beyond the monastic enclosure. He did not praise the Marthas bustling about domestic households and civic squares as worthy of divine visitation.

Bernard's introduction of Lazarus to the scene, from which he was absent in the gospel, was allegorical. He argued that the brother was omitted from the household in scripture because the Holy Spirit willed that house to be understood of the Virgin. It would have been incongruous for penitence to be present when she had never committed a sin. God forbid that her house have a speck of dirt needing Lazarus's broom! Although Bernard believed that Mary had contracted from her parents the stain of original sin, piety disallowed her to be less sanctified in the womb than Jeremiah or less full of the Spirit than John the Baptist. Her birthday would not otherwise be celebrated with such festive lauds. Since she was cleansed by grace alone from original sin, just as in baptism grace alone washes away its stain, her innocent heart could not have experienced penitence. Lazarus might abide with sinners; only Martha and Mary were invited into the Virgin's bedchamber. She took the part of Martha when she attended her pregnant and aged cousin Elizabeth in humble service and she took the part of Mary when she pondered in her heart the words spoken about her Son at his Nativity. In her singular and supreme person the Virgin united the business of Martha and the busy leisure of Mary, bearing within the glory of the king's daughter but decked without in colorful attire of golden borders. She was not one of the foolish virgins of the gospel parable but a prudent virgin who possessed a lamp and carried a vessel of oil. The house of the foolish virgins was swept and furnished but not vacant, since they lacked oil for their lamps. The bridegroom did not receive them into his house or admit them to the heavenly nuptials. But the Virgin, whose lamp was never extinguished, processed to meet him with a lamp so burning that the angels wondered at its miracle. She glowed ruddier with flame than all others, for her Son filled her with the oil of grace.[135]

---

134 Ibid. 3.4-7.

135 Ibid. 2.8.

Such reception of Jesus into the house of Martha and Mary was commonly allegorised of the incarnation through a mistranslation of scripture. In the phrase "he entered a village" (Luke 10:38) the place was rendered in the Vulgate version as *castellum*. That philology encouraged an interpretation of Jesus entering the castle of the Virgin, her womb. Preaching on her assumption, for which feast the pericope of Martha and Mary was the liturgical lesson,[136] Bernard had Jesus receiving Mary at his entry into the castellany town of the world. "In the world there was not a worthier place than the temple of the virginal womb into which Mary received the son of God; nor in the heavens a more regal throne by which the son of Mary elevates Mary." The castle he explained as the spacious expanse of the earth, the atrium of the armed prince Satan; yet a mere castle in comparison with the amplitude of the heavens from which the Word descended. Jesus entered that castle, even into the "most contracted inn of a virginal womb." With *diversorius* Bernard departed from the usual *stabulum* for "inn" to include the meanings of a retail or cookery shop, or a tavern. It was a hospitable place. Through Mary as mediatrix all people received the merciful Lord into their "houses." Each individual had a fortification (*castrum*) and a house (*domus*) at whose doors Wisdom knocked. If a person opened them, the Lord entered and supped there (Rev. 3:20). The fortification was the body. Its custodian had to sweep it clean with the broom of confession and to decorate it with the verdant plants of monastic observance, so to make it a home rather than a prison.[137]

Mary's womb, however, was a temple in the castellany town of the world, not a room in a house. Her reception of Jesus there merited her no household seat but an eternal throne. That allegorical transformation of the domestic to the ecclesiastical, of the lowly to the royal, aggrandized the incarnation beyond scripture. As Erasmus would correct the popular interpretation, Mary's humility was not personal virtue but social status.[138] The medieval alteration profoundly influenced imagination and art, however. Mary vested in chasuble and pallium as a priest, as a symbol of the Church, had been current in French iconography since wooden sculptures of the Romanesque style.[139] Her figuration of the Church was clerical, not lay—oddly so, since women were forbidden ordination to the priesthood.

---

[136] Roberta D. Cornelius, *The Figurative Castle: A Study in the Mediaeval Allegory of the Edifice with Especial Reference to Religious Writings* (Bryn Mawr, Pa.: Bryn Mawr College, 1930), pp. 37-48.

[137] Bernard of Clairvaux, *Sermo de assumptione* 2.2-6.

[138] For the scriptural concept see Klaus Wengst, *Humility: Solidarity of the Humiliated: The Transformation of an Attitude and its Social Relevance in Graeco-Roman, Old Testament-Jewish and Early Christian Tradition* (Philadelphia: Fortress, 1988). Erasmus is discussed below.

[139] See Ilene H. Forsyth, *The Throne of Wisdom: Wood Sculptures of the Madonna in Romanesque France* (Princeton: Princeton University Press, 1972), pp. 23-24 and figs. 112-21.

The scene of the annunciation in the gospel was in the city of Nazareth, its exact location unspecified. "In the sixth month the angel Gabriel was sent by God to a city in Galilee whose name was Nazareth, to a virgin betrothed to a man named Joseph, from the house of David, and the name of the virgin was Mary. And having entered *ad eam* the angel said: 'Hail, full of grace; the Lord is with you; blessed are you among women'" (Luke 1:26-28 Vulg.). Where did the angel enter? The city? a household, meaning the house of David? or her as a message? "I think," responded Bernard of Clairvaux, "in the sitting area of her chaste bedroom, where perhaps, having shut the door upon herself, she was praying to the Father in secret; for angels are wont to stand near those who pray and to delight in those whom they see raise pure hands in oration." The angel could penetrate her closed door; iron bars could not detain him because of his subtle substance. There was no need, Bernard concluded, to speculate that she left the door ajar.[140] Aquinas argued that the annunciation happened in Joseph's house, since by ancient custom Mary would have been conducted there at her betrothal with the right of admission.[141] Jean Gerson imagined her living in the home of Joseph's parents and conversing about the advent of the Messiah familiarly within that domestic circle.[142] Artists shunned Joseph's presence at the scene, however. Giovanni di Paolo's painting of him at the annunciation warming his hands before the fire is rare.[143] Popular sources, like the meditations on the life of Christ misassigned to Bonaventure, placed the annunciation in a "room of her little house."[144]

From classical usage the Vulgate version probably signified only the town. Antoninus, bishop of Florence, located the annunciation in the city, as the proper place of society and as prophetic of the Messiah's mission. But it occurred in the private room of a temple, in a sanctuary behind closed doors.[145] Medieval artists commonly mislocated in place and time the scene of the annunciation in a Christian church of Gothic architecture. In that

---

140 Bernard of Clairvaux, *In laudibus Virginis Matris* 3.1.

141 Thomas Aquinas, *Summa theologiae* 3a 29.2.

142 D. Catherine Brown, *Pastor and Laity in the Theology of Jean Gerson* (Cambridge: Cambridge University Press, 1987), p. 219.

143 Cynthia Hahn, "'Joseph Will Perfect, Mary Enlighten and Jesus Save Thee': The Holy Family as Marriage Model in the Mérode Triptych," *Art Bulletin* 68 (1986):61; Margaret B. Freeman, "The Iconography of the Mérode Altarpiece," *Metropolitan Museum of Art Bulletin* 16 (1957):137; Meyer Schapiro, "Muscipula diaboli: The Symbolism of the Mérode Altarpiece," *Art Bulletin* 27 (1945):183. See Giovanni di Paolo, Annunciation and expulsion, National Gallery of Art, Washington, D. C. Reproduced in Henry Sayles Francis, "A New Giovanni di Paolo," *Art Quarterly* 5 (1942):316 fig. 2.

144 Pseudo-Bonaventure, *Meditationes vitae Christi* 4; *Meditations on the Life of Christ*, trans. Isa Ragusa (Princeton: Princeton University Press, 1961), p. 16.

145 See Edgerton, "*Mensurare temporalia facit geometria spiritualis*: Some Fifteenth-Century Italian Notions about When and Where the Annunciation Happened," in *Studies in Late Medieval and Renaissance Painting in Honor of Millard Meiss*, ed. Irving Lavin and John Plummer, 2 vols. (New York: New York University Press, 1977), 1:119.

masterpiece of northern art, Jean duc de Berry's *Très riches heures*, the brothers Limburg recorded in their landscapes with intricate detail and bright color his ducal residences. They were especially attractive in the topography of the calendar pages depicting secular activities. Various châteaux graced the different months with their various pleasures, just as Gianozzo Alberti would praise them. In the scene for January the French landscape becomes a domestic interior. The convention of an elderly man eating before the hearth is elaborated into a lavish banquet in a ducal château, perhaps the Hôtel Bicêtre near Paris. The left wall and the ceiling are the only visible architecture of the great hall. An elegant Jean duc de Berry sits at table, profiled before an enormous fireplace with a circular screen of rushes. Behind the tip of the screen the fire blazes and sparks, while a courtier warms his hands. It is a glittering and merry scene of males at court. Even the bishop of Chartres, Martin Gouge, shares the rich table, as a page summons more food to the groaning board on which puppies lap the dishes.[146] Yet the duke's favorite château of Mehun, the residence where he stored many manuscripts and jewels, dominated a most undomestic scene, the miniature of Jesus' temptation in the wilderness.[147] A château, even when graced with episcopal presence, was like every house a morally perilous place.

Mary is not in a house in its depiction of the annunciation. She kneels at an embellished lectern in a Gothic chapel sculptured with fanciful gargoyles and patriarchal statues. Through its leaded windows there streams from the Father on high a golden light, the popular metaphor for her perpetual virginity; for, just as light penetrates glass without altering it, so did Jesus penetrate her womb without altering it.[148] In contemporary depictions of the annunciation by the Boucicaut Master her ecclesiastical and domestic places and roles are contrasted. In the lower scene of a miniature from his workshop a nimbused Mary sits on a chair in a pleasance spinning, the womanly task. She is without a mantle, but cherubim suspend the cloth of

---

146 See James M. Snyder, *Northern Renaissance Art: Painting, Sculpture, the Graphic Arts from 1350 to 1575* (New York: Harry N. Abrams, 1985), pp. 57-63. For the châteaux in the calendar see Millard Meiss, *French Painting in the Time of Jean de Berry: The Late Fourteenth Century and the Patronage of the Duke*, 2 vols., National Gallery of Art Kress Foundation Studies in the History of European Art, 2 (London: Phaidon, 1967), 2:pls.419-23. Limburg brothers, January, from the calendar of the *Très riches heures du Duc de Berry*, fol. 1v, before 1416, Musée Condé, Chantilly. Reproduced, 2:pl.489; Snyder, *Northern Renaissance Art*, p. 39 colorplate 10. For the calendrical convention see Associate of Brussels Initials Master, January, London, British Museum, Add. 29433, fol. 1. Reproduced by Meiss, pl. 718.

147 Limburg brothers, detail from the temptation of Christ with the château de Mehun, Chantilly, Musée Condé, *Très riches heures*, fol. 161v. Reproduced in Meiss, *Late Fourteenth Century and Patronage of the Duke*, 2:pl.424. Cf. Detail of Annunciation with château de Mehun, French, 1465, The Cloisters, New York. Reproduced ibid., pl. 430.

148 Ibid., p. 58 and p. 59 fig. 51. Cf. p. 58 fig. 49 Mary with the architectural model of a church.

honor embroidered with golden initials *M*; otherwise she is indistinguishable in her domestic duty from any female saint. In another version she is weaving inside a house with a bedchamber visible. In the upper scenes of the annunciation, however, Mary in a mantle kneels in prayer with a book before the altar in a church.[149] This separation of Mary at the loom and Mary at the lectern may reject the apocryphal scriptures, which posed her at the annunciation spinning thread for the veil of the temple.[150] It was the Boucicaut Master who first fully depicted a church in representations of the annunciation, designing it with high vaults and a great central arch.[151]

The ecclesiastical iconography was perfected by Jan van Eyck, who explored in an altarpiece for a chapel in St. Bavo in Ghent[152] the situation of the Virgin. This location of the annunciation has seemed a domestic interior. The rooms are well above street level, for rooftops are visible through the central windows; and the two annexed rooms are vaulted, a feature of secular architecture only occurring in the spaces in towers adjoining the façade. There is an arcade of porphyry columns. The living quarters of the Virgin is a royal hall, the urban palace of the celestial queen. Her chamber alludes to the temple of Solomon, the tower of David, the gate of heaven, the city of God. It is an interior belonging to Jerusalem on high. Yet its furnishings are ambiguous, suitable to either an ecclesiastical or domestic room. There is a laver of a design used by the priest to wash his hands before and after Mass. The vaulted compartments recall the annexes for receiving the offerings of a congregation and for the preparation and storage of the Eucharistic elements.[153] So the Virgin is not in a hall but in a sacristy. Be-

---

149 Boucicaut Master, Annunciation, angels and the Virgin weaving, Florence, Corsini Collection, Book of Hours. Reproduced in Meiss, *French Painting in the Time of Jean de Berry: The Boucicaut Master*, National Gallery of Art Kress Foundation Studies in the History of European Art, 3 (London: Phaidon, 1968), pl. 128. Boucicaut Master and Workshop, same title, Paris, Bibliothèque national, ms. lat. 10538, fol. 31. Boucicaut Master, Annunciation, Paris, Musée Jacquemart-André, ms. 2, fol. 53v. Reproduced, pl. 29.

150 *Protoevangelium of James* 11:1, *Pseudo-Matthew* 9, cited by David M. Robb, "The Iconography of the Annunciation in the 14th and 15th Centuries," *Art Bulletin* 18 (1936):481, without reference to these miniatures.

151 Meiss, *Boucicaut Master*, pp. 27-30.

152 This is commonly reproduced, but the best reference for large colored plates is Elisabeth Dhanens, *Hubert en Jan van Eyck* (Mercatorfords, 1980). See for the altarpiece designed to open, p. 73; for panels of Gabriel and Mary compressed, pp. 94-95 figs. 57-58. For other reproductions see Otto Pächt, *Van Eyck: Die Begründer der altniederländischen Malerei*, ed. Maria Schmidt-Dengler (Munich: Prestel, 1989), for the altarpiece designed to open, p. 214; Lotte Brand Philip, *The Ghent Altarpiece and the Art of Jan van Eyck* (Princeton: Princeton University Press, 1971), for the exterior and for the Virgin, figs. 2, 72, and pl. II; Siegfried Thalheimer, *Der Genter Altar* (Munich: C. H. Beck, 1967), for the exterior, Gabriel, and Mary, figs. 1, 7, 8.

153 Philip, *Ghent Altarpiece*, pp. 82-84, 91-92. For the piscina with laver, basin, and towel see fig. 89; Dhanens, *Hubert en Jan van Eyck*, p. 89 fig. 53. It is considered an ambiguous space by John L. Ward, "Hidden Symbolism in Jan van Eyck's *Annunciations*," *Art Bulletin* 57 (1975):211. For the chambers as pastophories see Carla Gottlieb, "En ipse stat post parietum nostrum: The Symbolism of the Ghent Annunciation," *Bulletin des musées royaux des beaux-*

side her is the piscina for sacramental ablutions and a towel; stored in a niche in the wall are the lectionaries and vessels for Mass. Although the room has a low ceiling, it is not a domestic interior. It is part of an ecclesiastical façade called a solarium in early descriptions of the upper chambers of westwork churches. Such churches were squeezed between two towers, the distinctive features of northern Gothic architecture. Beyond the figures of Gabriel and Mary are visible the projections of those flanking towers. In the panels between the towers are views across the roofs of a Netherlandish city.[154]

The cityscape through the window[155] is earthly, a faithful rendition of a view from house number 16 on the corner of the Koey-straet in Ghent, the possible site of Hubert van Eyck's own home. Ghent was the hometown of the donors of the art, Joos Vijd and his wife Elisabeth Borluut, who are portrayed prayerfully on panels in the lower register.[156] They commissioned the altarpiece from Hubert, whose brother Jan completed or executed it. The deed registered with the civil magistrates and ecclesiastical administrators stipulates a Mass to be celebrated in perpetuity at the altar of the chapel, in honor of God, the Blessed Virgin Mary, and all the saints, for the salvation of the donors and that of their ancestors. The couple was childless. They invested in the altarpiece to great expense.[157] Its artist Jan van Eyck was a diplomat at court, official artist for the duke Philip the Good in Bruges. At the time of his work on the altarpiece he lived in that city permanently in a fine purchased house. He was newly married.[158] Although the donors are a married couple, he portrays them kneeling at opposites. The citizens in the background, strolling the streets, or looking out of the windows of houses and shops, seem mundanely remote from the divine mystery in the symbolic space. Mary herself has her back to the streets of Ghent, as did Monica to the streets of Ostia.

His depiction of the annunciation is not even analogous to human experience as her marriage, frequently allegorised from the Song of Songs. The indicative item—the ring—is absent. The Virgin wears on her ample white mantle a brooch of sapphire with pearls and on her head a matching circlet, but no ring. Nor does the angel, who wears a more handsome version of her

---

arts de Belgique 19 (1970):82-90.

154 Snyder, *Northern Renaissance Art*, pp. 92-93.

155 Reproduced in Dhanens, *Hubert en Jan van Eyck*, p. 90 fig. 54; Philip, *Ghent Altarpiece*, fig. 88.

156 Philip, *Ghent Altarpiece*, p. 194; for the portraits, pp. 192-200; and for the painters' quatrain with commission, p. 41 and fig. 49. Portraits reproduced in Dhanens, *Hubert en Jan van Eyck*, pp. 98-99 figs. 59, 62; Thalheimer, *Genter Altar*, figs. 23, 24. For background see David Nicholas, *The Domestic Life of a Medieval City: Women, Children, and the Family in Fourteenth Century Ghent* (Lincoln: University of Nebraska Press, 1985).

157 Guy Bauman, "Early Flemish Portraits 1425-1525," *Metropolitan Museum of Art Bulletin* 43-4 (1986):20, and for their portraits, pp. 18-19.

158 Snyder, *Northern Renaissance Art*, pp. 89, 96-97.

dainty jewelry, offer her a ring; he bears a scepter of lilies. In his Annunciation in a Gothic cathedral she is also without a ring. Yet in van Eyck's paintings of the Madonna, the Virgin with the child Jesus, she does wear rings. The artist focused on a ring in his portrait of Jan de Leeuw, who holds a gold band set with a red stone between his fingers. The woman in his Arnolfini portrait wears two rings, as the man takes her other hand.[159] To whom in the art of van Eyck was the Madonna married? Joseph or Jesus? Who was the donor of her ring? The response to that question typifies the literal and allegorical senses of scripture, whose meanings were to differ and collide in renaissance and reformation exegesis. The harmony of medieval exegesis, in which Mary was wed to both—Joseph by the literal sense and Jesus by the allegorical sense, was to be challenged by a critical philology promoting an historical science.

The development of van Eyck's iconography displays Mary as the type of the Church. In his other Annunciation she is surprised at prayer in a cathedral by a coronate angel with a scepter, who features the queenly feathers of a peacock and is vested in a richly brocaded cope. Although the building has been identified with Notre Dame in Dijon and the with the cathedral of Tournai, its details are fictitious. The architecture forms a complex and erudite iconography of the incarnation. The personal figures are disproportionately large to the building, to express Mary in the church as the Church, as does his iconic Madonna. While the angel salutes her, a dove streams into the nave on the longest of seven rays from an upper window. The clerestory windows are Romanesque round arches; the lower ones, Gothic pointed arches. The architectural discrepancy, attributed to the symbolism of the Old and New Testaments, was a feature of several late medieval Belgian ecclesiastical structures.[160] An elaborate iconographical pro-

---

[159] Jan van Eyck, Annunciation, National Gallery, Washington, D. C., p. 357 fig. 221. Madonna with canon Joris van der Paele, Stedelijke Musea, Brussels, p. 225 fig. 147. Lucca Madonna, Städelsches Kunstinstitut, Frankfurt-am-Main, p. 234 fig. 152. Madonna in the church, Staatliche Museen, Berlin, p. 321 fig. 199. Madonna with the fountain, detail, Koninklijk Museum voor Schonekunsten, Antwerp, p. 301 fig. 188. A pair of gold wedding bands on the ring finger of Mary's left hand in the last painting is identified by Larry Silver, "Fountain and Source: A Rediscovered Eyckian Icon," *Pantheon* 41 (1983):96. Portrait of Jan de Leeuw, detail, Kunsthistorisches Museum, p. 240 fig. 156. Arnolfini portrait, detail, National Gallery, London, p. 201. All reproduced in Dhanens, *Hubert en Jan van Eyck*. For the Arnolfini portrait see recently Edwin Hall, *The Arnolfini Betrothal: Medieval Marriage and the Enigma of Van Eyck's Double Portrait*, Discovery, 3 (Berkeley: University of California Press, 1994); Linda Seidel, *Jan van Eyck's Arnolfini Portrait: Stories of an Icon* (Cambridge: Cambridge University Press, 1993).

[160] John Oliver Hand in idem and Martha Wolff, *Early Netherlandish Painting* (Washington, D. C.: National Gallery of Art, 1986), pp. 76-86; Thomas Lyman, "Architectural Portraiture and Jan van Eyck's Washington Annunciation," *Gesta* 20 (1981):263-71. Jan van Eyck, Annunciation, left wing of a probable triptych, c. 1434-1436, National Gallery of Art, Washington, D. C. Reproduced p. 77. For his Madonna in a church, Staatliche Museen, Berlin, see Dhanens, *Hubert en Jan van Eyck*, p. 317 fig. 195. In addition to sources like Dhanens, the paintings are collected for comparison in Carol J. Purtle, *The Marian Paintings*

gram fills the stained-glass windows, the murals, the decorations of the pavement and floor with their scriptural and zodiacal designs, and the capital of the corner pier, down to the detail of the footstool in the corner. The interpenetration of the physical and the spiritual in the painting imitates the very incarnation.[161] A dealer reported the painting as executed for Philip the Good for an unspecified religious monument in Dijon. The Virgin may portray the features of his wife, Isabella of Portugal. Its possible provenance from the ducal chapel of the Charterhouse of Champmol, near Dijon, may indicate noble or clerical associations.[162] The noble character of van Eyck's paintings reflect his own social position as court painter to the duke of Burgundy. Although the church is designed naturalistically, it does not represent any particular architecture, but rather is a transcendental image.[163] Stylistically it is not readily associated with the altarpiece in Ghent[164] commissioned by the bourgeois Vijds. The only concession to lowliness is Mary's bare head; her blue robe is furred with ermine. She is a clerical, not a congregational, version of the Church. Not only are no citizens visible through its windows, no worshipers are within its nave.

A transitional location for the annunciation in a house appeared in Florentine painting where the Virgin was portrayed in a portico. In an Annunciation by Giotto each figure, Gabriel and Mary, occupies a separate space in two bays of a portico, with drawn curtains at the rear suggestive of rooms beyond. No longer is the Virgin associated with abstract or ideographic backgrounds, or with settings outdoors. Her transition to a domestic interior occurs in an anonymous fresco in S. Maria Novella, Florence, where her bedroom is visible from the portico. Yet porticoes are still exterior settings. Interior settings of the annunication representing Mary's bed originated late in the fourteenth century in northern Italy. From them developed the bourgeois interiors of the Flemish masters. The first definitive and unified form was in the central panel of the Mérode triptych, with its realistic detailing of appointments in a room whose lack of accurate perspective makes it seem overcrowded.[165] The realistic details of a Netherlandish home had already

---

of Jan van Eyck (Princeton: Princeton University Press, 1982). For the origins of the concept see Joseph C. Plumpe, *Mater ecclesia: An Inquiry into the Concept of the Church as Mother in Early Christianity*, Catholic University of America Studies in Christian Antiquity, 5 (Washington, D. C.: Catholic University of America Press, 1943).

161 Ward, "Hidden Symbolism," pp. 196-220.

162 Hand, *Early Netherlandish Painting*, pp. 76-86.

163 Craig R. Harbison, "Realism and Symbolism in Early Flemish Paintings," *Art Bulletin* 66 (1984):589.

164 Hand, *Early Netherlandish Painting*, pp. 76-86.

165 Robb, "Iconography of the Annunciation," pp. 480-526. See also Panofsky, "The Friesdam Annunciation and the Problem of the Ghent Altarpiece," *Art Bulletin* 17 (1935):441-42. Giotto, Annunciation, Arena chapel, Padua; Annunciation, S. Maria Novella, Florence. Reproduced in Robb, "Iconography of the Annunciation," p. 483 fig. 3, p. 489 fig. 9. He attributed the Mérode altarpiece to the Master of Flémalle, p. 498 fig. 29; but most scholars now credit Robert Campin. The triptych is no longer in the Mérode collection, Brussels, but

accompanied the Virgin in the De Buz Book of Hours, where she sits in the company of a dog on a low stool before her loom with a box of weaving implements.[166]

The Mérode triptych is attributed to Robert Campin, a citizen of Tournai, married to Ysabiel de Stoquain or Elisabeth van Stockem, about seven years his elder. The couple was childless. Campin himself owned houses successively in the rue des Chapeliers, the rue des Puits-l'eau, and the rue des Carriers. He invested in municipal securities, was considered a notable member of his parish, and was active in his profession. He worked for the city, its churches, and its citizens. Tournai employed him in various positions, from mere heraldic painter to executor of important projects like the decoration of the images on which civic oaths were taken. He was elected dean of the union of painters under the banner of the goldsmiths, a position responsible for the formulation of the charter of the painters' guild. He was captain of his *Eswardeur* for two terms, a group elected by the parish which in turn elected the provosts, jurors, and magistrates with whom they formed the three ruling councils of the city. Campin became captain of his quarter and procurator of the convent of the Haute-Vie, a clerk of the accounts of the city, and warden of the church of St-Pierre.[167]

---

in The Cloisters, Metropolitan Museum of Art, New York. Reproduced frequently, as in the articles cited below; for color see Bauman, "Early Flemish Portraits," pp. 4-5. References to it will be cited from Martin Davies, *Rogier van der Weyden: An Essay with a Critical Catalogue of Paintings Assigned to him and to Robert Campin* (London: Phaidon, 1972). Robert Campin, Annunciation, central panel of Mérode triptych, The Cloisters, Metropolitan Museum of Art, New York, pl. 141. For many reproductions of the Virgin annunciate in an Italian domestic interior see Thornton, *Italian Renaissance Interior*.

Iconographical interpretations of the domestic interior as a Eucharistic sanctuary typically detail each item as symbolic. The use of textual sources is arbitrary and uninformed, and there are basic errors in Christian doctrine. The theory is fundamentally disoriented in supposing that images are contemplative, whereas contemplation is transcendent of images. The art can, of course, be meditative, or used for meditation; but that is different. For the iconography of the room as a disguised Eucharistic sanctuary see Philip, *Ghent Altarpiece*, pp. 82, 83, 94; for a wedding chamber as a shrine or a tabernacle, Gottlieb, "Respiciens per fenestras: The Symbolism of the Mérode Altarpiece," *Oud Holland* 85 (1970):65-84; idem, "Et ipse stat post parietum nostrum," pp. 75-76; for both authors accepted by Barbara G. Lane, *The Altar and the Altarpiece: Sacramental Themes in Early Netherlandish Painting* (New York: Harper & Row, 1984), pp. 42-50; for the room as a complex design of Isaian prophecies, Charles Ilsley Minott, "The Theme of the Mérode Altarpiece," *Art Bulletin* 51 (1969):267-71; and for miscellaneous iconography, William S. Heckscher, "The Annunciation of the Mérode Altarpiece, an Inconographic Study," in *Miscellanea Jozef Duverger: Bijdragen tot de Kunstgeschiedenis der Nederlanden*, 2 vols. (Ghent: Uit. vereniging voor de Geschiedenis der Textielkunsten, 1968), 1:35, 57, 59, 62, 64. See also Matthew Botvinick, "The Painting as Pilgrimage: Traces of a Subtext in the Work of Campin and his Contemporaries," *Art History* 15 (1992):1-18.

166 Virgin at the loom, De Buz Book of Hours, c. 1400, Cambridge, Mass., Harvard University Library, Ms. 42. Reproduced in Sandra Hindman, *Text and Images in Fifteenth-Century Illustrated Dutch Bibles*, Corpus sacrae scripturae neerlandicae medii aevi miscellanea, 1 (Leiden: E. J. Brill, 1977), fig. 52, and see pp. 96-97.

167 Lorne Campbell, "Robert Campin, the Master of Flémalle and the Master of Mérode," *Burlington Magazine* 116 (1974):634, 637; Theodore H. Feder, "A Reexamination through

For his role in the revolt against the patrician government of Tournai he was fined and condemned to make a pilgrimage to St-Gilles in Provence. The pilgrimage may have been commuted to a fine, as was usual.[168] The metaphor and mentality of pilgrimage are remote from his scene of the annunciation. Against the judgment of Augustine that no one could be at home in the world, not even in his own chair,[169] Mary is securely at home in his art. She is dethroned: seated cozily on the footrest of a bench placed before a hearth, intently reading scripture. An angel intervenes, while on rays emanating from the center of a cruciform oculus a naked infant bearing a cross streams toward her ear. A table in the middle of the room holds a book and a pouch with scrolls, a decorative maiolica pitcher with a stem of lilies, and a pewter holder with a candle whose smoking wick has just been extinguished. On the rear wall is a recess hung with a laver full of water, a carved rack with a towel, and windows with shutters in open and closed positions. The ceiling is wooden, the floor tiled. The left wing portrays the donor, identified from the coat of arms on the left rear window of the interior as an Ingelbrecht from Mechelen. He kneels on a garden path before the open door, witnessing the scene, with his wife modestly behind him. She is an addition. Perhaps Ingelbrecht commissioned the work before his marriage, then had his wife's portrait painted over the background. At the crenellated wall of the gatehouse is a further addition, a professional messenger with the coat of arms of Mechelen on his chest.[170] Such devotional paintings as their class could afford were developed from the half-length secular portrait, with its serenity and even rigidity of abstract background yielding to elaborate landscape and rich decor.[171] The middle panel depicts the central room of a burgher's house, such as the donors might have owned. They seem to have arrived home to be surprised by the event within.

Campin's depiction of the annunciation is so comfortable that the Virgin does not even react to the advent of the angel. Her conventional countenance of fear or wonder is lacking; she simply continues reading. The scene is sheer domesticity. The small dimensions of the triptych suggest that it was meant for Ingelbrecht's bedroom, or perhaps for the living room or

---

Documents of the First Fifty Years of Roger van der Weyden's Life," *Art Bulletin* 48 (1966):417, 420, 425. Campbell's reattribution of the triptych to an associate or assistant has not been accepted by the consensus. For problems of attribution see recently Christopher Baker, "The Robert Campin Symposium, National Gallery, London," *Apollo* 138 (1993):52-53.

[168] Campbell, "Robert Campin, the Master of Flémalle, and the Master of Mérode," p. 634; Feder, "Reexamination through Documents," p. 425.

[169] Augustine, *De civitate Dei* 1.15.

[170] For the donor panel see Bauman, "Early Flemish Portraits," p. 19; Heckscher, "Annunciation of the Mérode Altarpiece," pp. 45-46, 49; Helmut Nickel, "The Man beside the Gate," *Metropolitan Museum Bulletin* 24 (1966):237-44.

[171] See Sixten Ringbom, *Icon to Narrative: The Rise of the Dramatic Close-Up in Fifteenth Century Devotional Painting*, Acta academiae Aboensis, A-31 (Åbo: Åbo Akademie, 1965), pp. 45-47.

chapel of his house. It was not intended for public display. Its private usage is indicated by the donors at prayer before the Virgin's door, since an Annunciation with worshippers was untraditional. The scene is even more immediate: it transpires now, in their house, by their hearth. The donors are portrayed on the same scale as the angel and the Virgin, not as in earlier Italian models on a much smaller scale. They are intimate witnesses to the sacred event. The votive character of the art reflects the indissolubility of the holy and the ordinary characteristic of late medieval piety.[172] On the fireplace, flanking its recess, are the cowering figures of a man and a woman in grisaille. A generic type on fifteenth-century Flemish fireplaces, the couple resemble conventions for the month of February in the calendars and probably suggest the season of winter. They also resemble grotesques inspired by Gothic marginal illustrations and may allude to marriage under the old law or to Adam and Eve. The bench against which the Virgin rests is carved with configurations of a lion for male and a dog for female, as in a profusion of examples of those animals at the feet of married couples in medieval tombs.[173]

The bench is particular furniture of a homey character. Its clever back can be rotated, turned over, or reversed for use in one direction or the other without the heavy bench being moved. It could thus be installed permanently before the hearth for the master and others to warm either their fronts or their backs at will. A bench did not serve in medieval domestic life what a sofa does in a modern living room. A personal chair was ponderously placed beside the bed, but the bench invited anyone to sit down. It was an item of equality, if not of intimacy. The bench was more precious to its owner than the trestle table that was pushed against it at mealtime. "Of the two, bench and table, the bench has greater value: the table is subject to the bench, just as a prudent wife listens to her husband and is subject to him." So would moralize Gilles Carrozet in *Les blasons domestiques*.[174]

A bench was the commonest medieval form of seating, superior to the stool.[175] It had the most familiar character of all furniture, welcoming neigh-

---

[172] Jozef De Coo, "A Medieval Look at the Mérode Annunciation," *Zeitschrift für Kunstgeschichte* 44 (1981):123, 128-31, 114. See also idem, "Robert Campin: Vernachlässigte Aspekte zu seinem Werk," *Pantheon* 48 (1990):36-53. For the blending of the sacred and profane and the saturation of the daily with the religious see Johan Huizinga, *The Waning of the Middle Ages: A Study of the Forms of Life, Thought and Art in France and the Netherlands in the XIVth and XVth Centuries* (London: Edward Arnold, 1924), pp. 136-37, 139, 140.

[173] Heckscher, "Annunciation of the Mérode Altarpiece," pp. 49-50, 54-55. He interprets Campin's treatment of the hearth as negative: the mouth of hell, to which the bench acts as a barrier.

[174] De Coo, "Medieval Look at the Mérode Annunciation," pp. 115-16, arguing against the bench as the throne for the Virgin's celestial coronation by Gottlieb, "Disguised Symbolism in the Gulbenkian Altarpiece," *Revista coloquio artes de Fundaçao Gulbenkian* 32 (1977):32. In the bibliographical edition the citation of Carrozet is at p. 19.

[175] Penelope Eames, *Furniture in England, France and the Netherlands from the Twelfth to the Fifteenth Century* (London: The Furniture History Society, 1977), p. 206.

bors, visitors, guests, and even strangers into the household. The invention of the movable backrest enhanced its desirability. There were various mechanisms—van Eyck's painting of St. Barbara before the hearth shows a system different from the Virgin's bench in his Annunciation. The term for these benches in Netherlandish inventories was *wendlys* or *keerlys*, and the fourteenth-century charter of the joiners of Bruges allowed their sale. They seem to have been an appurtenance of wealthy homes into the fifteenth century in the Netherlands; also in France, where ducal and civic inventories mention a *banc tourné* or variants, and as far as Hungary. It may have been a local version on which Alberti in *De iciarcia* warmed to the fire, for a *ciscranna* is inventoried for the Medici town house in Florence and a pair of benches with swingable backs survives in S. Maria della Carmina. Extant Netherlandish examples from later in the century have seats that lift up for storage, doubling as chests. The benches served also as beds. They were used as stands for cradles, with a manoeuvre of position allowing access to the infant.[176] There was a Flemish custom of placing the bed of a woman just delivered of a child before the hearth,[177] so that Mary on the bench before the fireplace prophesies the Nativity.

The earliest representations of a bench with a movable back are all in French secular manuscripts of the early fifteenth century dating before Campin's Annunciation. They illustrate emphatically secular subjects: Hannibal drinking poison; Christine de Pisan viewing paintings in the Salle de Fortune; Sostrata worried about Pamphilia in labor; Syra the procuress warning Philotus against liberality. In later examples an Austrian breviary depicts a dinner guest seated on a keerlys vomiting; the most famous version was in Lucas Cranach, the elder's, painting of Cardinal Albrecht of Brandenburg as St. Jerome in his study. A bench with a movable backrest can have no meaning or use as the Madonna's celestial throne. A throne by definition is immovable, firm, unshaken. Nor can the Virgin's bench divide the space of the room from the hearth if its function is to turn, enlarging or reducing space. The exact rendition of such domestic items displays the realistic vision of the artist, curious and inquisitive about things. In Campin's portrayal of St. Barbara the mechanism of her bench is so clearly drawn that a carpenter could copy it.[178]

Yet in this Annunciation, as in all such depictions in a Flemish interior, the hearth is cold.[179] Perhaps the lack of a fire, despite the ornamental

---

176 De Coo, "Medieval Look at the Mérode Annunciation," pp. 116, 117, 119. The movable bench in the St. Barbara wing of Campin's Werl altarpiece was identified earlier by Eames, *Furniture*, p. 206. For the *ciscranna* see Thornton, *Italian Renaissance Interior*, pp. 171-73.

177 Huizinga, *Waning of the Middle Ages*, p. 207.

178 De Coo, "Medieval Look at the Mérode Annunication," pp. 119-20, 123-28, 116-17, 123, 121, 122.

179 See Rogier van der Weyden, Annunciation, Louvre, Paris. Reproduced in Davies,

andirons, classically reflects the absence in the incarnation of the male procreative force. Although Campin did not portray the Virgin before a blazing hearth, he did so paint the Madonna. She sits similarly before it on the footstool of a bench, which holds on cloths a book with a jewelled clasp. Her arm propped against a cupboard supports the infant, while with her right hand she prepares the nipple of her exposed breast to express milk. Her gaze is averted. Her tresses are loose, as at home. She wears a ring on her finger, and her furred robe is banded with embroidery and studded with gems. A plaited rush fire screen behind her head and shoulders enhances her presence. At its tip flames leap, while andirons flank its sides. A triangular table for a tray beneath the window on the tiled floors is the only other furnishing. Open shutters disclose the wall of her estate with the arch and roof of the gatehouse; beyond it, the streets of a town with horsemen and strollers, populous houses and shops, a church, and a rolling landscape.[180]

Her domestic bench allusive of Solomon's throne suggests leadership not liturgy; for he was a ruler, not a priest. Even the allegoriser Dante had Aquinas in paradise praising the wisdom of Solomon as supreme precisely because it involved prudence in government. Aquinas acknowledged it as superior to the wisdom of theologians like himself, who represented the ab-

---

Rogier van der Weyden, pl. 21; Odile Delenda, *Rogier van der Weyden: Roger de la Pasture* (Paris: Cerf, 1987), between pp. 32-33.

180 Robert Campin, Madonna before a firescreen, National Gallery, London. Reproduced in Jill Dunkerton et al., *Giotto to Dürer: Early Renaissance Painting in the National Gallery* (New Haven, Conn.: Yale University Press with National Gallery Publications, London, 1991), pl. 13; Davies, *Rogier van der Weyden*, pl. 160. For the interpretation of the room as a heavenly palace see Frances Pitts, "Iconographic Mode in Campin's London Madonna," *Konsthistorisk Tidskrift* 55 (1986):87-100. For the hearth as a symbol of the Eucharistic holocaust that is Christ baked in the Virgin's womb see Carra Ferguson O'Meara, "'In the Hearth of the Virginal Womb': The Iconography of the Holocaust in Late Medieval Art," *Art Bulletin* 63 (1981):76-79, 82-83, with extensive citation from Thomas Aquinas, especially *Summa theologiae* 1a, 2ae, q. 102 art. 3. Campin's iconography of the incarnation is not Thomistic, however. The advent of the infant, beaming into the interior of the Mérode Annunciation toward the Virgin's ear, is rather a variant on the heresy Aquinas condemned of the infant streaming passively through the aqueduct of the Virgin's womb. Both notions denied Christ's formation from her menstrual blood, thus his true incarnation. Antoninus, archbishop of Florence and a Dominican friar, protested the iconography in his own *Summa theologica* 3.2.10. It is cited without reference to this argument by Robb's appendix on the naked Christ child, "Iconography of the Annunciation," p. 526, and by Edgerton, "*Mensurare temporalia facit geometria spiritualis*," p. 115. Benedict XIV condemned the iconography as the Valentinian heresy, just as Aquinas argued. O'Meara's reduction of Campin's art to anti-Semitic propaganda, in which the Madonna nursing her child is the antithesis to the Jewess cooking hers, p. 87, is arbitrary. Lane extends O'Meara's interpretation to the shrine of the body of Christ and the sanctuary for transubstantiation, thus as an explanation of the Mass, in *Altar and Altarpiece*, pp. 4-8. For further criticism of her method and of the iconographical school in general see Robert Baldwin's review in *Renaissance and Reformation* 2 (1987):197-202; for her defense, Lane, "Sacred versus Profane in Early Netherlandish Painting," *Simiolus* 18 (1988):107-15. See further on realism vs. iconography Harbison, *Jan van Eyck: The Play of Realism* (London: Reaktion, 1991), pp. 9-18; David Carrier, "Naturalism and Allegory in Flemish Painting," *Journal of Aesthetics and Art Criticism* 45 (1987):237-49; and response, Robert Grigg, "Flemish Realism and Allegorical Interpretation," ibid., 46 (1987), 299-300.

stract knowledge that defined scholasticism.[181] The Madonna's bench in Campin's painting is civic. Its lions are perched in alignment with the center of the window, which opens onto the view of the town. The chalice on the Gothic carved furniture appears on a board added as late as the nineteenth century. The original design seems to have been a brass bowl on a domestic cupboard.[182] A domestic hearth, even with reference to the Eucharist, is not ecclesiastical in significance but domestic. The sacrament was not instituted in a church, as even Aquinas acknowledged, but in a home, and that an urban home.

Its earliest depiction was a panel by Dirk Bouts for an apsidal chapel of the collegiate church of St. Peter in Louvain. Although it was commissioned for a church, with the local faculty of theology supplying the iconography, its setting is domestic. The upper room is late Gothic in style, affording through its window a view of the grand place of Louvain with its town hall. Christ, blessing the host as in the Eucharistic rite, rather than breaking the bread as in the scriptural verse, is framed by a hearth and seated at a table with his disciples. The commission was from the confraternity of the blessed sacrament for the bicentennial of that feast. The confraternity was a lay, not clerical, organization of burghers, several of whose members are painted in attendance as servants and witnesses.[183] The concept is not liturgical but devotional. It invites the viewer, especially the confraternity, to imagine the sacramental celebration as a supper in their own homes. A scene of the Last Supper from the workshop of Pietro Lorenzetti in Assisi even reveals the kitchen next to the dining room. The servants before a burning hearth scrape the plates clean for the dog and cat to lick.[184] Its hearth provides the first example of light in a picture illuminated by a light

---

[181] Dante, *Paradiso* 13.95-105.

[182] For the alteration see Joseph Destrée, "Altered in the Nineteenth Century? A Problem at the National Gallery, London," *Connoisseur* 74 (1926):209-10; Panofsky, *Early Netherlandish Painting* 1:163-64.

[183] Dirk Bouts, Holy Sacrament altarpiece, central panel, Collegiate Church of St. Peter, Louvain. Reproduced in Shirley Nielsen Blum, *Early Netherlandish Triptychs: A Study in Patronage* (Berkeley: University of California Press, 1969), pl. VII and see pp. 59-70. See also Aloys Butzkamm, *Bild und Frömmigkeit im 15. Jahrhundert: Der Sakramentsaltar von Dieric Bouts in der St.-Peters-Kirche zu Löwen* (Paderborn: Bonifatius, 1989. Reproduced also in Lane, *Altar and Altarpiece*, p. 106 fig. 68, who identifies the place as a sanctuary, pp. 113-14. O'Meara interprets Christ replacing the hearth as a holocaust, "'In the Hearth of the Virginal Womb,'" pp. 75-76, 84 . See in general Creighton E. Gilbert, "Last Suppers and their Refectories," in *The Pursuit of Holiness in Late Medieval and Renaissance Religion*, ed. Trinkaus with Heiko A. Oberman, Studies in Medieval and Reformation Thought, 10 (Leiden: E. J. Brill, 1974), pp. 371-402. For Bouts's Annunciation in a private sanctuary see Diane Wolfthal, *The Beginnings of Netherlandish Canvas Painting: 1400-1530* (Cambridge: Cambridge University Press, 1989), p. 41 and pl. 61; Colin Eisler, "What Takes Place in the Getty Annunciation?," *Gazette des beaux-arts* 111 (1988):193-202; Robert Koch, "The Getty Annunciation by Dieric Bouts," *Burlington Magazine* 130 (1988):509-22.

[184] Workshop of Pietro Lorenzetti, Last Supper, S. Francesco lower church, Assisi. Reproduced in O'Meara, "'In the Hearth of the Virginal Womb,'" p. 81 fig. 5. For her interpretation of this scene as a holocaust see pp. 81-82.

within it, for the animals cast their shadows on the floor.[185] The kitchen beside the dining room is a realistic aspect, to the detail of the ewer on the cupboard, that associates the celebration of the Eucharist in the church with the eating of supper in a home.

That painting with the hearth as its fixed referential point was the prototype of the Flemish interiors.[186] The Madonna before the fire screen in Campin's portrayal offers her breast to the viewer, at whom her infant directly gazes.[187] She extends to all viewers the singular privilege of Bernard of Clairvaux, who was believed graced with drops of her milk.[188] There are no pictorial barriers to prohibit entering imaginatively into that room and sharing the intimacy of mother and child. Personal involvement in a scene, through meditation on textual and artistic images, was the popular devotion. On the donor wing of the Mérode altarpiece, Ingelbrecht gazes into the interior with brow furrowed in wonder, hat respectfully in hand. The door is not ajar to symbolize Mary as the gate who opened heaven, as in medieval allegory, but to allow the donor pictorial access to the scriptural scene. His wife tells her beads, conjuring the event in her imagination, for the annunciation is the first joyful mystery of the rosary she prays. In the Arnolfini portrait by Jan van Eyck prayer beads hang on the wall behind the couple, next to a mirror whose frame is carved with ten gospel scenes, from the Nativity to the Resurrection, for their meditation.[189] In the incarnational scene of Matthias Grünewald's altarpiece for the hospital in Isenheim, the Christ child himself fingers coral and gold beads, inviting imitation; while Antony abbot in the scene of his temptation has the rosary wrapped around his knuckles, which the basilisk bites to force release.[190] The desire for realism in religion was no longer a sop to the laity, as in Bernard of Clairvaux's condescension to art for the plebs in the parishes, who were deemed incapable of contemplation.[191] Now an abbess of Flines in a contract for a sculptured altarpiece of the Nativity stipulated the details of a Flemish home.[192] And in a copy of a Madonna in the church attributed to Jan Gos-

---

185 See Meiss, *The Great Age of Fresco* (New York: Praeger, 1970), p. 70.

186 Mario Praz, *An Illustrated History of Interior Decoration* (London: Thames & Hudson, 1987), pp. 90, 83, and p. 82 fig. 33.

187 Pitts, "Iconographic Mode in Campin's London Madonna," p. 90; O'Meara, "'In the Hearth of the Virginal Womb,'" p. 82; Lane, *Altar and Altarpiece*, p. 8. Originally the infant's eyes were turned toward the mother's breast. Heckscher, "Annunciation of the Mérode Altarpiece," p. 55.

188 For Bernard see Peter Morsbach, "Lactatio," in *Marienlexikon*, ed. Remigius Bäumer and Leo Scheffczyk (St. Ottilien: Eos, 1988-), 3:702-3. See also Paule-V. Bétérous," À propos d'une des légendes mariales le plus répandues: Le 'lait de la Vierge,'" *Bulletin de l'Association Guillaume Budé* 4 (1975):403-11.

189 Jan van Eyck, Arnolfini portrait, detail, National Gallery, London. Reproduced in Dhanens, *Hubert en Jan van Eyck*, pp. 200-1; Davies, *Rogier van der Weyden*, fig. 20.

190 Wilhelm Fraenger, *Matthias Grünewald* (Munich: C. H. Beck, 1983), pp. 89, 219.

191 Bernard of Clairvaux, *Apologia ad Guilelhem abbatem* 13.28.

192 See Campbell, "The Art Market in the Southern Netherlands in the Fifteenth Cen-

saert the abbot Christiaan de Hondt kneels in his room with a dog curled at his feet, his very crosier propped against the wall by a blazing hearth.[193]

In another Madonna before the hearth by Campin she is again situated in a bourgeois interior. The naked infant prone on her lap turns and warms to the modest fire burning on the andirons.[194] Mary extends her hand before the flames before diapering the child with the cloth on her lap.[195] Perhaps she tests the heat, to see if it is too intense on his bare back. In a reminiscent Birth of the Virgin by Jan de Beer a nurse is seated on the floor between the foot of St. Anne's bed and the hearth. She holds up to its flames the same right hand, while in her lap is the newborn babe in the identical position as the Christ child in Campin's painting. The scene is homey, as detailed in the bowl of porridge with a spoon, the wicker basket of swaddling cloths, and the ordinary furnishings of Anne's bedroom, in which plenteous women attend the new mother. The nurse's slipper is even off her foot.[196] The Madonna before the hearth in Campin's painting may be about to heat water for the infant's bath, for there is a lidded pewter jug on a tray table, and above it on a rod an ample towel. The scene contrasts with the other half of the diptych, the Trinity enthroned in a tent.

Yet another version, a tiny devotional panel, clarifies the room as domestic. The mother and child are cheek-to-cheek. She sits on a cushion on the footrest of a bench, her left foot comfortably slipped out of her sandal. In front of the hearth is a basin of water, and next to the Madonna on the tile floor is a wicker basket with swaddling cloths.[197] Probably she is about to bathe and swaddle her child, a favorite devotion with women. In hagiogra-

---

tury," *Burlington Magazine* 118 (1976):192-93; Harbison, "Realism and Symbolism in Early Flemish Painting," p. 588.

193 Copy attributed to Jan Gossaert, Madonna in the church, Galleria Doria, Rome. Reproduced in Dhanens, *Hubert en Jan van Eyck*, p. 319 fig. 197.

194 Master of Flémalle, Madonna of the fireplace, Hermitage, Leningrad. Reproduced in Dunkerton et al., *Giotto to Dürer*, p. 244 fig. 13b; Davies, *Rogier van der Weyden*, fig. 14; Meiss, *Late Fourteenth Century and Patronage of the Duke*, 2:pl.333.

195 Panofsky, *Early Netherlandish Painting*, 1:173.

196 Jan de Beer, Birth of the Virgin, Thyssen-Bornemisza collection. Reproduced in Eisler, *Early Netherlandish Painting: The Thyssen-Bornemisza Collection* (London: Sotheby, 1989), pl. 27. See also the servant turning the spit,who shields his face from the fire with upheld hand. Unknown artist, third quarter 15th c., cathedral, Atri, Italy. Reproduced in Thornton, *Italian Renaissance Interior*, p. 211 pl. 239. It seems improbable that Mary's hand upraised to the fire wards off the evil spirits of the hearth, as contends Hecksher, "Annunciation of the Mérode Altarpiece," p. 55; or that the infant turns from the fire as a prefiguration of the crucifixion, as claims O'Meara, "'In the Hearth of the Virginal Womb,'" p. 84. There is also a piscina hung with a laver and a carved rack and towel, as in Campin's Annunciation in the Mérode triptych. Against Gottlieb's assertion that the Virgin's room must be a sanctuary, since burghers did not install a piscina in their dining rooms, see the examples of such niches in fifteenth-century homes, as in Bruges, in Harbison, "Realism and Symbolism in Early Flemish Painting," p. 591 n. 18.

197 Alistair Smith and Martin Wyld, "Robert Campin's Virgin and Child in an Interior," *Burlington Magazine* 130 (1988):570-72. Reproduced also in Dunkerton et al., *Giotto to Dürer*, p. 44 fig. 40.

phy a female saint bathed the infant Jesus in a tub of tepid water and tended him as he swished about in it, splashing her all wet before she could even wash him. Toweling him dry she played intimately with him.[198] She did not ponder the tub as an allegorical baptismal font but experienced it as a source of personal delight. The towel was not a symbol of purity but a practical cloth. While absorbing the water on the infant's skin, it allowed her a means to caress him. Toweling him she played intimately. Touch was a sense in spiritual ascendancy. Sight had been the paradigm for contemplation as the analogue of intellection, the apprehension of a true idea. Meditation differed from the immediate achievement of that still point. It was a lengthy procedure in movement. It was ruminative, discursive, exploratory—like the eye moving from object to object in a painted Netherlandish interior. The roving eye acquired a tactile quality, for the exact painterly detailing of light on surfaces allowed it to linger on things.

Realism became a devotional aid. By an artistic shift from the subject it functioned to involve the viewer affectively. Eliciting and structuring the responses of beholders, it stimulated new states of consciousness.[199] There was in late medieval piety an alteration of prayer from contemplation, which was transcendental, intellectual, and iconoclastic, to meditation, which was incarnational, affective, and imaginative. A meditative Margery Kempe bathed the infant Jesus in her soul. In her imagination she personally begged about the town of Bethlehem for his swaddling cloths; watched a demonstration from Mary with her kerchief on how to swaddle; then offered to do it herself, promising that she would not bind him too tightly. The swaddling cloths were practical: they actually wrapped the infant, while reminding her to live "chaste and clean."[200] They were personally moral, not abstractly theological, in import. Her meditation of the poor mother nursing before the hearth was not significant until the child climbed from that lap and toddled over to Kempe's lap. It was only then that she burst into tears of devotion for the sorrowful mother and son of the passion. When a scene excited the devout imagination to a moral response it quickened with meaning.

The Madonna portrayed in a Flemish interior is no byzantine allegory. Her fire screen is not a halo[201] any more than the same device framing Jean duc de Berry in the calendar for January canonizes him. The pseudo sancti-

---

[198] See Herlihy, *Medieval Households*, p. 127.

[199] James H. Marrow, "Symbol and Meaning in Northern European Art of the Late Middle Ages and the Early Renaissance," *Simiolus* 16 (1986):150-69. See also Harbison, "Visions and Meditations in Early Flemish Painting," ibid. 15 (1985):87-118; idem, "Realism and Symbolism in Early Flemish Painting," p. 593.

[200] *Book of Margery Kempe* 1.85.

[201] For the halo see Pitts, "Iconographic Mode in Campin's London Madonna," p. 87; Lane, *Altar and Altarpiece*, p. 4; O'Meara, "'In the Hearth of the Virginal Womb,'" p. 75; Davies, *Rogier van der Weyden*, p. 253; Panofsky, *Early Netherlandish Painting*, 1:163.

fication of such religious art is docetist, in denial of the reality of the incarnation. The Madonna's room is a bourgeois interior not a disguised sanctuary. The cloth on her lap is a diaper, such as a sensible person would place under a baby's buttocks, not a corporal on the altar for the reception of the Eucharist.[202] There was a persistent classical topic of rearing "in the mother's lap," especially in the lap of a mother of rare chastity, who tenderly cared for and honorably educated her son. Her breast was a place of solace and not just sustenance.[203] Deliberate sanctification of the ordinary by the medieval invention of scriptural or liturgical parallels to justify its very existence was waning. Margery Kempe knew that the infant's cloth was not a corporal but a diaper because she had procured it herself and used it to just that purpose.

Just as the tale of Augustine's conversion nested tales within tales, so do these domestic interiors in art display pictures within pictures. In an Annunciation by Rogier van der Weyden on the bed curtain in the Virgin's bourgeois chamber there hangs above her pillows a metal medallion embossed with an image of God the Father.[204] Devotional images were popular in bedrooms as an invitation to a divine or saintly presence.[205] They also enhanced the role of the artist or artisan against criticism like Bernard of Claivaux's of the piety of "carnal" persons. Bishops had pastorally to tolerate such fools, he barely conceded. Commoners needed religious excitement by corporeal ornaments because they could not be elevated by spiritual concepts. To the wise person an image was like his meretricious sister Humbeline: "dung."[206] Values were changing, however. On the right wing of the Mérode Annunciation, in the position corresponding to its lay donor and his wife, is Joseph at work in his carpentry shop.[207] He is seated on a lat-

---

[202] For the Madonna's lap as an altar, the diaper a corporal for the Eucharistic host, see Lane, *Altar and Altarpiece*, pp. 16, 18, 35, 53, 64, 95. However, for an example of an infant with a cloth under its buttocks, who is being held up before the fire, see the miniature from *Historie de la belle Hélaine*, ms. 15th century, Paris, Bibliothèque national. Reproduced in Paul Lacroix, *France in the Middle Ages: Customs, Classes and Conditions* (New York: Frederick Ungar, 1963), p. 86.

[203] Dixon, *The Roman Mother* (London: Croom Helm, 1987), pp. 129-30.

[204] Rogier van der Weyden, Annunciation, Louvre, Paris. Reproduced in Davies, *Rogier van der Weyden*, pl. 21; and for identification of the medallion see p. 236. The room is considered "divine," "sacred space" in Blum, "Symbolic Invention in the Art of Roger van der Weyden," *Konsthistorisk Tidskrift* 46 (1977):105. For the solidarity and power of the Burgundian court in the Columba altarpiece, which includes an Annunciation, see Laurinda S. Dixon, "Portraits and Politics in Two Triptychs by Rogier van der Weyden," *Gazette des beaux-arts* 109 (1987): 181-90. See also in the Virgin's room the devotional altar with triptych, the painting tacked on the wall, and over the pillow of her bed the circular medallion in Joos van Cleef, Annunciation, Metropolitan Museum of Art, New York. Reproduced in Panofsky, "Friesdam Annunciation," p. 456 fig. 28.

[205] Kecks, *Madonna und Kind*.

[206] See Bernard of Clairvaux, *Apologia ad Guillelmum abbatem* 13.28.

[207] Robert Campin, Mérode triptych, right wing, The Cloisters, Metropolitan Museum of Art, New York. Reproduced in Davies, *Rogier van der Weyden*, pl. 143. For the interpretation of his role as sanctioning the sacral nature of marriage and the family see Hahn,

ticed bench, probably of his own making, boring holes in a board with a bit and brace. At his feet are a saw resting on a miniature stool, and a dowel and an axe on a half-hewn log. On the bench before him are finer tools—blade, pliers, chisel, tack hammer, gimlet, and nails—and a mousetrap. The open shutters of his upper room display a local city busy with passersby.

The mousetrap spiritually adumbrates his foster son. By his marriage to the Virgin, Joseph provided the ruse by which the devil was fooled about the divine identity of the Christ child. Jesus was supposed to be the son of Joseph the artisan, as all the villagers knew (Matt. 13:55). But, as Augustine preached, the cross was a mousetrap, and on it the devil was caught by the bait of Jesus' body.[208] The trap on Joseph's carpentry bench is, however, an accurate device for catching real mice. A bow saw with twisted twine and a wedged spring hold the blade taut. The wedge in the *U*-shaped opening is a catch, like those supporting the shutters above Joseph's head. A bit of cheese on a nail on the underside of the lid, delicately supported by the raised catch, provides the bait. When the mouse reaching for the cheese presses the catch, the lid is released to snap shut.[209] Another mousetrap on the windowsill of Joseph's shop advertises his craft to the populace. He is a joiner, a maker of household furnishings, rather than a constructor of large projects.[210] The item in his hand seems variously to be: the cover of a footstool for a warming tray, an instrument of the passion, the lid of a fisherman's box for bait, the floor of a doweled mousetrap, a fire screen, and the strainer of a winepress.[211] With its multiple holes for nailheads it resembles simply the door and shutters of the rooms in the triptych. It is an emblem of his trade. A joiner, Joseph is a clever man, who designed the fine movable bench on whose footrest his betrothed Mary sits at the annunciation. He likely also made the dining table with its sixteen edges and the fire screen. The religious significance of the board in his hand is that the just man is a maker. An illumination on the social estates at the turn of the six-

"'Joseph, Mary, Jesus,'" p. 55.

208 Schapiro, "Muscipula diaboli," pp. 182, 184, citing Augustine, *Sermo* 163, 130, 134.

209 John Jacob, "The Mérode Mousetrap," *Burlington Magazine* 108 (1966): 374. See also C. Roth, "Medieval Illustrations of Mouse-traps," *Bodleian Library Record* 5 (1956):244-51.

210 Irving L. Zupnick, "The Mystery of the Mérode Mousetrap," *Burlington Magazine* 108 (1966):129, 133.

211 Panofsky, *Early Netherlandish Painting*, 1:164; Charles de Tolnay, "L'autel Mérode du Maître de Flémalle," *Gazette des beaux-arts* 53 (1959):75, and Freeman, "The Iconography of the Mérode Altarpiece," *Metropolitan Museum of Art Bulletin* 16 (1957):138; Schapiro, "A Note on the Mérode Altarpiece," *Art Bulletin* 41 (1959):327-28; Zupnick, "Mystery of the Mérode Mousetrap"; Heckscher, "Annunciation of the Mérode Altarpiece," p. 48, and Hahn, "'Joseph, Mary, Jesus,'" pp. 60-61; Marilyn Aronberg Lavin, "The Mystic Winepress in the Mérode Altarpiece," in *Studies in Late Medieval and Renaissance Painting in Honor of Millard Meiss*, ed. Lavin and Plummer, 1:297-301. Disagreeing with these symbolic interpretations, De Coo notes that Joseph is not using the tools, "Medieval Look at the Mérode Annunciation," pp. 131-32.

teenth century would depict a carpenter in his workshop planing a board on a bench, with his tools fully displayed. His wife wearing an apron holds a distaff. On the floor a male child plays with the wood shavings in a basket.[212] There have no halos but the carpenter's family is worthy of art.

A proposal at the Council of Constance by Pierre d'Ailly and Jean Gerson that Joseph be elevated above the apostles to rank next to the Virgin had failed. Their argument for a universal feast of the marriage of Mary and Joseph also failed; but it was adopted locally, as in Bruges. Their true marriage was insisted on by Gerson in laudatory works and in a Mass. He called Joseph a *charlier*, his own family name. In 1479 the husband of Mary was introduced into the Roman breviary.[213] As the cult of Joseph developed, he shed his depiction as an old man (so as to be disinterested in sex with the Virgin) and his victimization as the butt of jokes. He was even bodily assumed into heaven to reunite the holy family as a model for the human family. In eternity Joseph attained universal hegemony, because the mother of God who was subject to him on earth remained submissive to him in heaven. In art and literature, although nearly invisible before late medieval culture, he attained the features of a youthful companion to Mary and a capable provider for the family.[214] Even in the Mérode wing, where he is still bearded as an elder, he is industrious. Jesus had in Joseph an artisan for a father to figure the Artisan of creation. As in the exegesis of Ambrose, although the human and the divine are not comparable, still "the symbol is perfect, since the Father of Christ works by the fire and the spirit and like a good artisan of the soul trims off our vices all around, takes the axe to the unfruitful trees, cuts off that which is worthless, saving the well-shaped shoots, and softening the rigidity of souls in the fire of the spirit, and fashioning humankind by different sorts of ministries for different uses."[215]

Although the cult of Joseph the laborer originated in consideration of Christ's humble origins, it owed to a new conception in the fifteenth century of labor as virtuous.[216] Campin may have signed his own name to his Annunciation on the Virgin's maiolica pitcher, in an anagram of pseudo Greek and Hebrew letters as DVPAYMKN or du Kampyn.[217] He carefully depicted

---

212 Detail from illuminated page of Jean Bourdichon, *Les quatre états de la société*, c. 1500, Bibliothèque de l'École national supérieure des beaux-arts, Paris. Reproduced in Thomas Hoving et al., *The Secular Spirit: Life and Art at the End of the Middle Ages* (New York: E. P. Dutton with the Metropolitan Museum of Art, 1975), p. 101.

213 Schapiro, "Muscipula diaboli," p. 184.

214 Herlihy, *Medieval Households*, pp. 127-30. For Joseph as a comic type see also Huizinga, *Waning of the Middle Ages*, pp. 152-53.

215 Hahn, "'Joseph, Mary, Jesus,'" pp. 55, 58, citing Ambrose, *Expositio evangelii secundum Lucam* 3.2.

216 Hahn, "'Joseph, Mary, Jesus,'" p. 64. See also Lynn White, Jr., "The Iconography of *Temperantia* and the Virtuousness of Technology," in *Action and Conviction in Early Modern Europe: Essays in Memory of E. H. Harbison*, ed. Theodore K. Rabb and Jerrold E. Seigel (Princeton: Princeton University Press, 1969), pp. 197-219, and on Joseph, pp. 199-201.

217 T.-L. de Bruin, "Le Maître de Flémalle et sa crypto-signature," *Gazette des beaux-*

its bulbous body, with a three-lobed opening and broad, flat handle; its pattern of three large oak leaves amid a floral design, with the hint of a central bird; and its broad bands down the sides with their untypical inscription.[218] It was a credit to the skill of the potter and to the industry of the Flemish household that could afford to grace its table with a Florentine import. Popular piety assumed an interest in the household of the holy family.

Although the Boucicaut Master located the annunciation in a Gothic cathedral, the birth of the Virgin was in an ordinary house. In a miniature from his workshop her mother St. Anne lies amid sheets, pillows, and coverlet in a bed of wooden frame with a dog curled at its foot. A midwife takes the infant Mary. A hearth with firewood, bellows, and andirons warms the scene.[219] Such domesticity is transferred to Mary's own home in the Hours of Catherine of Cleves, from about the turn of the fifteenth century, where she sits by the window weaving. The infant Jesus toddles in a homemade baby walker, while Joseph planes a plank of wood. The room is furnished with a cabinet of supplies for weaving, a shelf of plates, and a carpentry bench with tools of the trade. A hooded stone fireplace is built against the wall. In another of its miniatures Mary sits on a chair nursing, a yellow mat beneath her feet. Joseph sits on a barrel chair on bare tile with a bowl of gruel. The cylindrical, open gable-wall fireplace is decorated with two faces. In its recess a cast-iron pot hangs on a gallows over the flame, while a small one bakes on the hearth. There are tongs, a grill, a hook, a ledge, a warming niche, and bellows beside it. The Hours also include an illustration of St. Martha in an apron as a housewife or kitchenmaid holding a cast-iron pot and a wooden spoon. In the border she is spinning.[220] There is no sister Mary present.

In its illustration of the holy family by the hearth the toddling infant holds a banderole toward Mary proclaiming, "I am your solace." He and his mother are nimbused in gold, while Joseph, to whom he has his back, depreciatingly sports a red scarf.[221] But by the early sixteenth century, even in a Netherlandish painting of much lesser quality than van der Weyden's Annunciation, his vase on the mantle of the Virgin's fireplace has been replicated. The status of Joseph the artisan, absent from that scene, has improved. In a portrait of the holy family at the hearth he is emphasized by

---

arts 67 (1966):5-6.

[218] See Ellen Callman, "Campin's Maiolica Pitcher," *Art Bulletin* 64 (1982):629-31.

[219] Boucicaut workshop, Birth of the Virgin, Bourges, Bibliothèque municipale, ms. 34, fol. 46v. Reproduced in Meiss, *Boucicaut Master*, pl. 64.

[220] Hours of Catherine of Cleves, New York, Pierpont Morgan Library, Ms. 917. Reproduced by Plummer, ed., pls. 92, 93, 155. For such literature see Susan Groag Bell, "Medieval Women Book Owners: Arbiters of Lay Piety and Ambassadors of Culture," in *Women and Power in the Middle Ages*, ed. Erler and Maryanne Kowaleski (Athens: University of Georgia Press, 1988), pp. 149-97; rpt. from *Signs: Journal of Women in Culture and Society* 7 (1982):742-68.

[221] Hours of Catherine of Cleves, pl. 92.

his position on the same bench as Mary and Jesus. While the Madonna looks in the opposite direction at a book an angel props open, she lifts the infant to reach for an apple Joseph is peeling.[222] As in the Hours of Catherine of Cleves the fireplace is central to the composition; but all have their backs to it. The hearth could still be an ambiguous site. An oaken and leather bellows with the coat of arms of Amsterdam dating to the first half of the sixteenth century is preserved from a household or guild hall. Carved in high relief, once painted, is a depiction of the holy family's flight into Egypt.[223] The majority of the images of the holy family at labor are located in Egypt,[224] an incisive reminder that it too was under the curse of Adam (Gen. 3:17-19) to toil on the earth in exile.

Yet people were attracted to a domestic Mary. The cult of her very house at Nazareth became accessible, when at the end of the thirteenth century angels were believed to miraculously lift it from its foundations and transport it to an Italian hill called for its foliage Loreto. The deed avoided the profanation of her house during the conquest of the Holy Land by the Turks, who had already destroyed the basilica of the Annunciation. The relocation was part of a massive movement of relics. The cult of her house spread among friars and confraternities, and it was honored by Pope Julius II in a bull of 1510 augmenting the indulgences accruing to its feast of the annunciation. By then the house at Loreto had become enclosed in a basilica as a sanctuary, as if the house were unholy without such consecration. The pope was convinced that there the devout venerated not only the Virgin's image but also the very chamber in which she whom the angel saluted conceived the Savior. Leo X commissioned prestigious artists like Donato d'Agnolo Bramante and Luca Signorelli to embellish it and Andrea Sansovino to sculpt its walls. In his bull of 1519 he affirmed that the holy house was "the premier and most celebrated of all the sanctuaries," because the Virgin had transported by almighty power her statue and her house from Nazareth. The route was indirect, he explained, because the angels initially flew to Dalmatia, then to the forest of Recanti and the field of two brothers, before they settled it where it actually is, and where, thanks to the Virgin, almighty God continues to work miracles. During the Catholic Reformation Pope Julius III transferred the administration of the sanctuary to the Society of Jesus, which defended it rigorously. At the end of the sixteenth century the Sacred Congregation of Rites instituted on 10 December the feast of the

---

[222] Netherlandish, Holy Family, early sixteenth century, cathedral treasury, Le Puy. Reproduced in Wolfthal, *Beginnings of Early Netherlandish Canvas Painting*, pl. 53 and pp. 62-63.

[223] See Hoving et al., *Secular Spirit*, p. 29 fig. 15. Its scene is almost identical to one c. 1510 from Utrecht, now in the Rijksmuseum, Amsterdam.

[224] Hahn, "'Joseph, Mary, Jesus,'" p. 64. For an example see idem, "Joseph as Ambrose's 'Artisan of the Soul' in the Holy Family in Egypt by Albrecht Dürer," *Zeitschrift für Kunstgeschichte* 47 (1984):515-22.

translation of the Virgin's house.[225] Yet either the locals had moved their church from the valley to the hilltop, or a family named Angeli had financed the transport of an edifice by ship from Nazareth to Loreto. It was a popular place of pilgrimage, nevertheless, and since late in the fifteenth century for exorcism. In 1920 Pope Benedict XV elevated Mary with her house, under the title of Our Lady of Loreto, to the status of a patron. Of homeowners? homemakers? housebuilders? Aviators.[226]

The flight of the prestigious house impressed no less a humanist and reformer than Erasmus, who composed a liturgy in its honor. After the introit with its classical image of the laurel, Erasmus employed to the collect traditional images from scripture. He did not suggest in his cult of the Virgin's house that she was a house. In his sermon of praise, honor, invocation, and imitation he did emphasize that her marriage was to Joseph, not to Jesus. Her womb was the bridal chamber from which the Son issued, but "come from his bridal chamber he took as his wife the new Church." It was dowerless, captive, and polluted; but he purified its iniquity with his blood, redeemed its captivity with his death, and enriched its nakedness with spiritual gifts. "The soul of each one of us, beloved, is the spouse of Christ," Erasmus preached. Through unfeigned faith and sincere charity the members of the Church remained in the embrace of the spouse. Through the unification of the Spirit, just as Christ was one with the Father, so were all one with him. Erasmus concluded in hope of frequent gathering to praise the Virgin of Loreto, so that by the example of the Son and his mother "each one may return home better." The cult that would delight Mary and gladden her Son was the removal of vice and the acquisition of virtue.[227]

Erasmus earlier composed an entreaty in adversity to the Virgin Mother, in which he related among her hardships that she had given birth "not at home but in public."[228] In a prose litany of scriptural allusions he named her relations as daughter, betrothed, mother, and concubine.[229] With

---

[225] Italo Tanoni, "Le culte marial de la sainte maison de Lorette et son évolution," *Social Compass* 33 (1986):107-11. Among recent publications, which seem intended to promote cult, are Giuseppe Santarelli, *La santa casa di Loreto: Tradizione e ipotesi* (Loreto: Loreto, 1988); Floriano Grimaldi, *Pittori a Loreto: Committenze tra '500 e '600: Documenti*, Soprintendenza per i beni ambiantali e architettonici delle Marche, 3 (Ancona: n. p., 1988); idem and Katy Sordi, *Scultori a Loreto: Fratelli Lombardi, Antonio Calcagni e Tiburzio Vergelli: Documenti*, ibid., 2 (Ancona, n. p., 1987); Grimaldi, *La basilica della santa casa di Loreto: Indagini archeologiche geognostiche e statiche*, ibid., 1 (Ancona, n. p. 1986); Luca de Monterado, *Storia del culto e del pellegrinaggio a Loreto (XIVe-XVe siècles)* (Loreto: Congregazione universale santa casa, 1979).

[226] Tanoni, "Culte mariale de la sainte maison," pp. 113-14, 124-28, 119, 121.

[227] Erasmus, *Virginis Matris Lauretum cultae liturgia*, ed. Leon E. Halkin, in *Opera omnia* (ASD), 5-1:97-109, 101-2, 105-6, 197. For a survey of his Marian writings see idem, "La mariologie d'Érasme," *Archiv für Reformationsgeschichte* 68 (1977):32-55.

[228] Erasmus, *Obsecratio ad virginem matrem Mariam in rebus adversus*, in *Opera omnia* (LB), 5:1236E.

[229] Erasmus, *Paean Virgini Matris*, in *Opera omnia* (LB), 5:1231A.

"concubine" he denied by canon law any relationship to God by lawful marriage, thus acknowledging a difference in social status. He also distinguished it in stability and exclusivity from prostitution as an informal cohabitation with affection.[230] As an incarnational place, she was a most sacred temple and the mystical town the redeemer had visited under the figure of the sisters Martha and Mary. Her womb was a *scriniolum*, a small case or box for keeping booklets, papers, and letters—a fitting receptacle for the Word.[231] So Erasmus enjoined all persons: let your heart be the library of Christ.[232]

In his edition of the New Testament in Greek, with its translation into Latin, Erasmus corrected the Vulgate version to a significant paradigm for humanist theology. "In the beginning was the Speech," not the Word (John 1:1).[233] Yet he failed to elucidate the incarnational verse, only replicating the usual verb, "And that Speech was made flesh, and dwelt among us" (v. 14). The divine nature, he explained, was united to a human body in the hypostatic union. The human body was a "tabernacle" of the soul.[234] Although Erasmus announced his edition of scripture for private reading "at home,"[235] he did not restore revelation to its domicile. For the topical verse of John 14:23 Erasmus preserved the Vulgate translation of dwelling. "If anyone loves me he will keep my speech, and my Father will love him, and we will come to him, and we will make our dwelling at his home (*mansio apud eum*)." The permanence of that divine dwelling he elaborated in his paraphrase on the gospel. In the mutual love of the human person and the unified Father and Son, Jesus promised that "we will never be torn away from him. And not only will I return to visit the one who is mindful of my bidding, but the Father also and I will come to him by way of our common Spirit; and we will not come only to depart soon thereafter, but we will make our dwelling in him (*mansionem apud eum faciemus*) and will never leave him. What happens in the Spirit is both permanent and powerful." This exegesis departed from Augustine's sense of *mansio* as but a temporary lodging. Augustine in his treatise on the gospel had virtually ignored the verse, transforming the abode into a "manifestation," interior and brief, to

---

230 See James Brundage, "Concubinage and Marriage in Medieval Canon Law," *Journal of Medieval History* 1 (1975):1-17, without reference to Erasmus. Concubinage was not forbidden the laity until the Council of Trent.

231 Erasmus, *Paean Virgini Matris*, 5:1232B, 1230E, 1232B, 1227E. A *scrinium* was, in a fifteenth-century hymn on the annunciation, a box for Eucharistic hosts. Ingvar Bergström, "Medicina, fons et scrinium: A Study in Van Eyckian Symbolism and its Influence in Italian Art," *Konsthistorisk Tidskrift* 26 (1957):1-20.

232 Erasmus, *Ratio verae theologiae*, p. 194; cf. Jerome, *Epistolae* 60.10.

233 Boyle, *Erasmus on Language and Method in Theology*, Erasmus Studies, 2 (Toronto: University of Toronto Press, 1977).

234 Erasmus, *Annotationes in Novum Testamentum*, in *Opera omnia* (LB), 6:340A-B.

235 Erasmus, *Apologia*, in *Ausgwählte Werke*, p. 168.

lovers, not to aliens.[236] Aquinas also considered it a manifestation yet he acknowledged that dwelling denoted a firm adhesion to God. He came to persons through faith and compunction but not to remain with them; he abided in those who persevered in their predestination. Dwelling also indicated the familiarity of Christ to people, although Aquinas did not elaborate on that delight.[237] Erasmus's interpretation reiterated the ecclesiastical nature of that dwelling. Since the believer could not yet come to God in an eternal state, Jesus offered that "then in an invisible but powerful manner we will come to you, to dwell in the temple of your heart."[238] That word *templum* was "church". The humanists Alberti, Valla, Erasmus all preferred its Latinity to *ecclesia* from the Greek.[239]

Although Erasmus exhorted returning home from the liturgy of the Virgin's house a better person, the heart of the worshipper was a church, not a house, for God. At the annunciation Mary was in her chamber in a house but she was not domestically occupied. She was "at leisure in contemplation."[240] Erasmus retained the contemplative norm for the incarnation, although it is unscriptural, since the word never occurs. As its premier editor he had to have known that. He did not mistakenly ascribe contemplation to Mary, the sister of Martha, however. He described the sisters as equal in piety, only differently directed, like the diversity of gifts within the Church.[241] Their iconography, as in a moralized bible, portrayed their house as a large hearth over whose flames a pot hangs from a gallows. A seated Christ raises his hand in benediction to Mary crouched at his feet, while Martha stands in the orans posture.[242] It was not the worst depiction of a woman at a hearth. That was reserved for the Jewess cooking and eating her dismembered child.[243] Erasmus protested in his encomium of marriage about contemporary painting that impiously represented the scene of Jesus and his

---

236 Augustine, *In evangelium Iohannis tractatus* 66.2.

237 Aquinas, *Expositio in quatuor evangelia* ad caput 14, lectio 6.

238 Erasmus, *Paraphrasis in evangelium Iohannis*, in *Opera omnia* (LB) 7:611E-612A; *Paraphrase on John*, ed. Robert D. Sider, trans. Jane E. Phillips, Collected Works of Erasmus, 46 (Toronto: University of Toronto Press, 1991), p. 173. That translation incorrectly renders the paradigmatic *logos-sermo* (John 1:1) as "Word" passim.

239 Alberti, "Religio" in *Intercenales*, trans. Marsh, p. 19; *Libro della famiglia* 3, pp. 243-44; and for the Tempio Malatestiano in Rimini see Gadol, *Leon Battista Alberti*, pp. 95-98, 118-20. Valla, *De professione religiosorum* 3.5.

240 Erasmus, *Paraphrasis in evangelium Lucae*, in *Opera omnia* (LB), 7:289B. He notes that a girl lived with her betrothed even without sexual intercourse. *Annotationes in evangelium Lucae* 5:223B.

241 Erasmus, *Paraphrasis in evangelium Lucae* 7:378F.

242 Bible moralisée, late 13th century, London, British Library, Add. MS 18719, f. 25. Reproduced in Rosalind and Christopher Brooke, *Popular Religion in the Middle Ages: Western Europe 1000-1300* (London: Thames & Hudson, 1984), p. 137.

243 Luçon Master, Jewess eating her child, Geneva, Bilbiothèque publique et universitaire, fr. 190, II, fol. 101; Cité des dames workshop, Paris, Bibliothèque de l'Arsenal, ms. 5193, fol. 309; Boucicaut workshop and French illuminator, both Collection Kettaneh, New York. All reproduced in Meiss, *Boucicaut Master*, pls. 384-87.

apostles in the home of the two sisters. Martha was bizarrely portrayed chatting with John in a corner of the kitchen, one arm about his shoulder, while with the other she mocked the Lord speaking to Mary.[244] Erasmus also corrected by *oppidulum* the mistranslation in that pericope of *castellum*, which had promoted the allegories on the Virgin's womb as the castle of love. Jesus entered a certain small town or village, and a woman named Martha welcomed him into her house, he explained. That was not to be imagined as a powerful stronghold, like the structures popularly called "castle." Martha was reprehended not because she readied a banquet but because she was preoccupied with excessively diverse preparations in contrast to the one thing necessary.[245] What that was Erasmus did not specify, although in his *Enchiridion militis christiani* he characteristically indicated the sole sighting of life as Christ.[246]

As well as razing the castle as an architectural model for the incarnation, Erasmus demolished the aqueduct. Mary could not have served as one because she was not "full of grace." Erasmus corrected the angelic salutation to "Ave gratiosa," explaining that "she is not full of grace (*gratia plena*), but, as I have reconciled it with the verb, *gratificata*." He complained about Bernard of Clairvaux's astonishing speculation on the incorrect words. Homer used the term as beloved, Origen as rare honor. Scripture meant that Mary was embraced by a gratuitous favor of spirit.[247] Erasmus's complaint referred to Bernard's exegesis that Mary, who was full in her soul, became full in her womb with a spiritual and corporeal plenitude as a unique privilege. The angelic salutation "with thee," rather than "in thee," became Bernard's occasion for a philosophy of the divine presence. Although by his simple substance God was everywhere equally present, in rational creatures he had a presence that he did not in other creatures. He was in irrational creatures but not possessed by them; in rational creatures he could be possessed by cognition, the more so by love. Only in good souls was there a concordance of wills causing spiritual union. This union was true of every holy soul but especially of Mary's. Her consent was such that, not only her will but even her flesh, was married, effecting Christ from her substance and God's substance, so that he belonged wholly to both. Thus the angelic salutation.[248]

---

244 Erasmus, *Encomium matrimonii*, in *Opera omnia* (LB) 5:695. See Hans Buijs, "Voorstellingen van Christus in het huis van Martha en Maria in het zestiende-eeuwse Keukenstuk," *Nederlands Kunsthistorish Jaarboek* 40 (1989):93-128; P. F. K. Moxey, "Erasmus and the Iconography of Pieter Aertsen's *Christ in the House of Martha and Mary* in the Boymans-van Beuningen Museum," *Journal of the Warburg and Courtauld Institute* 34 (1971):335-36; Panofsky, "Erasmus and the Visual Arts," ibid. 32 (1969):211.

245 Erasmus, *Annotationes in Novum Testamentum* LB 6:275E.

246 Erasmus, *Enchiridion militis christiani*, p. 63. Boyle, *Erasmus on Language and Method in Theology*, pp. 72-81.

247 Erasmus, *Annotationes in Novum Testamentum*, 224A, 223D-F.

248 Bernard of Clairvaux, *In laudibus Virginis Matris* 4.3; 3.4.

Lorenzo Valla before Erasmus had suggested the corrected translation *gratificata*.[249] He also wielded its philology to mock the ignorance of the friars. In his *Encomium s. Thomae*, preached by invitation on an anniversary of Aquinas's death, he imitated the ancient practice of commencing an oration with an invocation the gods. He saluted, "Hail, Mary, full of grace." Yet Valla had corrected that mistranslation in his annotations on the New Testament, so that he was duping the Dominicans with false knowledge and taunting their inability to know better. He rehearsed the legend of how Aquinas's mother was approached in pregnancy by the friar who congratulated her falsely with a similar annunciation. Thomas would fulfill the excellence of his name, which meant either "abyss" or "twin". That prophecy was paralleled by the one to Dominic's pregnant mother about bearing a dog with a torch in its mouth. Dominic founded the house, Thomas paved it with marble; Dominic erected the walls, Thomas decorated them with beautiful paintings. Aquinas fled from nobility, wealth, family, parents, as if from the Sirens,[250] however; so that the artisan was no domestic. Aquinas was thus prophesied by false philology. Valla tacitly mocked Aquinas's *Expositio salutationis angelicae*, in which she was scholastically analyzed as "full of grace," surpassing the angels in three regards: the first of which could be divided into two parts, although the second and third dealt with the overflowing of grace from her soul to her body and from there to humanity.[251] Valla was critical of recent theologians with vain Aristotelian ideas who lacked that philosopher's expertise on language or in languages, Greek and Latin.[252] Valla thought housewives understood usage better.[253]

Although Erasmus retained the ecclesiastical model for the Virgin annunciate, he corrected the Vulgate version of her social status. In her poetic Magnificat (Luke 1:46-55), the Lord did not remark her humility but regard her lowly estate. She was a mere girl (*virguncula*), undistinguished by wealth, nobility of lineage, or public life. She lived in a small town disdained by the Jews, betrothed to a man of no worldly aristocracy, a worker in a trade.[254] Erasmus glossed her *humilitas* as *parvitas*, not virtuous humil-

---

[249] Lorenzo Valla, *Adnotationes*, p. 830. Jerry H. Bentley, "Biblical Philology and Christian Humanism: Lorenzo Valla and Erasmus as Scholars of the Gospels," *Sixteenth Century Journal* 8 (1977):22-23; see also Jacques Chomarat, "Les *Annotations* de Valla, celles d'Érasme et la grammaire," in *Histoire de l'exégèse au XVIe siècle*, Textes du colloque international tenu à Genève en 1976, ed. Olivier Fato and Pierre Fraenkel (Geneva: Droz, 1978), pp. 202-28.

[250] Valla, *Encomium s. Thomae*. For this work see also Salvatore I. Camporeale, *Lorenzo Valla tra medioevo e rinascimento: Encomion s. Thomae—1457, Memorie domenicane* 7 (1977).

[251] Thomas Aquinas, *Expositio salutationis angelicae*, pp. 28-30.

[252] Valla, *Repastinatio dialectice et philosophie* 1, proem. See G. R. Evans, "Lorenzo Valla and the Theologians," *Journal of Theological Studies* 38 (1987):436-37.

[253] Valla, *Dialecticae disputationes* 1.2.

[254] Erasmus, *Paraphrasis in evangelium Lucae* 7:288F-289A.

ity but humbled condition.[255] In his colloquy "Concio, sive Medardus" he defended his interpretation against a slanderous sermon, likened to dung, that alleged he had altered the Virgin's humility (*humilitas*) to vileness (*vilitas*). He contrasted her with learned, powerful, and wealthy noblemen who expected the Messiah from their own stock. The Lord gazed with merciful favor on "a maiden unknown to fame, poor, married to a carpenter, without even wealth of offspring." Of the scriptural word he advised, "Take it as referring to humble condition, not to a moral virtue." Humility in the ancient idiom did not mean the moral virtue, opposite to arrogance, called modesty, but rather an inferior secular lot. In the current sense it was the condition of lower-class, poverty-stricken "outsiders," despised persons who were humble, as being groundlings. The Virgin thus depreciated her own status and praised God's bounty to her. As Erasmus stated, "There is no mention of merits." In response to the slanderous sermon about his exegesis the learned in the congregation hissed at the preacher, and quite a few women got up indignantly from the pews and left the church muttering.[256] Yet the Virgin's lowly status did not recommend her to him as a home, even though Erasmus revered her house translated to Loreto.

He had visited her shrine at Walsingham, England,[257] a replica of her house at Nazareth that had been erected in the twelfth century by Richelde, a great lady of the parish.[258] In his colloquy "Peregrinatio religionis ergo" a letter by the hand of the Madonna's angelic secretary was deposited on the pulpit of Glaucoplutus, or Ulrich Zwingli the reformer. In it Mary expressed her gratitude for his persuasions against the invocation of the saints. She was exhausted by shameless demands from her. It was not, she complained, as if her Son were always an infant (as sculptured and painted nursing), who required his mother's consent to grant a petition, lest she deny him the breast. The protagonist Ogygius nevertheless pilgrimaged to her shrine at Walsingham to ask for "family safe and sound, a larger fortune, a long and happy life in this world, and eternal bliss in the next." His interlocutor Menedemus, or Stay-at-home, questioned whether a local Virgin would not suffice. The church in Antwerp, he noted was grander than the chapel in Walsingham. He was told that different gifts are bestowed in different places.[259]

At Walsingham the pilgrim noticed that the Virgin's house was of recent

---

255 Erasmus, *Annotationes in Novum Testamentum* 6:225F-227C.

256 Erasmus, "Concio, sive Medardus," in *Colloquia, ed. Halkin,* in *Opera omnia* (ASD), 1-3:656-64; *The Colloquies of Erasmus*, trans. Craig R. Thompson (Chicago: University of Chicago Press, 1965), pp. 469, 470, 474. See also *Lingua*, ed. J. H. Waszink, in *Opera omnia* (ASD), 4-1-A, p. 122.

257 Thompson, *Colloquies of Erasmus*, p. 286.

258 J. C. Dickinson, *The Shrine of Our Lady of Walsingham* (Cambridge: Cambridge University Press, 1956), pp. 7-9.

259 Erasmus, "Peregrinatio religionis ergo," in *Colloquia*, pp. 472-74; trans. Thompson, p. 291.

materials and construction, as he carefully inspected its walls, thatched roof, rafters, and crossbeams. "How is it known for certain that this *is* the cottage?" he asks the custodian. He was shown as clear proof a ratty old bearskin fastened to the posts. Ogygius's dullness to comprehend the proof extended to disbelief about the Madonna's milk reserved on the altar of the main church. It seemed but powdered chalk mixed with albumin. Yet prostrate he prayed for an infancy of simplicity that longed for the milk of evangelical teaching, so that he might attain to perfect maturity. In the shrine of the Virgin he personalized her purity by praying that "we too, through the grace of the Holy Spirit, may be made worthy to conceive the Lord Jesus spiritually in our inmost hearts, and never lose him once conceived." His interlocutor Menedemus, not itching for such pilgrimages, preferred his own "Roman stations." He explained: "Here's how I wander about at home. I go into the living room and see that my daughter's chastity is safe. Coming out of there into my shop, I watch what my servants, male and female, are doing. Then to the kitchen, to see if any instruction is needed. From here to one place and another, observing what my children and my wife are doing, careful that everything be in order. These are my Roman stations." To the pious comment that St. James would oversee such affairs if he but went on pilgrimage, Stay-at-home rejoined: "Sacred Scripture directs me to take care of them myself. I've never read any commandment to hand them over to saints."[260] Yet in criticizing the abuse of pilgrimage, and even its rationale, the reformer did not venture to suggest that life itself was not a pilgrimage.

Erasmus attended to domesticity in *Encomium matrimonii*, *Institutio christiani matrimonii*, and *Vidua christiana*. As he preached in his liturgy for the Virgin's house at Loreto, Christ did not honor marriage by his presence at the wedding feast in Cana so that Christians might dishonor it.[261] In his paraphrase of John's gospel Christ was a guest there to honor weddings, opposing those who would in the future condemn them as "filthy."[262] Erasmus wrote in his colloquies on a variety of household topics from the role of servants to wretched hospitality.[263] His interest in "Diversoria" was not in inns as a metaphor of spiritual pilgrimage but in the comparison of French and German social customs: how guests were variously treated in those accommodations.[264] In "Proci et puellae" on courtship the lovers considered a marriage more of the mind than of the body, as an education to virginity and perhaps to attainment of the continence Mary and Joseph practiced by tradition. At home as a couple they would provide moral example for their children.[265] There was no suggestion that they themselves were a

---

260 Ibid., pp. 477-80, 494; trans. Thompson, pp. 295, 297, 312.

261 Erasmus, *Liturgia Virginis Matris*, p. 104.

262 Erasmus, *Paraphrasis in evangelium Iohannis* 7:515-16.

263 Erasmus, e. g., "Herilia iussa," "Opulentia sordida," in *Colloquia*, pp. 158-61, 676-85.

264 Erasmus, "Diversoria," ibid., pp. 333-38.

265 Erasmus, "Proci et puellae," ibid., pp. 277-88.

holy home. In "Coniugium" it was a matter of wives humoring their husbands,[266] as Monica had Patricius.

Erasmus like Alberti was alert in household management to dangerous details such as the cosmetic use among aristocratic women of white lead.[267] He importantly deplored social injustice, like the scurrilous marriage for financial gain of a tender virgin daughter to a rascally elder with venereal disease.[268] Children, not only parents, could be at fault, however. In "Virgo misogamos" he counseled against the rash and romantic entry of a girl into the convent against parental wishes. "You have Christ at home," he stated. Human and divine ordinances and instructions were to obey one's parents. As Eubulus questioned Catherine, "Will you steal away from the authority of excellent parents for the purpose of giving yourself over to an artificial instead of true father, and adopting another mother in place of your real one?" She would be adopting in the convent not new parents but new masters, he declared, who would reduce her from the freedom the children of a household enjoyed to the status of a slave. Although the slavery of the ancient world had largely been abolished by Christian compassion, a new sort was revived, under the pretension of religion, he observed. Why, a nun even forfeited her baptismal name.[269]

Secular law did not release a daughter from parental jurisdiction but required parental consent for the purchase or sale of property, he argued. By what right, he inquired of Catherine, did she surrender herself, their nearest and dearest possession, to unknown others without parental consent? When she answered that natural laws did not apply to piety, he responded that piety was most forceful in baptism. Religious profession was morally neutral, really just an exchange of clothing. Catherine would give up her freedom in the household to pray at will in her own room, or when privacy tired to go forth publicly to church to listen to choral chant, to attend services, to hear sermons—selectively, from the preacher with the purest doctrine. The religious vows of poverty, chastity, and obedience could all be practiced at home. The only difference from the convent was the veil and its ritual.[270]

"Then you think it's not right for me to become the bride of Christ except with parental approval?" summarized Catherine. Eubulus urged from scripture a more radical consideration. "You've already 'married' Christ, I tell you, and *so have we all*. Who marries the same husband twice?" He also warned her to be careful "lest, while intending to marry Christ, you marry others." When Catherine rejoined that the monks regarded nothing

---

[266] Erasmus, "Coniugium," ibid., pp. 301-13.

[267] Erasmus, "Senatulus, sive Gunaikosunedrion," ibid., p. 633.

[268] Erasmus, "Agamos gamos, sive Coniugium impar," ibid., pp. 591-600.

[269] Erasmus, "Virgo misogamos," ibid., pp. 291-95; trans. Thompson, p. 108. For filial piety as the primary spiritual endowment of a prospective wife see *Christiani matrimonii institutio*, in *Opera omnia* (LB) 5:659.

[270] Erasmus, "Virgo misogamos," in *Colloquia*, pp. 295-96.

holier than the ascetic disregard of parents, Eubulus required from her a passage in scripture that taught it. "To flee from unrighteous parents to Christ is a sacred duty. But what sacred duty is it, pray, to flee from good parents to the monastic life, which often means from good to bad?" The girl was not convinced.[271] In a sequel to that colloquy she became "Virgo poenitens," repentant of her decision. Catherine had fled back home after a horrible incident in the convent she was too ashamed to divulge, but which by implication was a sexual advance from the monks or nuns.[272] To his final work, Erasmus affirmed that the souls of all the pious, not only consecrated religious, were brides of Christ.[273]

Although the friars told the innkeeper in "Ptochoplousioi," or prosperous beggars, that spiritual kinship was more extensive than natural kinship,[274] Erasmus expounded the duties of the latter in his colloquy "Puerpera." Pilgrimage to the dried milk of the Madonna at Walsingham yielded to a visitation to a home about the flowing milk of a mother. His colloquy was not womanly conversation but male instruction by a friend of the family to a new mother, only sixteen, who had hired a wet nurse. Fabulla was not without wisdom. She considered her delivery safe but not happy, until her son should prove himself an honest man; and she was pleased with the sex of her child, not by convention but as divine will. Fabulla believed that God had the leisure to attend women in childbirth, for he could do no better than to preserve by propagation what he had created. Her visitor Eutrapelus thought God would better attend to the affairs of state: the exiles of kings, the extensions of boundaries, the courts in bankruptcy, and the peasants in revolt. Reviewing factionalism and anarchy, with Luther in the figure of a wild boar wasting the vineyard, he exclaimed, "The whole earth is pregnant with I know not what calamity." God should mind his kingdom.[275]

Fabulla retorted, "What men think most urgent may seem insignificant to God." She argued cleverly against the superiority of males to females with the scriptural example of the creation of female after male as a figuration of Christ born after Adam: artists were superior in their later works. Woman was not subject to man, only wife to husband, and not as to a superior but as to an aggressor. Not only men are members of Christ, she said. Eutrapelus conceded that all humans shared that dignity by faith. Fabulla pressed the argument. All humans were created in the image of God expressed in mental gifts; yet men were drunken, thieving, adulterous, and especially bellicose. War was nothing compared to parturition. Her visitor

[271] Ibid., pp. 296-27; trans. Thompson, pp. 110 (italics mine), 111.

[272] Erasmus, "Virgo poenitens," ibid., pp. 298-300. For the monks as debauched and for the nuns as lesbians, see "Virgo misogamos," ibid., pp. 292-94.

[273] Erasmus, *Ecclesiastes, sive de ratione concionandi*, in *Opera omnia* (Leiden), 5: 1029D.

[274] Erasmus, "Ptochoplousioi," in *Colloquia*, p. 402.

[275] "Puerpera," ibid., pp. 454-55; trans. Thompson, p. 270.

left his reply to another occasion and inquired about her child, by custom with his nurse. Eutrapelus assumed the offensive with a traditional plea for the virtue of mother's milk, its most emphatic endorsement in the sixteenth century.[276]

Fabulla's counterclaim for the superiority of mental education to physical nourishment provoked Eutrapelus to a classical philosophical argument about the relationship of body to mind and soul. Although a chimney top seemed far from the hearth, if a person sat on it he would feel the heat of the fire; so were mental faculties affected by bodily organs. Only ask the storks, he invited. Spirits flew from the stomach to the brain and from that organ to the mind. The body was the instrument of the mind and its "dwelling." Jesus himself called his body a "temple." The apostle Peter called it a "tabernacle." Others called it a "tomb," a "prison," or a "garrison," as if it were a citadel. Eutrapelus moralized that the pure of heart dwelled in a temple, those uncaptured by bodily passions in a tent. Those so blinded by mortal sins as to lack the air of evangelical freedom were in a tomb; those struggling against their sins without avail, in a prison; those struggling with vigilance, in a garrison.[277]

Fabulla observed that if the body was the dwelling of the mind, then many persons were ill housed. Eutrapelus agreed they were "houses dripping, dark, and exposed to every wind; smoky, damp, damaged, dilapidated—in short, rotten and infected." Yet the prime requirement for happiness was "a comfortable mode of living." Even if people could not transmigrate from their bodies except in death, they could through skill and care make the dwellings of their minds more habitable. The analogy was with the renovation of houses: changing windows, raising floors, plastering walls or hanging them with tapestries, ridding dirt by fire or fumigation. For a ruinous old body such change was very difficult, so that it mattered extremely that a young body receive proper care from birth. That meant, he argued in an Aristotelian discourse on the nature of the soul, by the mother as nurse. "So," Fabulla asked, "the mind's in the body as I'm in the house?" Eutrapelus answered, "Yes."[278]

Erasmus did not reason from that analogy to the divine indwelling in persons as in a house. The divine dwelling remained a church, architecturally and morally. Nor did his paraphrases on the gospels for the laity consider such familiarity. Erasmus did moralize doctrine and personalize truth, as in the example of the schoolboy who considered the parable of the sower and prayed that he himself might become its good ground. But although Gaspar began each morning by making the sign of the cross on his

---

276 Ibid., pp. 455-57; trans. Thompson, pp. 270, 267. See also *Ecclesiastes* 948B.

277 "Puerpera," pp. 458-63.

278 Ibid., pp. 463-66; trans. Thompson, pp. 278, 281. For the analogy that the spirit is in the body as the head of the household is in his house see also *Ecclesiastes* 944B.

forehead in his own room, he was careful on route to school to visit a church for the repetition of the prayers already said at home. He prayed for scholastic success to Jesus as a boy of twelve teaching in the temple. Gaspar was not uncritical of the habit of daily Mass; he disapproved its use as a superstitious guarantee of success at secular commerce.[279] Yet he did not repeat the insistence of Lionardo Alberti in dialogue that it was no more important than household discussion.

Adults could pray at home convincingly, however, even if they were not divine housing. In a popular colloquy, "Convivium religiosum," Erasmus restored religious dialogue to the classical site of a villa. Augustine had located his philosophical dialogues at one,[280] arguing against his mother that it was appropriate to sing conversional psalms even in its latrine. Yet that propriety was not because every domestic place was holy but because humans appealing to God were themselves unclean places.[281] The villa at Cassiciacum was a philosophical, not a domestic, site. There Augustine decided to reject marriage and, liberated from the defilement of women, to love only wisdom.[282] The description of Erasmus's place recalled the literary tradition of Horace's Sabine farm and Cicero's Tusculan villa. It may have been adapted from homes of friends that Erasmus visited: that of Johannes Froben in Basel, or of Thomas More in Chelsea, Johannes von Botzheim in Constance, or John Colet in Shene. Or it may have been inspired by a place of his own. An inveterate traveler to publishers and patrons, Erasmus settled agreeably in a country estate at Anderlecht, near Brussels, from May to November of 1521, in whose study he may have composed this colloquy.[283] The textual villa was a wonderful place in a smiling countryside where philosophers, disdaining the smoky cities that attracted priests in search of monetary profit, gathered for mental advantage. These philosophers were all lay and married. They had been invited for lunch at Eusebius's "modest but well-cultivated place." It proved to be an elegant estate, surpassing the grounds of Alkinoös's palace in providing a verdant feast of pears and other bounty. Not only was there nourishment for the body but also for the soul in that emblematic villa. Every corner was stamped with its master's design in a revival of the classical topic. The frescoes in the galleries painted with natural scenes were didactic: "a wonderful variety, and nothing inactive, nothing that's not doing or saying something." The trompe-d'oeil marble of

[279] Erasmus, "Confabulatio pia," in *Colloquia*, pp. 176, 173-74, 180, 176. Since Gaspar was an English schoolboy, the reference honored Aelred of Rielvaux's treatise on that pericope.

[280] See R. J. Halliburton, "The Inclination to Retirement—the Retreat at Cassiciacum and the 'Monastery' of Tagaste," *Studia patristica* 5 (1962):329-40.

[281] Augustine, *De ordine* 1.8.22-23.

[282] Augustine, *Soliloguia* 10.17, 14.25.

[283] Thompson, *The Colloquies of Erasmus*, p. 46. For its restoration see Jean-Pierre vanden Branden, *La Maison d'Érasme: Anderlecht*, Musea nostra, 28 (Brussels: Credit Communal, 1992).

its pillars even warned that appearances deceived, as did the painted cement of the stream. Draining the kitchen and carrying its waste to the sewer, the artificial channel suggested that people were callous when they polluted the fountain of scripture with sin and passion. As Eusbius explained, "Other men have luxurious homes; I have one where there's plenty of talk." From the door of the courtyard, to the beckoning shrine on the path, to the markers on the herbs in the garden, to the frescoes in the library and upper galleries were everywhere scriptural verses. Host and guests feasted on its exegesis in the presence of Christ, who was invited to join them at table, mingling with the food and drink but especially penetrating their hearts.[284] The abbot Bernard of Clairvaux had preached the interpretation of scripture to his monks; these lay humanists of Erasmus conferred about it among themselves.

Although the exegesis had transpired in a villa, believers were still declared analogues of ecclesiastical, not domestic, architecture: "Christ's living temples."[285] Yet the interpretation of scripture did not at least interrupt the eating of salad: the holy and the homey were compatible. The host at the moral conclusion of the banquet was practical in his charity. The leftovers were sent to a neighboring family in need, while he departed for one village to counsel a dying friend and for another to conciliate a stubborn quarrel.[286] If Bernard of Clairvaux meditated on scripture in the wood and field, with trees alone for masters, Erasmus had declared in his humanist manifesto *Antibarbari* that he must rather learn from townspeople.[287] There was in Erasmus's amiable piety a familiarity of the sacred with the secular, as in Campin's paintings of the Madonna in a bourgeois interior.

---

[284] Erasmus, "Convivium religiosum," in *Colloquia*, pp. 231-65; trans. Thompson, pp. 48, 53, 51.

[285] Ibid., p. 256; trans. Thompson, p. 70. Cf. Erasmus's argument for money better spent on the poor than donated to wealthy monasteries with Bernard of Clairvaux's *Apologia ad Guilelhem abbatem* 13.28.

[286] Erasmus, "Convivium religiosum," p. 265. For fuller interpretation of the colloquy see Boyle, *Erasmus on Language and Method in Theology*, pp. 129-41.

[287] William of St.-Thierry, *Vita prima* 1.4.23; Erasmus, *Antibarbari* in *Opera omnia* (ASD) 1-1, p. 135.

CHAPTER FOUR

CASTLE

"For castles, Castile." The proverb reflected the architecture of plains and promontories invaded and conquered since the age of Augustine and of their native reconquest and settlement. Upon that agonistic model Teresa de Ahumada y Cepeda constructed herself. She had not always imagined her interior a castle nor did she ever live in such an edifice, although the enclosed convents she so resolutely founded derived, like Bernard's monastic ideal of Clairvaux, from the Roman fortification (*castrum*). A castle (*castellum*) was its diminutive, but the more than two thousand built in Spain comprised a formidable mass. Teresa, who religiously adopted "de Jesús" for her surname, was born in 1515 in the most impressive walled city of Europe, Avila. Its ramparts of native granite extended for almost two miles, encircling the entire city, with eighty-eight monumental towers. There were nine staunchly fortified main gates; the most imposing, with twin towers named for the patronal san Vicente, loomed over the road to Madrid. The monument was erected in the final decade of the eleventh century by two thousand laborers, some prisoners of war, under Jewish, Muslim, and Christian masons, who reconstructed in oriental design fortified ramparts dating to Roman occupation. The king, Alfonso VI, had ordered a son-in-law, Raymond a knight of Burgundy, to build the defenses and to populate the town for control of the territory north of Toledo following its reconquest. Toledo was itself walled, as were Burgos, Alcalá de Henares, and dozens of villages; but Avila was the potentate. In a province whose fortifications were essential it best represented the close alliance of the Spanish nobility with their allies beyond the Pyrenees. Avila was the precursor of such notable distant cities as Carcassone in France, Conway in Wales, Dubrovnik in Croatia, and Visby in Sweden.[1] Although a panorama in 1570 emphasized its outstanding wall,[2] there was no castle in Avila except in the mind of Teresa de Jesús. The entire city was a fortress focused

---

[1] See Alberto A. Weissmüller, *Castles from the Heart of Spain* (London: Barrie and Rockliff, 1967), pp. 55, 13, 106, 108, 109 fig., 111, without reference to Teresa de Jesús. For the walls and gates see Manuel Gomez-Moreno, *Catálogo monumental de la provincia de Avila*, 3 vols. (Avila: Institución gran duque de Alba, Dirección general de bellas artes y archivos, 1983), 2:9-15; Juan Martin Carramolino, *Historia de Avila, su provincia y obispado*, 3 vols. (Madrid, 1872-73), 1:428-69, 2:211-36; for the geography and geology, 1:59-103, and for a description, 421-578.

[2] Richard L. Kagan, ed., *Spanish Cities of the Golden Age: The Views of Anton van den Wyngaerde* (Berkeley: University of California Press, 1989), p. 354.

on its cathedral, the jambs of whose very portals depict warriors brandishing clubs and shields. The Romanesque edifice with its blunt crennelated tower blends in with the civic wall to create a gigantic tower for defense. Peculiar to Avila, not only is the cathedral fortified but also it forms an integral part of the enclosure of the plaza. Behind the main altar runs a system of trapezoidal arches supported by a semicircular wall. It sustains the platform or terreplein of an immense flanking tower, whose slope is formed by the wall, with battlements in its capping.[3] Avila was founded on principles of Roman encampment, its squared plan synonymous with order.[4]

Teresa de Jesús was the daughter of Alonso Sánchez de Cepeda and his second wife, Beatriz de Ahumada, the third of the ten children she bore since her marriage at the age of fourteen. Patrilineally Teresa de Jesús was the granddaughter of Juan Sánchez, a wealthy merchant and tax farmer of Toledo. He was of a social status that the religious order she founded would by Inquisitional statutes of blood eventually exclude, a convert from Judaism. With national reunification, the monarchs Ferdinand and Isabel had ordered the conversion or expulsion of all Jews and Muslims in their territories, and Sánchez had submitted to compulsory baptism.[5] The Inquisition was authorized to monitor the integrity of the "new" Christians, as they were socially distinguished, rather than assimilated,[6] and it spied him in lapsed practice. Although Sánchez's precise offense is unknown, a converted Jew might betray himself by forgetting to light a fire on his hearth on the Sabbath. An inquisitor once led a governor to the top of a civic tower and indicated the houses that, despite the cold weather, lacked on that Jewish holy day smoke curling from the chimney.[7] Sánchez at his trial was pro-

---

[3] For the cathedral see Gomez-Moreno, *Catálogo monumental*, 1:65-132; 2:16-227; Angel Barrios García, *La catedral de Avila en la edad media: Estructura socio-jurídica y eco-onómica (Hipótesis y problemas)* (Avila: Caja central de ahorros y préstamos, 1973); Carramolino, *Historia de Avila*, pp. 441-42; and for its religious institutions, Tomás Sobrino Chomón, *Documentos de antiguos cabildos, cofradías y hermandades abulenses* (Avila: Obra cultur al de la Caja de ahorros de Avila, 1988).

[4] Fernando Marías, "City Planning in Sixteenth-Century Spain," in *Spanish Cities of the Golden Age*, ed. Kagan, pp. 91, 92.

[5] Jodi Bilinkoff, *The Avila of Saint Teresa: Religious Reform in a Sixteenth-Century City* (Ithaca, N. Y.: Cornell University Press, 1989), p. 109. For background see Pilar Leon Tello, *Judios de Toledo*, 2 vols., Instituto "B. Arias Montano," series E, 4 (Madrid: Consejo superior de investigaciones científicas, 1979); *Simposio "Toledo judaico,"* 2 vols. (Toledo: Centro universitario de Toledo, 1972); Antonio Dominguez Ortiz, *La clase social de los conversos en Castilla en la edad moderna*, Monografías histórico-sociales, 3 (Madrid: Consejo superior de investigaciones scientíficas, 1955); in general, *Les problèmes de l'exclusion en Espagne (XVIe-XVIIIe siècles): Idéologie et discours*, Colloque international, Sorbonne, 13, 14 et 15 mai 1982, ed. Augustin Redondo, Travaux du Centre de recherche sur l'Espagne des XVIe et XVIIe siècles, 1 (Paris: Sorbonne, 1983).

[6] See Juan Blazquez Miguel, *Inquisición y cryptojudaismo* (Madrid: Kaydeda, 1988); Albert A. Sicroff, *Los estatuos de limpieza de sangre: Controversias entre los siglos XV et XVII*, trans. Mauro Armiño, rev. ed., La otra historia de España, 5 (Madrid: Taurus, 1985).

[7] Fernand Braudel, *The Mediterranean and the Mediterranean World in the Age of Philip II*, trans. Siân Reynolds, 2 vols. (New York: Harper & Row, 1972), 2:807.

nounced guilty and sentenced to walk with his children in penitential procession to churches on seven consecutive Fridays. After that humiliation he packed his household.[8]

Housing in Toledo of the period corresponded in plan, distribution, and function to an ancient Mediterranean model of Italic origin. It had a typological permanence preserved across cultures as diverse as Hispanic-Roman, Muslim, and medieval Christian, so that the architecture was not a renaissance revival but a classical survival. The ancient house was organized around a patio onto which opened dependencies of two or more stories. The patio was of regular design, square or rectangular, an element of rational defense against the unsystematic character of the urban web of Toledo, with its irregular, narrow, and broken streets. In the interiors of the urban network—in the squares—patios were like open cells admitting light and air into the residences. Houses were usually detached and removed from the street, without any relation to it of the principal rooms for reception or for living; only slowly in the second half of the sixteenth century would balconies and galleries appear on the blind façades. The total orientation of the house was centripetal: onto the patio. Housing only remarked the social importance of the families who lived in Toledo by size. A very large residence had a major patio and a large number of dependencies, so distinguishing a great seignorial home from one of lesser income.[9] As the house, so the city. In the functional differentiation of Spanish cities Toledo, as the seat of the primate, was the very type of the convent city. The influence of religious institutions was so overwhelming that within its walls the city turned inward.[10] Such was the design of Teresa de Jesús' familial legacy.

Her grandfather moved to Avila, where in the bustling Cal de Andrín, the commercial district for converts off the small market, he flourished with a shop for woolens and silks. He had joined a small but active class whose number and influence increased. Although most of that community was humble, even impoverished, Sánchez lived luxuriously as a gentleman and arranged for his children good marriages. At the turn of the sixteenth century he won a plea in the appeal court entitling him to the status of nobility.[11] Such an appeal was designed to demonstrate in an individual, not the merit but the existence of, nobility, either of lineage or of service. Nobility of service was not civic but vassalic, with fidelity and loyalty as its prime

---

[8] Bilinkoff, *Avila of Saint Teresa*, p. 109.

[9] Pedro Navascués Palacio, "Tipología de la casa toledana en el rinascimiento," in *La maison de ville à la renaissance: Recherches sur l'habitat urbain en Europe au XVe et XVIe siècles*, Actes du colloque tenu à Tours du 10 au 14 mai 1977, De architectura, 1 (Paris: Picard, 1983), pp. 77-78. See also Marías, *La arquitectura del renacimiento en Toledo, 1514-1631*, 4 vols., Publicaciones del Instituto provincial de investigaciones y estudios toledanos, serie primera, monografías, 10 (Toledo: Instituto provincial de investigaciones y estudios toledanos, 1983-84).

[10] Marías, "City Planning in Sixteenth-Century Spain," pp. 101-2, 103.

[11] See Bilinkoff, *Avila of Saint Teresa*, pp. 110, 10.

requirements. It was selfless service voluntarily offered to the king, not to the community, and at the risk or loss of life and property, in familial hardship or personal danger. The military ideal of defense was paramount. Education did not figure in the concept of nobility nor did charity. It was a matter of noble living, with the trappings of wealth, houses, servants, slaves, and horses, without formulaic detail of level, or degree, or source of income.[12]

Nobles were believed descendants of the Visigothic and Germanic knights who had participated in the reconquest of the peninsula. Nobles thus possessed special qualities of blood. The status was also conferred by the crown, theoretically in acknowledgement of those qualities but practically in recognition of military service. By the reign of Charles V, commencing the year after Teresa de Jesús' birth, whoever could afford the payment acquired the status, for it was openly sold as a means of revenue for the crown. Nobility conferred social prestige, legal privilege, and immunity from direct royal taxation. Castilian nobility ranked from powerful grandees and opulent aristocracy of title to impoverished individuals who contended with starvation. It was not a homogeneous class of economic equals. Nobles could be ordinary working people.[13] The status was also granted to fathers of a dozen children, who were called the "codpiece aristocracy." At the close of the reign of Philip II in 1598 the high nobility counted one hundred persons, inclusive of wives and children only about four-to five hundred. Yet the entire nobility numbered perhaps one hundred thirty thousand, so that necessarily a large proportion was of poor aristocrats. They lived in tumbledown houses with scutcheons carved in stone, sacrificing to an ideal of not dirtying their hands with dishonorable labor, manual or trade. The lower populace ridiculed them for their pretense of tables set with fine linen but little food.[14]

Such was not the pathetic existence of Teresa de Ahumada y Cepeda's family. Her father continued in the woolen trade,[15] securing his business to the foundation of the Castilian economy. The principal revenues of the crown were from taxes on the woolen industry, so that laws favored pastoral, rather than agricultural, practice, encouraging the raising of sheep by indulging the meseta, or herders' guild. Since late medieval business the bourgeoisie and some of the aristocracy were involved in importing the

---

[12] I. A. A. Thompson, "Neo-noble Nobility: Concepts of *hidalguía* in Early Modern Castile," *European History Quarterly* 15 (1985):379-86.

[13] David E. Vassberg, *Land and Society in Golden Age Castile* (Cambridge: Cambridge University Press, 1984), pp. 91-92.

[14] Braudel, *Mediterranean and Mediterranean World*, 2:727, 715; Annie Molinié-Bertrand, "Les 'Hidalgos' dans le royaume de Castile à la fin du XVIe siècle: Approche cartographique," *Revue d'histoire économique et sociale* 52 (1974):51-82. See also Thompson, "The Purchase of Nobility in Castile, 1552-1700," *Journal of European Economic History* 8 (1979):313-60.

[15] See Bilinkoff, *Avila of Saint Teresa*, p. 114.

product of wool.[16] The rapid growth in the population and economy of Avila in the sixteenth century was largely due to the expansion of Castile's woolen trade. A major route of transhumance under royal protection—that originating in La Rioja and linking Burgos and Segovia, the financial centers—passed through the province. Merino wool of high quality was exported for manufacture to foreign parts, especially Flanders; some was retained as raw material for a native industry. Production of cheap, coarse woolens for local consumption employed dozens of men and women of Avila, about twenty percent of the population in the sixteenth century, but in the decade when Teresa de Jesús constructed her imaginative castle more than thirty percent. Most of Avila's residents were artisans, especially fabricators of woolen cloth. They worked as weavers, dyers, carders, combers, spinners, and fullers. A lawsuit against her father and brothers for failure to pay certain taxes vindicated their noble status. Testimony was that they lived as gentlemen, married to distinguished women who were themselves the daughters of gentlemen. They retained in their households servants and wet nurses. They had served the king with horses and arms.[17]

When Teresa de Jesús composed her epideictic *Vida suya*,[18] as her confessors ordered and licensed, she began with a confession of personal wickedness that she believed should have been countered by her virtuous, God-fearing parents. She wrote that she was was attracted at the age of six or seven to virtue, by the good vernacular books that her father, an avid reader, provided, and by her mother's instruction in prayer and the cult of the saints. Her parents favored virtue and were replete with it. Her father abounded in charity to the poor and in pity for the sick, a charity that originated at home with his treatment of his servants. The egregious nature of his magnanimity was displayed in his refusal to accept slavery. When he once had in the household a slave owned by his brother, he was so compassionate that he cherished her as one of his own children. He could not bear her captivity. Teresa de Jesús praised her father as strictly honest, free in speech from swearing or gossiping—in sum, a very decent man. Her mother was also very virtuous, despite chronic illness and considerable trial. She

---

[16] Vassberg, *Land and Society*, p. 152; Bilinkoff, *Avila of Saint Teresa*, p. 5; J. N. Hillgarth, *The Spanish Kingdoms*, 2 vols. (Oxford: Oxford University Press, 1976-78), 2:8. See also Carla Rahn Phillips, "Spanish Merchants and the Wool Trade in the Sixteenth Century," *Sixteenth Century Journal* 14 (1983):259-82.

[17] Bilinkoff, *Avila of Saint Teresa*, pp. xii, 4-6, 64-67. See in general Kagan, *Lawsuits and Litigants in Castile, 1500-1700* (Chapel Hill: University of North Carolina Press, 1981).

[18] For the hermeneutics see Marjorie O'Rourke Boyle, "A Likely Story: The Autobiographical as Epideictic," *Journal of the American Academy of Religion* 52 (1989):23-51; idem, "The Prudential Augustine: The Virtuous Structure and Sense of his *Confessions*," *Recherches augustiniennes* 22 (1987):129-50. For other recent interpretations see Carole Slade, *St. Teresa of Avila: Author of a Heroic Life* (Berkeley: University of California Press, 1995); Alison Weber, *Teresa of Avila and the Rhetoric of Femininity* (Princeton: Princeton University Press, 1990).

was exceptionally modest, disregarding her great beauty by wearing the costume of an elderly woman. She was pacific and most understanding and she died at thirty three a truly Christian death.[19] Teresa de Jesús before her religious profession bore her mother's name by a caprice of the Inquisition that valorized women. Medieval nobility had been based on male lineage. With the racist notion that the seed infecting Jews and Muslims was propagated through both the maternal and paternal lines, families added the appellation of the mother to avoid suspicion. Spanish culture became the only one in which the woman at marriage did not lose her name but transmitted it to her descendants.[20]

The dozen children—three sisters, nine brothers— enhanced her father's nobility by royal decree of the codpiece. The offspring imitated their parents' virtue, except for herself, Teresa de Jesús confessed, although she was the most beloved of her father. Her siblings did not impede her divine service, however. With a favorite brother about her age she used to read the lives of the saints. The two were so attracted by martyrdom as an easy and quick method of attaining heaven that they plotted to abscond to Muslim land and to beg the infidels to chop off their heads. But their parents were an absolute obstacle to that adventure. The children were terrified and absorbed by their imagination of eternal pain and glory, to which they devoted much time, repeating with relish the words "forever and ever and ever." Teresa de Jesús recalled that in childhood the truth had been impressed on her by rote.[21]

Thwarted as martyrs, the pair conspired to become hermits. In the kitchen garden she and her unnamed brother—her family and kin were all anonymous—played not house but hermitage.[22] The local hermitage was Nuestra Señora de las Vacas, whose ancient structure was a simple nave constructed of mud walls,[23] a type children could have imitated building in their yard. Although Teresa and her brother heaped up pebbles in the spacious kitchen garden of the house, their structure toppled. When she played with other girls, she enjoyed the make-believe of monasteries, as if they were nuns, although that was not such a good game as martyrs or hermits. Teresa

---

[19] Teresa of Avila, *Vida suya* prol., 1.1-2. For background see Isabel Beceiro Pita and Ricardo Córdoba de la Llave, *Parentesco, poder y mentalidad: La nobleza castellana: Siglos XII-XV* (Madrid: Consejo superior de investigaciones científicas, 1990).

[20] Janine Fayard and M-C. Gerbet, "Fermeture de la noblesse et pureté de sang en Castile à travers les procès de *hidalguía* au XVIème siècle," *Histoire, économie et société* 1 (1982):51-75.

[21] Teresa of Avila, *Castillo interior* 1.3-4. Their sobriety in conversation reflects moral injunctions against laughter or joking with a brother. See Julia Fitzmaurice-Kelly, "Woman in Sixteenth-century Spain," *Revue hispanique* 70 (1927):578.

[22] Teresa of Avila, *Castillo interior* 1.5.

[23] Jesús Ruiz-Ayúcar et al., *La Ermita de nuestra Señora de las vacas, de Avila, y la restauración de su retablo* (Avila: Diptación provincial de Avila, 1987), pp. 7, 9 and photo p. 11; Gomez-Moreno, *Catálogo monumental*, 1:166-69.

donated what alms she could and she privately prayed her devotions, especially the rosary, to which her mother had attached the children. When at eleven or twelve her mother died, the afflicted daughter begged tearfully before an image of the Virgin for her to replace her mother.[24] Juridically the disappearance of a mother did not affect the family in government or direction, since she did not participate in the father's title or exercise. Upon her death, the father conserved his paternal authority and increased his faculties as administrator, even beneficiary, of her inheritance.[25] Affectively, however, there was loss for Teresa. That loss was the decisive beginning of her substitution of celestial for terrestrial kin, so conventional in the asceticism of the hermitage and the monastery, and already adumbrated in the relationship to her brother as a co-martyr and her playmates—likely cousins—as nuns. Children since the Roman empire had built sandcastles and cried when they collapsed. They had played in imitation of adult roles, with Christians acting at bishops and monks, rather than pagan judges and soldiers.[26] But Teresa the child was in earnest.

The severance of Teresa with the world was not immediate. Like Augustine she blamed her parents for her dalliance, because they did not always provide a perfect model of virtuous deeds. She confessed that she hardly imitated upon attaining the age of reason her mother's good qualities, while her bad ones harmed her greatly.[27] Teresa de Jesús did not typically cite a failure of nursing in infancy, although Spanish law and morality criticized the usual practice of wet nursing.[28] She focused rather on the age of reason, the years between six and eight, which were a turning point in discipline for adult responsibilities.[29] Since girls required stricter discipline than boys, vice was traced to effeminate training and maternal spoiling.[30] The particular maternal fault she cited was indulging in the fashionable books of chivalry, reading for distraction from the great household occupations. Although her mother did not ignore her domestic task for those books, she did busy her children with them. With Teresa they became a habit, as she wasted hours round the clock in a useless pastime, so absorbed in reading that her con-

---

24 Teresa of Avila, *Castillo interior* 1.3-7.

25 Enrique Gacto, "El grupo familiar de la edad moderno en los territorios del mediterráneo hispánico: Una vision jurídica," in James Casey et al., *La familia en la España mediterránea (siglos XV-XIX)* (Barcelona: Crítica, 1987), p. 44.

26 See Thomas Wiedemann, *Adults and Children in the Roman Empire* (London: Routledge, 1989), pp. 148, 150-51.

27 Teresa of Avila, *Vida suya* 2.1-2.

28 Fitzmaurice-Kelly, "Woman in Sixteenth-Century Spain," pp. 567-69; Heath Dillard, *Daughters of the Reconquest: Women in Castilian Town Society, 1100-1300* (Cambridge: Cambridge University Press, 1984), pp. 156-57.

29 For the age of reason and early education see Kagan, *Students and Society in Early Modern Spain* (Baltimore, Md.: Johns Hopkins University Press, 1974), pp. 8, 5-30.

30 Fitzmaurice-Kelly, "Woman in Sixteenth-Century Spain," p. 624. See also in general Edna M. Sims, "Resumen de la imagen negativa de la mujer en la literatura española hasta mediados del siglo XVI," *Revista de estudios hispánicos* 11 (1977):433-49.

tentment depended on a supply of new titles.

Typically she blamed as the source of moral corruption the female sex, archetypally the fertile female, the mother. From the small maternal fault she imitated, Teresa de Jesús blamed the cooling of her own religious desires and consequently the beginning of her failure in everything. Her father disapproved of chivalric novels (she had to be warned to hide the books when he was around), so that she also portrayed the husband conventionally as morally superior to his wife. Upon her literary education followed the typical censure of female vanity: how Teresa, desiring to please others and to look attractive, began to wear full dress, to care for her hair and manicure, to use scents.[31] Spanish confessional manuals judged the use of cosmetics severely as a mortal sin. Sumptuous dress on maidens, if vain, and not worn on parental orders to catch a husband, could also be a mortal sin.[32] Parents were counseled to rear their daughters with simple, modest clothing worn with lowered eyes.[33] Teresa de Jesús' analysis of her domestic slide from virtue copied the tirades of the clergy against women reading chivalric novels as doctrinal heterodoxy. The literature was judged a cause of deformity toward unhappiness, because the illicit love it celebrated differed from humanistic and moralistic proposals for marriage. Francisco de Osuna allowed women to read, but not those books.[34] It was from his *Tercer abecedario*, in

---

31 Teresa of Avila, *Vida suya* 2.1-2. For morality and literacy see Sara T. Nalle, "Literacy and Culture in Early Modern Castile," *Past and Present* 125 (1989):65-96; Keith Whinnom, "The Problem of the 'Best-Seller' in Spanish Golden-Age Literature," *Bulletin of Hispanic Studies* 57 (1980):189-98; D. W. Cruickshank, "'Literature' and the Book Trade in Golden-Age Spain," *Modern Language Review* 73 (1978):799-824.

32 José Sánchez Herrero, "Los cuidados de la belleza corporal femenina en los confesionales y tratados de doctrina cristiana de los siglos XIII al XVI," in *Les soins de beauté: Moyen âge, début des temps modernes*, Actes du IIIe colloque international Grasse, 26-28 avril 1985, ed. Denis Menjot (Nice: Université de Nice, 1987), pp. 280-85. Teresa de Jesús' editor Luis de León was of this severe opinion in *La perfecta casada* 11.

33 Fitzmaurice-Kelly, "Woman in Sixteenth-Century Spain," pp. 574-75, 583, 607-14; and for female finery see Bartolomé Bennassar, *The Spanish Character: Attitudes and Mentalities from the Sixteenth to the Nineteenth Century* (Berkeley: University of California Press, 1979), pp. 170-71, 173.

34 See Mariló Vigil, "La vida cotidiana de la mujeres en el barroco," in *Nuevas perspectivas sobre la mujer*, Actas de las primeras jornadas de investigación interdisciplinaria, 2 vols. (Madrid: Universidad autónoma de Madrid, 1981), 2:159-60; Asunción Rallo Gruss, "Los 'Coloquios matrimoniales' de Pedro Lujan (Mujer y espacio privado en el siglo XVI)," in *Realidad histórica e invención literaria en torno a la mujer* (Málaga: Diputación provincial de Málaga, 1987), p. 57, without reference to Teresa. For the moral judgment on chivalric literature see Edward Glaser, "Nuevos datos sobre la crítica de los libros de caballerías en los siglos XVI y XVII," trans. Concepción Yáñez, *Anuario de estudios medievales* 3 (1966):393-410; Cruickshank, "'Literature' and the Book Trade," p. 806; Daniel Eisenberg, *Romances of Chivalry in the Spanish Golden Age* (Newark, Del.: Juan de la Cuesta, 1982), pp. 89-110; B. W. Ife, *Reading and Fiction in Golden-Age Spain: A Platonist Critique and Some Picaresque Replies* (Cambridge: Cambridge University Press, 1985), pp. 11-17; and for a related genre, Elizabeth Rhodes, "Skirting the Men: Gender Roles in Sixteenth-Century Pastoral Books," *Journal of Hispanic Philology* 11 (1987):131-49. For a general survey of literacy see Margaret L. King, *Women of the Renaissance* (Chicago: University of Chicago Press, 1991), pp. 172-88.

deliberate rejection of chivalric literature, that Teresa de Jesús learned recollected prayer.[35]

Although her father was strict about disallowing the children visitors, he was not so prudent, she judged, about their first cousins, who were frequent guests in the house. She associated dangerously with relatives a little older than she, who were poised for immersion in the vanities of the world. They went about everywhere together, for they loved her greatly. Her kin engaged her in chats about their affections, happenings, and childs' play, exposing her soul to harm. She warned about such associations, since the natural inclination was toward the worst, and she blamed her father for not having shielded her from those relatives. Rather than imitate an older sister who was very modest and good, she mimicked a frivolous kinswoman who was forever about the house, although Teresa's mother tried hard to avoid entertaining her, so as to prevent a baneful influence on her daughter. Yet that was her choice relative for conversation around the age of fourteen or fifteen, and they indulged each other in pastimes and confidences.[36] Teresa de Jesús' criticism reflected the moral topics of bad companions and female loquacity. Daughters were to speak when spoken to, with gentle voice and subdued laughter, and only the truth, never gossip.[37] The moralist Luis de León advised the head of household never, ever to allow another female into his home to converse with his women, because they always caused a thousand harms. The husband and father should secure his dwelling with latches, crossbars, and bolts.[38] That very author became the editor of Teresa de Jesús' *Castillo interior*.[39]

Yet the paternal practice in the household of Ahumada y Cepeda of indulging relatives reflected its social marginality. The network of interests and solidarities in Spanish society was tightly woven of ties of blood and bonds of kinship. The converts from Judaism followed the basic principles of social structure as did the majority but by their circumstances they were obliged to reinforce them. Merely belonging to an ethnic minority was already a factor of segregation. Severe religious repression aggravated it. As thrust to the social margins, the converts relied on internal cohesion as the essential condition for survival. They practiced a closed endogamy to establish solidarity among members of a community and among communities. Mixed marriage was very infrequent. The courtship of Teresa by her cousin

---

35 Teresa of Avila, *Vida suya* 4.7.

36 Ibid. 2.2.

37 See Fitzmaurice-Kelly, "Woman in Sixteenth-Century Spain," pp. 576-77, 578; Vigil, "Vida cotidiana de las mujeres," p. 156; idem, *La vida de las mujeres*, pp. 20, 26.

38 Luis de León, *Perfecta casada*, p. 79; cited by Maria Angeles Duran, "Lectura económica de fray Luis de León," in *Nuevas perspectivas sobre la mujer*, 2:273.

39 For his edition of Salamanca, 1588, see Teresa of Avila, *Obras completas*, ed. Silverio de santa Teresa, 4:xlviii-xlix.

was to the norm.[40]

Before that age she would not have offended God by mortal sin, although she confessed her sense of honor stronger than her piety. She coveted reputation extremely but she did not preserve it—she only did not loose it entirely. Her friendship with the female cousin was opposed by her father and a sister; yet, although they reproached her, they could not deny a relative social access to the home. The cousinly conversations so altered her that she was almost bereft of virtue in a soul naturally virtuous, she admitted, because the cousin had impressed on it her own traits. She lost the fear of God but not of reputation, which fear tormented her. Supposing her deeds unknown, she dared to act frequently against honor and against God. Yet Teresa de Jesús confessed herself shrewd in mischief, faulting herself and not her relative, because her own malice sufficed, with maids at hand to assist her in every sort of wrongdoing. None of the household staff benefited her by good counsel; she was vain, they were self-interested. Naturally she loathed immodesty but she did indulge in pleasant conversation. The danger of evil was present, given the occasion; and, with it, danger to her father and brothers.[41]

A father who discovered his daughter and her lover misbehaving under his roof was entitled, as in the Roman legal code, to kill them. Or a father might discover, as did hers, that he cherished his daughter more than his honor.[42] There were dual notions of honor. The ecclesiastical sentiment was related to a guiltless conscience: honor was in the regard of God alone. Essential was the subjective aspect, because it was within ecclesiastical jurisprudence to control only those sanctions that derived from religion. The worldly conception of honor was concerned to maintain the pecking order, by defense against humiliation and by avoidance of shame. It was the work of the nobility, who from the origination of military power attained the rank and possessions to exercise sanctions. The definition of honor as virtue exemplified a culture of guilt; the definition of honor as precedence exemplified a culture of shame.[43] Teresa de Jesús' circumlocution about her honor concerned chastity, inaccessibility to males as the sole basis of female honor in Spanish society.[44] Masculine honor was an issue of precedence. Males

---

[40] See Jaime Contreras, "Family and Patronage: The Judeo-Converso Minority in Spain," in *Cultural Encounters: The Impact of the Inquisition in Spain and the New World*, ed. Mary Elizabeth Perry and Anne J. Cruz (Berkeley: University of California Press, 1991), pp. 137-38.

[41] Teresa of Avila, *Vida suya* 2.3-6.

[42] Malveena McKendrick, *Woman and Society in the Spanish Drama of the Golden Age: A Study of the mujer varonil* (London: Cambridge University Press, 1974), pp. 16, 17.

[43] J. G. Peristiany and Julian Pitt-Rivers, "Introduction" to *Honor and Grace in Anthropology*, ed. idem, Cambridge Studies in Social and Cultural Anthropology, 76 (Cambridge: Cambridge University Press, 1992), pp. 7-8.

[44] See Dillard, *Daughters of the Reconquest*, pp. 168-92; and in general for the legal background, Rafael Serra Ruiz, *Honor, honra e injuria en el derecho medieval español*,

sought to establish their names in the forefront of the group, actively and positively attaining status, prestige, or respect. The role of women of honor was sexual purity, freedom from even gossip that might destroy reputation. Female duty was negative and passive, avoiding action that might stain the family's reputation. While male honor was defined and defended against rivals, female honor was conserved and sheltered against the envious and their slander. The defense of female honor was the role of men, whose own honor was desecrated by any injury or affront to mother, wife, daughter, or sister.[45]

The situation for females was restraint, rather than comfort, with threats and accusations, prohibitions and punishments more common than rewards for behavior.[46] A girl was not to play with boys or accept their gifts; when older, she was never to speak with any male, not even with a relative in the presence of her mother.[47] Women could end in the public jail for a dozen years merely on the suspicion of adultery, so that they were obstinate in defending an honor dependent on the good opinion of others. They tended to avoid any type of relationship with men, above all with those outside the family.[48] Teresa consulted a confessor and others, who assured her that she had done nothing morally wrong, since the matter only involved a conversational friendship with a cousin in prospect of marriage. But as an adult and as a nun she judged it "vanity" and "danger."[49] Her flirtation with unchastity—dishonor—originated in the bosom of her family: in the fault of a mother who mentally escaped her tasks with chivalrous novels, rather than virtuous treatises; of a father who imprudently allowed morally vacuous relatives access to their home; of a particular kinswoman of flighty affective conversation; and of maids who conventionally performed for their mistresses the role of go-between with lovers.[50]

Teresa de Jesús never described or even located her home. It was in the city; the wealthy nobility of Avila shunned the countryside as boring.[51] In

---

Anales de la Universidad de Murcia, Derecho 23 (Murcia: Universidad de Murcia, 1969).

[45] Pitt-Rivers, "Honour and Social Status," in *Honour and Shame: The Values of Mediterranean Society*, ed. Peristany (Chicago: University of Chicago Press, 1966), pp. 25, 36, 42, 45; idem, "Postscript: The Place of Grace in Anthropology," in *Honor and Grace in Anthropology*, p. 226. For the argument that the male control of female sexuality through concepts of honor and shame was a symbol for the organization of solidarity in pastoral societies see Jane Schneider, "Of Vigilance and Virgins: Honor, Shame and Access to Resources in Mediterranean Societies," *Ethnology* 10 (1971):1-24.

[46] Julio Caro Baroja, *Las formas complejas de la vida religiosa: Religión, sociedad y carácter en la España de los siglos XVI y XVII* (Madrid: Akal, 1978), p. 51.

[47] Fitzmaurice-Kelly, "Woman in Sixteenth-Century Spain," p. 576.

[48] Pereiro Barbero, "El entorno afectivo de la mujer en el siglo de oro al través de los testamentos," in *Realidad histórica e invención literaria en torno a la mujer* (Málaga: Diputación provincial de Málaga, 1978), pp. 31, 32

[49] Teresa of Avila, *Vida suya* 2.9; 2.6.

[50] For the role see Michael J. Ruggiero, *The Evolution of the Go-Between in Spanish Literature through the Sixteenth Century*, University of California Publications in Modern Philology, 78 (Berkeley: University of California Press, 1966).

[51] See Vassberg, *Land and Society*, pp. 92, 105, without reference to Teresa de Jesús.

the seventeenth century the Carmelites, with the bishop as financial patron, constructed a church of Santa Teresa de Jesús and a convent on its site. The order had debated that plan, because her small familial lot could not be widened—bounded as it was by the civic wall, a plaza, and public streets. Yet the consultant architect, friar Alonso de san José, thought the site accommodating enough. The baroque façade eventually faced the small plaza; the gate named for Antonio Vela was renamed for the saint. The initial stone of her church was laid by the architect on her patronal feast of St. Joseph in the very apartment in which she had been born. It became the chancel of the church, which also housed underneath her crypt. Although sixteenth-century conventual foundations, like her own of the convent of San José, had been outside the city walls, the new edifice was promoted within its precincts from devotion to her. The location of the only domestic place Teresa de Jesús ever blessed (with pious make-believe), the vegetable garden for the kitchen, became uncertain. One source placed it as the site of the main chapel, another as the cloistered garden.[52]

The urban displacement of homes with convents was a complex process caused by demographic crisis, the loss of industry and trade, the increasing importance of the agrarian sector in the economy, and the emigration of elites, allowing abandoned space to become occupied by religious foundations. The renaissance city, secular and public, yielded to the counter-reformation city, religious and private.[53] The allocation to the Carmelites of her familial land was allowed because of a drastic demographic crisis that reduced the population of Avila to less than half[54] of its size when Teresa de Jesús had invented her interior castle. During her lifetime the population had doubled, through migration of nobles from country estates to urban palaces with social connections and luxurious goods, and with them an entourage of servants and peasants. There were between twelve and thirteen thousand residents at its peak in 1572.[55] Yet the alteration of the domestic to the ecclesiastical on the site of her home copied a new and dire pattern of depopulation. The province of Avila had few very important villages; only the capital surpassed in the sixteenth century a thousand hearths, in the seventeenth less than half of that figure. External causes blamed were plague, war, departures for the Indies, foreign merchandise, and the expulsion of the Muslims. Internal causes reckoned too heavy a system of taxation, entailed estate, the attraction of the court and its leisure, the excessive number of priests and religious, and the questioning of marriage. The number of clergy and religious was often invoked and deplored for the depopulation of the

---

52 María José Arnáiz Gorroño et al., *La iglesia y convento de la santa en Avila*, Monografías de arte y arquitectura abulenses, 1 (Avila: Institución "gran duque de Alba," Diputación provincial de Avila, 1986), pp. 29-66.

53 Marías, "City Planning in Sixteenth-Century Spain," p. 105.

54 Arnáiz Gorroño et al., *Iglesia y convento de la santa*, p. 32.

55 Bilinkoff, *Avila of Saint Teresa*, p. 54.

elites. The provincial census of 1591 counted more than fifteen thousand professed religious in convents, almost a third of those in convents for women. The creation of new orders and the foundation of convents during a depopulation, dating from the last third of the sixteenth century through the first half of the seventeenth, was much criticized. Castilians abandoned agriculture, commerce, manual work, and military service to seek refuge in convents from indigence and idleness. In that period of recession and of demographic and economic crisis there was a massive inactive population. With half the people it needed, Castile had double the religious.[56]

Demands were made to the king that, with papal approval, he disallow the admission to convents of persons less than sixteen years of age and their profession before twenty years of age. Remedies proposed for the decline in marriages and the birthrate included the severe punishment of adultery, prostitution, and debauchery. Men were urged to acquire more respect for women. The suppression of the obligatory dowry was considered, since upright women were languishing as spinsters for lack of one. Women, in turn, were admonished to expect less luxurious clothing from their husbands. Illegitimate offspring were not to be exposed but reared. All babies were to be treated carefully, especially foundlings, who with the rate of infant mortality at forty per cent almost always died. So necessary was it thought to promote marriage that royal privileges were asked to be granted with the third child,[57] rather than the twelfth.

Such was the social situation in which Teresa de Jesús created yet another religious order, with thirty foundations by her death. The razing of her familial home of a dozen children to construct a church and convent for perpetually vowed virgins was in that context an antisocial act and symbol. The excavation struck right to the origins of the city, for the house backed onto the civic wall. By medieval precedent the construction of homes, especially those of the most notable lineages, was near to the walls, with whose defense the owners were charged. The system extended along the entire eastern sector of Avila, including the fortress and the cathedral, from the gate of Carmen to what became the plaza of Sta. Teresa de Jesús. Families were clearly grouped: next to the ancient episcopal palace, the towers and façades with the six bezants of the Velada y Gómez Davila; in the major gate of San Vicente, the distinct branch of the Aguilas; by Mosén Rubí, the Bracamontes; in the plaza of the saint, the family for which it was originally called, the Velas.[58] Neither the Carmelites nor the citizens thought to rename

---

[56] Molinié-Bertrand, *Au siècle d'or l'Espagne et ses hommes: La population du royaume de Castille au XVIe siècle* (Paris: Economica, 1985), pp. 171-73, 351, 377-88. See also in general Lynn Hollen Lees and Paul M. Hohenburg, "Urban Decline and Regional Economies: Brabant, Castile, and Lombardy, 1550-1750," *Comparative Studies in Society and History* 31 (1989):439-61.

[57] Molinie-Bertrand, *Au siècle d'or l'Espagne et ses hommes*, pp. 388-89.

[58] See Abelardo Merino Alvarez, *La sociedad abulense durante el siglo XVI: La no-*

it the Plaza de los Cepedas y Ahumadas. Her family was forgotten; the daughter who abandoned it was honored. The burial place of her parents is contested between the convents of San Francesco and San José; in either case they were interred outside the civic walls.[59]

Teresa's own flirtation with marriage was curbed after three months of assignations with her courting cousin. She was taken by her father to a convent that educated noble girls, although not such naughty ones as herself, she thought. The move was on the quiet; only she and a relative knew. She was not in disgrace with her father (although he suspected something), as she explained, because he loved her so exceedingly and because she was an expert at dissimulation. In fear for her honor, Teresa was secretive about her activities, although she confessed herself mindless of the omniscience of God. At the convent school she initially felt very pained for her plight, the more so from fearing that the nuns knew about her vanity. Within only a week there, however, she was "much more content than in my father's house."[60]

Although utterly hostile to the idea of becoming a nun, she remarked on the modesty, piety, and prudence of the sisters at Nuestra Señora de la Gracia. She was tempted by messages from her relatives; but, since their opportunity to reach her was slight, they soon gave up trying. Her bad companions at home were soon replaced by the good company of the nun in charge of the lay dormitory. She had professed as a religious because of the saying "Many are called, but few are chosen" (Matt. 22:14); and she conversed about the rewards for those who relinquished everything for Christ. Thus was Teresa de Jesús introduced to religious life as a matter of prestige and prize. She did not want to be a nun but she feared marriage. So she warmed to the idea of joining a good friend of hers in a less strict convent, that of Encarnación, which she did eventually enter.[61] The convent was a common refuge from the prospect of bad marriage.[62] Teresa de Jesús copied the Castilian cultural heroine, the woman adverse to love and marriage: the bandit, warrior, huntress, avenger, or scholar.[63]

She vacillated in the notion of religious life vainly and sensually, rather

---

bleza, Discursos leídos ante la Real academia de la historia en la recepción pública del señor don Abelardo Merino Alvarez el dia 11 de abril de 1926 (Madrid: Patronato de huérfanos de los cuerpos de intendencia e intervención militares, 1926), p. 147.

59 Leonardo Herrera, "El sepulcro de los padres de santa Teresa en la iglesia del ex convento de san Francisco de Avila," *Boletin de la Real academia de la historia* 71 (1917):534-35; Bernardino de Melgar, "Sepultura de Alonso Sánchez de Cepeda," ibid. 67 (1915):475-86; idem, "La sepultura de d. Alonso de Cepeda," ibid. 66 (1915):309; Herrera, "La sepultura de los padres de santa Teresa de Jesús," ibid, p. 308.

60 Teresa of Avila, *Vida suya* 2.6-8. For that convent see Gomez-Moreno, *Catálogo monumental*, 1:201-2.

61 Teresa of Avila, *Vita suya* 2.8-3.3.

62 Graciela S. Daichman, *Wayward Nuns in Medieval Literature* (Syracuse, N. Y.: Syracuse University Press, 1986), p. 98.

63 See McKendrick, *Woman and Society in the Spanish Drama*.

than morally and spiritually, she wrote, until serious illness forced her home again. During convalescence she visited the village home of a sister who doted on her and who, with a husband solicitous of Teresa's comfort, wanted her to reside there permanently. But a paternal uncle, a widower who lived on the road, intervened by inviting her to his home for several days.[64] He played the traditional role of a father's brother: severity and gloom.[65] When he bid her to read him some ascetic literature on contempt for the world, she complied only to be pleasing. But the books recalled her to the truth of childhood, when she had played hermit in the garden, about the nullity of everything, the vanity of the world with its brief finish. Teresa feared that if she died she would go to hell. In her will she was not inclined to be a nun but she perceived that it was the best and securest state. Gradually she forced herself to take it. For three months she battled with herself, paralleling the three months of flirtation with her cousin. She reasoned that the trials and pains of being a nun could not be worse than purgatory and that she well deserved hell; so if she lived on earth as if in purgatory, at death she would go straight to heaven. In choosing a state in life Teresa de Jesús confessed herself moved more by servile fear than love. She was battered by temptations against her decision, and her frail health lapsed into fevers and faints.[66]

What restored her vitality was her fondness for good books. She read in the letters of Jerome, which so encouraged her that she determined to tell her father that she was about to take the habit. Teresa was so honorable that she would not relent once she had declared her decision to him. She was certain of that. Yet he so loved her that she could not accomplish her will with him, not even through the mediation of others. She could only obtain his permission to do what she wished after his death.[67] Roman law was extraordinarily influential on the ordinances in force in Spain, ever since the official recognition in late medieval society of the *Siete partidas*, although customary formulas for the authentic provincial law still survived. The family was considered a strictly domestic group circumscribed by the persons who lived in the same house: the spouses and their descendents. It was governed by the primacy of the husband and father, who exercised the directive offices affecting the internal functioning of the group and its extensions to the outside. The superior authority of the father over the members of the family rendered it an assembly in which, in practice, the decisions of the

---

[64] Teresa of Avila, *Vida suya* 3.2.

[65] See Maurizio Bettini, *Anthropology and Roman Culture: Kinship, Time, Images of the Soul*, trans. John Van Sickle (Baltimore, Md.: Johns Hopkins University Press, 1991), pp. 14-38.

[66] Teresa of Avila, *Vida suya* 3.2-6.

[67] Ibid. 3.7.

head always prevailed. Wife and children were to be submissive and obedient.[68]

The father had the obligation to educate, rear, and feed his legitimate descendents and to establish the dowry of his daughters. His most important powers toward his children were a moderate punishment in use of his right of correction and the authorization of marriage as a form of controlling the exit from the nuclear family to constitute a new one or to integrate another. This marital authority was absolute while the children were minors. It was so important that, in distinction to the other paternal powers, it was susceptible of exercise by the mother if she were widowed. The marriage of minors contracted without paternal, or on his death maternal, permission was generally punished with disinheritance. Disinheritance was principally conceived under the law as a means of dissuasion, so that children would not gravely rupture the duties of submission and the respect owed to superiors. Its causes coincided in all the Spanish territories: to attempt a crime against the life of the parents; to maltreat, attack, or seriously injure them; to accuse them in a criminal trial, except for treason or heresy; to commit adultery with a stepmother; to commit a crime of treason, apostasy, or heresy; and for daughters— sons also in Castile—to marry without paternal consent or to live dissolutely. In Castile were added the charges of not redeeming a captive father, not going surety for an imprisoned one, not lending assistance should he lose his reason, and preventing him from making a will.[69]

Disinheritance, and with it the loss of the dowry required for entrance to a convent, was the threat constraining Teresa. There were several possible terminations to paternal authority: a forced end, when a father prostituted a daughter, or exceeded his right of correction by cruelty, or abandoned a child; a legal end, at the age of majority, which was twenty five, or by matrimony; and a voluntary accord of emancipation between a father and a child.[70] Such a free agreement was her most realistic hope and her sure aim; but her father refused to grant it. Teresa was afraid of herself and of her weakness. Since waiting would not avail against relenting in her decision, she sought another way: she ran away from home. She persuaded a brother to become a friar against the vanity of the world, and together they fled at dawn to the convent where a friend was. Teresa de Jesús recalled that there was more sentiment in leaving the house of her father than she could imagine for her own death. It seemed that every bone dislodged within her body. Since she lacked the love of God to replace that of father and kin, had grace not assisted her, her impulse toward the convent would not have sufficed for the deed. It gave her courage against herself.[71] Although Teresa

---

[68] Gacto, "Grupo familiar de la edad moderna," pp. 36, 37, 39.

[69] Ibid., pp. 43, 58-59. For women forced into the convent by parents see Daichman, *Wayward Nuns*, pp. 78-80; Vigil, *Vida de las mujeres*, pp. 209-11; idem, "Vida cotidiana de las mujeres," pp. 158, 161-62.

[70] Gacto, "Grupo familiar de la edad moderno," p. 44.

[71] Teresa of Avila, *Vida suya* 3.7; 4.1.

experienced that in acting against father and family she was coincidentally acting against herself, she accomplished the unnatural severance.

Augustine had taught that a girl could enter the convent against the will of her parents,[72] but in the letters of Jerome she found her staunchest documentation. They pronounced it impossible for anyone to attain salvation at home. Exit from home to the monastery was by stepping on a father's back. Against the commonsense argument that if everyone remained a virgin the world would end, Jerome thought that a wonderful aspiration. He defended monastic seclusion, because the only safety from human weakness was strict removal from worldly temptations. Like Augustine he was sexually experienced before his conversion to asceticism but he had broken with his family. After a trial in the desert against imaginative temptations of urban dancing girls, Jerome became the invited instructor and advisor of a circle of chaste and aristocratic Roman women. He preferred virgins, whose reading of scripture developed into study of philology and allegory under his direction, and into personal familiarity and spiritual trust. Jerome shunned the houses of wanton women, unattracted by their silken garments, sparkling jewelry, cosmetic faces, and gilded displays. He preferred women mourning and fasting, squalid with filth in sackcloth and ashes, purblind from weeping. He praised widows for deserting their own children.[73] There was Marcella, whose house in the wealthy and noble quarter of the Aventine was a meeting place; and Paula, whose house he termed a "domestic church." She had terminated sex with her husband Toxotius after delivering him a male heir, her fifth child. But it was her daughter Eustochium, the first young Roman woman of rank to vow virginity by keeping to her own room,[74] who received the letter that likely determined Teresa's direction.

It praised daughters for deserting their fathers. Jerome exhorted a departure from land and kin in imitation of the patriarch Abraham but he warned that the exodus would be insufficient "unless you forget your people and your father's house." A virgin was not to look back homeward or to linger, lest she be consumed. A praiseworthy father would charge his daughter, "'Do not remember your father,'" for a father was diabolical and his works were lustful. All those born of parents were by nature black. Only by leaving her childhood home, by forgetting her father, and by being reborn in Christ would the king desire her beauty and lead her to his chamber where he would make her white. Eustochium he pronounced the Lord's bride. She should disdain the households of married women because she was holier than they. Marriage was lesser, and even disadvantageous, for women: with

---

[72] F. van der Meer, *Augustine the Bishop: The Life and Work of a Father of the Church*, trans. Brian Battershaw and G. R. Lamb (London: Sheed & Ward, 1961), p. 215, citing Augustine, *Sermones* 161.12; *Enarrationes in psalmos* 44.3.

[73] Jerome, *Epistolae* 14.2; 45.2-4.

[74] J. N. D. Kelly, *Jerome: His Life, Writings, and Controversies* (London: Duckworth, 1975), pp. 288, 289, 21, 34, 91-97, citing Jerome, *Epistolae* 30.14; 100 101.

pregnancy, crying babies, amorous jealousies, and the burdens of household management. While marriage replenished the earth, the company of virginity was in heaven. Virginity was the natural state, marriage the fallen condition. "I praise wedlock, I praise marriage," he pleaded, "but it is because they produce me virgins." The temple of a virgin's body was a dearer to God than any vessel of gold or silver. "Let no one prevent you, neither mother nor sister nor kinswoman nor brother."[75] Nor father.

Even in Jerome's lifetime he was severely criticized by the secular clergy when Blesilla, a virgin in his spiritual charge, collapsed and died from rigorous fasting.[76] His cult, which exploded in the fourteenth century with a spurious work exalting him as the epitome of asceticism, in the sixteenth century was on the wane through humanist appropriation of him as an exemplary editor and exegete. It was tenacious, however, in Spain, where the royal Escorial would house the largest collection of his relics, and where the eponymous order of the austere Jeronymites was founded.[77] That was the religious order Teresa de Jesús' ascetic uncle left home to join, illicitly so, since it had enacted statues of blood against converts from Judaism.[78] Her father could not have appreciated his avuncular interference in the matter of his daughter. Teresa de Jesús attributed the paternal opposition to her entry of the convent to love. Perhaps that love had judged her natively unfit for religious life, as her psychological battles with profession and its physical symptoms of fevers and faints suggested. Yet the ideology of asceticism circularly rejoined that its very goal was to strive against nature, so that once she entertained its premise she was caught in its conclusion.

She ran away from home to Encarnación, a misnomer for a place of flight from the world, since the doctrine of the incarnation was the divine hypostasis of the flesh, not its human rejection. Perhaps the convent invented its name in repudiation of its site. It was constructed upon the city's Jewish cemetery, which the Catholic monarchs had donated to the nuns. Encarnación was founded by Elivra González de Medina, the former concubine of Nuño González del Aguila, the cathedral canon and archdeacon. He was the son of a formidable family of ecclesiastics and councilors, and lord of an extensive estate. Although he bequeathed his property to his concubine, at his death their son contested the will in protracted lawsuits, so that she established her own house as a place for devout women. From two companions,

---

[75] Jerome, *Epistolae* 22.1-2, 16, 19-20, 24; *Select Letters of St. Jerome*, trans. F. A Wright (New York: G. P. Putnam's Sons, 1933), pp. 55, 95, 107.

[76] Jerome, *Epistolae* 39.5; 45.4.

[77] See Eugene F. Rice, Jr., *Saint Jerome in the Renaissance*, Johns Hopkins Symposia in Comparative History, 13 (Baltimore, Md.: Johns Hopkins University Press, 1985). For his reliquary see Rosemarie Mulcahy, "Frederico Zuccaro and Philip II: The Reliquary Altars for the Basilica of San Lorenzo de El Escorial," *Burlington Magazine* 129 (1987):502-9.

[78] The Jeronymites in 1486 excluded Jewish converts. Sicroff, *Estatuos de limpieza de sangre*, p. 105, without reference to the uncle.

her establishment increased to a house of fourteen women under Carmelite rule with her as the "mother." After the construction and consecration of the official convent in the year of Teresa de Jesús' birth, the number expanded enormously, so that in 1535, when she entered at age twenty, it housed more than one hundred nuns.[79] Yet celibate women in sixteenth-century Spain were a minority. There were unmarried women (*soltera*) who lived alone or with a sibling or other family member, such as Teresa's sister had invited her to do. The poorest were placed as servants, and most were enumerated as poor. Then there were women or girls (*beata*) living piously in their house alone or with other similar women, such as Elvira had initiated. In the census they were counted as equal with other citizens, but most as poor. Some lived with a widowed mother or, with a brother or brother-in-law. Some of the quasi religious were retired in monasteries or communities in town; most were terciaries under the Franciscan rule.[80]

When Teresa in the kitchen garden plotted martyrdom with her brother, they likely sought to imitate Avila's patronal san Vicente and his sisters Sabina and Criseta, who had been crucified and dismembered during the Roman persecutions.[81] The possibilities for religious witness by its female citizens were in the sixteenth century very much reduced. Teresa de Jesús sensed even as a child that she would have had to run away to Muslim territory; as an adult she ran away to the convent. Encarnación was one of the largest in the city and it reproduced urban social conditions by perpetuating issues of class, caste, and honor. Avila was a manufacturing and mercantile city but with a rural air, for municipal ordinances still fined residents whose pigs roamed the streets to forage in vineyards and gardens. It was an aristocratic city with a few elite families dominating its political institutions, especially the municipal council. Through planning and patronage an oligarchy also dominated the cathedral chapter, the most extensive and wealthy religious institution of the bishopric. Those aristocrats also financed monastic foundations. Elite benefactors—landowners, councilors, prelates—endowed religious houses by ordering prayers for their kin and their clientele, just as the Burgundian knights had done at Clairvaux. They appointed the chaplains of the place and they decorated the walls of the chapel with their familial escutcheons, just as the Rucellai had at S. Maria Novella in Florence. The religious, freed by the money of patronage from manual labor, obliged with vocal prayer in anniversary masses, commemorations, and petitions for their benefactors, their kin, and their clients.[82]

---

79 See Bilinkoff, *Avila of Saint Teresa*, pp. 41-42. See in general Nicolás González y González, *El monasterio de la Encarnación de Avila*, 2 vols. (Avila: Caja central de ahorros y préstamos, 1976); Gomez-Moreno, *Catálogo monumental*, 1:204-7; 2:490-96.

80 Molinié-Bertrand, *Au siècle d'or l'Espagne et ses hommes*, pp. 349-50.

81 For the saints see Merino Alvarez, *Sociedad abulense*, p. 85.

82 See Bilinkoff, *Avila of Saint Teresa*, pp. 112-13, 11, 15, 32, 49-50. For an analysis of the Castilian municipality see Helen Nader, *Liberty in Absolutist Spain: The Habsburg Sale of*

The convent Teresa de Jesús entered was of that custom, having been rescued from financial crisis by aristocratic lay patronage. The endowment of the licentiate Bernardo Robles willed the Carmelites there eight hundred thousand maravedis to construct a principal chapel and to pay other expenses. In exchange his will specified scrupulously his manner and place of burial in the memorial chapel. It required a nun in perpetual adoration before the Eucharist praying for the repose of his soul—and she had to hold a candle in the process. Since the executors were his heirs, they were charged with withholding payment if the nuns should fail his stipulations. The Carmelites obliged in hourly shifts around the clock for several months, until they appealed to the pope for commutation, since their rule required nocturnal silence. Although the vigils terminated, the nuns resumed them when the family threatened to cease payment. During Teresa de Jesús' residence, there were thirty years of negotiations between the nuns and the heirs, until when she was prioress the convent finally won its plea.[83] Repetitive prayer for the deceased in Spain escalated to a hundred or thousand Masses.[84] Surrogation was entrenched by the stratification of society, with its division of labor and with its ideology of purity as privileged.

So was the ideology of the wealthy as privileged entrenched at Encarnación. The renunciation of material possessions was not required upon entrance. The nuns were even permitted sizeable revenue from landed properties and other sources; many were attended there by personal servants, even slaves. Nor was the renunciation of familial status even entertained. The values and behavior of aristocratic upbringing prevailed in the paramountcy of prestige and reputation. The nuns addressed one another by their surnames, even by the titular doña, which Teresa de Ahumada y Cepeda was guaranteed as the daughter of a noble. Her father did not disinherit her but supplied the convent twenty-five fanegas of grain or two hundred gold ducats annually, a substantial income. He paid the costs of her entrance and profession, like the dowry he would have spent on her marriage. Teresa de Jesús enjoyed in the convent a spacious private apartment befitting her familial station. It was situated on two levels connected by a staircase and it included facilities for cooking and dining, so that it must have had a hearth. She lived there with her youngest sister Juana and several other relatives, while still other relatives joined them in their parlor for conversation. There was no vow of enclosure as in the Benedictine rule of stability, so that the nuns could absent themselves even for prolonged periods if impecunious or ill, as Teresa de Jesús soon became from chronic fainting. Other nuns were impecunious. While the upper-class nuns lived in secluded quarters of rela-

---

Towns, 1516-1700, Studies in Historical and Political Science, 1 (Baltimore, Md.: Johns Hopkins University Press, 1990).

[83] See Bilinkoff, *Avila of Saint Teresa*, pp. 50-51.

[84] Bennassar, *Spanish Character*, pp. 71-72.

tive comfort, the lower-class nuns slept in a common dormitory. Since the communal funds were slight, those without private incomes were almost destitute, while their "sisters" maintained a style similar to that of the homes they had only physically abandoned. Occasional, but acute, conflicts arose.[85]

The social problems were as old as the convent next to Augustine's episcopal palace, where differences among the nuns—from dowry to diet—had occasioned the pride of the aristocrats toward the poor.[86] Teresa de Jesús supposed the problem in her convent was the papal relaxation of the original Carmelite rule.[87] And so she sought reform through renewal, particularly the principle of enclosure. The nuns were to be strictly separated from society. Her reformed rule did not accomplish social severance, however, except superficially by physical enclosure. Social relations were merely transferred from carnal to celestial kin, as they had been historically in the ascetic withdrawal from the family. Her spirituality remained freighted with the aristocratic values of elitism, in a hierarchy where value was reckoned by proximity to a centralist monarch. The populace was uncritically affectionate toward Philip II for electing to live among them, in permanent retreat at Madrid in the geometrical center of the peninsula.[88] For his sedentary and static style of government other contemporaries compared him to a spider motionless at the center of a web.[89] They unlikely alluded to Leon Battista Alberti's paternal metaphor. When the Italians considered the ruler of that most powerful empire—extending north-south from Antwerp to Angola, including Spain and Italy, and extending overseas to Mexico, Peru, Brazil, the Philippines, and the East Indies—they colloquially quipped, "God has turned into a Spaniard."[90]

Teresa de Jesús was no progressive individual. She obeyed priestly authority to the extent of giving "the fig" to visions she personally believed divine.[91] That was an obscene gesture with the fingers in mockery of the female genitals.[92] Giovanni della Casa in his important manual on courtesy,

---

85 See Bilinkoff, *Avila of Saint Teresa*, pp. 113-15; and also for class distinctions in convents, Vigil, *Vida de las mujeres*, pp. 221-22.

86 See van der Meer, *Augustine the Bishop*, p. 223.

87 Bilinkoff, *Avila of Saint Teresa*, p. 114. See in general A. D. Wright, "The Religious Life in the Spain of Philip II and Philip III," in *Monks, Hermits and the Ascetic Tradition*, ed. W. J. Shiels, Studies in Church History, 22 (Oxford: Basil Blackwell for the Ecclesiastical History Society, 1985), pp. 251-74.

88 See for Philip II Braudel, *Mediterranean and Mediterranean World*, 2:676-77; J. H. Elliott, *Imperial Spain, 1469-1716* (New York: New American Library, 1977), pp. 247-51.

89 Braudel, *Mediterranean and Mediterranean World*, 2:676; Geoffrey Parker, *Philip II* (London: Hutchinson, 1978), pp. 24-25. For further study see Mia J. Rodríguez-Salgado, *The Changing Face of Empire: Charles V, Philip II and Habsburg Authority, 1551-1559* (Cambridge: Cambridge University Press, 1988).

90 Parker, *Philip II*, pp. 61, 158, 62; Elliot, *Imperial Spain*, p. 248.

91 Teresa of Avila, *Vida suya* 29.5-6.

92 For an indigenous example of an amulet with "the fig" against the evil eye see W. L. Hildburgh, "Images of the Human Hand as Amulets in Spain," *Journal of the Warburg and Courtauld Institutes* 18 (1955):69. For a contemporary drawing of "the fig" see Michelan-

Galateo, worte that well-mannered women avoided even saying the word "fig".[93] Teresa de Jesús begged God's forgiveness for making "the fig" to him as a Jewish insult. She obeyed the clerical order to do it, however, reasoning that God had ordained her confessor in his place.[94] Teresa de Jesús collapsed the hierarchy—from God, to king, to father, to husband—into a single figure, his Majesty of the interior castle. She internalized the hierarchy of status, regarding all the nuns descendant in lineage and dignity from the king by their creation. Not all the nuns were royally graced, however, so that they dwelt conventually in different and unequal abodes. Their placement close to, or far from, the king remained a matter of precedence, of honor, of prestige, of favors and of merits, of rewards and of punishments, and of patronage. Philip II, who reserved the rights of ecclesiastical patronage against papal supremacy,[95] kept Teresa de Jesús' own *Vida suya* by his bedside until his death, when it was removed to the impressive library at the Escorial.[96] Her very canonization would be patronized by the royalty.[97]

Avila had acquired the title "of the king" on its coat of arms and royal privileges from its association with medieval Castilian monarchs,[98] who had resided there.[99] Teresa de Jesús would establish his divine Majesty in Avila. She snatched the foundation of her reformed convent out of the fires: hell perversely imagined as a kitchen with cupboard and oven.[100] The municipal oven was a daily destination for Castilian townswomen, who brought their loaves for collective baking there. A dietary staple, bread was a principal product of female labor, of both housewives and tradeswomen. Although its dough was mixed domestically, bread was baked municipally, and the bakery was a place for women to meet other women and to exchange

---

gelo, Archivio Buonarroti, folio 40Bv. Reproduced in Robert J. Clements, *The Poetry of Michelangelo* (New York: New York University Press, 1965), fig. 1. For "the fig" in general see Desmond Morris, Peter Collett, and Peter Marsh, *Gestures: Their Origins and Distribution* (London: Jonathan Cape, 1979), pp. 148-60; Macdonald Critchley, *Silent Language* (London: Butterworths, 1975), pp. 115-17. A basic monograph is Jose Leite de Vasoncellos, *A figa: Estudo de etnografia comparativa* (Porto: Araujo, 1925).

93 Giovanni della Casa, *Galateo* 232.

94 Teresa of Avila, *Vida suya* 29.5-6.

95 See H. E. Rawlings, "The Secularisation of Castilian Episcopal Office under the Habsburgs, c. 1516-1700," *Journal of Ecclesiastical History* 38 (1987):53-79.

96 Parker, *Philip II*, pp. 54-55, 46-47.

97 See Francisco López Estrada, "Cohetes para Teresa: La relación de 1627 sobre las Fiestas de Madrid por el Patronato de España de santa Teresa de Jesús y la polémica sobre el mismo," in *Congreso internacional teresiano 4-7 octubre 1982*, ed. Teófanes Egido Martinez et al., 2 vols. (Salamanca: Universidad de Salamanca, 1983), 2:637-81. See also Silverio de santa Teresa, *Procesos de beatificación y canonización de Santa Teresa de Jesús*, 3 vols. (Burgos: Monte Carmelo, 1934-35).

98 Carramolino, *Historia de Avila*, 2:5.

99 Merino Alvarez, *Sociedad abulense*, pp. 170-71, 148-49.

100 For the cultural topic see Gerd Bauer, "In Teufels Küche," in *Essen und Trinken in Mittelalter und Neuzeit*, Vorträge eines interdisziplinären Symposions vom 10.-13. Juni 1987 an der Justus-Liebig-Universität Giessen, ed. Irmgard Bitsch, Trude Ehlest, and Xenia von Ertzdorff (Sigmaringen: Jan Thorbecke, 1987), pp. 126-42.

news or gossip. Socialization around the oven could erupt into violence between rival households, however, as defamatory epithets escalated into assault.[101] The oven of Teresa de Jesús' imagination was such a violent place. Once at prayer, in a twinkling she supposed herself in the place the devils had prepared as just punishment for her sins. The entrance seemed a very long and narrow alley like a very low, dark, and close oven. Its floor was muddy and malodorous and filthy with crawling vermin. At the end of the passage was a hollow in the wall like a cupboard, with Teresa de Jesús cramped in it. The sight was nothing compared with her feeling, which exceeded all the excruciating pains of her paralysis and other ailments. She felt "a fire in the soul." And she realized that the torment would continue without end, just as she had learned by childish rote in the garden: "for ever, and ever, and ever." In the order of pains, that realization was nothing in comparison with the agony of her soul: a tightening, a suffocation, an affliction so sensible and so desolate as to be ineffable. The wresting of the soul from the body could not explain it, for her very soul was sundering. The fire within and her desperation were extreme as she felt herself burning and crumbling. In such a destructive place there was nowhere to sit or lie down in that hole in the wall. The very walls, which were frightful, then pressed down on her and smothered her until there was darkest darkness. The Lord did not wish her to see more of hell just then, she wrote. Probably she lost consciousness. The change of diet and routine from home to convent had immediately caused her poor health. Her girlish fainting spells increased, so that loss of consciousness, virtual or total, became frequent. She also complained with the fainting of chest pains,[102] like the sensation of a tightening, crushing pressure, and of the suffocation she then experienced in imaginary hell.

The foundation of her convent was the aftermath of that terror. Like the hell of her imagination it would be a tightly enclosed place. The cubbyhole that constricted her would be replaced by the cell; the destructive fire and her despair, by a purgative fire and hope. She would substitute for hellish fears of punishment conventual hopes of reward. As she reasoned, being burned on earth was slight in comparison with being burned in eternity. So terrible was her fear of hell that, even in memory of that vivid fantasy, the natural heat ebbed from her body. She considered the experience a divine mercy, because it helped her abandon fear of the tribulations and trials of this life and because it strengthened her to endure thankfully liberation from such eternal and horrible pains. Since then, everything seemed to Teresa de Jesús easy in comparison with her imaginative suffering in hell. Nor did bookish descriptions of hellish pains, like the devils tearing at human flesh with pincers, avail her as did that one fantasy. From it she acquired acute

---

[101] See Dillard, *Daughters of the Reconquest*, pp. 151, 153, 158, 159.

[102] Teresa of Avila, *Vida suya* 32.1-3; 4.5.

pain toward condemned souls, especially the "Lutherans," by baptism still members of the Church, so that she would suffer many deaths willingly to free one soul from those grievous torments. In such an important matter no one should be satisfied in doing "everything that we are able to do on our part," she wrote. Nothing should be neglected, and might the Lord be pleased to give the grace to do it![103] Her concept of nuns was as ancient as the civic rationale for the Vestals: the enclosure of virgins as propitiation against fire out of control.

The foundation of her reformed convent followed upon her horrific fantasy of the sufferings of the wicked: herself. Desirous of the means and manner of doing penance for such evil, and of meriting something to gain the good of heaven, she wished "to flee people." She deliberated how she could "totally separate myself from the world." It was a delightful disquiet, she wrote, a spiritual heat. In considering what she could do for God, her first thought was "to follow the call that his Majesty had given me to religion, keeping my rule with the greatest perfection I could." Yet, although God was well served in the populous convent of Encarnación, from necessity the nuns frequently left to stay elsewhere. The rule was not observed in its original rigor but as mitigated by the papal bull. Another objection of hers was the considerable luxury of a large and delightful house. Yet another nun remarked that, although they could not be discalced, they could still form a monastery. With similar desire Teresa de Jesús conferred with a widowed companion, doña Guiomar de Ulloa, who devised to provide the income for a reformed institution. But Teresa de Jesús was content in her present convent—her cell (apartment) was to her liking—and so she delayed, while the pair agreed to commend the idea to God.[104]

Once after communion, wrote Teresa de Jesús, his divine Majesty commanded her to procure the reformed convent with all her energies. He grandly promised that her effort would not fail and that he would be well served in it. She should name the convent for "San Joséf," who would guard one door, while our Lady guarded the other. Christ would go about the place with the nuns. The convent would be a star of great splendor. Teresa de Jesús was to tell her confessor what God ordered and that he should not oppose or hinder it. The vision and speech had such a great effect on her that she did not doubt it was the Lord's will, for she was aware of the discomfort and labor of a new convent when she was content in her own. The Lord frequently reappeared to speak with her about the foundation with such clear reasons and arguments that she finally declared to her confessor in writing what had transpired. He thought it was not feasible financially; but Teresa de Jesús' female patron conferred about its income with

103 Ibid. 32.4-7.
104 Ibid. 32.8-10.

the provincial, who readily agreed to it under his jurisdiction.[105]

The Church was powerful and, like the nobility, it owed much of its influence to wealth through ownership of property. Although some ecclesiastical lands dated to the Roman era, its most important gifts originated from generous royal grants in recognition of its support during the reconquest. After the reconquest it acquired property through the bequests of individuals; ecclesiastical ownership in the sixteenth century, concentrated near and in the cities, was on the rise. Taxpayers complained, because ecclesiastical land was exempt from many forms of taxation, thus burdening the ordinary lay citizenry.[106] Avila erupted into what Teresa de Jesús styled "the great persecution" of repartee and laughter at the absurdity of a reformed convent. The Carmelite provincial ceded to public opinion of its grand folly and withdrew his support of the project. The nuns at Encarnación murmured that Teresa de Jesús was insulting them: she was well enough off, they said, especially since there were others there better than she; she was uncharitable toward her own convent; she should solicit income for it rather than establish a new place; no, she should be tossed into its prison. Her patron was denied absolution unless she removed the scandal she had caused as a collaborator. Undaunted, the pair consulted a Dominican friar, who sided with them.[107]

And so the foundation was begun. Initially it was a small house in the barrio of san Roque belonging to a cleric. It was purchased for Teresa de Jesús by Juan de Ovalle, a brother-in-law, who moved in there with his wife Juana de Ahumada and their children. Teresa de Jesús, under the pretext of visiting her relations, began with his direction the work of converting the tiny house on its tiny site into the perfect monastery with the pretty views that she envisioned. There was little money; so to raise a mud wall her patron pawned a scarlet spread to pay for the cost of construction.[108] Once when Teresa de Jesús was needy and uncertain, St. Joseph himself, as "my true father and lord," appeared to her and made her understand that she would lack nothing. Although she had not a penny to pay workmen, she was instructed to hire them. She was provided with a surprising source of money from Ecuador, from a brother living there. Teresa de Jesús thought the house too small for a monastery and she wanted to purchase the adjacent house for a church but the Lord upbraided her for greed.[109] Avarice among religious women in accepting gifts from lovers in exchange for favors was a staple of satire. Nuns were mocked as insatiably greedy.[110] In her imagina-

---

105 Ibid. 32.11-13.

106 Vassberg, *Land and Society*, pp. 109-13.

107 Teresa of Avila, *Vida suya* 32.14-33.2.

108 Luis Cervera Vera, *Complejo arquitectónico del monasterio de san José en Avila* (n. p.: Ministerio de cultura, 1982), pp. 14-16.

109 Teresa of Avila, *Vida suya* 33.11-12.

110 Daichman, *Wayward Nuns*, p. 128.

tion Christ reprovingly cited how often he had slept in the open for lack of shelter. An astonished Teresa de Jesús conceded that he was right and so concluded that the house was perfect after all. She drafted plans and dismissed the purchase of further property.[111]

The initial foundation, outside the civic walls to the north, was a structure on two levels. Downstairs were the chapel and choir, upstairs the cells and offices. Walls formed of mud with stone buttresses and some meager pebbles were soon raised around the house. With papal authorization of the foundation, several nuns took the habit with Teresa de Jesús in the convent of "our most blessed father St. Joseph." The Eucharist was installed and Mass celebrated, although the church did not encompass more than ten steps: with a paltry and narrow altar in the porter's box, and a straw grille separating the nuns in the choir from the celebrant. The convent seemed to clerical visitors like the inn at Bethlehem.[112] The cell of Teresa de Jesús was of stucco walls hung with a crucifix and a cup; it had a tiled floor, wooden ceiling with rafters, and wooden window with shutters. It was furnished with a bed, a mat, and a stone bench on which she composed her interior castle.[113]

Then "persecution" resumed. The corregidor, the councilors, the caballeros and the commoners, the cathedral chapter of Avila—all wanted the reformers ejected. The nuns at Encarnación criticized the rival convent, as did the inhabitants of the other monasteries. When the stir settled, the Carmelite provincial and the papal nuncio authorized her definitive stay in the reformed cloister. Teresa de Jesús enlarged the premises some; the citizens gradually dropped their lawsuit and acknowledged the convent as a work of God. The Carmelite general enthusiastically approved the foundation and authorized her to found more.[114] Like most acquisition of ecclesiastical property, the convent was piecemeal and fragmented, interspersed among lands owned by individuals and municipalities.[115] Unlike the careful cartularies for Clairvaux, San José lacks documentation of its acquisitions of houses, gardens, and plots, or of the names of their vendors. Its initial acquisition was another house with a corral, separated by other properties from the original site. It was by purchasing properties between those points that the place grew. The ultimate holdout for completing the perimeter was a miniscule and ancient house, whose inhabitants perturbed the nuns' retire-

---

[111] Teresa de Avila, *Vida suya* 33.12.

[112] Cervera Vera, *Complejo arquitectónico del monasterio*, pp. 17-18; Silverio de santa Teresa, *Historia del Carmen descalzo en España, Portugal y América*, 15 vols., Vol. 2: *Santa Teresa en san José de Avila (1562-1567)* (Burgos: Monte Carmelo, 1935), pp. 138-39.

[113] Tomas Alvarez and Fernando Domingo, *Sainte Thérèse d'Avila: La grande aventure des fondations* (Burgos: Monte Carmelo, 1980), p. 13 photo. See also Gomez-Moreno, *Catálogo monumental*, 2:520-29.

[114] Teresa of Avila, *Vida suya* 36. Bilinkoff, *Avila of Saint Teresa*, pp. 137-40.

[115] See Vassberg, *Land and Society*, p. 113.

ment by constantly prying. After the death of Teresa de Jesús the house collapsed, and the Carmelites bought it.[116]

With the principal house renovated, the nuns had hermitages erected in the vegetable garden As Teresa de Jesús had childishly played, they were also to topple. The hermitages were small, isolated, withdrawn, as the fundamental complement in all Carmelite monasteries. But the municipal council denounced them as damaging the civic water supply and it ordered their demolition, against the nuns' petition. Later other hermitages were to be erected on the site of a dovecot and some lots, one of them named posthumously for Teresa de Jesús. The main cloister was erected on the plots of the orchard and consisted in two levels of simple architecture constructed in stone. The lower had windows, the upper, columns of Tuscan order joined in the middle with plain railings. In the middle was raised a simple stone cross. The entire garden, which served for the recreation of the community and for the cultivation of produce for its frugal table, was surrounded by high mud walls of masonry raised in successive eras.[117] Enclosure was the total concept. Of particular concern to Teresa de Jesús was the common practice of nuns exiting the walls.[118] Men were ingenious in penetrating the cloister; women, ingenious in abetting them. Nuns were much lampooned in literature, both moralistic and entertaining, for their laxity, especially in intercourse, pregnancy, and abortion.[119] As Erasmus satirized, over dinner in a home the nuns would become gay with wine, laugh at coarse jokes, and behave dissolutely. After-dinner games, dances, and songs led suggestively with flirtations, nods, and kisses to very unvirginal affairs. The nuns he mocked were "visiting relatives."[120]

Familial visitation was a common excuse for leave from the cloister. Teresa de Jesús herself used it to inspect surreptitiously the renovations to the house purchased by her brother-in-law that would become San José. Her justification was exiting a cloister to establish a cloister. The reformed convent was to be no domestic place. Once Juan de Ovalle's family had moved out, no other family moved in. Teresa de Jesús pitied as poor the owners of villas who lived in grand houses. Life in her convent was to resemble that of "our King, who had no house, except the porch of Bethlehem where he was born and the cross on which he died. Such houses afforded little recre-

---

116 See Cervera Vera, *Complejo arquitectónico del monasterio*, pp. 18-27.

117 Ibid., pp. 28, 32. See also Fidel Fita, "El gran pleito de santa Teresa contra el Ayuntamiento de Avila (Años 1562-1564)," *Boletin de la Real academia de la historia* 66 (1915):266-81; José Molinero, "Actas municipales de Avila sobre la fundación del monasterio de san José por santa Teresa (Años 1562-1564)," ibid., p. 155; and for the civic aqueduct and fountains, Carramolino, *Historia de Avila*, 1:465-66.

118 Teresa of Avila, *Vida suya* 32.9.

119 See Daichman, *Wayward Nuns*.

120 Erasmus, "'Ichthuophagia,'" in *Colloquia*, ed. Leon E. Halkin, in *Opera omnia* (ASD), 3-1: 525; *The Colloquies of Erasmus*, trans. Craig R. Thompson (Chicago: University of Chicago Press, 1965), p. 344.

ation."[121] Although the notion of Jesus as homeless was unscriptural, it had a pathetic appeal in art, to the detail of his drooping head in crucifixions.[122] Teresa de Jesús' knowledge of his birthplace was not scriptural either; for she termed it a "porch" or "portico" (*portal*), a reference that reflected not text but image. Renaissance paintings of the Nativity often transferred its site from the narrative stable to an architectural porch. Her term indicated how vividly her piety was dominated by the imaginative scene, rather than the scriptural text. She railed against the iconoclasm of the Huguenots because they were destroying "portraits" of Christ.[123] She believed that art rendered authentic likeness, just as her imagination represented his Majesty.

It was his Majesty who had commanded the foundation of the convent, and exactly to his order Teresa de Jesús had placed in its chapel the prescribed images over the doors.[124] Sculpture was commonly placed on the deep shelf provided by the top of the projecting cornice of a renaissance doorway, as in Vittorio Carpaccio's painting of the famous dream of St. Ursula.[125] Over one door of the reformed Carmelite convent stood guard a gilded statue of the Madonna; over the other, St. Joseph costumed in silk with a sombrero and staff. On the very altar was set a picture of him.[126] Joseph was accorded unusual dignity in Spanish devotion, through an Arabic version of the apocryphal gospel whose infancy narrative allowed his arrival in Bethlehem a full chapter. His traditional occupation as a carpenter was piously embellished: once when he cut a timber too short, he and the Christ child stretched it to fit. Joseph was painted early there;[127] a Spanish panel was the prototype of Dutch scenes of the holy family at work. While the Virgin weaves at the loom, Joseph fashions a mousetrap.[128] The cathedral of Avila displayed a painting of the holy family with reference to a lost one by Raphael.[129] Even Philip II painted a canvas of Joseph that hung in

---

[121] Teresa of Avila, *Camino de perfección* 2.9.

[122] James H. Marrow, *Passion Iconography in Northern European Art of the Late Middle Ages and Early Renaissance: A Study of the Transformation of Sacred Metaphor into Descriptive Narrative*, Ars neerlandica, 1 (Kortrijk: Van Ghemmert, 1979), pp. 167-69.

[123] Teresa of Avila, *Vida suya* 9.6.

[124] Ibid. 32.11.

[125] Peter Thornton, *The Italian Renaissance Interior: 1400-1600* (London: Weidenfeld and Nicolson, 1991), p. 33. Vittorio Carpaccio, Dream of St. Ursula, 1490s, Accademia, Venice. Reproduced p. 134 pl. 140.

[126] Teresa of Avila, *Vida suya* 32.11. Silverio de santa Teresa, *Santa Teresa en san José de Avila*, p. 138.

[127] Georgiana Goddard King, "The Virgin of Humility," *Art Bulletin* 17 (1935):478-79.

[128] Barbara G. Lane, "An Imaculatist Cycle in the Hours of Catherine of Cleves," *Oud Holland* 87 (1973):193-94. Martin Toner, Holy family at work in Egypt, Villalonga Mir collection, Palma, Majorca. Reproduced p. 191 fig. 2. See also Marzal de Sax, Annunciation, Provincial Museum, Zaragosa. Reproduced in Cynthia Hahn, "'Joseph Will Perfect, Mary Enlighten and Jesus Save Thee': The Holy Family as Marriage Model in the Mérode Triptych," *Art Bulletin* 68 (1986):56 and 57 fig. 3.

[129] Gomez-Moreno, *Catálogo monumental*, 2:116-18. Reproduced no. 172.

the parish church of the town of El Escorial.[130]

Whatever his attraction to a monarch, Joseph as an artisan was a plausible patron for a nun who designed and founded convents. Women were even hired in construction, although at lower wages than men: as masons, carpenters, and carriers.[131] When Joseph appeared to instruct Teresa de Jesús about the hiring of workmen and to assure her about the completion of the construction, she named him "my true father." When she and her companions professed their vows in its chapel, with his picture on its altar, she called him "our most glorious father Joseph."[132] He served as the paternal figure in her displacement of her family. The divine instruction to found the convent indicated Mary and Joseph at the doors and Jesus within: the holy family. Joseph replaced her own natural father. Teresa de Jesús did not usually refer to God, not even the first person of the Trinity, as father. That was "his Majesty." Meditation on the address of the Lord's prayer, "Our father, who art in heaven," occasioned only a lesson for the nuns to disregard lineage.[133]

The convent she had termed a "castle" in *Camino de perfección*[134] became her model for the human soul in *Castillo interior o las moradas*. It was not a familial castle. Teresa de Jesús acknowledged that the identity of the human self was from parentage and citizenship, so that the person ignorant of them was confounded and bestial. She derived the identity of herself and her nuns, however, from their divine origin and heavenly destiny. If they were ignorant of their creation in the image and likeness of his Majesty, they were more than confounded and bestial. As his daughters they were to belong to the mother of God. They were to imitate her by reflecting on her grandeur and good as patron of their order of Carmel and they were to take her as their intercessor. Teresa de Jesús addressed the nuns as "daughters" and as "sisters." In the outer rooms of the castle, she wrote, the devils would prompt remembrance of "impediments" to their vocation, among them "friends and parents." Although valuation of them was worthwhile, faith taught fulfillment. Valid memory of the family represented its termination in death (much as Teresa's deceased mother was replaced by the heavenly Mother). The death of members of family meant to her oblivion by their survivors, graves trod upon, worms teeming in their corpses. The will inclined the soul that was well loved by its family to repay it with love. But the true lover who was God never abandoned the soul, she wrote. One could not gain a better friend. "The whole world is full of falsehood," she rued, its contentments burdened with labor, care, and contradiction.[135]

---

[130] Parker, *Philip II*, p. 45.

[131] See Dillard, *Daughters of the Reconquest*, p. 161.

[132] Teresa of Avila, *Vida suya* 33.12; 36.5.

[133] Teresa of Avila, *Camino de perfección* 27.6.

[134] Ibid. 2.

[135] Teresa of Avila, *Castillo interior* 1.1.2; 3.1.3; 1.2.12; 2.1.3. For the rejection of family

Understanding taught the soul that "outside this castle it will not find security or peace; so to avoid going through strange houses, because one's own is so full of goods, if one wishes to enjoy it." A nun would find interiorly "everything she needs in her house, especially having such a guest, who will make her lord over all goods, providing she desires not to get lost like the prodigal son eating the husks for swine." In the faculties of her soul she would have "great and true friends and relations." An effect of the prayer of union would be a change of her pusillanimity with relatives, friends, and the villa. They would now be regarded as a "weight": as only a necessary obligation to perform, so as not to oppose God. Relatives and friends would weary the soul, for it had sampled that creatures could not give it true rest. Yet Teresa de Jesús regarded herself as not so conformed to the divine will that if her father or brother should die she would feel nothing. When a person could do nothing more about such suffering, she explained, it made a virtue out of necessity, like the philosophers. The Lord only asked in such circumstances for love of God and neighbor, and the more certain sign of that was whether one loved the neighbor as arising from love of God.[136]

Yet neighbors were restricted from the convent of San José by a constitution that regulated enclosure to the details of doors and keys. The nuns were to deal with other persons for edification, not recreation, and in the guard of another nun. Worldly matters were to be disregarded, even unspoken, under penalty of nine days imprisonment in the convent cell, with a lashing administered on the third day in the refectory. The nuns were to avoid much conversation with relatives, even close relatives, for danger of preoccupation with their affairs. Should their kin not be satisfied with holy conversation, their visits should be short and seldom.[137] Teresa de Jesús intended the nuns to serve each other in their select community, not to aspire to apostolic or charitable works outside it. As she warned them in conclusion of her interior castle, such exterior desires were devilish. She countered the aspirations of her nuns to teach and to preach, as men did, with the conviction that those were satanic stratagems to deflect them from the possible tasks at hand. They were only to pray for outsiders.[138] Yet her own relatives contributed to its very chapels; so that, while Teresa de Jesús shunned their person, she accepted their money. A relation, Francisco de Saliedo, at his expense constructed and endowed a chapel of new design on the site of the primitive one. He elected it as his burial place and he willed the convent a great part of his goods. Her brother Lorenzo, a cultured man who

as a worldly value incompatible with religious life see also Teófano Egidio Lopez, ed., *El linaje judeoconverso de santa Teresa: Pleito de hidalguía de los Cepeda* (Madrid: Espiritualidad, 1986), pp. 142-52.

136 Teresa of Avila, *Castillo interior* 2.1.3; 2.1.4; 5.2.8; 5.3.7; 5.3.8.

137 Teresa of Avila, *Constituciones* 15-20.

138 Teresa of Avila, *Castillo interior* 7.4.14.

lived in Ecuador richly and powerfully, and very well related by marriage, had greatly assisted her economically with the foundation of San José when it was merely her desire. In his will he commissioned a patronal chapel for his burial to be well constructed and adorned with golden borders and plateresque work to his sister's taste.[139]

Teresa de Jesús had cast herself as an architect in designing the renovations to the house that became the convent. Now she was inventor of a spirituality, empowered by obedience to her superiors to compose something for the nuns of the reformed Carmelite convents. They required the determination of some doubts about prayer, it was argued, and women better understood such language from one another. She discounted her spiritual remarks as "irrelevant" to outsiders. The laity were meddlers in worldly affairs, so absorbed in property, or honor, or commerce, that, although they sincerely sought to regard and enjoy the beauty of the soul, in conformity with their estate they did not abandon such things and escape such "impediments." The nuns in the convent were free from such "obstacles." Yet she allowed that there were many souls in the world desirous of not offending his Majesty, even guarding against venial sin. They did penance, made hours of recollection, spent time well, exercised themselves in charitable works toward their neighbors, and were decent in speech and dress and household management. Those persons were already in the third dwelling of the soul and would not be denied entry into its final place, she considered.[140]

The interior castle of her design was unlanded and not oriented. Teresa de Jesús wrote only that it was in "exile," in a "slough of miseries."[141] Soil and climate were negligible in the Mediterranean region, for sun and rain accomplished all.[142] Architectural treatises since antiquity had accorded primacy to siting, especially the celestial factors of sun and rain. Housing was conceived as shelter from those elements. As Leon Battista Alberti wrote, in the beginning people searched for settlements, contrived habitations, and deliberated "a shelter from the sun and the rain," so that they erected walls upon which to place a roof.[143] As a model for the soul Teresa de Jesús' castle was situated not terrestrially but cosmically, with reference to the sun, which composed its center. Rain dripped or poured into its rooms through conduits from celestial fountains. The castle was without a roof, open limitlessly to the heavens. Without such protection it was penetrated not only by natural elements but also by supernatural beings. Holy and unholy aerial creatures vied for its possession. Only by erecting walls as barriers between its apartments could she endeavor to shut out the demons from her interior,

---

139 Cervera Vera, *Complejo arquitectónico del monasterio*, pp. 44-45, 48-49.

140 Teresa of Avila, *Castillo interior* praef.; 1.2.10; 3.1.5, 6.

141 Ibid. 1.1.3; 7.3.1; 6.6.1; 1.2.8; 5.2.10.

142 Braudel, *Mediterranean and Mediterranean World*, 1:30.

143 Alberti, *De architectura* 1.2; *On the Art of Building in Ten Books*, trans. Joseph Rykwert, Neil Leach, and Robert Tavernor (Cambridge, Mass.: M I T Press, 1988), p. 8.

as she had locked out the world from the cloister; yet still they descended to menace her by air.

At the center of the castle, or the soul, was the ever resplendent sun, introduced as his Majesty.[144] Christian churches were traditionally oriented toward the rising sun to eclipse Roman homage to Apollo, the solar and imperial deity, with honor to the light of Christ.[145] The principle was not always feasible; the basilica at Hippo Regius faced west;[146] the church of Sta. Teresa de Jesús on the site of her home, unlike all other churches in Avila, faced northeast.[147] Although solar imagery was important in prophetic and contemplative traditions of righteousness and illumination, it faded in Teresa's castle as a dominant metaphor. She explained initially that the sun penetrated every corner of the edifice, although it was only dimly perceived in the outer apartments. The evil creatures lurking there did not allow the soul to avert its eyes, so that living there it was like entering a place flooded with light after staring at the ground: one could scarcely open one's eyes. And she wrote extensively about visions in her imagination and in her understanding.[148] But she did not explore or exploit the symbolism of light as did the contemplative literature influenced by Neoplatonist epistemology. Her reticence was probably wariness to disassociate her experience from that of the "illuminated" (*alumbrados*), whose doctrine had been promoted by another Castilian woman, Inez de la Cruz, and condemned by the Inquisition as heretical. The sect was considered quasi Lutheran.[149] Teresa de Jesús was careful in the letter appended to *Castillo interior* to solicit prayer for "light for the Lutherans."[150]

In her castle the sun as "the origin of virtue" afforded "heat to our works." She wrote of the "warmth" of the Holy Spirit and of the will being "enkindled" to a felt presence. Initially the soul sensed a brazier emitting aromatic odors as its sparks. Its light was not perceived nor was its source, but its warmth and fragrance penetrated the entire soul. Sometimes even the body participated in the enjoyment. In the apartment of the spiritual espousals the fire kindled in the burning brazier that was God spewed a spark into the soul to make it feel that fire. It left the soul in a painless pain, for

---

144 Teresa of Avila, *Castillo interior* 1.2.3; praef.

145 For the concept see Franz Joseph Dolger, *Sol salutis: Gebet und Gesang im christlichen Altertum*, Liturgiewissenschaftliche Quellen und Forschungen, 16-17 (1925; reprint ed., Münster: Aschendorff, 1972); idem, *Die Sonne der Gerechtigkeit und der Schwarze: Eine Religionsgeschictliche Studie zum Taufgelobnis*, ibid., 14 (1918; reprint ed., Münster: Aschendorff, 1970).

146 A.-G. Hamman, *La vie quotidienne en Afrique du nord au temps de saint Augustin*, new ed. (Paris: Hachette, 1985), p. 42.

147 Arnáiz Gorroño et al., *La iglesia y convento de la santa*, p. 60.

148 Teresa of Avila, *Castillo interior* 1.2.10, 6-7.

149 See Antonio Márquez, *Los alumbrados: Origenes y filosofía (1525-1559)*, 2d ed. (Madrid: Taurus, 1980).

150 Teresa of Avila, *Castillo interior*, appendix 4.

it was not set alight. The very center of the castle was like a fire shooting flames upward.[151] God was not a hearth but a brazier, which was since Minoan civilization a portable, not a fixed, fire. The source of light and heat to her castle was not like her convent's kitchen, illuminated by a window[152] and furnished with a deep hearth, with pots on tripods and long-handled brass pans hanging from hooks on the masonry wall.[153] It was a brazier, a large metal bowl for burning charcoals, the principal domestic alternative to the fireplace for heating. The utensil was versatile: with a long handle it became a warming pan for the bed; on a small stand, a chafing dish; in a box, a warmer for hands or feet. It could also be converted into a burner or censer for perfume by fitting a small pan filled with scented pastilles above the container of coals. Burners for wood of aloes, oil of cypress, or scent of musk were a feature of glamorous residences.[154] That usage coincided with Teresa de Jesús' image. Although fire was a traditional metaphor for divine activity in the soul, it had in Avila a special preciousness. Firewood and coal were commodities in high demand and short supply, carefully supervised by municipal officials.[155]

More copious in the interior castle was aqueous imagery. Water was also a precious commodity, since in the sixteenth century most of Spain was quite dry. But the climate was variable and subject to great extremes, so that the peasant was either praying for rain or its cessation.[156] In Avila there was a parallel geographical situation: residents on the crown of the hill were petitioning for water, while those at its foot complained of flooding. The municipal council constructed wells, pipes, and fountains, and it consulted experts for new sources and means of storage, while it processed the statue of Nuesta Señores de Sonsoles in penitence.[157] The core of the foundation of the convent of San José as privacy in prayer had been challenged when the council ordered the demolition of its hermitages, because their construction near the aqueduct damaged the civic supply of water. Water for drinking or irrigation, whether from a natural spring or a manmade well, was public property controlled by public officials.[158] Even the conditions for the nuns' kitchen garden were unfavorable. The vegetative layer of the soil was thin because of the granite bed that configured the base of Avila. Then there was the general lack of water, although the nuns conserved a primitive well at the north of the cloister. Of singular importance to the convent was the well of the Samaritan woman (John 4:7-42), situated at the north of the gar-

151 Ibid. 1.2.3; 1.2.5; 5.2.3; 4.2.6; 6.7.8; 6.2.4; 7.3.8.
152 Cervera Vera, *Complejo arquitectónico del monasterio*, p. 30.
153 Alvarez and Domingo, *Sainte Thérèse d'Avila*, photo p. 14.
154 Thornton, *Italian Renaissance Interior*, pp. 26-27, 251.
155 See Bilinkoff, *Avila of Saint Teresa*, p. 61.
156 Vassberg, *Land and Society*, pp. 197-98.
157 Bilinkoff, *Avila of Saint Teresa*, p. 58.
158 See Vassberg, *Land and Society*, pp. 54-55., without reference to her.

den but outside the walls. It was next to the ancient municipal aqueduct, whose waters irrigated the nuns' scant plantations. There were also three Moorish cisterns that caught rainwater and flowed through granite conduits to the cultivated plots. Such agricultural skill and organization were infrequent in convent gardens. Another cache of water was in the northwestern corner of the garden, possibly issuing from a fount supplied by the aqueduct. Teresa de Jesús herself found and piped the water from a deep well to quench the thirst of her community.[159]

She spiritually diverted Bernard of Clairvaux's metaphor of the pregnant Virgin as an aqueduct of grace by piping water figuratively within herself. Nothing was more fitting to expound some scriptural matters than water, she argued. Although she had little knowledge or talent, she wrote, she was such a friend of that element that she had observed it with more notice than other things in nature.[160] Teresa de Jesús had abundant opportunity to observe water, since the year she completed *Castillo interior* was preceded by three of unusually cold and rainy weather.[161] A soul, she continued, had two fountains or troughs brimming with water, but differently so. One water flowed from a distance through many conduits built with craft; the other occurred at the origin of the water and filled the soul silently. Since the spring was of great volume, it filled the trough and overflowed it in a broad stream. It involved neither craft nor the construction of conduits; but water always issued from it. The water from the conduits represented the contentments drawn from meditation, because it was carried by thoughts, which aided the self through creatures but fatigued the understanding. Since it issued from human diligence, it made noise when it filled the soul with benefits. In the other fountain the water came from its origin in God as supernatural favor, effecting supreme peace and quiet and suavity deep in the interior of the self. The soul did not know whence or how it came, only that its delight and contentment differed from sentiments in the heart. It overflowed through all the abodes of the castle and its population of powers to arrive at the body, where the exterior person began in God but ended in self. It arose not from the heart but from a profound interior thing, the center of the soul. There were great secrets in the self, she wrote, amazing and incomprehensible, so that human knowledge of God must be trivial. The sensuality of her analogy was only an aid toward understanding.[162]

Yet sensuality was a spirituality, as dramatized by Francisco de Mora, the architect of the monastery of San José after her demise. When the nuns presented him for veneration a relic of her arm, secretly he plucked off a fingernail the size of a chickpea, wrapped it in paper, and hid it in his devo-

---

[159] Cervera Vera, *Complejo arquitectónico del monasterio*, pp. 32-34.
[160] Teresa of Avila, *Castillo interior* 4.2.2.
[161] See Vassberg, *Land and Society*, p. 198, without reference to her.
[162] Teresa of Avila, *Castillo interior* 4.2.3-4.2.6.

tional book of hours.[163] What she wrote with that arm, the autograph of *Castillo interior*, also suffered a sensual fate. After preservation for some centuries in a gold cover, it was transferred to a sumptuous crystal reliquary. The reliquary was surmounted with a large, faceted crystal and encased in a gold castle, based on marble and crenellated with round towers and a turreted entrance: an exterior castle.[164] Although her interior castle was designed as spiritual, Teresa de Jesús described it sensually, and even sensationally. Although she declared her intellection of its divine indwelling, her language was typically figurative rather than theoretical.

The immediate denotations of a castle in Spain were militaristic and monastic. The earliest peninsular architecture was a strong tower for the defense of frontiers, coasts, or cities. When it was constructed by a family or a lord, it was seignorial. More complicated constructions became classified by ownership. Some, not residential but purely military, were built or owned by the king for the protection of his authority or territory, although those situated on heights were occupied by troops only in danger. Under nominal jurisdiction of the king were castles owned and maintained by individual nobles or religious orders. Then there were royal and seignorial castles as headquarters for an estate or as personal residences. Those were designated as a "castle-palace" because they emphasized comfort as well as security. Most were fortified until the sixteenth century or later, when some were converted to simple residences, while others were abandoned for mansions in more accessible locales. Seignorial estates were usually located on level ground with adaptations amenable to residence. Some nobles maintained separate mansions in the towns, retreating to the castle only when threatened by attack. By the sixteenth century castle-palaces tended toward elegant living with more windows, stone and wooden fretwork, and galleries and staircases that were decorative as well as utilitarian. Chapels were enlarged and beautified.[165] Although the earliest examples had been constructed by the Arabs with an aesthetic, rather than functional, design, their Christian counterparts expressed by the fifteenth century the ascendancy to power of the clergy and nobility. Before then, those estates had owned few castles; now their construction became ambitious familial projects. Design was generally symmetrical, depending on the terrain, with brick exteriors of Muslim influence, as in the interior decor and technique. With the turn of the sixteenth century the renaissance taste of nobles and prelates dictated within the squat, solid fortress the luxurious rooms of Italianate marmoreal style.[166]

---

163 For the anecdote see Cervera Vera, *Complejo arquitectónico del monasterio*, p. 60. See also idem, "Las obras y trabajos de Francisco de Mora en Avila," *Archivo español de arte* 60 (1987):402-4.

164 Alvarez and Domingo, *Sainte Thérèse d'Avila*, photo p. 115.

165 See Washburn, *Castles in Spain*, pp. 2-3, 8.

166 Weismüller, *Castles from the Heart of Spain*, pp. 29-30, 42, 32, 45, 42, 39.

Since Teresa de Jesús designated within the interior castle the "palace" of the king, her architectural model was of that type. Yet it was not very residential, certainly not domestic. Christian castles in Spain since the primitive types, on elevated topography with walls sometimes integrated with those of a town, relied for strength on the main tower. Called the "tower of homage," it was similar to the French donjon or the English keep, which served as the residence of the feudal lord and as the ultimate defense of the castle. Feudalism was not successful in Spain, however, despite attempts at implementation, because of the granting of charters of rights and obligations to towns. The charters defined the relation of the town and its inhabitants to the overlord, introducing the freedom of the populace to the detriment of the authority of the nobility. Architectural developments of castles in other countries, such as the fortified gate or the movement forward and ultimate disappearance of the keep, were not paralleled in Spain. The majority of structures there retained the keep with its inner and outer wards or baileys. An important element, even in the castle-palace, was attached to the symbol of the tower of homage. In the early keeps a king might have to share his sleeping quarters with his courtiers, for lack of adequate facilities for comfort. By the end of the medieval era keeps were rich living quarters. They were not permanently used as residences, however; some never were.[167] The celebrated royal edifice, just constructed in restoration of Augustine's aesthetics—to the very detail of ordered fenestration—was the Escorial. The complex included a house for Philip II, with a master bedroom viewing the altar; but it was a mausoleum to his father, commemorating a victory in battle.[168] It was no ordinary renaissance palace, but a dynastic tomb, like the Egyptian pyramids. The king never intended or used it as his principal residence; he only visited it on religious occasions.[169]

When Teresa de Jesús indicated that the king in the castle-palace was a "guest," she accurately reflected the social impermanence of such a dwelling. Nor was the soul stable for even its owner. Her activity was not to reside but to "walk" (*andar*) in it,[170] just as his Majesty had promised that Christ would "walk" with the nuns in the convent of San José she was to found.[171] The ambulatory exercise of the nuns in the convent replicated that of wives in the house. As a moralist dictated, wives were to be "content with what is their part, and familiar with their house and walking in it because God made

[167] Ibid., pp. 32, 35, 39, 45.

[168] George Kubler, *Building the Escorial* (Princeton: Princeton University Press, 1982), pp. 131-34, 87-89, 12. For his father's famous edifice see Earl J. Rosenthal, *The Palace of Charles V in Granada* (Princeton: Princeton University Press, 1985).

[169] Brown, "Philip II as Art Collector and Patron," in *Spanish Cities of the Golden Age*, ed. Kagan, p. 26.

[170] Teresa of Avila, *Castillo interior* 2.1.4; *Camino de perfección* 28.10; *Castillo interior* 1.2.7

[171] Teresa of Avila, *Vida suya* 32.11.

them for her alone." Yet, although he conversely thought women were created with soft limbs to sit in a corner,[172] Teresa de Jesús did not concur with that. The soul was not to retire into a corner of itself but to amble through its rooms, above and below and at the sides, because God dignified them all. It should not constrict itself by spending too much time in a single spot, except for the initial important abode of humility. It was an edifice in which the nuns were continually walking in fatigue on a wearisome journey. Even the entry to the final abode was a "spiritual road."[173] The castle as an architectural model collapsed into the civil engineering of a "road," as in her *Camino de perfección*,[174] and as in the Benedictine rule of the monastery as a highway. The medieval oxymoron of instability in stability prevailed.

Yet the concept of motion transcended monasticism. The sole unity of the Mediterranean region was created by human movement along routes with relations. Its busiest plateaus were centered in the Spanish peninsula in old and new Castile, crossed with tracks teeming with a populace on the move in caravans of muleteers transporting wares and passengers. They journeyed on north-south routes of transhumance and transport, along which the towns were aligned. Cartage enabled the province to maintain an association with the periphery of the peninsula, especially with ports for the woolen trade abroad. Traffic determined the economy. The roads in Spain were also cluttered with vagrants: students, adventurers, beggars, cutpurses, travelers, civil servants minus posts, captains minus companies, and donkeys with empty saddlebags. Soldiers too were wayfarers, both experienced hands and fresh recruits.[175] Yet, while the departures of males were regular and their absences long on business and adventure, Castilian women were more permanent. Because of the danger of attack and the scarcity of accommodations in travel, women stayed at home, knitting ordinary society in continuity and settlement.[176] Teresa de Jesús and her nuns walked to exhaustion but never outside the confines of the castle.

In a society in movement precisely where the king dwelled centrally within the interior castle was indicated by her metaphor of the brazier. Although the castles of Castile were ruined, in the province of Avila one at Oropesa preserves a fireplace with chimney on the second floor. At the castle-palace of Mombeltran, forty miles southwest of the city of Avila, extant in the largest room of the second story is also the chimney of a great fireplace.[177] Since her king was a brazier of fire, he was portable anywhere; but his personal palace was constructed in her imagination on the second story.

[172] Luis de León, *Perfecta casada*, pp. 129-30, cited by Angeles Duran, "Lectura económica de fray Luis de León," pp. 271-72.

[173] Teresa of Avila, *Castillo interior* 1.2.8; 3.2.7; 7.1.1.

[174] Ibid. 1.1.3.

[175] Braudel, *Mediterranean and Mediterranean World*, 1:276, 277, 54-55; 2:741.

[176] Dillard, *Daughters of the Reconquest*, pp. 167, 163.

[177] See Washburn, *Castles in Spain*, pp. 155, 39, 113, without reference to her.

Teresa de Jesús described the interior castle as having ground and upper floors.[178] Access to the strong tower, or keep, was usually on that second level.[179] That tower was the center of the defensive castle, in virtually all Spanish examples the great looming tower of homage where the commander swore fealty to his lord. It could even be maintained as a separate unit, because it was protected by an advantageous site; by entry on the upper floor, sometimes by drawbridges; and by well-provided storerooms.[180] The keep was a veritable fortress and it could be disproportionate to its castle, as high as one hundred thirty feet. It was notable in Spain for its elegance.[181]

The basic plan of the castle, aloof on the Castilian plains where defense relied on massiveness, was square or rectangular with round towers at the corners. Symmetry was the principle of design, with native ingenuity displayed in stellar or circular castles.[182] Teresa de Jesús described the interior castle as containing many apartments, on the ground and upper floors and at the sides, with the principal one in the center and middle of all those.[183] That castle was invented with architectural verisimilitude but not in social realism. The castle was at its zenith by the middle of the fifteenth century, after which it declined with political unification.[184] Spanish monarchs aimed at absolute supremacy of the crown over the nobility. For the centralization of authority, they ordered the destruction of many of the finest strongholds, so that under Ferdinand and Isabel and under Charles V castles were as policy systematically leveled.[185] By the middle of the sixteenth century those structures not already dismantled by royal decree were abandoned widespread. Patrician families constructed civilian palaces in replacement. The government provided for defense military forts whose accommodations were limited to the garrison.[186] Teresa's model for the soul as a castle was in the year of its invention—1577—undomestic. It was also socially anachronistic, like her foundation of the convent of San José to revive the medieval rule of enclosure.

The palaces of magnates during the reign of Philip II differed from the castle. The entrance had a grand portal depicting the coat of arms of the owner—in Avila escutcheons by the hundred—with pavement of finely inlaid pebbles. Access to the patio was through a door: to one side a large

---

178 Teresa, *Castillo interior* 1.1.3.

179 See Weismüller, *Castles from the Heart of Spain*, p. 32, without reference to her.

180 Washburn, *Castles in Spain*, p. 5. For the tower of homage see also Edward Cooper, *Castillos señoriales en la corona de Castilla*, rev. ed., 3 vols. in 4 (Junta de Castilla y León: Consejería de cultura y turismo, 1991), 1-1:35-39.

181 Weismüller, *Castles from the Heart of Spain*, p. 51. For castles in Avila see Cooper, *Castillos señoriales*, 1-2:355-75.

182 Weismüller, *Castles from the Heart of Spain*, pp. 49, 35.

183 Teresa of Avila, *Castillo interior* 1.1.3.

184 Weismüller, *Castles from the Heart of Spain*, p. 13.

185 See Washburn, *Castles in Spain*, p. 10.

186 Weismüller, *Castles from the Heart of Spain*, p. 45, 54.

window with a wrought-iron grate, to the other the descent to the cellars, stables, and basements. Up several steps were walls covered in plaster reliefs in two colors in a mix of styles. The patio had an Arabic fountain, marble columns forming two to four galleries, on the high walls some plaster works, arched windows with central pillars, decorative painted tiles, and brick floors. Stairways with Moorish paneling led to vast corridors and spacious salons decorated with tapestries, armory, and artistry. The palace featured a monumental chimney of marble where burned an oaken log, around which the family and servants gathered at nightfall to pray the rosary. Before the reign of Ferdinand and Isabel private edifices did not boast conveniences or even manifest aesthetics. In her childhood and youth the future queen lived in the province of Avila in a palace humbly built of mud, brick, and wood. It had a tiny patio, low rooms, and scant decor, demonstrative of the poverty of life and manner of even the highest personages of the late medieval era. Aristocrats then lived in true fortresses reflecting the exigencies of a civic life that could suddenly become militaristic, with the streets as battlegrounds.[187]

The architecture of noble houses in Avila displayed ancient doors with ogives, robust towers with only loopholes, enormous voussoirs and historic decoration of blazons with heralds, and the machicolations and merlons of battlement. A typical late medieval palace had a turret absorbing the entire place, huge square battlements, and sentinels in the corners—all to raise a siege to defend its broad, arched gateway. A home was completely castellated. A seignorial mansion in the rude renaissance style of the decades during which Teresa de Jesús was born and raised was of granite, very austere, very severe. Its corridors were centered around a patio, with stairs in the front and a garden in the rear. Beneath the tower, the entrance hall had all the elements of a strong house. It was nearly square, with a door opening to the street on an angle. A peephole, like a small grated window of the type in the cells of a prison, was placed on an odd angle: for spying an attacker and for letting arrows fly through it for his dispersal. A handsome patio, a level above ground, had galleries all around on two floors, with arches below and lintels above. A grand salon richly displayed the current artistry, even paintings imported from Brussels and Rome. The development of interiors and furnishings corresponded to the disuse of militaristic aspects in the exteriors. The arched passageways, somber rooms, clumsy chests, the cold and damp of early in the century—all eased toward comfort. Stone benches were embedded in walls next to windows overlooking the streets. Living quarters were organized along great corridors with beautiful galleries and ample salons. Furnishings included leather armchairs with large nailheads, tables, desks of various sizes and styles, and everywhere tapestries: of the

[187] Merino Alvarez, *Sociedad abulense*, pp. 146-48. For the houses of the repopulators and notables see also Carramolino, *Historia de Avila*, 1:444-64.

narratives of patriarchs, the triumphs of Petrarch, and the victories of rulers.[188]

In the modest homes of Avila's nobility, lacking grand and rich tapestries, canvases hung on whitewashed stone walls. The art had only obscure marks or signatures. Scenes were terrorful images of Christ's passion or of saintly lives. At the head of each bed in an alcove was a branch of palm and a container of blessed water. Any home, rich or poor, had an image of the Madonna with a burning lamp or candle,[189] such as the one to which Teresa de Jesús tearfully fled when her mother died.[190] The only furnishing she transferred from her home to the castle were such images, which frequently appeared on the walls of her mind. Visions were just like paintings, she wrote.[191] They allowed her access to the status opposite to her conventual task of embroidery, samples of which—golden liturgical vestments—are extant from her trained fingers.[192] The fine art of painting was superior to the applied art of needlework, since it belonged to the privileged, rather than the working, class; and was proper to males, rather than females. Art with thread was lesser than art with paint; for embroidery was done in the domestic sphere for love, while painting was executed in the public sphere for money. Painting was individual, displaying personality; embroidery collective, displaying presence.[193] Yet there was a gifted female artist—married too—resident at the Spanish court who portrayed even Philip II.[194] Teresa de Jesús preferred the painterly images in her mind as the only decoration of her interior castle. There was not a stick of furniture there: no bridal bed with silken hangings such as Bernard of Clairvaux described, nor varied cushions for the indwelling Trinity such as Margery Kempe provided. There was not a rude chair to sit upon, for Teresa de Jesús agreed with Augustine that on earth a person could never rest.

The interior castle was not allegorical but schematic. She did not exploit details of architecture or articles of furnishing to discourse on virtues or vices in the medieval style. The castle served Teresa de Jesús as a mnemonic device for experiences of prayer, just as architectural models like palaces had classically served the invention of discourse. The orator

---

188 Ibid., pp. 149-52.

189 Ibid., pp. 154, 147.

190 Teresa of Avila, *Vida suya* 1.7.

191 Ibid. 28.3.

192 See Alvarez and Domingo, *Sainte Thérèse d'Avila*, photo p. 22.

193 Rozsika Parker, *The Subversive Stitch: Embroidery and the Making of the Feminine* (London: Women's Press, 1984), pp. 5, 81.

194 Ilya Sandra Perlingieri, *Sofonisba Anguissola: The First Great Woman Artist of the Renaissance* (New York: Rizzoli, 1992), pp. 117-67; María Kusche, "La antigua galería de retratos del Pardo: Su importancia para la obra de Tiziano, Moro, Sánchez Coello y Sofonisba Anguissola y su significado para Felipe II, su fundador," *Archivo español de arte* 65 (1992):11-14; idem, "Sofonisba Anguissola en España: Retratista en la corte de Felipe II junto a Alonso Sánchez Coello y Jorge de la Rua," ibid. 62 (1989):391-420.

memorized by assigning his topics to the parts of an impressive edifice: each structure, each room, each object. He then recovered his knowledge or its sensation by recalling the topics sequentially in a hunt through memorial corridors, according to principles of order and association.[195] Teresa de Jesús confessed herself in the preface a writer of poor memory. The organization of the castle was marked by lapses and digressions.[196] If fabrication was the female task, her work was not well spun or woven. The more important abodes of the castle were disordered theologically. The fifth abode, or prayer of union, was experientially more intimate with God than the sixth or seventh abodes. It was the divine possession of the soul, whereas the latter only involved visions in the imagination or the understanding. Teresa de Jesús evidently ranked them higher than the fifth by different norms: the sixth because it was unbodily, the seventh because it was habitual. The incorporeality and duration of experience were sublimer in her judgment than the intimacy of union. The habitual consciousness of the indwelling Trinity, which she identified as the supreme state of spiritual marriage,[197] was merely the ordinary premise for Augustine's speculation. She terminated *Castillo interior* where he commenced *De Trinitate*. She did not achieve his identification of the principle of divine union as the Holy Spirit, as charity. For Teresa de Jesús the Spirit was conventionally inspirational; charity was human works and human proofs.

The interior castle, besides its divisions, had a door. The entry to its beauteous and delightful interior was through prayer and consideration. Teresa de Jesús was perplexed about the contradiction of entering the soul when the soul was already within her. She nevertheless judged that some persons were lingering in the courtyard of the castle with the guards, not knowing or even considering what lay within or its design. They were like paralyzed persons intent on the insects crawling the walls.[198] The metaphor was grim, for Castilian crops were regularly destroyed by insect pests, aphids, and worms. Most dramatic were the plagues of locusts. A major infestation could cause total crop failure and even kill livestock through contamination of their supply of food and water. There was no effective control despite many attempted methods. Fields were periodically ravaged as populations of locusts increased and decreased with their cycles; the migratory swarms causing the severest damage followed unusually hot weather with drought. Many areas of old Castile suffered a plague of locusts in 1573-

---

[195] See Frances A. Yates, *The Art of Memory* (Chicago: University of Chicago Press, 1966), pp. 1-7, 9-10. See also E. Michael Gerli, "*El castillo interior* y el *arte de la memoria*," in *Santa Teresa y la literatura mística hispánica*, Actas del I congreso internacional sobre Santa Teresa y la mística hispánica, ed. Manuel Criado de Val, Historia de la literatura española desde sus fuentes, 6 (Madrid: EDI-6, 1964), pp. 331-37.

[196] Teresa of Avila, *Castillo interior* praef.; 1.2.1-2; 4.1.2; 7.1.1, 3-4.

[197] Ibid. 7.1.6.

[198] Ibid. 1.1.3; 2.1.11.

74;[199] in the spring of 1571 the city of Avila sent money and representatives, including a priest to conjure the insects, when the pests destroyed most of the annual harvest.[200] Her nuns would have been impressed by her metaphor of evil, since the populace had just experienced it. Vermin even penetrated the walls of her castle to the first abode, precious as it was.[201] The nuns' bodies were dirty, their skin crawling with vermin; but the bugs were believed to originate within them. According to the current medical theory, lice did not exist in nature independently of bodies, to which they were then attracted by lack of hygiene. Vermin were generated from corrupt substances within bodies, then secreted to the surface of the skin by exhalations. They swarmed from the inside to the outside, as signs of innate decay and impending death.[202] Women were believed more prone than men to vermin because of their poor digestion and phlegmatic humor.[203] Verses attributed to Teresa de Jesús implored God not to create lice.[204]

The outer abode also had reptiles,[205] probably the basilisk, a small harmless lizard with a conical hood that acquired a lethal reputation and served in monastic morality to symbolize vainglory.[206] And there were snakes,[207] associated in the most popular legend about diamonds, told in the romance of Alexander and retold in the travelogue of Marco Polo. When that king was in India, he ventured into a diamond pit guarded by snakes of such fatal power that their gaze killed. Alexander outwitted them by holding up mirrors as shields; the snakes beheld their own image and died.[208] Teresa de Jesús ascribed evil to creepy, crawly creatures, such as menaced the paintings

---

199 See Vassberg, *Land and Society*, p. 199, without reference to Teresa de Jesús.

200 Bilinkoff, *Avila of Saint Teresa*, p. 154.

201 Teresa of Avila, *Castillo interior* 1.2.10.

202 See Georges Viagrello, *Concepts of Cleanliness: Changing Attitudes in France Since the Middle Ages*, trans. Jean Birrell (Cambridge: Cambridge University Press, 1988), pp. 42-45. Nuns were forbidden to bathe for cleanliness—it was only permitted in illness or for health— since the earliest Spanish treatment of the cosmetic topic. Leander, *De institutione virginum et contemptu mundi* 20, cited by Sánchez Herrero, "Cuidados de la belleza corporal femenina," p. 277.

203 Piero Camporesi, *The Incorruptible Flesh: Bodily Mutation and Mortification in Religion and Folklore*, trans. Tania Croft-Murray and Helen Elson, Cambridge Studies in Oral and Literate Culture, 17 (Cambridge: Cambridge University Press, 1988), p. 82.

204 Cervera Vera, *Complejo arquitectónico del monasterio*, p. 18.

205 Teresa of Avila, *Castillo interior* 1.2.14; 3.2.8.

206 See Adam Wienand, "Heils-Symbole und Dämonen-Symbole im Leben der Cistercienser-Mönche," in *Die Cistercienser: Geschichte, Geist, Kunst*, ed. Ambrosius Schneider et al. (Cologne: Wienand, 1974), pp. 505-7.

207 Teresa of Avila, *Castillo interior* 3.2.7; cf. 5.1.5.

208 Berthold Laufer, *The Diamond: A Study in Chinese and Hellenistic Folk-lore* (Chicago: Field Museum of Natural History, 1915), 10-21; *Diamonds, Myth, Magic, and Reality*, ed. Jacques Legrand (New York: Crown, 1980), pp. 16-17. For their ancient use and value see also Laufer, *Diamond*, pp. 42-46; Legrand, ed., *Diamonds*, pp. 12-15; Godehard Lenzen, *The History of Diamond Production and the Diamond Trade*, trans. F. Bradley (London: Barrie & Jenkins, 1970), 1-7, 15-25; Leonard Gorelick and A. John Gwinntt, "Diamonds from India to Rome and Beyond," *American Journal of Archaeology* 92 (1988):547-52.

of Hieronymous Bosch on the walls of the royal palace, El Escorial.[209] Their indeterminate movement was conventionally contrary to holiness.[210] The aerial creatures of her invention were also grounded. She introduced herself as a parrot, a caged bird, and she also compared herself to one with broken wings. In the abode of union the soul became a small dove but its activity was to generate heat for warming others, so that her concept was brooding in a nest, not flight from it. Even in the principal palace, where the most secretive affairs between the soul and God transpired, he was communicating only with persons as "smelly worms."[211] That was the ancient prototype of the unclean, swarming creatures.[212] The gnawing worm in rotting flesh symbolized the decay of death, and the lyricist Florencia Pinar had compared a worm hooking and tearing at the entrails to a crafty and cruel love.[213] In the second half of the sixteenth century there also gaped a profound divide between rich, vigorous, noble dynasties, which owned vast property, and the mobile mass of the poor and disinherited. They were disparaged as human insects, "caterpillars and grubs."[214]

A certain worm Teresa de Jesús adopted as a metaphor for the transformation of the soul from carnal to spiritual, the silkworm.[215] Yet it was a contrary metaphor for spiritual elevation. Its caterpillar, unlike all other caterpillars, lacks any real power of locomotion. In its adult phase as moth it is unable to fly, its small wings incapacitated from centuries of domestication. If excited, the male of the species can vibrate them; but no flight ensues.[216] Teresa de Jesús' knowledge was quite unscientific. She supposed that the silkworm moth flew. For the egg she had "seed" and she ignored the chrysalis. She explained that she had never seen sericulture, only heard about it, so that if her description was "twisted" (like silken threads) she was not at fault. She indicated that the nuns would certainly have heard

---

209 See Brown, "Philip II as Art Collector and Patron," p. 28; Antonio Matilla Tascon, "Felipe II adquiere pinturas del Bosco y Patinir," *Goya* 203 (1988):258-61; Elisa Bermejo Martínez, *La pintura de los primitivos flamencos en España* 2 vols. (Madrid: Consejo superior de investigaciones científicas, 1980-82), 2:109-35.

210 See Mary Douglas, *Purity and Danger: An Analysis of the Concepts of Pollution and Taboo* (London: Ark, 1984), p. 56. For mortals as grubs crawling on the earth beneath the lofty divine Majesty see also John Calvin, *Institutiones religionis christiani* 2.6.4.

211 Teresa of Avila, *Castillo interior* 1.1.3; 5.4.10; 6.4.7; 6.4.10.

212 Douglas, *Purity and Danger*, p. 56. For worms see also Camporesi, *Incorruptible Flesh*, pp. 78-82, 112-18.

213 Alan Deyermond, "Spain's First Women Writers," in *Women in Hispanic Literature: Icons and Fallen Idols*, ed. Beth Miller (Berkeley: University of California Press, 1983), pp. 49, 48, citing Florencia Pinar from Hernando del Castillo, *Cancionero general*, fol. clxxxv verso. Cf. Teresa of Avila, *Castillo interior* 5.3.6.

214 Braudel, *Mediterranean and Mediterranean World*, 2:755.

215 Teresa of Avila, *Castillo interior* praef.; 3.1.5; 5.3.1; 1.1.3; 5.2. A silkworm becomes a moth, not a butterfly. The silkworm moth is rendered "butterfly" in all translations and interpretations examined.

216 John Feltwell, *The Story of Silk* (Phoenix Mall, Gloucestershire: Alan Sutton, 1990), pp. 1, 37, 57.

about the marvels of sericulture, which only God could have invented. In her epideictic wonder the dead seeds came alive with the foliation of the mulberry tree, and the caterpillars fed on the leaves until fully grown. Attaching their bodies to twigs, the insects spun silk from their mouths into cocoons that enveloped them. The gross and ugly caterpillars died, and from the cocoons emerged a very pleasant moth. That natural cycle was her spiritual moral.[217]

Teresa de Jesús' excuse of her model was indifferent to factuality. An elementary source, Pliny's *Naturalis historia*, had left the matter of silkworms in women's hands.[218] And indeed, the largest number of female workers, who were in the textile industry, were in silks, with many of its trades exclusive to them, although always supervised by men. They were spinners, weavers, and fashioners of ribbons, kerchiefs, fringes, tassels, laces, girdles, caps, and purses.[219] Even Spanish nuns worked in silks.[220] In the seventeenth century silkworms would be in the exquisite hands of Maria Sibylla Merian, who captured and studied caterpillars to paint them from life in miniature masterpieces, and who in scientific achievement discovered the metamorphosis of the silkworm.[221] Yet religious authors before Teresa de Jesús, such as Marco Girolamo Vida in *De bombyce* and Ludovico Lazarelli in *Bombyx*, had considered the insect;[222] and it appeared in Guillaume de Saluste Sieur du Bartas's influential *La creation du monde ou première sepmaine*.[223] Michelangelo Buonarroti penned a sonnet in which he imagined himself as a silkworm that could shed its skin to clothe his beloved's hand and foot with gloves and slippers.[224] But such books were not available to Teresa de Jesús, by her own obscurantist decision for enclosure—a decision that repudiated the very fondness for books that had propelled her

---

[217] Teresa of Avila, *Castillo interior* 5.2.1-8. For the double thread with twisting as *torcido* see Manuel Garzon Pareja, *La industria sedera en España: El arte de la seda del Granada* (Granada: Gráficas del Sur, 1972), p. 372.

[218] Pliny, *Naturalis historia* 11.26.75-11.27.78.

[219] Diane Bornstein, *The Lady in the Tower: Medieval Courtesy Literature for Women* (Hamden, Conn.: Archon, 1983), p. 100.

[220] Perry, *Crime and Society in Early Modern Seville* (Hanover, N. H.: University Press of New England, 1980), p. 214.

[221] For her see Natalie Zemon Davis, *Women on the Margins: Three Seventeenth-Century Lives* (Cambridge, Mass.: Harvard University Press, 1995), pp. 140-202; Sharon Valiant, "Maria Sibylla Merian: Recovering an Eighteenth-Century Legend," *Eighteenth Century Studies* 26 (1993):467-79; Londa Schiebinger, *The Mind Has No Sex?: Women in the Origins of Modern Science* (Cambridge, Mass.: Harvard University Press, 1989), pp. 68-79.

[222] Thomas Moffet, *The Silkewormes and their Flies*, pp. xii-xiii.

[223] Guillaume de Saluste Sieur du Bartas, *La creation du monde ou première sepmaine* 5.885-900. For studies see Jan Miernowski, *Dialectique et connaissance dans La sepmaine de Du Bartas: "Discours sur discours infiniment divers"* (Geneva: Droz, 1992); *Du Bartas: Poète encyclopédique du XVIe siècle*, Colloque internationale, Faculté des lettres et sciences humaines de Pau et des pays de l'Adour, 7, 8 et 9 mars 1986, ed. James Dauphiné (Lyon: Manufacture, 1986); idem, *Guillaume de Saluste du Bartas: Poète scientifique* (Paris: Belles Lettres, 1983).

[224] Michelangelo Buonarroti, *Rime* 94. See Clements, *Poetry of Michelangelo*, p. 204.

into the convent. In her description of the caterpillar spinning its cocoon she indicated that its house was Christ. "It seems to me," she wrote, "that somewhere I read or heard that our life is hidden in Christ, or in God, which is the same thing, or that our life is Christ. As to whether this is so or not, it matters little for my purpose."[225] Her oblique reference was biblical (Col. 3:3-4). Teresa de Jesús read but, by her deliberate rejection of Latin learning, only in the vernacular.[226] In her obscurantism she deprived herself of scripture, since the Inquisition forbade vernacular versions.[227] In substituting sericulture for scriptural culture, she was like the character a century later in John Dryden's *The Conquest of Grenada*:

"I scarcely understand my own intent:
But Silk-worm-like, so long within have wrought,
That I am lost in my own Webb of thought."[228]

Her hearsay about the silkworm was likely from her family, which had been engaged in merchandising silks since her paternal grandfather. Or she may have learned the comparison from John of the Cross, a chaplain and confessor. His ancestors, like hers, had belonged to the corporation of silk merchants in Toledo; his father was a silk weaver.[229] Trial by the Inquisition had merely occasioned the relocation of her grandfather's silk business from Toledo to Avila. In the years beginning the decade in which Teresa de Jesús composed her interior castle the Inquisition expelled from Granada the very cultivators of silk, so that her model was socially cogent. Those cultivators were the compulsorily baptized Muslims, denigrated as Moriscos rather than Christians, and watched by the authorities, as were the converted Jews of her own family. The converted Muslims had lived peaceably in the southern province for more than forty years, until their situation progressively worsened. Their economy was severely handicapped by a ban on the export of silk fabric, then by a drastic increase in taxation on the silk industry. The economic measures coincided with Inquisitional pressing of charges against crypto-Muslims. Then royal policy condemned their very civilization. The Arabic language and tradition, such as the customary veiling of women in public, were prohibited. The promulgation intended to eliminate residual Islamic practices and to intimidate the populace.[230]

---

[225] Teresa of Avila, *Castillo interior* 5.2.4.

[226] Teresa of Avila, *Carta* 112. Latin was taught in all the municipal towns as requisite for matriculation at university. Nalle, "Literacy and Culture," p. 74.

[227] Virgilio Pino Crespo, *Inquisición y control ideológico en la España del siglo XVI*, La otra historia de España, 9 (Madrid: Taurus, 1983), pp. 272-83.

[228] John Dryden, *Conquest of Grenada, The Second Part*, in *Works*, 11:118.

[229] See Gerald Brenan, *St John of the Cross: His Life and Poetry* (Cambridge: Cambridge University Press, 1973), pp. 3, 4, 95, without reference to this suggestion.

[230] Braudel, *Mediterranean and Mediterranean World*, 2:790-91; Vassberg, *Land and Society*, pp. 177-78. For fiscal policy see Modesto Ulloa, *La hacienda real de Castilla en el reinado de Felipe II*, 2d ed. (Madrid: Fundación universitaria española seminario "Cisneros," 1977), pp. 359-73. For background see Caro Baroja, *Los moriscos del reino de Granada*

In rebellion Moriscos massacred that populace and its priests, burlesqued ritual, desecrated churches, constructed a mosque, and crowned a king. Raids and manhunts ensued on both sides, with indiscriminate killing. Philip II dispensed the old Christians the right to loot the property of the new Christians, including their bales of silk. The uprising was militarily crushed with a mass surrender of the rebels at the beginning of the decade in which Teresa de Jesús created her silkworm. Muslim property and possessions were sold to nobility and church, including monasteries, to the profit of the royal exchequer. Chained in long convoys, the people—between sixty and one hundred fifty thousand—were expelled from Granada and forcibly dispersed throughout Castile for assimilation.[231] A thousand were settled in Avila.[232] After their expulsion the silk industry declined. The colonists who assumed the sericulture were accustomed to the expansive agriculture of dry-farmed cereals, whereas Muslim agriculture was based on the intensive gardening of orchards and crops from trees, like the mulberry for silk.[233] In Avila the converted Muslims never exceeded more than fifteen percent of the population, with most in farming but many in metalworking. They controlled the manufacture of the pots and pans[234] at the convent's very hearth.

The converted Muslims were not the only persecuted sericulturists. The Huguenots played a central role in silk production. Across the Spanish border in Lyon, a capital of the industry, they were forbidden to practice their skills.[235] Teresa de Jesús wrote that the divine command for a reformed convent after her hellish fantasy was fortified by damaging news from France, how the "Lutherans" were wreaking havoc. Correct reference was to the Huguenots; in either case, "a wretched sect." Anguished, she implored the Lord to remedy the growing evil, as if she were someone who could do something. She would have died a thousand times to save one soul being lost there, she wrote. "But I saw that I was a base woman and the impossi-

---

(Ensayo de historia social) (Madrid: Instituto de estudios políticos, 1957). For the history of the textile see Garzon Pareja, *Industria sedera en España*; Cyril Bunt, *Spanish Silks* (Leigh-on-Sea: F. Lewis, 1965); Florence Lewis May, *Silk Textiles of Spain, Eighth to Fifteenth Century* (New York: Hispanic Society of America, 1957).

231 Braudel, *Mediterranean and Mediterranean World*, 2:791-92; Vassberg, *Land and Society*, p. 178; Andrew C. Hess, *The Forgotten Frontier: A History of the Sixteenth Century Ibero-African Frontier* (Chicago: University of Chicago Press, 1978), pp. 145-47; K. Garrad, "La industria sedera granadina en el siglo XVI y su conexión con el levantamiento de los Alpujarras (1568-1571)," *Miscelánea de estudios árabes y hebraicos* 5 (1956):73-98; Bernard Vincent, "Combien de Morisques ont été expulsés du royaume de Grenade?," *Mélanges de la casa de Velásquez* 7 (1971):397-99; idem, "L'expulsion des morisques du royaume de Grenade et leur répartition en Castille (1570-1571)," ibid. 6 (1971):210-46; Elliott, *Imperial Spain*, pp. 288-94; Parker, *Philip II*, pp. 104-9.

232 Parker, *Philip II*, p. 107.

233 Vassberg, *Land and Society*, pp. 179, 181.

234 Bilinkoff, *Avila of Saint Teresa*, p. 11.

235 Feltwell, *Story of Silk*, pp. 157-58. For women as silk weavers see Davis, "Women in the Crafts in Sixteenth-Century Lyon," *Feminist Studies* 8 (1982):58.

bility of success in what I desired in the service of the Lord." So she determined "to do the tiny thing that was in me, which is to follow the evangelical counsels with the total perfection that I could." She was "confident in the great goodness of God, who never fails to assist whoever decides to abandon everything for him." Teresa de Jesús was convinced that the Huguenots were false witnesses, sentencing Christ to death again. "The world is burning," she exclaimed. The principal reason why the Lord had convened the nuns at San José was that human force of arms was insufficient to attack "this fire of those heretics." Necessary was the noble tactic employed in time of war when the enemy had overrun the entire land: retreat to a very well-fortified city from which to launch attacks.[236] Yet the Huguenots, as the noblewoman Charlotte Arbaleste attested, had like the Carmelites sucked in the faith with their mother's milk.[237] Only the year before Teresa de Jesús wrote *Castillo interior* the Spanish army killed six thousand Huguenots and torched eight hundred of their homes. Those events altered the history of the silk industry by propelling skilled survivors into voluntary exile, especially to England.[238] Silk stockings were fashionable there with the royalty (Queen Elizabeth wore black ones) and now affordable by the nobility.[239]

Silk was used in the sixteenth century decoratively for banners and embroideries, carpets and paintings. Its high-tensile strength served for guy ropes and the strings of musical instruments. The Samurai warriors whom explorers and missionaries would encounter fastened the metal plates of their armament with its tough filament.[240] For the soul to be a silkworm was to be productive in a labor that was as graceful as it was durable. Yet the metaphor was spun from Teresa de Jesús' misbelief precisely about work and grace. The construction of her convent and castle was ascetic. She determined "to do the tiny thing that was in me," defined as the perfect observation of the evangelical counsels. Her aspiration was in perfect alignment with semipelagian thought: to do what was within one's power. Teresa de

---

236 Teresa of Avila, *Camino de perfección* 1.2; 1.5; 3.1; cf. *Castillo interior* 5.2.10-11.

237 See Davis, "Boundaries and the Sense of Self in Sixteenth-Century France," in *Reconstructing Individualism: Autonomy, Individuality, and the Self in Western Thought*, ed. Thomas C. Heller, Morton Sosna, and David E. Wellbery (Stanford, Calif.: Stanford University Press, 1986), p. 56.

238 Feltwell, *Story of Silk*, pp. 158-59; and for the origins of the industry there see Marian K. Dale, "The London Silkwomen of the Fifteenth Century," *Economic History Review* 4 (1933):324-35. See also Barbara Diefendorf, *Beneath the Cross: Catholics and Huguenots in Sixteenth-Century Paris* (New York: Oxford University Press, 1991).

239 Feltwell, *Story of Silk*, p. 145; Joan Thirsk, *Economic Policy and Projects: The Development of a Consumer Society in Early Modern England* (Oxford: Clarendon, 1978), pp. 120, 125-27; idem, "The Fantastical Folly of Fashion: The English Stocking Knitting Industry, 1500-1700," in *Textile History and Economic History: Essays in Honour of Miss Julia de Lacy Mann*, ed. N. B. Harte and K. G. Ponting (Manchester: Manchester University Press, 1973), pp. 50-73.

240 Feltwell, *Story of Silk*, pp. 128-29, 132, 136-37.

Jesús believed that if she did her little part, God would not fail to provide his grace, not only for herself but for the conversion of the "Lutherans." Her mentality replicated in ordinary language the condign merit Luther rejected. As he advisedly cited the gospel (Luke 14:28), building a structure required computing the cost and assessing the capability.[241]

Teresa de Jesús urged the beginner at prayer to work diligently and to be determined and disposed to conform her will to God. Such conformity was the supreme perfection attainable, the entire human good; the more conformed soul would receive the more from God. "Let us endeavor to do what is in ourselves," she counseled. Then contradicting that semipelagianism she advised, "Confide in the mercy of God, and nothing in the self." Her interior castle swayed between those extremes, the semipelagianism of the ascetic tradition and the inability of her spiritual experience. The soul was victorious both through divine mercy and through human perseverance, she wrote in compromise. Reward conformed to love, a love not fabricated in the imagination but proved by works. While his Majesty had no need of human works, he did have need of willful determination. The soul should have a good disposition and persevere in it but it should also consider itself a useless servant, to whom he need not grant any favors. Love was not delight but determination; yet God granted favor to whom he willed, often to the least attentive. Great divine favors were not obtainable by poor human services. They occurred at divine, not human, will, although only to those rebuffing worldly things. The Lord did not reserve for himself the many other deeds people in their misery could perform with his aid, such as penance, good works, and prayer. The practice of virtues was necessary. The soul that did not dispose itself failed.[242] The nuns in their monastic station were to be workers, not like the vagrants who threatened urban and rural stability, doing no work because they said there was none, and so gaming in public squares.[243] Vagrancy, causing a persistent shortage of labor, contributed to a major defect of Castilian textiles, their excessive cost.[244]

The silkworm illustrated her admitted "profound confusion." In the spiritual union that its moth symbolized his Majesty became the very abode that the soul constructed for itself. "I wish to say that we are able to abandon ourselves and place ourselves in God, since I say that he is the abode, and we ourselves are able to construct it to place ourselves in it. And, yes, we are!" The human effort of abandoning the self to construct an abode, like the silkworm spinning its cocoon, was "slight work that is nothing." Yet to it his Majesty united himself, conferring on it such exalted value that he be-

---

241 Luther, *De servo arbitrio*, p. 105.

242 Teresa of Avila, *Castillo interior* 2.1.8; 3.1.1; 3.1.7; 3.2.8; 4.1.7; 4.2.9; 4.3.3; 4.3.5; 5.1.2; 7.2.8.

243 Braudel, *Mediterranean and Mediterranean World*, 2:741.

244 Elliott, *Imperial Spain*, p. 181.

came the reward of the work. Since he paid the greater price, he desired to unite those trifling human labors with the supreme ones he had suffered in his passion, so that they became one. Teresa de Jesús thus wrote of advancement through the rooms of the castle as "meriting more and more." As she judged, "True union may very well be obtained with the Lord's favor, if we exert ourselves to procure it by having no will except attachment to the will of God." Union of her will with his will she declared her constant desire. It was the clearest and safest union, since his will was complete perfection. "May it please his Majesty to give us the grace to merit to arrive at this state; for it is in our hand, if we will."[245]

Yet the assurance of that semipelagian reasoning faltered as Teresa de Jesús elaborated the sublimer rooms of the interior castle. When her favors became more detested than believed by others, she was enlightened that the soul had no good except that given it by his Majesty, so that forgetful of self she could praise him as if they happened to a third party. In persecution she could only wait on his mercy fighting for the victory. She did not fight; all weapons seemed in the hands of her enemies. The soul clearly learned its misery and the very little it was able to do of itself, should the Lord forsake it. There was no need of reflection; the experience of inability made her understand the self as trivial and miserable. Yet in response she formulated: "Who owes much, must pay much." The soul paid little of its obligation, she thought, and that little was full of faults, failings, and feebleness. It should strive to forget its work, recall its sins, and place itself in the mercy of God. It had nothing with which to pay, in its poverty and misery, for it had nothing it had not received. It needed to beg pity and mercy from him on sinners. Teresa de Jesús begged God tearfully to take her from such exile. Living in the matrimonial room of the interior castle, the soul experienced as a great penance "everyday pain and confusion to see the little it was able to do and the much it was obliged to do." Although spiritual marriage effected in the soul self-oblivion, it caused "pain in seeing that its efforts can do nothing," for it desired to do all it could.[246]

Teresa de Jesús did not comprehend grace as gratuity. She considered it a favor, yet one to be both earned and repaid. Some of her experience manifested gratuity, however. She termed that experience "supernatural" to distinguish it from religious exercises such as vocal prayer and good works. Those she must have considered "natural," although theologically they were also by supernatural grace. The design of her interior castle was divided—between the courtyard and the first three abodes, then the fourth to seventh abodes—on the principle that with the fourth abode commenced "supernatural" matters. At that juncture she entrusted herself to the Holy

[245] Teresa of Avila, *Castillo interior* 7.4.16; 5.2.5; 5.3.2; 5.3.3; 5.3.5; 5.3.7.
[246] Ibid. 6.1.4-5; 6.1.10; 6.1.11; 6.5.4; 6.5.6; 6.6.1; 7.2.9; 7.3.8.

Spirit and asked him to commence speaking for her.[247] In her architectural schematic the courtyard and initial abodes—as natural—were located on the ground floor. The final abodes with their raptures into heaven—as *supernatural*—were on the upper floor; with the fourth abode imagined, perhaps, as a transitional stairway. Although Teresa de Jesús did not explicate that design, its division coincided with her semipelagian belief. In a letter appended to *Castillo interior* she indicated that the nuns could not enter all the abodes through their own efforts, however laborious, if the Lord of the castle did not place them there.[248] She implied that they could enter some of the abodes through their own efforts, at least the initial three. In her exposition of the silkworm in the fifth abode, of prayer of union, she argued for the value of human effort toward that union, and even for "meriting more and more." In the sixth abode of spiritual espousal her confidence failed, however; and in the seventh abode of spiritual marriage she named its children, but not its cause, "works! works!"[249]

In the preface Teresa de Jesús had identified herself as a parrot and she parroted throughout the castle the semipelagianism she had learned, although her experience sometimes contradicted it. She was not only spiritually but socially conditioned to semipelagian belief. Her word for grace was "favor". Her notion that a divine favor could be earned, although slightly, and that its repayment was obligatory, however poor, was a cultural idea. It was not baldly a nominalist argument. Teresa de Jesús more likely derived it, not from the Spanish adherents of William of Ockham but from the Spanish courtiers of Philip II and the descendant pecking order of payments and obligations, rewards and punishments, on which her society depended. The very word in Castilian for formal "you", *Usted*, was a contraction of "your mercy", *vuestra merced*. Her concept of grace as a "favor" was not a literal gift, only a quasi gift. The cultural rationale seems to have been thus: To preserve and honor the dignity of its recipient, it was tacitly pretended or assumed that he deserved the "favor"; in turn, he obligatorily repaid it with some deed, also considered a "favor." The concept was as ancient as the clientele gathering in the peristyle of Augustine's family home to receive the daily dole from his father as patron. The baskets of goods he proffered were gifts, but they were gifts earned and repaid in an elaborate Roman system of patronage and clientele. The notion of a gift as not really gratuitous seems indigenous to her Mediterranean culture; it contradicted Luther's logic of a gift as strictly gratuitous. Grace was not only spiritual but cultural, its theology tenaciously rooted in anthropology.[250]

---

[247] Ibid. 4.1.1; cf. 5.4.11; 6.1.1.

[248] Ibid. epilogue 2.

[249] Ibid. 5.2.5-5.3.7; 6; 7.4.6.

[250] For Luther's logic and semiotics see Boyle, "The Chimera and the Spirit: Luther's Grammar of the Will," in *The Martin Luther Quincentennial*, ed. Gerhard Dünnhaupt (Detroit, Mich.: Wayne State University Press for *Michigan Germanic Studies*, 1985), pp.

Teresa de Jesús' false solution to the contradiction between culture and experience was to base the interior castle in humility as virtue. Its initial rooms were self-knowledge, since the most important thing on earth was humility, to which it led. The safe and level path was to contrast divine grandeur with human baseness. Humility was necessary even for the soul in the royal chamber; for humility, like the bee in the hive, was ever working. Christ was a model of humility. To imagine entering heaven without entering the self, knowing and reflecting on its misery and seeking mercy, was foolhardy. Humility was ointment to its wounds, and those who possessed it were assured healing by the divine physician. It was the very virtue that procured grace. "Humility! humility!" she exclaimed. "By this the Lord allows himself to be vanquished for whatever we wish from him." By humility and detachment the soul could procure divine favors without striving for them. The soul was to solicit such favors like the indigent poor before a mighty and rich emperor, then to lower its eyes and hope with humility for a gracious response. God was quite fond of that virtue because he was supreme truth, and because humility was to walk in the truth of human misery and nothingness. That was the path of self-knowledge.[251] Yet self-knowledge was a classical, not scriptural, concept, although the ascetic tradition adopted it.[252] Nor was humility in scripture moral virtue but social status, as renaissance and reformation exegesis had ably demonstrated about the Virgin annunciate.

Teresa de Jesús' construction of the interior castle on an ascetic basis of humility occasioned her very terror of moral failure and its consequent punishment. It was a place fraught with immense fear of dangers. The soul constantly begged against failure, understanding that no good deeds originated in itself. There was no security in the castle, only tenacity on its path. The soul suffered the great misery of always having to pass in this life like those who had enemies at the gate, neither able to sleep or eat without weaponry, so that they did not chip away at its strength. In such a miserable life it was impossible even to pray for escape. The beatitude the nuns sought was secure only with the blessed in heaven. Even the saints lapsed into grave sin, so that there was no security on earth. The realization terrified Teresa de Jesús. "For sure, my daughters, I am in such fear writing this that I do not know how to write nor how to live when I recall that, which is

17-31. For insights that stimulated my statement of the culture of grace in this paragraph, although his theology is confused, see Pitt-Rivers, "Place of Grace in Anthropology," pp. 215-46. For the gift as not gratuitous see also Marcel Mauss, *The Gift: Forms and Functions of Exchange in Archaic Societies*, trans. Ian Cunnison (London: Cohen & West, 1970). The possibility that the Protestant-Catholic conflict over grace reflected a difference between cultural practices and values concerning gifts requires investigation.

[251] Teresa of Avila, *Castillo interior* 1.2.8; 1.2.10; 2.1.11; 3.2.6; 4.2.9; 4.3.5; 6.10.7; epil. 2.

[252] See Pierre Courcelle, *Connais-toi, toi-même de Socrate à saint Bernard*, 3 vols. (Paris: Études augustiniennes, 1974-75).

frequently." She asked for prayer that his Majesty abide in her always, for a life as badly spent as hers had no security. There was no remedy for it, other than to plead his Majesty and to rely on the merits of his Son and the Madonna, whose habit she wore. Yet Mary as a model and patron guaranteed the nuns no security, she realized. Enclosure from the world, and the penance and prayer practiced in the convent, were good practices; but they were insufficient reason to stop fearing. Ever in mind should be the verse, "Blessed is he who fears the Lord" (Ps. 112:1).[253] The asceticism toward merit that occasioned her fear she then reversed on itself, so that her fear became circularly the occasion for further merit. She counseled and she cultivated fear precisely "to gain more merit," for the greater the fear, the greater the reward. If a soul strove with determination to perform difficult tasks, his Majesty would "pay" it even in this life.[254]

The soul was diligently to petition God to hold it in his hand; for if he should ever let go of it, it would fall into the abyss. It was never to have confidence in itself but to walk fearfully. Even in spiritual espousal, the soul secure in its interior was severely afflicted by fear of diabolical ensnarement. Because of such deceptions "it is always good to behave with fear," she wrote. For herself, she avowed, "I suppose danger everywhere." Although those gathered in the monastery were blessed in being physically removed from wretched times and a miserable life, there was always wretchedness in the mind. It was good to be fearful, to walk carefully, never to be self-confident, she advised. The soul in spiritual marriage should be more careful than ever not to lose the favor by divine displeasure. Such great mercy was not perfectly fulfilled on earth and could be lost by withdrawal. In spiritual marriage the soul was not sure of salvation, nor safe from failure, except when his Majesty held it in his hands so that it did not offend him. Insecurely it walked with much more fear than before to guard itself against the slightest offense. The more favored, the more fearful.[255]

Her fear was derived from the agon that defined asceticism. The interior castle was inhabited by the senses and powers of the soul, who were its vassals. The powers served as the mayors, the stewards, and the masters of the rooms. They were also its guards for fighting, for it was a place of diabolical combat. Although people walked with the desire of not offending God and of doing good works, the devil could still conquer souls.[256] Since the literature of the desert fathers the devil had two methods of attack: brute

---

[253] Teresa of Avila, *Castillo interior* 1.2.5; 3.1.2; 3.1.3; 3.1.4.

[254] Teresa of Avila, *Vida suya* 4.2.

[255] Teresa of Avila, *Castillo interior* 5.4.9; 6.6.2; 6.6.2; 6.6.8; 6.8.8; 7.1.8; 7.2.1; 7.2.9; 7.3.14; 7.4.16.

[256] Ibid. 2.1.10; 4.3.2; 1.2.3; 1.2.10. For allegories of the soul and its wardens see also Roberta D. Cornelius, *The Figurative Castle: A Study in the Mediaeval Allegory of the Edifice with Especial Reference to Religious Writings* (Bryn Mawr, Pa.: Bryn Mawr College, 1930)., pp. 20-36.

force and angelic wile. Wiliness was especially feared, from the scriptural verse of the transformation of the devil into an angel of light (2 Cor. 11:14), a monition that was current in the discernment of spirits.[257] Teresa de Jesús cited it immediately and feared it the more, although she also wrote of diabolical brute force. The castle was a place of "terrible battery," for the demons by a thousand methods inflicted pain. Against their assault the nuns were to "be manly,"[258] like Perpetua in the arena or Monica in the home. As angelic creatures, virgins were especially enrolled as warriors in the cosmic contest between good and evil spirits. Their very virtue was shield and strength, with fabulous tales of women thrashing or outwitting the devil.[259] The virile woman was preserved in medieval Spanish culture in the lore of the Amazons, in the romance of Alexander, and in local legends about shepherdesses.[260] From classical myth and renaissance poetry she emerged as the darling of the drama.[261]

A victory of the city of Avila against its invaders was attributed to such a valiant woman. Early in the reconquest, when the men were absent at war, the wife of the royal governor, Jimena Blázquez, organized and inspired the women of the city. Vested in the helmets and armor of their husbands, they climbed the battlements and banged their pots and pans horribly. When the Muslims heard the din, they feared Avila had twice their number of warriors and fled the site without a battle. The city, for the military valor of those women, was dubbed "Avila of the knights."[262] The common personal weapons were not culinary, however, but the short bow, spear or pike, sword, dagger, mace and axe for clearing the path, and boiling liquids of lead, pitch, or oil.[263] Teresa de Jesús advised the nuns to defend the interior castle armed with the cross. They should embrace it as their spouse had shouldered it. Those women who were the better able to suffer in manly

---

257 For the verse applied to Luther see Boyle, *Rhetoric and Reform: Erasmus' Civil Dispute with Luther*, Harvard Historical Monographs, 71 (Cambridge, Mass.: Harvard University Press, 1983), pp. 132-42.

258 Teresa of Avila, *Castillo interior* 1.2.10; 2.1.1; 2.1.2; *Camino de perfección* 7.

259 John Bugge, *Virginitas: An Essay in the History of a Medieval Ideal*, International Archives of the History of Ideas, series minor, 17 (The Hague: Martinus Nijhoff, 1975), pp. 58-67.

260 Estelle Irizarry, "Echoes of the Amazon Myth in Medieval Spanish Literature," in *Women in Hispanic Literature*, ed. Miller, pp. 53-66. For the definition of the virile woman by Teresa de Jesús' editor see Luis de León, *Perfecta casada* 1b. For an example of a soldier-nun, Catalina de Erauso, see Perry, "The Manly Woman: A Historical Case Study," *American Behavioral Scientist* 31 (1987):86-100. For a survey see Megan McLaughlin, "The Woman Warrior: Gender, Warfare and Society in Medieval Europe," *Women's Studies* 17 (1990):193-209.

261 McKendrick, "Women against Wedlock: The Reluctant Brides of Golden Age Drama," in *Women in Hispanic Literature*, ed. Miller, pp. 115-46; C. Bravo-Villasante, *La mujer vestida de hombre en el teatro español (siglos XVI-XVII)* (Madrd: Sociedad general española de librería, 1976).

262 Bilinkoff, *Avila of Saint Teresa*, pp. 2-3.

263 Washburn, *Castles in Spain*, p. 25.

fashion would be the more liberated. There was diabolical combat everywhere within the castle. Teresa de Jesús' universal agon was manifest in her discussion of righteous persons as "tried" even by his Majesty. Desirous that his chosen souls should feel their misery, he withdrew slightly his favor. Her remedy was to test oneself before the Lord did.[264] Trial and instruction through pain was an ancient concept, a contest to which Teresa de Jesús did not discover an alternative. The soul combated both devil and God.

The devil also deceived in the guise of an angel of light. He produced his wiles and deceits in the imagination, she wrote, frequently in women and illiterates, who were ignorant of the faculties, the imagination, and a thousand other interior matters. He would endeavor to deter spiritual betrothal, for, once the soul was surrendered to the spouse, the devil became fearful. From experience he learned that combat would be to his loss and her gain. There were holy persons who had fallen by the devil's subtlety and cunning. Religious life offered no security from his stratagems, since there was "no enclosure so enclosed" that he could not enter it, no desert so remote that he could not travel there. Only in the matrimonial abode could the soul relax its fear, since it was so habitually united to his Majesty that it acquired fortitude.[265] Such diabolical wiliness reflected not only ascetic psychology but actual practice of warfare against Spanish castles. Weaponry for frontal assault included war machines against the wall, the battering ram, the crossbow, bones and picks, and the flooding of the moat. Although most castles were capable of withstanding a long siege, a cunning attacker had a chance of success with other methods. The most popular was mining to create a breach in the wall.[266] Teresa de Jesús imagined the castle besieged and undermined until the soul entered the keep, the matrimonial palace.

That was the seventh abode, the marital number.[267] The castle was made for marriage. Her choice of constructional material was not its most enduring one, stone carefully fitted. Nor was it the quicker and cheaper method, a coarse mixture prepared of rough stones in mortar or clay, faced with fitted stone or with rough stone smoothed on the outside and set with mortar.[268] Such rude matter only composed its outer walls, the body. Her building ma-

264 Teresa of Avila, *Castillo interior* 2.1.1; 4.3.10; 3.2.1; 3.2.2; 3.2.3.

265 Ibid. 5.1.1; 6.3.16; 5.3.10; 5.4.6; 5.4.7; 5.4.8; 6.1.2.

266 Washburn, *Castles in Spain*, p. 15. For artillery, munitions, and war machines see also David C. Goodman, *Power and Penury: Government, Technology and Science in Philip II's Spain* (Cambridge: Cambridge University Press, 1988), pp. 109-41.

267 See Russell A. Peck, "Number as a Cosmic Language," in *Essays in Numerical Criticism in Medieval Literature*, ed. Caroline D. Eckhardt (Lewisburg, Pa.: Bucknell University Press, 1980), p. 24. Seven was the sum of three and four, the first male and female real numbers, hence marriage. It had many other relevant associations; e. g., in Robert Campin's Annunciation of the Mérode triptych the infant soul streams into the Virgin's room on seven rays of light.

268 Washburn, *Castles in Spain*, p. 9; Weismüller, *Castles from the Heart of Spain*, p. 32.

terials were farfetched. She imagined the soul "a castle completely of diamond or of very clear crystal."[269] Valued for their hardness, diamonds had been used since antiquity for a technology of drilling and engraving that was revived in the sixteenth century for glass. The diamond was scarce among the populace from Rome to the Renaissance, by sumptuary laws the privilege of royalty, nobility, and clergy. The French and English courts were dripping with diamonds; Teresa de Jesús' use of the jewel for a royal palace was fitting. Agnes Sorèl, mistress of Charles VII of France, who also posed for a vulgar portrait as the Madonna, was the first woman notably to wear a diamond. Renaissance fashion dictated it as the essence of a pendant, but it also predominated in rings. Diamond rings were adopted as emblematic of royal ideas, beginning with their use by the Medici family. The Tudors distributed diamonds as pledges of love and loyalty; Mary gave her husband Philip II a legendary one in the shape of a pyramid. Diamonds were not native to Spain, however, but shipped with spices on boats manned by galley slaves from the Indian mines to Antwerp's cutters.[270] Teresa de Jesús' description of the castle "where there are many rooms, just as in heaven there are many abodes"[271] indicated a celestial source for its diamond. In the apocalyptic vision: "'Come here and I will show you the bride that the Lamb has married.' In the Spirit he took me to the top of an enormous high mountain and showed me Jerusalem, the holy city, coming down from God out of heaven. It had all the radiant glory of God and glittered like a some precious jewel of crystal-clear diamond" (Rev. 21:9-11).

The crystalline quality of her soul coincided with medieval allegories of the virtuous castle besieged by vice,[272] especially unchastity. The most famous vernacular castle, in Jean de Meun's *Roman de la rose*, was assaulted by Venus aiming her bow at the loophole in the tower between ivory

---

[269] Teresa of Avila, *Castillo interior* 1.1.1; 1.1.2. Cf. the divinity as a diamond in *Vida suya* 40.10. For the origins of crystal see Mary Luella Trowbridge, *Philological Studies in Ancient Glass* (Urbana: University of Illinois Press, 1922), pp. 53-55, 79-83; rpt. in University of Illinois Studies in Language and Literature, 13. See also Edwin Atlee Barker, *Spanish Glass in the Collection of the Hispanic Society of America*, Hispanic Society of America Publications, 102 (New York: Putnam, 1917).

[270] See Gorelick and Gwinnet, "Diamonds from India to Rome and Beyond"; Joan Younger Dickinson, *The Book of Diamonds: Their History and Romance from Ancient India to Modern Times* (New York: Bonanza, 1965), pp. 154, 156, 159, 161, 52-55, 5; *Diamonds*, ed. Legrand, pp. 252-61; Lawrence L. Copeland, *Diamonds, Famous, Notable, Unique* (Los Angeles: Gemmological Institute of America, 1966), p. 9; Lenzen, *History of Diamond Production and the Diamond Trade*, pp. 33-41. For Sorel's portrait see Margaret Scott, *Late Gothic Europe, 1400-1500*, History of Dress, 1 (London: Mills & Boon, 1980), pp. 150-51. Reproduced p. 145 pl. 76. For royal adoption beginning with the Medicis see Diana Scarisbrick, *Rings: Symbols of Wealth, Power, and Affection* (New York: Harry N. Abrams, 1993), pp. 43-45. For contemporary metallurgy on diamonds see Vannuccio Biringuccio, *De la pirotechnia* 2.13.

[271] Teresa of Avila, *Castillo interior* 1.1.1.

[272] See Cornelius, *Figurative Castle*; Fritz Saxl, "A Spiritual Encyclopedia of the Later Middle Ages," *Journal of the Warburg and Courtauld Institutes* 5 (1942):110-11.

columns symbolic of a maiden's legs.[273] The castling and enclosure of females in Castilian society, testified by Teresa de Jesús' experience at home and by her choice of the convent, was precisely a guard of chastity. The celebrated religious allegory was the Virgin as the castle of love. The scriptural verse about Jesus' visit to the home of Martha and Mary occasioned it by mistranslation; for, although the text had "he entered a town and a certain woman named Martha received him" (Lk. 10:23), the Vulgate *castellum* for "town" was popularly rendered "castle". There was a facile transition from that verse to the allegory of Jesus entering the castle of Mary, her virginal womb, at the incarnation.[274] The substance of her castle was crystalline: in the frequent image of the divine penetration of her body like sunlight through a windowpane so that her virginity was not ruptured. In a metaphor attributed to Bernard of Clairvaux, "Just as the brilliance of the sun fills and penetrates a glass window without damaging it, and pierces its solid form with imperceptible subtlety, neither hurting it when entering nor destroying it when emerging: thus the word of God, the splendor of the Father, entered the virgin chamber and then came forth from the closed womb." And just as a ray penetrating a glass acquired color, so the Son entering her chaste womb emerged from it pure, but colored by her in the nature of a man.[275]

The attribute of Mary's perpetual virginity in late medieval art became a crystal flask, of bulbous shape like a pregnant womb, with a narrow spout like a tight vagina. It appears illuminated in Jan van Eyck's Annunciation in the Ghent altarpiece, on a bench in the sacristy just below the windowsill. There the artist uses natural light striking the Virgin from the right, symbolizing through its penetration of the window her incorruptible virginity.[276] The carafe decorates Rogier van der Weyden's Annunciation in a bourgeois Flemish home, on the very mantle of the hearth.[277] It also appears, half-filled with colored liquid, in a place Teresa de Jesús frequented while deciding her vocation. In an Annunciation on the retable of the

---

[273] Jean de Meun, *Roman de la rose* 20785-816.

[274] Cornelius, *Figurative Castle*, pp. 37-48.

[275] Cited by Millard Meiss, "Light as Form and Symbol in Some Fifteenth-Century Paintings," *Art Bulletin* 27 (1945):76, 177, without primary documentation. Art historians routinely cite this from Meiss. I have been unable to locate the text readily in the critical edition of Bernard of Clairvaux.

[276] Jan van Eyck, Annunciation, 15th century, Ghent. Reproduced in Meiss, "Light as Form and Symbol," pp. 179-80; Lotte Brand Philip, *The Ghent Altarpiece and the Art of Jan van Eyck* (Princeton: Princeton University Press, 1971), p. 87 and fig. 82, although the light striking the glass carafe is not a "well-known symbol of Christ's immaculate conception" but of Mary's perpetual virginity. See also Michèle Labergère, "La fenêtre, foyer lumineux chez van Eyck," *Gazette des beaux-arts* 105 (1985):97-98; Albert Châtelet, "Fenêtre et fontaine dans l'Annonciation: À propos de Jean van Eyck et du Maître de Flémalle," *Études d'art médieval offerts à Louis Grodecki*, ed. André Chastel (Paris: Ophrys, 1981), pp. 317-24.

[277] Rogier van der Weyden, Annunciation, Louvre, Paris. Reproduced in Martin Davies, *Rogier van der Weyden: An Essay with a Critical Catalogue of Paintings Assigned to him and to Robert Campin* (London: Phaidon, 1972), pl. 21.

chapel of Nuestra Señora de Gracia, where she studied as a girl, the carafe is on a shelf in the Virgin's room.[278] In Robert Campin's image of the Madonna before the hearth there is also striking treatment of light—the fire, the candle on the chimney, the daylight through the open shutters of the window, triple sources of illumination similar to those in his painting of St. Barbara.[279] That panel portrays the saint, like his Virgin annunciate, reading on a reversible bench before a hearth in a cozy bourgeois room.[280] The artist attended to the sources and effects of light as it touched the edges of the furniture and stretched to the end of the keerlys, the tip of the window shutter, and the wall beyond.[281] Objects on the chimney—the statue of the Trinity and the candle, the laver and towel against the wall, are all symbolic. In the distance out the window is Barbara's attribute, the tower.[282] An illuminated carafe on the mantle refers to the guarantee of her sanctity, her virginity.

There was a monastic metaphor of light reflected and refracted through a vase filled with water as the illumination of a meditative mind. In a miniature in a book of hours a similar vase graces a niche behind the desk of Thomas Aquinas as he writes.[283] Yet Barbara's flask in Campin's painting is not divinely illuminated; it casts a definite shadow. It shows a square sunspot at the level of the water, halfway up its globe, so that it is illuminated naturally by light from an undepicted window across the room. A crystal vase and glass also appear on the ledge of an open window in a Castilian painting of Flemish influence portraying St. Katherine, crowned on a cathedra with open book and steely sword in hand.[284] The iconography displayed the ideology associating virginity with illumination, whether visionary or contemplative. The monastic vow implied the Gnostic belief in

---

[278] Annunciation, retable, chapel of Nuestra Señora de Gracia, Avila. Reproduced in Gomez-Moreno, *Catálogo monumental*, 2:137.

[279] Alistair Smith and Martin Wyld, "Robert Campin's Virgin and Child in an Interior," *Burlington Magazine* 130 (1988):570.

[280] Robert Campin, St. Barbara before the hearth, 15th century, panel of Werl altarpiece, Prado, Madrid. Reproduced in Davies, *Rogier van der Weyden*, pl. 153.

[281] Ibid., p. 36.

[282] Meiss, "Light as Symbol and Form," p. 176. For the candle beside the image of the Trinity as perhaps symbolic see Andrew Breeze, "The Trinity as Taper: A Welsh Allusion to Langland," *Notes and Queries* 37 (1990):5-6.

[283] Brian Madigan, "Van Eyck's Illuminated Carafe," *Journal of the Warburg and Courtauld Institutes* 49 (1986):226, 229. He argues that the water in Barbara's vase is divinely illuminated, p. 229. He cites Richard of St. Victor, *Benjamin minor* 5.11; and French Master H, St. Thomas in his cell, Turin book of hours, fol. 73v, as reproduced in Albert Châtelet, *Early Dutch Painting*, pp. 199, 202, which was not available. But see Châtelet, *Les primitifs hollandais: La peinture dans les Pays-Bas du nord au XVe siècle* (Fribourg: Office du livre, 1980), reproduced p. 38 fig. 28 and see catalogue 24, p. 199.

[284] Painting of St. Katherine, cathedral, Salamanca. Reproduced in Aurea de la Morena, "Representación de la santidad femenina a fines de la edad media en la pintura castellana," in *La condición de la mujer en la edad media*, Actas del coloquio celebrado en la Casa de Velázquez, del 5 al 7 de noviembre de 1984 (Madrid: Universidad complutense, 1986), p. 447 photo 2.

original sin as sexual intercourse, with sexuality and death as its effects. Asexuality thus became requisite for attaining immortality. The angelic innocence lost by the primordial parents in Eden was recreated and perfected on earth by virgins, whose restoration of their creation in the divine image admitted them to contemplation and prophecy.[285] Teresa de Jesús' inaugural voice, "I no longer wish you to converse with humans but with angels,"[286] coincided with that ideology. She understood the angelic state as complete separation from the body, although she conceded that the human soul should not so flee corporeality as to consider the humanity of Christ harmful, and thus abandon it for his divinity.[287] Her emphasis on humility, rather than chastity, as the foundational virtue of the interior castle reflected the competing theology of Augustine, who altered original sin from the ontological to the psychological order and identified it not as lust but as pride.[288] Teresa de Jesús' model and material of the castle as crystal, however, were constructed of the Gnostic dualism he rejected. For her spiritual union depended on both virtues.

Spiritual union she praised as a sleep of the faculties of the soul to the world and to the self, so that for its duration there was neither sensation, nor thought, nor understanding, nor desire. It was a delicious death to the world, so as to live more in God. So united was his Majesty to the essence of the soul in that abode that the devil would not dare to enter it—or even know of its secret; although small slender lizards, trifling thoughts arising from the imagination, could intrude. It differed from all worldly pleasures as did the coarseness of the body from the marrow of its bones. God so fastened himself in the interior of the soul that, when it returned to itself, it could not doubt that it was in God and God in it. Through that favor Teresa de Jesús acquired the information and belief that God was in everything by presence, power, and essence. Union was the wine cellar of the Song of Songs (2:4), a placement by his Majesty who entered the center of the soul without passing through any door, unimpeded by the sleeping senses and faculties. Or it was like a wax impressed with his seal: the soul disposed by being soft to the touch, without impediment, only consent.[289] With that image of the divinely impressed wax she departed from Aquinas's doctrine of the female soul as not created immediately in the divine image.

Union was not yet spiritual betrothal. Although espousal was a coarse comparison, Teresa de Jesús explained that she knew no other to convey her meaning than the sacrament of marriage. The corporeal affairs of the married were a thousand leagues distant from spiritual marriage and its contentments,

285 Bugge, *Virginitas*, pp. 5-21, 41-47.
286 Teresa of Avila, *Vida suya* 24.5.
287 Teresa of Avila, *Castillo interior* 6.7.6; 6.7.14.
288 See Bugge, *Virginitas*, pp. 25-26.
289 Teresa of Avila, *Castillo interior* 5.1.3; 5.1.4; 5.1.5; 5.1.8; 5.1.9; 5.1.11; 5.2.12.

however. It was completely love with love, in operations most pure and so delicate and suave as to be ineffable. In secular society, when a couple became engaged, there was discussion of the compatibility and desirability of the match, and even a trial of separation. So did his Majesty visit the soul briefly in union, that it might better understand him. Such visitations rendered the soul more worthy for the customary giving of the hands, so enamoring it that it did not disturb the divine engagement. Teresa de Jesús did not explain how the soul was so visited by God in its center when he was already dwelling there. She proceeded to the sixth and seventh abodes of betrothal and marriage, which were unseparated by any closed door. The soul wounded with love for its spouse procured more space for their solitude. Yet although his Majesty's visits engraved a heartfelt desire to enjoy such encounters again, he disregarded such desire. He wanted the betrothal to "cost" dearly in exterior and interior trials, as Teresa de Jesús personally detailed.[290]

Desirous to withdraw from the contentment and conversation of earth, the soul experienced locutions and visions in its imagination and understanding. Teresa de Jesús compared that abode to a royal or noble closet displayed with many types of glass and earthenware. It was like her experience of the house of the duchess of Alba, where she was once ordered to stay by her superiors during a journey. On entry Teresa de Jesús was amazed at the furnishings and decor and she learned to praise the Lord for a variety so abundant as to cause oblivion. In rapture his Majesty stole her soul for himself as his own matter, ultimately his spouse. In that abode there was no interference from the senses or powers, since the doors of those dwellings were completely shut, even the gateways of the castle and its surrounds, so that only his abode remained accessible. Although ecstasy transpired briefly, the will was so absorbed and the intellect so ravished that love alone was intelligible. Everything else was so fatiguing that, like the silkworm moth, the soul found no lasting site and, at any ignition of the fires of love, it flew. She did not explain the discrepancy between the vision in her understanding of Christ at her side and her belief in the divine indwelling as deeply interior.[291]

Before the consummation of spiritual marriage, in which the silkworm moth died, God pitied the soul suffering with desires and brought it into his personal abode. As in heaven, he had in the soul a living room, like another heaven, where he alone dwelled. In the other abodes he had only united the soul to himself in its superior part; here he joined it at its center with a ces-

---

[290] Ibid. 5.4.3; 5.4.4; 6.4.4; 6.6.1; 6.1.2-6.1.11.

[291] Ibid. 6.2.6; 6.6.3; 6.4.2; 6.4.8; 6.4.9; 6.4.13; 6.4.14; 6.6.1; 6.6.8. Her editor compared the female in the home to fragile glassware placed for safety on a high shelf. Luis de León, *Perfecta casada* 3. He also castigated wives as spendthrifts for the vogue of acquiring such glass, ibid. 2.

sation of all potencies. In that place he removed the scales from its eyes in an intellectual vision of the Trinity, all three persons and each one distinct. The spirit was enkindled like a cloud of exceeding clarity to understand through a wondrous information that all three persons were one substance and power and wisdom and single God. What was held by faith the soul understood as if by sight, although neither corporeally nor imaginatively. The persons there communicated and spoke and gave the soul to understand the saying of the Lord in the gospel: that He and the Father and the Holy Spirit would come to dwell with the soul who loved him and kept his commandments (John 14:23).[292] Thus wrote Teresa de Jesús of Avila on the topical verse of divine indwelling at home in the believer.

To hear and believe those words was so different from understanding their truth in that manner, she exclaimed. Daily she was more amazed at her clear understanding of how the trinitarian persons never departed but were in the interior of her soul. "In the very very interior," she wrote, "in something very profound that it does not know how to explain, because it is unlearned, it feels in itself this divine company." The soul became more involved in the service of God and, when its occupations ended, it adverted to that divine company, although not so clearly as initially. Teresa de Jesús compared the situation to a person who had been in a very bright room with others; once the window shutters were closed, it was in the dark but still knew that the others were present. Sight was not in the power of the soul, except when the Lord wished to open the window of understanding. The essence of her soul never moved from that apartment, no matter the labors and business, so that her soul seemed to her divided like Martha and Mary—the one enjoying quietude at its pleasure, the other engaged in tasks. The sisters cooperated to show hospitality to the Lord by feeding him well to retain his presence. Mary only sat at his feet because she had already performed the task of washing his feet and drying them with her hair.[293]

Teresa de Jesús' notion of hospitality embraced a vision at communion in which the Lord assured her that after his Resurrection he had indeed visited and comforted his mother,[294] an unscriptural fancy favoring the iconography of van der Weyden.[295] In a vision on Palm Sunday, when she could not swallow the host because of her absorption, she sensed her mouth filling with blood and her face and entire body being covered with it, as if the Lord had just shed it upon her. He said he was rewarding her for her hospitality.

---

[292] Teresa of Avila, *Castillo interior* 7.2.5; 7.1.3; 7.1.5; 7.1.6.

[293] Ibid. 7.1.7; 7.1.9; 7.1.10; 7.4.12. The last conflates the Marys of different pericopes (Luke 10:38-42 and 7:37-38).

[294] Teresa of Avila, *Relaciones espirituales* 12.

[295] Rogier van der Weyden, Christ Visiting his Mother, Metropolitan Museum of Art, New York. See Martin Davies, *Rogier van der Weyden: An Essay with a Critical Catalogue of Paintings Assigned to Him and to Robert Campin* (London: Phaidon, 1972), p. 248; Bermejo Martínez, *Pintura de los primitivos flamencos en España*, 1:273 fig. 57.

For thirty years in communicating on that feast Teresa de Jesús had invited him to remain with her, although she was a "bad inn."[296] Inns were always bad;[297] but in Castile they were important female establishments, such as those in Toledo that housed merchants and served as shops for their wares, or those on the road to Santiago de Compostela that catered to pilgrims.[298] Her sentiment of hospitality to Christ as retaining the host physically in her mouth departed culturally and spiritually from Augustine's injunction of hospitality as charity: welcome a stranger into your home, if you would have Christ as a guest.[299] It reverted to a primitive notion of sacrifice, before the gods consented that the portion reserved and consumed for them be allotted to the needy in the invention of charity.[300]

Not swallowing the host had also been expressly condemned as anathema and sacrilege by two early Spanish councils.[301] It was associated in popular culture with magic, as in case of the medieval wife who kissed her husband while retaining the host in her mouth to procure his love.[302] The amatory magic was still current.[303] Teresa de Jesús explained that she acted as a personal host to the eucharistic host because the Jews had been so inhospitable in welcoming Christ enthusiastically, then abandoning him to dine elsewhere.[304] There was no scriptural evidence that the Jews failed to invite him to dinner; her judgment was anti-Semitic.[305] Her imaginative reception of Christ's blood into her body on Palm Sunday rejected her Jewish familial bloodline. The imaginary blood in her mouth was not wholly unusual, since communicants with difficulty swallowing the host were permitted to wash it down with wine (blood) from the chalice.[306] It may have been more significant: the mouth smeared with blood and full of drank blood was the sign of the epileptic.[307]

---

[296] Teresa of Avila, *Relaciones espirituales* 22.

[297] See Marcelin Defourneaux, *Daily Life in Spain in the Golden Age*, trans. Newton Branch (New York: Praeger, 1971), pp. 15-16.

[298] Dillard, *Daughters of the Reconquest*, p. 163.

[299] Augustine, *Sermones* 236.3; 225.3; *In epistolam Joannis ad Parthos* 10.6; 40.10.

[300] See Mauss, *Gift*, pp. 15-16.

[301] Council of Saragossa (A. D. 380) 3, I Council of Toledo (A.D. 400) 14, in *Canones apostolorum et conciliorum saeculorum IV-VII*, 2:13; 1:205.

[302] See Peter Browe, "Die Eucharistie als Zaubermittel im Mittelalter," *Archiv für Kulturgeschichte* 20 (1930):134-54. See also Michel de Montaigne, *Journal de voyage en Italie*, 1:98-99.

[303] Guido Ruggiero, *Binding Passions: Tales of Magic, Marriage, and Power at the End of the Renaissance* (New York: Oxford University Press, 1993), pp. 90-94.

[304] Teresa of Avila, *Relaciones espirituales* 22.

[305] For local anti-Semitism see also Bilinkoff, *Avila of Saint Teresa*, pp. 11-14.

[306] See Miri Rubin, *Corpus Christi: The Eucharist in Late Medieval Culture* (Cambridge: Cambridge University Press, 1990), p. 82, without reference to Teresa de Jesús. For the Eucharistic bread changing into bloody flesh in the mouth of the recipient see Browe, *Die Eucharistischen Wunder des Mittelalters*, Breslauer Studien zur historischen Theologie, n. f. 4, 1 (Breslau: Müller and Seiffert, 1938).

[307] Owsei Tempkin, *The Falling Sickness: A History of Epilepsy from the Greeks to the Beginnings of Modern Neurology*, 2d ed. rev. (Baltimore, Md.: Johns Hopkins University

It was at communion that Teresa de Jesús experienced spiritual marriage through an imaginative vision of the sacred humanity of Christ, as instructive of the sovereign gift to her soul. The favor might be received by others differently, she thought. The risen Lord represented himself to her at communion in a form of great splendor and beauty and majesty. He told her that "now was the time that she she take his things as hers and that he would take care of her things."[308] In another version dating to the convent of Encarnación she was disappointed because the celebrant of the Mass divided the host to share it between her and another nun. She thought he was mortifying her because she had expressed a preference for large hosts. The Lord assured her that no one would separate her from him. Although he had addressed her as "daughter," in the same conflation of relationships that characterized the imagination of Margery Kempe, he then appeared to Teresa de Jesús imaginatively and wed her as wife. "He gave me his right hand and said to me, 'Behold this nail, which is the mark that you will be my spouse from today. Until now you have not merited it; from here on, not only will you look to my honor as creator and as king and as your God, but as my true bride. My honor is yours and yours, mine.'" On another occasion the Lord indicated that, as his bride, she could ask whatever she desired, and he would grant it. As proof he gave her a handsome ring with a stone like an amethyst, but of a brilliance very different from an earthy gem, and he placed it on her finger.[309] Rosy fingernails, described as amethysts,[310] belonged to the canon of female beauty.[311] The amethyst was classically believed to assist suppliants before a king.[312] At the Spanish court it was not precious, however. The inventory of Philip II's younger sister Juana listed a bracelet with an amethyst but linked only with lapis, carnelian, and jacinth. In comparison, Juana had a large and valuable diamond.[313] The very editor of

---

Press, 1971), pp. 12, 23, 23, 102, 103.

308 Teresa of Avila, *Castillo interior* 7.2.1.

309 Teresa of Avila, *Relaciones espirituales* 31, 34. For the extravagant vogue for multiple rings see Scarisbrick, *Rings*, p. 42; Katherine Morris Lester and Bess Viola Oerke, *Accessories of Dress* (Peoria, Ill.: Chas. A. Bennett, 1954), pp. 335-43. The Spanish wore jewelry excessively as a sign of status. Bennassar, *Spanish Character*, p. 171.

310 Philip Sidney, *The Countess of Pembroke's Arcadia*, p. 291, cited by James V. Mirollo, *Mannerism and Renaissance Poetry: Concept, Mode, Inner Design* (New Haven, Conn.: Yale University Press, 1984), p. 150.

311 For the topic of *effictio* see M. B. Ogle, "The Classical Origin and Tradition of Literary Conceits," *American Journal of Philology* 34 (1913):125-52; idem, "The White Hand as a Literary Conceit," *Sewanee Review* 20 (1912):459-69. For an example of ruby fingernails see Agnolo Firenzuolo, *Delle bellezze delle donne* 2.

312 Pliny, *Naturalis historia* 37.40.124. It was also named in a Spanish commentary on scripture the gem of Venus because of the luxury and allurement of its color. Francisco Rueo, *De gemmis* 2.1.11.

313 Yvonne Hackenbroch, *Renaissance Jewellery* (London: Sotheby Parke Bernet, 1980), p. 318. See for his jewels F. J. Sánchez Cantón, *Inventarios reales: Bienes muebles que pertenecieron a Felipe II*, Archivo documental español, 10-11 (Madrid: Real academia de la historia, 1956-59).

Castillo interior compared the precious virtue of wifely perfection to the ruby, diamond, or emerald—but not the amethyst.[314] Teresa de Jesus' ring was depreciatory: she was not worth a diamond to match the material of her castle.

At the entry to the royal palace Teresa de Jesús warned the soul not to postpone the celebration of spiritual marriage, for it brought so many "goods."[315] Economic benefit rather than marital affection was the concept from Roman law still prevalent in Castilian society,[316] and she appropriated it to describe the ultimate relationship of the soul with God. The divine directive that "she should take his things, and he would take care of hers"[317] replicated legal endowment and dowry. Betrothal, the intermediate step between consent and nuptials, had as its most important visible sign an endowment or commitment, in charter or word, of property from the bridegroom. His endowment of the bride was *arras*, after the pledge a buyer transferred to a seller to secure delivery of the goods—here the bride. Endowment ranged from lands to items, with a customary noble gift a handsome leather tent as a movable residence. It was the bridegroom's obligation in Castilian society also to pay for the nuptials, especially the feast, and to clothe the bride down to her shoes. His expenses were legally limited, however, so to benefit especially the bachelors whom the towns sought to attract to domestic permanence. There was also a civic desire to limit the display of wealth, as in other sumptuary legislation, by restricting the size of the wedding procession, the number of guests, the amount of food and drink served, and the gifts exchanged between host and guests. The male endowment was the only necessary condition of betrothal; the woman did not formally transfer any property until marriage. Then she brought her bridal trousseau of land, clothing, and silver plate, if she were aristocratic; or cooking utensils, quilts, and linens, if she were common. An aristocratic woman of medieval Toledo included furred cloaks, silk and taffeta jackets and dresses richly embroidered, and thirty-six wifely coifs, plain and golden.[318]

---

314 Luis de León, *Perfecta casada* 1b.

315 Teresa of Avila, *Castillo interior* 7.1.2.

316 Bennassar, *Spanish Character*, pp. 182-91. For the dowry as an inevitable evil see Fitzmaurice-Kelly, "Woman in Sixteenth-Century Spain," pp. 586-87.

317 Teresa of Avila, *Castillo interior* 7.2.1.

318 Dillard, *Daughters of the Reconquest*, pp. 46-55. See also Estrella Ruiz-Galvez Priego, *Statut socio-juridique de la femme en España au XVIème siècle: Une étude sur le mariage chrétien faite d'après l'Epitome de matrimonio de Diego de Covarrubias y Leyva, la legislation royale et les moralistes* (Paris: Didier érudition, 1990), pp. 12-32. For surveys see María Isabel Lopez Diaz, "Arras y dote en España: Resumen histórico," in *Nuevas perspectivas sobre la mujer*, 1:83-98; Beceiro Pita and Córdoba de la Llave, *Parentesco, poder y mentalidad*, pp. 170-77; Diane Owen Hughes, "From Brideprice to Dowry in Mediterranean Europe," in *The Marriage Bargain: Women and Dowries in European History*, ed. Marion A. Kaplan (New York: Huntington Park, 1985), pp. 13-58. For moralists against lavish weddings and their banquets see Fitzmaurice-Kelly, "Woman in Sixteenth-Century Spain," pp. 593, 594.

When Teresa de Jesús entered the convent of Encarnación her dowry was bedding and clothing. For her profession at San José she wore a coarse woolen habit.[319] The exchange of goods—"his things" and "her things"—that characterized her spiritual marriage was economic, if unequal. Yet it lacked the crucial asset of Castilian conjugal economics—"their things"—the partnership of jointly owned acquisitions. Although the husband officially administered the couple's assets, the wife participated actively by work and money in a cooperative venture of mutual profit.[320]

Teresa de Jesús' description of the Lord taking her right hand alluded to the Roman wedding custom, in which the iconographic handclasp was a public display of closeness and trust.[321] It canonically obeyed the joining of the hands scholastically required as the sign of mutual consent.[322] In Castilian practice the nuptials could conclude with the priest remitting the bride to the bridegroom by joining their hands in mutual consent to the marriage.[323] Christ's display to her of the mark of the nail on his hand replicated the Resurrection on the main retable of Avila's cathedral, where the wound on his hand uplifted in benediction is prominent.[324] In a marital context her visualization suggested his redemptive payment in blood for her. The giving of the ring, as in Teresa de Jesús' celestial amethyst, had also been customary since Roman marriage. It was placed on the finger whose vein was believed to run to the heart,[325] the finger called "the doctor" because of the claim that fainting women could be revived by massaging it.[326] In Castilian custom there was a blessed betrothal ring, preferably and distinctively one for each partner. Teresa de Jesús omitted the provision of hers for the bridegroom. And there was no secular betrothal kiss, the binding act toward consummation in the agreement to marry, with its subtle legal consequences for gifts.[327]

---

319 Bilinkoff, *Avila of Saint Teresa*, pp. 114, 108. For nuns' dowries see also Vigil, *Vida de las mujeres*, p. 220.

320 For conjugal economics see Dillard, *Daughters of the Reconquest*, pp. 68-95. For background see John A. Crook, "'His and Hers': What Degree of Financial Responsibility Did Husband and Wife Have for the Matrimonial Home and their Life in Common, in a Roman Marriage?," in *Parenté et stratégies familiales dans l'antiquité romaine*, Actes de la table ronde des 2-4 octobre 1986, Paris, Maison de sciences de l'homme, ed. Jean Andreau and Hinnerk Bruhns, Collection de l'École française de Rome, 129 (Rome: École française de Rome, 1990), pp. 153-72.

321 See Treggiari, *Roman Marriage*, pp. 120-21; Suzanne Dixon, *The Roman Family* (Baltimore, Md.: Johns Hopkins University Press, 1991), p. 65.

322 For the development from the Roman *dextrarum iunctio* to the scholastic *traditio* see Edward Hall, *The Arnolfini Betrothal: Medieval Marriage and the Enigma of Van Eyck's Double Portrait*, Discovery, 3 (Berkeley: University of California Press, 1994), pp. 32-47.

323 Dillard, *Daughters of the Reconquest*, p. 64.

324 Berruguete and Santacruz, Resurrection, main retable, cathedral, Avila. Reproduced in Gomez-Moreno, *Catálogo monumental*, 2:115 no. 168.

325 Treggiari, *Roman Marriage*, pp. 148-48.

326 Dickinson, *Book of Diamonds*, pp. 150-51.

327 See Dillard, *Daughters of the Reconquest*, pp. 47, 58-60.

Her spiritual marriage lacked social character. It borrowed no social analogy from carnal marriage, in which the betrothal was publicized before witnesses, parents or other relatives. Kin were absent from her nuptials. There transpired nothing of the festive and communal occasion of a Castilian wedding, widely attended by the townspeople, who on a Sunday were off work. There was no procession of the married couple on horseback through the streets, no feast, or joust, or revelry.[328] There was no escort from the house of her father to that of her husband, which custom dated to the practice of the Roman upper-class.[329] Her imagination even excluded the celestial witnesses—the angels and saints, especially the Virgin Mary—who traditionally thronged scenes of spiritual marriage in literature and art. Teresa de Jesús had introduced the interior central abode of the castle as the principal place where transpired the "very secret" affairs between the soul and God.[330] Hers was a clandestine marriage, the model the Council of Trent had legislated against, by stipulating the publication of bans and a ceremony in the church of the bride's parish in the presence of two witnesses with a blessing by the priest.[331] As that conciliar decree was adopted in Spain, diocesan tribunals punished the couple in a clandestine marriage with public fasting and penance.[332] Yet traditionally it had been valid and indissoluble[333] and popularly it was, in its circumvention of parental consent, a sign of passionate love.[334] By a reduction of the lay model of familial authority that allowed the Church the control of marriage, gift, and inheritance, the consent of the partners, not the parents, was canonically enshrined at Trent.[335]

Teresa de Jesús' clandestine marriage was not only asocial but antisocial in the version in which the Lord, contradicting the priest who fractured the host, assured her that no one would part her from him.[336] It was not only

---

328 See ibid., pp. 46, 60-61, 65-66.

329 Ruiz-Galvez Priego, *Statut socio-juridique de la femme*, p. 241.

330 Teresa of Avila, *Castillo interior* 1.1.3.

331 Council of Trent, 24th session.

332 James Casey, "Le mariage clandestin en Andalousie à l'époque moderne," in *Amours légitimes amours illégitimes en España (XVIe-XVIIe siècles)*, Colloque international, Sorbonne, 3, 4, 5 et 6 octobre 1984, ed. Redondo, Travaux du Centre de recherche sur l'Espagne des XVIe et XVIIe siècles, 2 (Paris: Sorbonne, 1985), pp. 57-58. See also Federico R. Aznar Gil, *La institución matrimonial en la Hispania cristiana bajo-medieval (1215-1563)*, Bibliotheca salmanticensis, estudios, 123 (Salamanca: Universidad pontífica Salamanca, 1989), pp. 173-289; Ruiz-Galvez Priego, *Statut socio-juridique de la femme*, pp. 154-69.

333 Dillard, *Daughters of the Reconquest*, p. 39.

334 Joseph Pérez, "La femme et l'amour dans l'Espagne du XVIe siècle," in *Amours légitimes amours illégitimes*, ed. Redondo, pp. 23-24.

335 For the history of the issue of consent see Dillard, *Daughters of the Reconquest*, pp. 37-46; Jack Goody, *The Development of the Family and Marriage in Europe* (Cambridge: Cambridge University Press, 1983), pp. 151-53, 155, 193. For catechesis on marriage in provincial councils and diocescan synods in the fifteenth and sicteenth centuries see Aznar Gil, *Institución matrimonial*, pp. 59-65.

336 Teresa of Avila, *Relaciones espirituales* 31.

anticlerical but unsisterly, since the priest administered the other half of her host to another nun. That celebrant may have indeed been mortifying her, as she suspected, for he was John of the Cross, who criticized religious sensuality as immaturity of faith. Her charismatic experiences were a textbook of the "spiritual gluttony" he rejected.[337] Her designation of her betrothal ring as an amethyst repudiated him, since the amethyst was scripturally one of the twelve stones adorning the embroidered judgmental breastplates of the high priests (Ex. 28:19, 39:12).[338] By bestowing on Teresa de Jesús an amethyst, the Lord gave her his own sacerdotal judgment. In her imagination of spiritual marriage there was no clerical role analogous to that of secular marriage. No officiating priest sprinkled purifying salt on a nuptial bed; or blessed again a charter and rings outside or inside the church door; or received the bride from her kin as signifying their consent; or veiled the couple in symbolic blessing and yoked their shoulders with cord; or recited prayers and pronounced the formal benediction.[339]

Despite her wanting or vague comparisons with carnal marriage, she discriminated the spiritual relationship by its social stages. The imaginative vision in which the Lord wed her by endowment differed from similar representations, she wrote, which had left her bewildered and frightened. That powerful impression differed from them as marriage did from betrothal.[340] In Castilian society betrothal was virtually marriage, a binding agreement to marry, usually consummated sexually before the nuptials. Canonically a formula of future or present words distinguished the two stages. The status of betrothal was about the same as that of marriage, however; its unilateral termination was usually illegal, except for female adultery.[341] Such comparisons were the best to the purpose, she thought, nevertheless In the matrimonial abode there was "no more memory of the body than if the soul were not in it, but the spirit alone." The appearance of the humanity of the Lord was through the medium of the senses and powers. In spiritual marriage there was a secret union in the very center of the soul where God himself was and needed no door to enter. There he appeared in an intellectual, not imaginative, vision, as in his risen passage into the upper room where the disciples had been gathered (John 20:19-21). The secret was so great and its mercy so elevated that it immediately communicated ineffable delight. It

337 See John of the Cross, *El subido de monte Carmelo* 2.18.4; 2.19.11. For the horrible death of a greedy man who presumed to take the large host, rather than the common one, see Montaigne, *Journal de voyage en Italie*, 1:105-6.

338 This was commented in Epiphanius, *De XCII. gemmis, quae erant in veste Aaronis*, reprinted in 1565 with a *Corollarium* by Conrad Gesner in his collection of literature on gems.

339 See Dillard, *Daughters of the Reconquest*, pp. 61, 62-64. For the nuptial customs see also Ruiz-Galvez Priego, *Statut socio-juridique de la femme*, pp. 238-43.

340 Teresa of Avila, *Castillo interior* 7.2.2.

341 Dillard, *Daughters of the Reconquest*, pp. 60, 56, 57-58. See also Ruiz-Galvez Priego, *Statut socio-juridique de la femme*; and for the current catechesis of provincial councils and diocesan synods see Gil, *Institución matrimonial*, pp. 59-65.

manifested the glory of heaven in a more exalted manner than any vision or enjoyment. The spirit was made one with God, so united to his creature that they could not be separated. Betrothal and union were different from marriage, for they often involved separation. In the favor of marriage the soul was always with God in its center. Union was like two candles so joined that they burned with the same light; the wick, the flame, and the candle were one, but could be separated. Marriage was like rainfall into a river or fountain indivisible from it, or like a stream into the sea. Its effect was a secret but clear aspiration that God gave life to the soul.[342]

Although she appealed to a maternal model, in which streams of milk from the divine breast sustained the soul and comforted all inhabitants, the castle was no familial place. And although spiritual marriage was like daylight streaming into a room by two separate windows to become one light, it was not a domestic scene. The king was in his palace, unfailingly at his post, but the kingdom was at war and in pain. Departing from the military architecture of the castle, Teresa de Jesús did compare the operation of the soul to the construction of a royal temple. "In this temple of God, in this dwelling place" were equivalent concepts. She wrote of the undisturbed repose of the soul there, of its delight in the "tabernacle."[343] The interior castle was a dwelling, but not a home, however. Even in spiritual marriage Teresa de Jesús was uncomfortable, tormented by unknown sins, fearful of ejection from the castle. Marital stability was lacking. Socially a bridegroom's repudiation of his betrothed after intercourse was not only severely fined: he was outlawed.[344]

And so for security Teresa de Jesús constructed her castle by works. Its foundation was humility. Without it the Lord would not construct a tall building for fear of its toppling to the ground; while in humility the stones were laid so firmly that the castle would not fall. Yet she asserted, "For this does the spiritual marriage serve: that it always give birth to works, works."[345] Women's work in Castilian towns was a product of some domestic capability such as baking or textiles, or it was auxiliary and subsidiary to that of the husband.[346] Teresa de Jesús conceived the work of her nuns as prayer for the salvation of the "Lutherans,"[347] so that as spouses they were helpmates by prayer to the Lord's grace. "Do you know what it is to be truly spiritual?" she asked in climaxing the construction of the castle. "To become slaves of God." The nuns were to be "marked with his brand, which was the cross." Since they had given him their liberty, they were able to be "sold as slaves to everyone, as he was." That was no harm but a great favor,

---

342 Teresa of Avila, *Castillo interior* 7.2.3; 7.2.4; 7.2.6.

343 Ibid. 7.2.6; 7.2.4; 7.2.10; 7.3.11; 7.2.10; 7.2.11; 7.3.12; 7.3.13.

344 See Dillard, *Daughters of the Reconquest*, pp. 57-58.

345 Teresa of Avila, *Castillo interior* 7.4.8; 7.4.6.

346 Dillard, *Daughters of the Reconquest*, p. 162.

347 Teresa of Avila, *Vida suya* 32.6.

Teresa de Jesús thought. Any soul that was not determined for slavery was not making much progress. Those who were not enslaved to the exercise of virtue, especially humility in the performance of works, were perpetually stunted as dwarfs.[348]

Slaves were historically included in Castilian charters of betrothal. The aristocratic woman of Toledo with the thirty-six coifs numbered slaves among the household items of her bridal trousseau.[349] Yet wives were not slaves: even Aristotle's *Politica* distinguished them, and medieval and renaissance commentators agreed.[350] Castilian custom and attitude could differ, however. Enslavement of the bride to the bridegroom was the penalty for her adultery before marriage.[351] A Spanish canonist classed women as the natural slaves of their husbands.[352] Teresa de Jesus' own mentor at recollection argued as the premise for husbands to silence wives: "We are men and you are women. We are masters and you are slaves."[353] Before her another woman had pronounced, "Behold, I am the slave of the Lord" (Luke 1:38). She was the Virgin annunciate, whose scriptural usage of slavery identified her humble social status of poverty and oppression (v. 48).[354]

Teresa de Jesús created an ideology of marriage as slavery that was socially incoherent. Marriage of a slave woman to her master, or to a free man with her master's permission, in reality emancipated her.[355] If Teresa de Jesús was (imaginatively) a married slave, then her husband Christ was necessarily also a slave. Her rationale seems to have been an association of slavery with his imprisonment during the passion—because of his flogging. Christ's flagellation loomed importantly in devotion from the erection of its supposed column of oriental jasper in S. Prassede at Rome early in the thir-

---

348 Teresa of Avila, *Constitutiones* 22; *Castillo interior* 6.4.10; 7.4.3; 7.4.8; 7.4.6; 4.3.9; 1.2.9; 7.4.8; 7.4.9. See also Erica Tietze-Conrat, *Dwarfs and Jesters in Art*, trans. Elizabeth Osborn (London: Phaidon, 1957).

349 Dillard, *Daughters of the Reconquest*, pp. 48, 55.

350 Aristotle, *Politica* 1.1. See Ian Maclean, *The Renaissance Notion of Woman: A Study in the Fortunes of Scholasticism and Medical Science in European Intellectual Life* (Cambridge: Cambridge University Press, 1980), pp. 19, 76; also W. W. Fortenbaugh, "Aristotle on Slaves and Women," in *Articles on Aristotle*, ed. Jonathan Barnes, Malcolm Schofield, and Richard Sorabji, 4 vols., Vol. 2: *Ethics and Politics* (London: Duckworth, 1975-79), pp. 135-39.

351 Dillard, *Daughters of the Reconquest*, p. 56. But the subservience of the bride, symbolized by the veiling of her head in the nuptials, was explicitly mitigated by the priestly enjoinment to the bridegroom in his final benediction: "I give you a wife, not a servant," p. 64.

352 See Anthony Pagden, *The Fall of Natural Man: The American Indian and the Origins of Comparative Ethnology* (Cambridge: Cambridge University Press, 1982), p. 46.

353 Francisco de Osuna, *Norte de los estados*, fol. CXVII, cited by Fitzmaurice-Kelly, "Woman in Sixteenth-Century Spain," pp. 560-61, without reference to this argument.

354 See Joseph Vogt, *Ancient Slavery and the Ideal of Man*, trans. Thomas Wiedemann (Oxford: Basil Blackwell, 1974), pp. 146-51.

355 See William D. Phillips, Jr., *Slavery from Roman Times to the Early Transatlantic Trade* (Minneapolis: University of Minnesota Press, 1985), p. 102, without reference to Teresa de Jesús.

teenth century. The saint of the Catholic reform, Charles Borromeo, who was titular of that church, said Mass daily in its chapel of the flagellation next to the very column.[356] Among its artistic versions was a mural "Ecce homo" that Teresa de Jesús commissioned as prioress at the convent of Encarnación.[357] That or a pathetic portrait of Jesus condemned to the pillory had occasioned her conversion from laxity.[358] The image functioned in her *Vida suya* like the conversional topic of the opening of the book in Augustine's *Confessions*. There was a tradition of the skin of Jesus as a parchment stretched on the frame of the cross, marked with scourging like the strokes of a pen and decorated with wounds like the rubrics on a page. Although that deed or charter scripturally (Gal. 5:1) and traditionally liberated humanity from sin,[359] for Teresa de Jesús it became a writ of enslavement. Of all the episodes of Christ's passion, the supreme rhetorical development in medieval tracts was his flagellation. From the brief evangelical mention of his scourging was elaborated a complex and brutal ritual. There multiplied teams of scourgers and various implements: rods, thorns, and thistles; chain and rope with attached weights, or iron hooks called scorpions; dried ox sinews or tendons. The infliction of the wounds and their appearance was detailed; his blood was described as spraying and drenching the participants like rainfall, so that they were up to their ankles in gore.[360] A Flagellation on the main retable of Avila's cathedral depicts the scourgers with vehemence and vigor.[361]

Flogging had been in Roman society the primary symbolic distinction between the adult as free or enslaved; as exempted from, or vulnerable to, corporal punishment. The slave was in a relationship of exploitation, his obedience based on fear of routine whipping. The child or student who suffered such occasional correction of misbehavior was still in a relationship of familial piety. Flogging was not only pain but dishonor. Beyond a shocking cruelty intended to maim or to kill, it inflicted social and psychological anguish by insulting dignity. As an invasion and violation of a person, it was profound humiliation.[362] It was common Spanish punishment for minor

---

[356] For the column in S. Prassede, Rome in devotion and art see Émile Mâle, *L'art religieux de la fin du XVIe siècle du XVIIe siècle et du XVIII siècle: Étude sur l'iconographie après le concile de Trent*, 2d ed. rev. (Paris: Armand Colin, 1951), pp. 263-66; Rodolf Beny and Peter Gunn, *The Churches of Rome* (London: Weidenfeld and Nicolson, 1981), p. 33.

[357] Gomez-Moreno, *Catálogo monumental*, 1:206, photo 495.

[358] Ibid., 1:218, photo 534; 2:529.

[359] E. g., Catherine of Siena, *Le lettere* 11.

[360] Marrow, *Passion Iconography*, pp. 134-42.

[361] Attributed to Pedro Berruguete, Flagellation, main retable, cathedral, Avila. Reproduced in Gomez-Moreno, *Catálogo monumental*, 2:115, photo 167.

[362] Richard Saller, "Corporal Punishment, Authority, and Obedience in the Roman Household," in *Marriage, Divorce, and Children in Ancient Rome*, ed. Beryl Rawson (Oxford: Clarendon Press for the Humanities Research Center, Australian National University, Canberra, 1991), pp. 151-64. For cruelty to slaves see also Keith R. Hopkins, "Novel Evidence for Roman Slavery," *Past and Present* 138 (1993):3-27.

crimes, in the galleys and in the mines; and especially for women, who were usually spared harsher sentences.[363] Flogging short of death was practiced by masters against domestic slaves to regulate conduct.[364] It was also an alternative in Castile to the enslavement of the adulterous female to her betrothed.[365] It may have been an assault on wives;[366] just cause for violence against them was debated.[367] Flogging could be spectacular. Crowds at public appearances of the favorite dwarf at Philip II's court, Magdalena Ruiza, chanted "Whip her, whip her" to provoke and frighten the mentally retarded woman. Flogging was also an ascetic practice: at his deathbed the king had his father's scourge, clotted with imperial blood.[368] Scourging the soul was known in the current female spirituality of the province of Avila. Its celebrated beata, María de santo Domingo, in decrying herself as enslaved to the body prayed Christ to whip her hard so that she would not be sluggish.[369] In the convent of Teresa de Jesús those nuns who overly socialized with relatives were communally flogged.[370]

Their social dishonor through corporal shame symbolically countered the universal tendency to avoid enslaving members of the same society. Christians could not legally enslave other Christians.[371] Yet that is what her spirituality advocated: nuns enslaved to God and others. A slave was since Roman law defined as property, subject to the control of the master. Alien to the dominant society, a slave was without ties or possibilities of kinship. Even its progeny remained enslaved property.[372] Teresa de Jesús' espousal of slavery to God and others was the ultimate repudiation of kinship. Her rejection of the pity toward slaves that so egregiously distinguished her father's virtue denied his affection and judgment. With a spirituality of slavery she accomplished the valuational upheaval of her familial household, where slavery had been intolerable. Her testimony to that provided an early record of Castilian domestic slavery,[373] although she

---

363 Ruth Pike, *Penal Servitude in Early Modern Spain* (Madison: University of Wisconsin Press, 1983), pp. 3, 5, 7, 21, 36.

364 Phillips, *Slavery*, pp. 162-63, 100; A. C. de C. M. Saunders, *A Social History of Black Slaves and Freedmen in Portugal 1441-1555* (Cambridge: Cambridge University Press, 1982), p. 108.

365 Dillard, *Daughters of the Reconquest*, pp. 56-57.

366 See Vigil, *Vida de las mujeres*, pp. 102-3.

367 Fitzmaurice Kelly, "Woman in Sixteenth-Century Spain," pp. 599-602; and for daughters as legitimately stroked with a rod on the shoulder for misbehavior, p. 577.

368 See Parker, *Philip II*, pp. 169, 197-98.

369 María de santo Domingo, *Libro de la oración*; Mary E. Giles, *The Book of Prayer of Sor María de Santo Domingo* (Albany: State University of New York Press, 1990), p. 148. For her see also Bilinkoff, "A Spanish Prophetess and Her Patrons: The Case of María de santo Domingo," *Sixteenth Century Journal* 23 (1992):21-34.

370 Teresa of Avila, *Constitutiones* 15-20.

371 See Phillips, *Slavery*, pp. 6, 146, without reference to the convent.

372 See ibid., pp. 5-7, 13, 164.

373 Dominguez Ortiz, "La esclavitud en Castilla durante la edad moderna," in idem, *Estudios de historia social de España*, 4 vols. (Madrid: Consejo superior de investigaciones cien-

derived it from the rhetorical topic of the two brothers of opposing morals, regressing to Cain and Abel.[374] In the year before Teresa de Jesús composed her interior castle there were in Avila eighty nine persons in domestic service, or 6.8 per cent of its population.[375] That some were slaves is testified by their manumission in the will of Sancho Dávila, the city's prominent militarily man, "the scourge of the war."[376] After a medieval decline in slavery, at the beginning of the fifteenth century there was new impetus for it from the birth of capitalism, with its increasing demand for manual labor. With the Portuguese exploration of black Africa there flourished from mid-century a slave trade from its west coast. The market was Seville, which had the largest contingent of black slaves on the peninsula—perhaps one to thirty inhabitants—and on the continent. Natives came from the Canaries. War with the Muslims provided another source. Many prisoners from the Balkans and other eastern areas also arrived on the Iberian peninsula through Italian commercial centers. By the end of the medieval era there were already numerous slaves.[377]

Slavery thrived under papal approval, with the Church a massive institution of slaveholding in the Iberian colonial empires. The only prominent prelate to condemn slavery outright was the archbishop of Mexico, Alonso de Montufar,[378] so that the morality of Teresa de Jesús' father was extraordinary. Avoiding unconditional condemnation of the institution, lenient moralists merely signaled abuses and sought moderation. Aristotle's politics figured most importantly in its justification, a text never impugned, only interpreted for application and accommodation of its principles. A distinction was made between natural and legal servitude: subjection of ignorant and uncivilized persons to the power of the wise and strong; and subjection

---

tíficas, 1952), 2:383; José Antonio Saco, *Historia de la esclavitud desde los tiempos mas remotos hasta nuestros días*, 2d ed., 5 vols. (Havana: Alfa, 1937), 3:362.

374 See "Fratrum inter se irae sunt acerbissimae," Erasmus, *Adagia* 1.2.50, in *Opera omnia* (LB) 2. For Philo's important transformation of the biblical brothers into rival dualistic principles see Ricardo J. Quinones, *The Changes of Cain: Violence and the Lost Brother in Cain and Abel Literature* (Princeton: Princeton University Press, 1991), pp. 32-83.

375 Serafín de Tapia Sánchez, "Estructura ocupacional de Avila en el siglo XVI," in *El pasado histórico de Castilla y Léon*, 3 vols., Vol. 2: *Edad moderna*, ed. Jesús Crespo Redondo (Burgos: Junta de Castilla y Léon, 1983), p. 205. For the domestic staff of a medieval household see Dillard, *Daughters of the Reconquest*, pp. 155-57.

376 Merino Alvarez, *Sociedad abulense*, pp. 154, 61.

377 Dominguez Ortiz, "Esclavitud en Castilla," pp. 369, 373-74, 372, 376-77; Phillips, *Slavery*, pp. 160-63. For slavery in the Middle Ages and the fifteenth century see also ibid., pp. 43-65, 88-113; Saco, *Historia de la esclavitud*, 3:265-98, 345-62. The Muslims had black slaves despite royal prohibition. Saco, *Historia de la esclavitud*, 3:357-58, 360.

378 C. R. Boxer, *The Church Militant and Iberian Expansion 1440-1770*, Johns Hopkins Symposia in Comparative History, 10 (Baltimore, Md.: Johns Hopkins University Press, 1978), pp. 30-32. See also John Francis Maxwell, *Slavery and the Catholic Church: The History of Catholic Teaching concerning the Moral Legitimacy of the Institution of Slavery* (Chichester: Barry Rose, 1975); Richard Gray, "The Papacy and the Altantic Slave Trade: Lourenço da Silva, the Capuchins and the Decisions of the Holy Office," *Past and Present* 115 (1987):52-68.

from war, sale, or other circumstances. The biblical sisters Martha and Mary were argued as divine authority for Aristotle's division of human activities into action and contemplation, hence for his theory of natural slavery. The concept of birth to slavery by proper nature was judged repugnant, however; and especially after the controversy by Bartolomeo de las Casas it was hardly ever invoked. Other slavery was justified by citation of biblical, patristic, and medieval texts, especially a *Regimento de principis*, falsely attributed to Aquinas, although all the major scholastics did accept slavery. Yet Roman law in the Justinianian version provided some protection of the slave against killing or maiming by the master. In its medieval Spanish development the slave earned the right to bodily integrity, to contract marriage even against the master's will, to form a family, and in certain cases to have an expendable income and some juridical capacity.[379]

Slavery was more persistent and vigorous in the Iberian kingdoms because of shared borders with non-Christian states that could be legally raided. The prisoners of war who built the very walls of Avila were slaves.[380] Domestic slavery in Spain peaked in the sixteenth century and in the first half of the seventeenth century.[381] Ownership of slaves was an aristocratic, and even clerical, luxury: a prestigious decoration to the home, like the splendid tapestries that displayed wealth. A slave cost thirty-to one-hundred ducats; in the decade of Teresa de Jesús' composition a journeyman worked a year to earn seventy.[382] As the prominent theologian Francisco de Vitoria wrote, "I do not see why one should be so scrupulous over this matter. . . . It is enough that a man be a slave in fact or in law, and I will buy him without a qualm."[383] Dramas cast slaves as ordinary servants, treated as members of the household, confidants and accomplices to the loves of their mistress.[384] Comedies featured false slaves,[385] a ruse popularized by María de Zayas y Sotomayor's *La esclava de su amante*. In the guise of a Muslim slave named Zelima, the heroine experienced years of adventure, with capture by Corsairs, until she became the property of the family of her lover and obtained their permission to enter a convent.[386] Captivity to love was a poetic

379 See Dominguez Ortiz, "Esclavitud en España," pp. 406-8. For the argument from Martha and Mary see Pagden, *Fall of Natural Man*, pp. 40-41.

380 Phillips, *Slavery*, p. 107.

381 Dominguez Ortiz, "Esclavitud en Castilla," p. 397; Phillips, *Slavery*, pp. 160-69.

382 Bennassar, *Spanish Character*, pp. 106-17.

383 Francisco de Vitoria, "Carta al padre fray Bernardino de Vique," f. xvr, in "Coleccion de dictámenes inéditos" 174, cited by Pagden, *Fall of Natural Man*, p. 33.

384 Dominguez Ortiz, "Esclavitud en España," pp. 397, 385. For servants see also Miguel Herrero, *Oficios populares en la sociedad de Lope de Vega* (Madrid: Castalia, 1977), pp. 23-88; Vigil, *Vida de las mujeres*, pp. 122-26.

385 P. W. Bomli, *La femme dans l'Espagne du siècle d'or* (The Hague: Martinus Nijhoff, 1950), p. 292.

386 Zayas y Sotomayor, *La esclava de su amante*. For her see recently Mercedes Maroto Camino, "Spindles for Swords: The Re/discovery of María de Zayas' Presence," *Hispanic Review* 62 (1994):519-36.

conceit fashionable from Petrarch's lyrics of bondage by yokes, chains, snares, and nets—all symbols of Laura's tresses.[387] Legal bondage was a reality signaled not in metaphor but in flesh. Spanish drama recorded the custom of branding with a red-hot iron the forehead or cheek of slaves, especially those who had attempted escape. The common brands were the letter *S* and the mark of an intertwined nail that took on the aspect of a red flower.[388] Yet, from the beginning, slaves collected by Portuguese traders along the west African coast were branded on their right arms with a cross.[389] It was such a branding with the cross that Teresa de Jesús demanded for herself and her nuns. Searing the flesh also recalled the ordeal of the iron, which was the medieval Castilian method for proving the chastity of women.[390]

Slaves were to become common in Castilian convents for women in the next century.[391] In the New World hundreds of them lived in the convents of colonial Peru, not from the ideal of virginity, but from the reality of bondage by wealthy nuns who owned them. The population of a convent there spanned the social spectrum from white heiress to black slave. The slaves obtained shelter and food, and escape from poverty and abuse—but not always, for there erupted scuffles and even violence. In one such fight a nun ripped to shreds the dress of a slave owned by other nuns. At a grand convent in Lima called Encarnación, like the one Teresa de Jesús entered in Avila, a slave Pascuala had her face scratched and her head gashed with a stone pried loose from the courtyard. In another convent a mulatto maid of an important nun of the black veil, a lady, was refused entry into the religious life. She was only allowed to become a donate, a buffer state without vows one step up from the servants and slaves, a maid still but in a habit. The nuns who followed Teresa de Jesús' reformed rule at the convent there,

---

387 Boyle, *Petrarch's Genius: Pentimento and Prophecy* (Berkeley: University of California Press, 1991), pp. 64-66.

388 For the brands see Bomli, *Femme dans l'Espagne*, p. 291. Portuguese slaves were branded like cattle upon shipment, then branded again at each subsequent sale. The crown branded its slaves on the arms, others on the cheeks. Facial branding was mentioned as a common practice in a Portuguese drama. Saunders, *Social History of Black Slaves and Freedmen in Portugal*, p. 108.

389 Phillips, *Slavery*, p. 156. For the branding of slaves in Roman practice see p. 29; in general, Ruth Melinkoff, *The Mark of Cain* (Berkeley: University of California Press, 1981), pp. 23-24; as a punishment in medieval France, Paul Lacroix, *France in the Middle Ages: Customs, Classes and Conditions* (New York: Frederick Ungar, 1963), p. 417; and as a punishment of criminals in early modern Germany, Richard van Dülmen, *Theatre of Horror: Crime and Punishment in Early Modern Germany*, trans. Elisabeth Neu (Cambridge: Polity, 1990), p. 49.

390 See Dillard, *Daughters of the Reconquest*, pp. 197-98, 209. The ordeal continued in the Spanish kingdoms despite a papal canon of 1215 condemning it. The right of benediction of the rod was simply transferred from priests to judges. Robert Bartlett, *Trial by Fire and Water: The Medieval Judicial Ordeal* (Oxford: Clarendon, 1986), p. 19.

391 Dominguez Ortiz, "Esclavitud en Castilla," p. 385.

Las Descalzas, also had servants.[392] Women were expected to be motherly to their maids, kind but dignified, firm but gentle, and to be served from respect not fear.[393] Female mastery had its nadir in Catalina de los Rios Lisperguer, who flogged her slaves daily, then for torture immersed their flayed bodies in urine. Forty died at her hands. She herself was buried in state in the local Augustinian church, of which she was a benefactor, garbed prestigiously in the habit of a nun.[394]

The spirituality of slavery was developed by Antônio Vieira, a Jesuit diplomat and advisor to the Portuguese court, himself a descendent of black Africans. Although he believed slaves were created in the divine image, he styled them "children of God's fire" because they were branded with the mark of slavery as oppression and as illumination. The redemption of Christ gained them liberation from the servitude of the soul but not of the body. He compared slaves barefoot and ragged to members of a religious order—in poverty, obedience, abstinence, and vigils—under the rule of their masters. Since every religious order had a purpose, a vocation, and a special grace, he preached to slaves, "The grace of yours is whips and punishments."[395] No labor or life was more like Christ's passion than slavery, he continued, which could be sanctified by imitation of the divine exemplar. Christ was naked, maltreated, in irons and in prisons, with lashings and insults to wound him. For the martyr's prize, slaves should imitate him, so that after a life of privation and punishment they might be rewarded in heaven. In serving their master they were not obeying a man but one who served God.[396] The ideology of slavery in the New World continued the devotion to the passion in the Old World, reduced to compliance under physical pain.

The interior castle as a place of servitude was no concluding embellishment but integral to its design. Teresa de Jesús' alternative to her architectural construct was the natural creation. As she instructed, her castle was a tree of life planted in the living waters of God. The dwellings did not have to be explored in sequence. Their focus was the center, as if the castle were

---

[392] Luis Martín, *Daughters of the Conquistadores: Women of the Viceroyalty of Peru* (Albuquerque: University of New Mexico Press, 1983), pp. 199, 209, 184-85, 177. For nuns in the New World see also Electa Arenal and Stacey Schlau, *Untold Sisters: Hispanic Nuns in Their Own Works*, trans. Amanda Powell (Albuquerque: University of New Mexico Press, 1989).

[393] Fitzmaurice-Kelly, "Woman in Sixteenth-Century Spain," pp. 620-21; Ruth Kelso, *Doctrine for the Lady of the Renaissance*, rev. ed. (Urbana: University of Illinois Press, 1978), pp. 113-15.

[394] Boxer, *Women in Iberian Expansion Overseas, 1415-1815: Some Facts, Fancies and Personalities* (New York: Oxford University Press, 1975), pp. 46-47.

[395] *Children of God's Fire*, pp. 163-74, citing *Obras completas do padre Antônio Vieira*, 12:301-34.

[396] Katia M. de Queirós Mattoso, *To Be a Slave in Brazil, 1550-1888*, trans. Arthur Goldhammer (New Brunswick, N. J.: Rutgers University Press, 1986), pp. 99-100.

a palmetto whose outer layers might be peeled down to its edible core.[397] The actual tree she planted in the convent garden was a hazelnut that yielded an annual crop.[398] Her literary palm was symbolic, traditional as the tree of life.[399] Its artistic design, in embroidery extant from Avila, was frequently stylized with large fronds.[400] The palm tree had been associated since classical religion with Artemis, protector of virgins in their preparation for marriage and their erotic transformation into women.[401] Since the palm was believed the only plant that reproduced sexually, it symbolized faithful lovers, the female never bearing fruit without the male.[402]

The oil palm was in origin west African, dating before ironworking and cultivated since A. D. 550, the end of the Roman house. It was indeed the tree of life. With the yam, its kernel was the most important regional food crop; but the entire plant was useful: cooking oil was pressed from the pericarp and kernel; sap was collected at the base of the inflorescences for wine; the shell and residual fibre of the pericorp were harvested for fuel, the leaves for thatching, the fine fibres of the leaflets for fishing lines; the trunk for rafters, fences and bridges; and the fibers from the base of the stem for cordage and fish traps.[403] The palm was the staple of the society and culture exploited for slaves. It would not be until the nineteenth century that another woman would write a book on *Palmetto-Leaves.* But her appreciation of the spirituality of actual slaves would abolish the servility of Teresa de Jesús. Her name: Harriet Beecher Stowe.[404] Teresa de Jesús concluded her castle as a "poor wretch,"[405] since Augustine's age a mild curse for a slave.[406] A "wretch" (*ruin*) derived from a "ruin" (*ruina*), a collapsed castle. She imagined herself at its exit by death, not in paradise but only in purgatory: burning.[407]

---

[397] Teresa of Avila, *Castillo interior* 1.1.2; 1.2.8.

[398] Cervera Vera, *Complejo arquitectónico del monasterio*, p. 34.

[399] See Wolfgang Fleischer, *Untersuchungen zur Palmbaumallegorie im Mittelalter*, Münchner germanistische Beiträge, 20 (Munich: W. Fink, 1976), pp. 117-28.

[400] Maria Angeles Gonzales Mena, *Catálogo de bordados* (Madrid: Instituto Valencia de don Juan, 1974), p. 111; Garzon Pareja, *Industria sedera en España*, p. 271.

[401] Christiane Sourvinou-Inwood, "Altars with Palm-Trees, Palm-Trees, and *Parthenoi*," in idem, "*Reading*" *Greek Culture: Texts and Images, Rituals and Myths* (Oxford: Clarendon, 1991), pp. 99-143.

[402] J. Prest, *The Garden of Eden: The Botanic Garden and the Re-Creation of Paradise* (New Haven, Conn.: Yale University Press, 1981), p. 81.

[403] See M. A. Sowunmi, "The Beginnings of Agriculture in West Africa: Botanical Evidence," *Current Anthropology* 26 (1985):127; Adam Jones, *From Slaves to Palm Kernels: A History of the Galhinas Country (West Africa), 1730-1890*, Studien zur Kulturkunde, 68 (Wiesbaden: Franz Steiner, 1983), pp. 19, 166.

[404] Harriet Beecher Stowe, *Palmetto-Leaves*, pp. 292-95. For her domesticity see Gillian Brown, *Domestic Individualism: Imagining Self in Nineteenth-Century America*, New Historicism, 4 (Berkeley: University of California Press, 1990), pp. 13-60.

[405] Teresa of Avila, *Castillo interior* 7.4.16.

[406] Augustine, *Enarrationes in psalmos* 96.12; 73.12, cited by van der Meer, *Augustine the Bishop*, p. 135.

[407] Teresa of Avila, *Castillo interior* 7.4.16; epilogue 4.

EPILOGUE

That burning conclusion reversed traditional piety. Religion had classically embraced a reciprocity of affection and obligation among all members of family: not only filial submission but also parental fostering. Piety was a natural law of esteem.[1] Aeneas had rescued his family from the flames by carrying on his back his father, who clasped the ancestral gods, while his son walked beside him and his wife behind.[2] The epigraphy of Spain during Roman occupation specified familial sentiments of affection that were strong and open, with piety in the superlative degree—*pientissimus*—as the most frequent endearment for parents.[3] The traditional ethic of generosity posited that kin, simply as kin, had irresistible claims of mutual support and consideration. Kin were ideally to share, without coercive sanctions or contractual obligations. Amity was established on moral, not jural, values. Christian charity approximated it;[4] but with the ascetic severance of the believer from the natural family for a spiritual surrogate, or for stark isolation, its anthropological foundation was razed. Unlike the vestal virgin, the cloistered nun tended no civic hearth. With her imagination of a matrimonial keep a nun emphasized personal interiority. The construct of a castle imitated Augustine's injunction to seek God within the self, rather than in other creatures. "Enter, enter, my daughters in the interior," Teresa de Jesús urged. "Pass beyond your small works, because as Christians you must do all this and much more, and it suffices that you be vassals of God." She designed the interior castle to reflect the soul as created in the image and likeness of God (Gen. 1:26), a "king so powerful, so wise, so pure, so full of goodness," who delighted in his spiritual abode. The great beauty and capacity of a soul created in his image and likeness were as incomprehensible as their divine paradigm. A soul was incomparable.[5]

---

[1] See Richard P. Saller, "Corporal Punishment, Authority, and Obedience in the Roman Household," in *Marriage, Divorce, and Children in Ancient Rome*, ed. Beryl Rawson (Oxford: Clarendon Press for the Humanities Research Centre, Australian National University, Canberra, 1991), pp. 147-49.

[2] Vergil, *Aeneid* 2.707-29. For sixteenth-century art see Jürgen Rapp, "Adam Elsheimer 'Aeneas rettet Anchises aus dem brennenden Troja': Ein Stammbuchblatt in Deckfarbenmalerei," *Pantheon* 47(1989):118-23 figs. 10-19.

[3] Leonard A. Curchin, "Familial Epithets in the Epigraphy of Roman Spain," in *Mélanges offerts en hommage au Reverend Père, Etienne Gareau*, Cahiers des études anciennes, 14 (Ottawa: Université d'Ottawa, 1982), pp. 179-82.

[4] Meyer Fortes, *Kinship and the Social Order: The Legacy of Lewis Henry Morgan* (Chicago: Aldine, 1969), pp. 237-39, 251.

[5] Teresa of Avila, *Castillo interior* 4.3.6, referring to Augustine, *Confessiones* 10.27; 3.1.6; 1.1.1. For background see José Manuel Neito Soria, *Fundamentos ideológicos del*

Yet theologians did compare, sometimes with bad analogies, like Thomas Aquinas from numismatics or Teresa de Jesús from sericulture. Fundamentally erroneous was Augustine's philosophical analogy of the soul. In misconstruing scripture it mislaid the foundations of Western culture concerning human purpose and dignity. Just as buildings were erected by observation and experience without knowledge of structural theory, so exegeses were invented without knowledge of historical criticism. The modern scholarly consensus roundly rejects any interpretation of the creation of humans in the divine image with reference to the soul or its faculties. "And God said, 'Let us make humans in our image, after our likeness'" (Gen. 1:26). There is in the use of the plural form no revelation of the Trinity but rather a divine address to the heavenly host. A single opinion considers the verse vaguely relational, while another maintains that it affords no definition of human nature. By a remarkable agreement among exegetes, however, scripture reveals the divine mandate that humans exercise dominion over creation as God's very representatives on earth. In ancient parallels "image" referred to the role of the king as the divine deputy. Scripture extended it to all humanity. People were to tend creation as gardeners cultivated the soil.[6] This functional, rather than metaphysical or psychological, exegesis of human origins ruins Augustine's premise. A dichotomous creation of humans into body and soul, with the soul as ruler, has in Genesis no justification. Irrelevant, then, was the protracted dispute among theologians and philosophers concerning in which faculty of the soul, intellect or will, human dignity principally resided. The ideology of contemplation versus action, with the social or unsociable institutions it established, collapses like the faulty Roman tenements he decried.

Speculation on the paradigmatic verse of creation in the divine image historically eclipsed consideration of scripture that *was* relational. The gospel promise of divine indwelling as at home (John 14:23) was rejected with disbelief or deafness. Its denial was institutionalized by the displacement of the assembly of worship from the home to the basilica. Disorientation toward the immaterial as the sole or primary religious value caused abandonment of, or ambiguity about, the material: fundamentally the home as the basic human place, the site of generation. Discomfort at home and, more radically, mobility and exile from it further alienated the gospel

---

poder real en Castilla (siglos XIII-XVI) (Madrid: Eudema, 1988).

[6] For an exegetical survey see Gunnlaugur A. Jónssen, *The Image of God: Genesis 1:26-28 in a Century of Old Testament Research*, trans. Lorraine Svendsen, rev. Michael S. Cheney, Coniectanea biblica, OT series, 26 (Lund: Almquist & Wiksell, 1986). For the king as gardener see also Nicholas Wyatt, "'Supposing Him to Be the Gardener' (John 20,15): A Study of the Paradise Motif in John," *Zeitschrift für die neutestamentliche Wissenschaft* 81 (1990):35-36. Creation as a Trinitarian act was in art isolated and rare. See Adelheid Heimann, "Trinitas creator mundi," *Journal of the Warburg and Courtauld Institutes* 2 (1938-39):42-52. See also in general Jeanne Kay, "Human Dominion over Nature in the Hebrew Bible," *Annals of the Association of American Geographers* 79 (1989):214-32.

promise of divine domesticity. The Protestant reformation restored the home to some scriptural dignity, but only as natural, not as supernatural.[7] With the abolition of the religious vow of chastity as privileged, marriage became normative; but it was demoted from the status of a sacrament. And, although the movement abolished the practice of pilgrimage to shrines, it enhanced the ideology of pilgrimage to heaven by its antithesis of nature and grace, immanence and transcendence, here and there.

The first home economist, Catherine E. Beecher, sister of the abolitionist, emphasized convenience and comfort in planning houses that would be functional for their users. She criticized the disadvantages of a large structure, in which the furnishings were located at such distances that "half the time and strength is employed in walking back and forth."[8] Her criticism of domestic discomfort may serve metaphorically for a Christian society that expended itself in traversing enormous distances from home to locate God: out the front door. If historical epochs are defined by human feelings of hominess or homelessness in the universe,[9] then a single epoch stretched from Augustine of Thagaste to Teresa of Avila. And, if as a Roman statesman moralized, the house naturally displays the character of its inhabitants,[10] then Christians were opaque. Or they substituted, as they did, places other than the home as the religious model. The prophets for historical change were not the exegetes but the artists: the poet who challenged asceticism to create at his villa a spirituality of the secular; the architect who reasoned household management as religious as church attendance; the painter who imagined the Madonna in a bourgeois room, warming the naked God-man before a fire. In the long peregrination, Christianity was not a religion of the hearth but of the brazier.

---

[7] Although the analysis is mine, for a compatible study of Protestant reform see Lyndal Roper, "'Going to Church and Street': Weddings in Reformation Augsburg," *Past and Present* 106 (1985):62-101.

[8] See for home economics Witold Rybczynski, *Home: A Short History of an Idea* (New York: Viking, 1986), pp. 158-62, citing Catherine E. Beecher, *A Treatise on Domestic Economy for Use of Young Ladies at Home and at School* (New York, 1869 ed.), p. 34. For a sampler of recent literature see "Home: A Place in the World," *Social Research* 58 (1991); *Domestic Architecture and the Use of Space: An Interdisciplinary Cross-Cultural Study*, ed. Susan Kent (Cambridge: Cambridge University Press, 1990); *Dwellings, Settlements, and Tradition: Cross-Cultural Perspectives* (Lanham, Pa.: University Press of America, 1989); *Housing, Culture and Design*, ed. Setha M. Low and Erve Chambers (Philadelphia: University of Pennsylvania Press, 1989); Paul Oliver, *Dwellings: The House Across the World* (Oxford: Phaidon, 1987); Giuseppina Rullo, "People and Home Interiors: A Bibliography of Recent Psychological Research," *Environment and Behavior* 19 (1987):250-59.

[9] Martin Buber, "Das Problem des Menschen," cited by Grete Schaeder, *The Hebrew Humanism of Martin Buber*, trans. Noah J. Jacobs (Detroit, Mich.: Wayne State University Press, 1973), p. 29.

[10] Cassidorus, *Epistolae* 7.5, cited by Spiro Kostoff, "The Architect in the Middle Ages, East and West," in *The Architect: Chapters in the History of the Profession*, ed. idem (New York: Oxford University Press, 1977), p. 68.

PRIMARY SOURCES

Aelred of Rielvaux. *De Iesu puero duodenni*. Ed. A. Hoste. In *Opera omnia*, 1:245-78. Ed. idem, C. H. Talbot, and Gaetano Raciti. 2 vols. Corpus christianorum series latina, continuatio medievalis, 1-2. Turnhout: Brepols, 1971-89.

Alberti, Leon Battista. *Opere volgari*. Ed. Cecil Grayson. 3 vols. Bari: Gius. Laterza & Figli, 1960-73.

——. *De re aedificatoria*. In *Alberti Index*, 4: *Faksimile*. Ed. Hans-Karl Lücke. 4 vols. Veröffentlichungen des Zentralinstituts für Kunstgeschichte in München, 6. Munich: Prestel, 1975.

Ambrose. *Hexameron*. Ed. Karl Schenkl. Corpus scriptorum ecclesiasticorum latinorum, 32-1. Vienna, 1897.

——. *Expositio evangelii secundum Lucam*. Ed. Mark Adriaen. Corpus christianorum series latina, 14. Turnhout: Brepols, 1957.

The Ancrene Riwle: The Corpus Ms.: Ancrene Wisse. Trans. M. B. Salu. London: Burns & Oates, 1955.

Angela of Foligno. (*Librum de vere fidelium experientia*). *Le livre de l'expérience des vrais fidèles*. Ed. M.-J. Ferré. Paris: E. Droz, 1927.

Antoninus. *Summa theologica*. 4 vols. 1740; reprint ed. Graz: Akademische Druck-u. Verlaganstalt, 1959.

Apicius. *De re coquinaria*. Ed. Mary Ella Milham. Leipzig: B. G. Teubner, 1969.

(Apocryphal gospels). *Evangiles apocryphes*. Ed. Paul Peeters. 2 vols. Paris: Auguste Picard, 1914-24.

Aristotle. *Opera*. Ed. Immanuel Bekker. 11 vols. Oxford, 1837.

——. *Ethica nichomachea*. Ed. Ingram Bywater. Oxford, 1894.

Augustine. *Opera*. In *Patrologia latina*, vols. 31-47.

——. *Confessionum libri tredecim*. Ed. Lucas Verheijen. Corpus christianorum series latina, 27. Turnhout: Brepols, 1981.

——. *De civitate Dei*. Ed. Bernard Dombart and Alphonse Kalb. 2 vols. Corpus christianorum series latina, 47-48. Turnhout: Brepols, 1955.

——. *Contra academicos, De beata vita, De ordine, De magistro, De libero arbitrio*. Ed. W. M. Green and K.-D. Daur. Corpus christianorum series latina, 29. Turnhout: Brepols, 1970.

——. *De trinitate libri XV*. Ed. W. J. Mountain. 2 vols. Corpus christianorum series latina, 50-50A. Turnhout: Brepols, 1968.

——. *Enarrationes in psalmos*. Ed. Eligius Dekkers and Iohannes Fraipont. 3 vols. Corpus christianorum series latina, 38-40. Turnhout: Brepols, 1956.

——. *In evangelium Iohannis tractatus CXXIV*. Ed. Radbodus Willems. Corpus christianorum series latina, 36. Turnhout: Brepols, 1956.

Basil of Caesarea. (*Hexameron*). *Homélies sur l'Hexaéméron*. Ed. Stanislaus Giet. Sources chrétiennes, 26. Paris: Cerf, 1949.

——. (*In Hexameron beati Basilii*). Trans. Eustathius. *Ancienne version latine des neuf homélies sur l'Hexameron de Basile de Césarée*. Ed. Emmanuel Amand de Medieta and Stig Y. Rudberg. Texte und Untersuchungen zur Geshcichte der altchristlichen Literatur, 66. Berlin: Akademie, 1958.

Bede. *Hexameron*. In *Patrologia latina*, 91:1-190.

——. *Historia ecclesiastica gentis anglorum*. Ed. George Moberly. 2 vols. Oxford, 1896.

Benedict. *Regula*. Ed. Timothy Fry. Collegeville, Minn.: Liturgical Press, 1980.

Bernard of Clairvaux. *Opera omnia*. Ed. Jean Leclercq, H. Rochais, and C. H. Talbot. 8 vols. Rome: Cistercienses, 1955-77.

Bernardino of Siena. *Opera omnia*. Ed. Pacificus M. Perantanus. 9 vols. Florence: Ad Claras Aquas, 1950-56.

Biringuccio, Vannuccio. *De la pirotechnia.* Venice: Venturino Roffinello, 1540.
Bonaventure (Pseudo). (*Meditationes vitae Christi*). *Meditations on the Life of Christ: An Illustrated Manuscript of the Fourteenth Century.* Ed. Isa Ragusa and Rosalie B. Green. Princeton: Princeton University Press, 1961.
Buonarroti, Michelangelo. *Rime.* Ed. Enzo Noè Girardi. Scrittori d'Italia, 217. Bari: Laterza, 1960.
Calvin, Jean. *Opera quae supersunt omnia.* Ed. Eduard Reuss, Eduard Cunitz, and Johann Wilhelm Baum. Corpus reformatorum. Brunswick: C. A. Schwetschke, 1863-1900.
Canones et decreta sacrosancti oecumenici, et generalis concilii tridentini sub Paulo III, Iulio III, Pio IIII pontificibus max. Rome, 1564.
Canones apostolorum et coenobiorum saeculorum IV-VII. Ed. Herm. Theod. Bruns. 2 vols. in 1. Berlin, 1839.
Cassian, John. (*De institutis coenobiorum*). *Institutions cénobitiques.* Ed. Jean-Claude Guy. Sources chrétiennes, 109. Paris: Cerf, 1965.
Cassiodorus. *Variarum libri XII.* Ed. Ake Jason Fridh and James Werner Halpern. Corpus christianorum series latina, 96. Turnhout: Brepols, 1973.
Catherine of Siena. *Le lettere di S. Caterina da Siena.* Ed. Piero Misciattelli with Niccolò Tommasèo. 6 vols. Florence: C/E Giunti-G. Barbèra, 1970.
Cato, Marcus Porcius. (*Rerum rusticarum*). *On Agriculture.* Ed. William Davis Hooper, rev. Harrison Boyd Ash. Cambridge, Mass.: Harvard University Press, 1934.
Chalcidius. *Timaeus/Plato a Calcidio translatus et commentarioque instructus.* Ed. J. H. Waszink. Plato latinus, 4. London: Warburg Institute; Leiden: E. J. Brill, 1962.
Chaucer, Geoffrey. *The Text of the Canterbury Tales.* Ed. M. Manly and Edith Richert. 8 vols. Chicago: University of Chicago Press, 1940.
Chevalier de La Tour Landry. *Le livre du chevalier de La Tour Landry pour l'enseignement de ses filles.* Ed. A. Montaiglon. Paris, 1854.
Chrétien de Troyes. *Cligès.* Ed. Stewart Gregory and Claude Luttrell. Cambridge: D. S. Brewer, 1993.
Christine de Pisan. *Le livre de trois vertus.* Ms. 1528, Boston Public Library.
Cicero. *Academica.* Ed. James S. Reid. Rev. ed. London, 1885.
——. *De finibus bonorum et malorum.* Ed. Io. Nicolaus Madvigius. Hildesheim: Georg Olms, 1963.
——. *De oratore.* Ed. Augustus S. Wilkins. In *Rhetorica*, 1. Oxford: Clarendon, 1902.
——. (*Hortensius*). *Ciceros Hortensius.* Reconstructed by Laila Straume-Zimmerman. Europaische Hochschulschriften, 15; klassische Sprachen und Literatur, 9. Bern: Herbert Lang, 1976.
——. *Orationes.* Ed. Albert Curtius Clark. Oxford: Clarendon, 1909.
——. *Paradoxa Stoicorum, Academicorum reliquiae cum Lucullo, Timaeus, De natura deorum.* Ed. Otto Plasburg. Leipzig: Teubner, 1908.
Children of God's Fire: A Documentary History of Black Slavery in Brazil. Ed. Robert Edgar Conrad. Princeton: Princeton University Press, 1983.
"Colección de dictámenes inéditos." Ed. V. Beltrán Heredia. In *Ciencia tomista* 43 (1931):27-50, 169-80.
Columella. *Rei rusticae.* Ed. E. S. Forster and Edward H. Heffner. 3 vols. Cambridge, Mass.: Harvard University Press, 1941.
Corrozet, Giles. *Les blasons domestiques*. 1539; reprint ed. Paris, 1865.
Dante Alighieri. *La commedia secondo l'antica vulgata.* Ed. Georgio Petrocchi. 4 vols. Milan: Mondadori, 1966-68.
Della Casa, Giovanni. *Galateo ovvero de' costumi.* Ed. Emmanuela Scarpa. Ferrara: Franco Cosimo Panini, 1990.
Diego de san Pedro. *Diego de san Pedro's Carcel de amor: A Critical Edition.* Ed. Ivy A. Corfis. London: Tamesis, 1987.
Diogenes Laertius. *Vitae philosophorum.* Ed. H. S. Long. 2 vols. Oxford: Clarendon, 1964.
Dryden, John. *Works.* Ed. Edward Niles Hooker and H. T. Swedenberg, Jr. 19 vols. Berkeley: University of California Press, 1956-89.
Epiphanius. *De XII gemmis, quae erant in veste Aaronis.* Zurich, 1565.
Erasmus, Desiderius. *Opera omnia.* Amsterdam: North Holland, 1971-.
——. *Opera omnia.* Ed. Johannes Clericus. 11 vols. Leiden, 1703-6.

——. *Ausgewählte Werke*. Ed. Hajo Holborn with Annemarie Holborn. Munich: C. H. Beck, 1964.

Evagrius Ponticus. (*Logos praktikos*). *Traité pratique ou le moine*. Ed. Antoine Guillaumont and Claire Guillaumont. 2 vols. Paris: Cerf, 1971.

Falcone, Giuseppe. *La nuova, vaga, et dilettevole villa* . 1559; reprint ed. Venice: L. Spineda, 1612.

Firenzuolo, Agnolo. *Delle bellezze delle donne*. Ed. Delmo Maestri. In *Opere*, pp. 713-89. Turin: Unione Tipografico-Editrice, 1977.

Fonte, Moderata. *Il merito delle donne*. In *Donna e società nel seicento: Lucrezia Marinella e Arcangela Tarabotti*, pp. 159-96. Ed. Ginevra Conti Oderisio. Biblioteca di cultura, 167. Rome: Bulzoni, 1979.

Francisco de Osuna. *Norte de los estados*. Burgos, 1541.

——. *Tercera parte del libro llamado abecedario spiritual*. In *Escritores místicos españoles*, 1:319-587. Ed. Miguel Mir. Nueva biblioteca de autores españoles, 16. Madrid: Bailly, 1911.

Frontinus. (*De aquis urbis Romae*). *The Strategems and the Aqueducts of Rome*. Ed. Mary B. McElwain. New York: G. P. Putnam's Sons, 1925.

Gesner, Conrad. *De rerum fossilium, lapidum et gemmarum maxime, figuris et similitudinis*. Zurich, 1565.

Gregory the Great. *Homiliae in Hiezechihelem prophetam*. Ed. Mark Adriaen. Corpus christianorum series latina, 142. Turnhout: Brepols, 1971.

Guillaume de Lorris and Jean de Meun. *Le roman de la rose par Guillaume de Lorris et Jean de Meun*. Ed. Felix Lecoy. 3 vols. Paris: Champion, 1966-75.

Guillaume de Salluste. *The Works of Guillaume de Salluste Sieur du Bartas*. Ed. Urban Tigner Holmes, Jr., John Coriden Lyons, and Robert Whinte Linker. 3 vols. Chapel Hill: University of North Carolina Press, 1935-40. Reprint ed. Geneva: Slatkine, 1967.

Hali Meidenhad. Ed. O. Cockayne. Early English Texts Society, 18. London, 1866.

Halys. *Liber regialis*. Lyons: J. Myt, 1523.

Hernando de Castillo, ed. *Cancionero general recopilado por Hernando de Castillo, Valencia, 1511, facimile*. Ed. Antonio Rodríguez-Moñino. Madrid: Real academia española, 1958.

Hildegard of Bingen. *Liber divinorum operum simplicis hominis*. In *Patrologia latina*, 197:739-1038.

Hippocrates. (*De aeris, aquis, locis*). In *Hippocrates*, 1:70-137. Ed. W. S. Jones. 6 vols. New York: G. P. Putnam's Sons, 1923.

Homer. *Opera*. Ed. David B. Monro and Thomas W. Allen. 2d and 3d eds. 4 vols. Oxford: Clarendon, 1919-20.

Horace. *Opera*. Ed. Edward C. Wickham and H. W. Garrod. 2d ed. Oxford: Clarendon, 1912.

Hours of Catherine of Cleves. Ed. John Plummer. New York: George Braziller, 1966.

"I haue a new garden." In *Secular Lyrics of the XIVth and XVth Centuries*, pp. 15-16. Ed. Rossell Hope Robbins. Oxford: Clarendon, 1952.

Irenaeus. *Adversus haereses*. Ed. F. Sagnard. 7 vols. Paris: Cerf, 1952.

Jerome. (*Epistolae*). *Lettres*. Ed. Jerome Labourt. 6 vols. Paris: Belles lettres, 1949-58.

John of the Cross. *Obras de san Juan de la cruz*. Ed. Silverio de santa Teresa. 5 vols. Biblioteca mística carmelitana, 10-14. Burgos: Monte Carmelo, 1929-51.

Julian of Norwich. *A Book of Showings to the Anchoress Julian of Norwich*. Ed. Edmund Colledge and James Walsh. 2 vols. Studies and Texts, 35. Toronto: Pontifical Institute of Mediaeval Studies, 1978.

Kempe, Margery. *The Book of Margery Kempe*. Ed. Sanford Brown Meech and Hope Emily Allen. Early English Text Society, 212. London: Oxford: University Press, 1940.

——. *The Book of Margery Kempe 1436: A Modern Version*. Ed. W. Butler Bowden. London: Jonathan Cape, 1936.

Landino, Cristoforo. *Disputationes camaldulenses*. Ed. Peter Lohe. Istituto nazionale di studi sul rinascimento, Studi e teste, 6. Florence: Sansoni, 1980.

La Tour-Landry, Geoffroy de. *Le livre du Chevalier de La Tour Landry pour l'enseignement de ses filles*. Ed. A. Montaiglou. Paris, 1854.

Leander. *De institutione virginum et contemptu mundi.* Ed. Angel Custodio Vega. Scriptores ecclesiastici hispano-latini veteris et medii aevi. Madrid: Augustinianus Monasterium Escurialensis, 1948.

El linaje judeoconverso de santa Teresa (Pleito de hidalguía de los Cepeda). Ed. Teofanes Egidio Lopez. Madrid: Espiritualidad, 1986.

Ludolf von Sachsen. *Vita Jesu Christi ex Evangelio et approbatis ab Ecclesia Catholica doctoribus sedule collecta.* Ed. L. M. Rigollot. 4 vols. Paris, 1878.

Luis de León. *La perfecta casada.* Ed. Elizabeth Wallace. Decennial Publications, second series, 6. Chicago: University of Chicago Press, 1903.

Lujan, Pedro de. *Coloquios matrimoniales del licenciado Pedro de Lujan..* Ed. Asunción Rollo Gruss. Anejos del Boletin de la Real academia española, 48. Madrid: Aguirre, 1990.

Luther, Martin. *De servo arbitrio.* In *Luthers Werke in Auswahl,* 4:94-293. Ed. Otto Clemen. 6 vols. Berlin: Walter de Gruyter, 1950.

Lydgate, John. *The Minor Poems of John Lydgate.* Ed. Henry Noble McCracken. Early English Text Society, e. s. 107. London: Kegan Paul, Trench, Trübner for the Early English Text Society, 1911.

The Making of King's Lynn: A Documentary Survey. Ed. Dorothy M. Own. British Academy Records of Social and Economic History, 9. London: Oxford University Press for the British Academy, 1984.

María de santo Domingo. *Libro de la oración de sor María de santo Domingo.* Ed. José Manuel Blecua. Madrid: Hauser y Menet, 1948.

Marvell, Andrew. *The Poems and Letters of Andrew Marvell.* Ed. H. M. Margoliouth. 3d ed. rev. Pierre Legouis and E. E. Duncan-Jones. Oxford: Clarendon, 1971.

Mechtild of Hackenborn. *(Liber specialis gratiae). Revelationes Gertrudinae ac Mechtildianae.* Ed. Benedictine Monks of Solêmnes. Paris, 1875.

Le menagier de Paris. Ed. Georgine E. Brereton and Janet M. Ferrier. 2 vols. Oxford: Clarendon, 1981.

Merian, Maria Sibylla. *(Metamorphosis insectorum surinamensium).* Elisabeth Rücker and William T. Stern. *Maria Sibylla Merian in Surinam: Commentary to the Facsimile Edition of 'Metamorphosis insectorum surinamensium' (Amsterdam, 1705) Based on Original Watercolors in the Royal Library Windsor Castle.* 2 vols. London: Pion, 1980-82.

Minucius Felix. *Octavius.* Ed. G. Quispel. Leiden: E. J. Brill, 1949.

Moffet, Thomas. *The Silkewormes and their Flies.* Ed. Victor Houliston. Medieval and Renaissance Texts and Studies, 61. Binghamton, N. Y.: Medieval and Renaissance Texts and Studies, 1989.

Monastic Sign Languages. Ed. Jean Umiker-Sebeok and Thomas A. Sebeok. Approaches to Semiotics, 76. Berlin: Mouton de Gruyter, 1987.

Montaigne, Michel de. *Oeuvres complètes.* Ed. Arthur Armaingaud. Vols. 7-8: *Journal de voyage en Italie.* 12 vols. Paris: L. Conard, 1924-41.

Morelli, Giovanni di Pagolo. *Ricordi.* Ed. Vittore Branca. Florence: F. Le Monnier, 1969.

Nicolaus Cusanus. *Trialogus de possest.* In *Opera omnia,* 11-2. Ed. Renata Steiger. 16 vols. Leipzig: Felix Meiner, 1932.

Ovid. *Metamorphoses.* Ed. O. Korn and J. H. Muller. 2 vols. in 1. Berlin: Weidmann, 1915-16.

——. *Fasti.* Ed. James George Frazer. Cambridge, Mass.: Harvard University Press, 1961.

Palladius. *Lausiac History.* Ed. Cuthbert Butler. Cambridge: Cambridge University Press, 1898-1904.

Passio sanctarum Perpetuae et Felicitatis. Ed. A. A. R. Bastiaensen. In *Atti e passioni dei martiri,* pp. 107-47. n. p.: Fondazione Lorenzo Valla, Arnoldo Mondadori, 1987.

Patrologiae cursus completus, series latina. Ed. J.-P. Migne. 221 vols. Paris, 1800-75.

Peter the Venerable. *(Epistolae). The Letters of Peter the Venerable.* Ed. Giles Constable. 2 vols. Cambridge, Mass.: Harvard University Press, 1967.

Petrarch. *Epistolae familiares: Le familiari.* Ed. V. Rossi and Umberto Bosco. Edizione nazionale, 10-13. Florence: Sansoni, 1933-42.

——. *(Epistolae metricae).* In *Poesie minori del Petrarca,* 2-3. Ed. Domenico Rossetti. 3 vols. Milan, 1829-34

——. *(Epistolae variae).* In *Lettere di Francesco Petrarca,* 5:203-490. Ed. Giuseppe Fracassetti. 5 vols. Florence, 1863-67.

——. (*Liber sine nomine*). *Petrarcas "Buch ohne Namen" und die papstliche Kurie: Ein Beitrag zur Gesitesgeschichte der Frühренaissance*. Ed. Paul Piur. Halle: Max Niemeyer, 1925.

——. (*Testamentum*). *Petrarch's Testament*. Ed. Theodor E. Mommsen. Ithaca, N. Y.: Cornell University Press, 1957.

Petronius. *Satyricon*. Ed. Konrad Müller. Munich: E. Heimeran, 1961.

Philippe de Navarre. *Quatre âges de l'homme*. Ed. Marcel de Fréville. Paris, 1888.

Pliny. *Naturalis historia*. Ed. H. Rackham, W. H. S. Jones, and D. E. Eichholz. Cambridge, Mass.: Harvard University Press, 1938-42.

Pliny, the younger. *Epistularum libri decem*. Ed. R. A. B. Mynors. Oxford: Clarendon, 1963.

Plutarch. *Moralia*. Ed. Harold Fredrik Cherniss. 17 vols. Cambridge, Mass.: Harvard University Press, 1976.

——. *Vitae parallelae*. Ed. Robert Flacelière, Emile Chambry, and Marcel Juneaux. 16 vols. Paris: Belles lettres, 1957-83.

Possidius. *Sancti Augustini vita scripta a Possidio episcopo*. Ed. Herbert Theberath Weiskotten. Princeton: Princeton University Press, 1919.

I processi inediti per Francesca Bussa dei Ponziani (Santa Francesca Romana) 1440-1453. Ed. Placido Lugano. Vatican City: Biblioteca Apostolica Vaticana, 1945.

Processus canonizationis s. Thomae, Neapoli. Ed. M.-H. Laurent. *Fontes vitae s. Thomae Aquinatis*, fasicule 4. Ed. Dominic M. Prümmer. Toulouse: Privat, n. d.

Quintilian. *Institutiones oratoriae*. Ed. M. Winterbottom. 4 vols. Oxford: Clarendon, 1970.

Raymond of Capua. *Vita s. Catharinae Senensis*. In *Acta sanctorum*, 12:862-967. Ed. Joanne Carnandet. New ed. Paris, 1866.

Recueil des chartes de l'abbaye de Clairvaux: XIIe siècle. Ed. Jean Waquet. 2 vols. Troyes: Archives départmentales de l'Aube, 1982.

Richard of St.-Laurent . *De laudibus beatae Mariae virginis*. Inter *Opera Alberti magni*, 36. Ed. Augustus and Aemilius Borgnet. 38 vols. Paris, 1898.

Rucellai, Giovanni. *Giovanni Rucellai ed il suo zibaldone*. Vol. 1: *Il zibaldone quaresimale*. Ed. Alessandro Perosa. 2 vols. Studies of the Warburg Institute, 24. London: Warburg Institute, 1960.

Rueo, Francisco. *De gemmis, aliquot, iis praesetim quarum divus Iohannes apostolus in sua Apocalypsi meminat*. Zurich, 1565.

Ruiz, Juan. *Libro de buen amor*. Ed. Manuel Criado de Val and Eric W. Naylor. Clásicos hispánicos, 2, 9. Madrid: Consejo superior de investigaciones científicas, 1972.

Sallust. *Catalina, Iugurtha, fragmenta ampliora* . Ed. Alphonsus Kurfess. Leipzig: B. G. Teubner, 1968.

Salutati, Coluccio. *De seculo et religione*. Ed. B. L. Ullman. Nuova collezione di testi umanistici inediti o rari, 12. Florence: Leo S. Olschki, 1957.

Savonarola, Girolamo. *Prediche sopra Amos e Zaccaria*. Ed. Paolo Ghighlieri. 3 vols. Rome: A. Belardetti, 1971-72.

Seneca. *Opera quae supersunt omnia*. Ed. Friedrich Haase. 3 vols. in 2. Leipzig, 1852-53.

——. *Thyestes*. In *Tragoediae*, pp. 293-333. Ed. Otto Zwierlein. Oxford: Clarendon, 1986.

Seneca, the elder. *Controversiae*. Ed. M. Winterbottom. 2 vols. Cambridge, Mass.: Harvard University Press, 1974.

Sidney, Philip. *The Countess of Pembroke's Arcadia*. Ed. Maurice Evans. Harmondsworth, Middlesex: Penguin, 1977.

Signa loquendi: Die cluniacensischen Signa-Listen. Ed. Walter Jarecki. Saecula spiritalia, 4. Baden-Baden: Valentin Koerner, 1981.

Sugar, Abbot. (*Opera*). *Abbot Sugar on the Abbey Church of St.-Denis and its Art Treasures*. Ed. Erwin Panofsky. 2d ed. Ed. Gerda Panofsky-Soergel. Princeton: Princeton University Press, 1979.

Teresa of Avila. *Obras*. Ed. Silverio de santa Teresa. 9 vols. Biblioteca mística carmelitana, 1-9. Burgos: Monte Carmelo, 1915-24.

——. *Obras completas*. 2d ed. rev. Ed. Otger Steggink and Efren de la Madre de Dios. Madrid: Biblioteca de autores cristianos, 1967.

Theocritus. (*Opera*). *Theocritus*. Ed. A. S. F. Gow. 2 vols. Cambridge: Cambridge University Press, 1950-52.

Thibaut, Messire. *Le roman de la poire*. Ed. Christiane Marchello-Nizia. Paris: Société des anciens textes français, 1984.

Thomas Aquinas. *Opera omnia*. Rome: Polyglota S. C. de propaganda fide, 1882-1948.

——. *Expositio salutationis angelicae*. Ed. Joannes Felix Rossi. Monografia del Collegio Alberoni, 11. Piacenza: Collegio Alberoni, 1931.

Valla, Lorenzo. *Opera omnia*. Ed. Eugenio Garin. 2 vols. Monumenta politica et philosophica rariora, 1, 5-6. Turin: Bottega d'Erasmo, 1962.

——. *De professione religiosorum*. Ed. Mariarosa Cortesi. Thesaurus mundi, biblioteca scriptorum latinorum mediae et recentioris aetatis, 25. Padua: Antenore, 1986.

Varro. (*De agri cultura*). *Économie rurale*. Ed. Jacques Heurgon and Charles Guiraud. 2 vols. Paris: Belles lettres, 1978-85.

Vieira, Antônio. *Obras completas do padre Antônio Vieira*. 15 vols. Porto: Chardon, 1907-9.

Vergil. *Opera*. Ed. R. A. B. Mynors. Rev. ed. Oxford: Clarendon, 1972.

——. *Georgics*. Ed. idem. Oxford: Clarendon, 1990.

William of St.-Thierry et al. *Vita prima*. In *Patrologia latina*, 185-1:225-466.

Xenophon. *Opera omnia*. Ed. E. C. Marchant. 5 vols. Oxford: Clarendon, 1961-63.

Zayas y Sotomayor, María de. *La esclava de su amante*. In *Desengaños amorosos*, pp. 127-255. Ed. Alicia Yellera. Madrid: Catedra, 1983.

——. *Novelas amorosas y ejemplares*. Ed. Agustín G. de Amezúa y Mayo. Madrid: Aldus, 1948.

INDEX OF NAMES

INDEX OF SUBJECTS

Studies in the History of Christian Thought

EDITED BY HEIKO A. OBERMAN

1. McNEILL, J. J. *The Blondelian Synthesis.* 1966. Out of print
2. GOERTZ, H.-J. *Innere und äussere Ordnung in der Theologie Thomas Müntzers.* 1967
3. BAUMAN, Cl. *Gewaltlosigkeit im Täufertum.* 1968
4. ROLDANUS, J. *Le Christ et l'Homme dans la Théologie d'Athanase d'Alexandrie.* 2nd ed. 1977
5. MILNER, Jr., B. Ch. *Calvin's Doctrine of the Church.* 1970. Out of print
6. TIERNEY, B. *Origins of Papal Infallibility, 1150-1350.* 2nd ed. 1988
7. OLDFIELD, J. J. *Tolerance in the Writings of Félicité Lamennais 1809-1831.* 1973
8. OBERMAN, H. A. (ed.). *Luther and the Dawn of the Modern Era.* 1974. Out of print
9. HOLECZEK, H. *Humanistische Bibelphilologie bei Erasmus, Thomas More und William Tyndale.* 1975
10. FARR, W. *John Wyclif as Legal Reformer.* 1974
11. PURCELL, M. *Papal Crusading Policy 1244-1291.* 1975
12. BALL, B. W. *A Great Expectation.* Eschatological Thought in English Protestantism. 1975
13. STIEBER, J. W. *Pope Eugenius IV, the Council of Basel, and the Empire.* 1978. Out of print
14. PARTEE, Ch. *Calvin and Classical Philosophy.* 1977
15. MISNER, P. *Papacy and Development.* Newman and the Primacy of the Pope. 1976
16. TAVARD, G. H. *The Seventeenth-Century Tradition.* A Study in Recusant Thought. 1978
17. QUINN, A. *The Confidence of British Philosophers.* An Essay in Historical Narrative. 1977
18. BECK, J. *Le Concil de Basle (1434).* 1979
19. CHURCH, F. F. and GEORGE, T. (ed.) *Continuity and Discontinuity in Church History.* 1979
20. GRAY, P. T. R. *The Defense of Chalcedon in the East (451-553).* 1979
21. NIJENHUIS, W. *Adrianus Saravia (c. 1532-1613).* Dutch Calvinist. 1980
22. PARKER, T. H. L. (ed.) *Iohannis Calvini Commentarius in Epistolam Pauli ad Romanos.* 1981
23. ELLIS, I. *Seven Against Christ.* A Study of 'Essays and Reviews'. 1980
24. BRANN, N. L. *The Abbot Trithemius (1462-1516).* 1981
25. LOCHER, G. W. *Zwingli's Thought.* New Perspectives. 1981
26. GOGAN, B. *The Common Corps of Christendom.* Ecclesiological Themes in Thomas More. 1982
27. STOCK, U. *Die Bedeutung der Sakramente in Luthers Sermonen von 1519.* 1982
28. YARDENI, M. (ed.) *Modernité et nonconformisme en France à travers les âges.* 1983
29. PLATT, J. *Reformed Thought and Scholasticism.* 1982
30. WATTS, P. M. *Nicolaus Cusanus.* A Fifteenth-Century Vision of Man. 1982
31. SPRUNGER, K. L. *Dutch Puritanism.* 1982
32. MEIJERING, E. P. *Melanchthon and Patristic Thought.* 1983
33. STROUP, J. *The Struggle for Identity in the Clerical Estate.* 1984
34. 35. COLISH, M. L. *The Stoic Tradition from Antiquity to the Early Middle Ages.* 1.2. 2nd ed. 1990
36. GUY, B. *Domestic Correspondence of Dominique-Marie Varlet, Bishop of Babylon, 1678-1742.* 1986
37. 38. CLARK, F. *The Pseudo-Gregorian Dialogues.* I. II. 1987
39. PARENTE, Jr. J. A. *Religious Drama and the Humanist Tradition.* 1987
40. POSTHUMUS MEYJES, G. H. M. *Hugo Grotius, Meletius.* 1988
41. FELD, H. *Der Ikonoklasmus des Westens.* 1990
42. REEVE, A. and SCREECH, M. A. (eds.) *Erasmus' Annotations on the New Testament.* Acts — Romans — I and II Corinthians. 1990
43. KIRBY, W. J. T. *Richard Hooker's Doctrine of the Royal Supremacy.* 1990
44. GERSTNER, J. N. *The Thousand Generation Covenant.* Reformed Covenant Theology. 1990
45. CHRISTIANSON, G. and IZBICKI, T. M. (eds.) *Nicholas of Cusa.* 1991
46. GARSTEIN, O. *Rome and the Counter-Reformation in Scandinavia.* 1553-1622. 1992
47. GARSTEIN, O. *Rome and the Counter-Reformation in Scandinavia.* 1622-1656. 1992
48. PERRONE COMPAGNI, V. (ed.) *Cornelius Agrippa, De occulta philosophia Libri tres.* 1992
49. MARTIN, D. D. *Fifteenth-Century Carthusian Reform.* The World of Nicholas Kempf. 1992

50. HOENEN, M. J. F. M. *Marsilius of Inghen.* Divine Knowledge in Late Medieval Thought. 1993
51. O'MALLEY, J. W., IZBICKI, T. M. and CHRISTIANSON, G. (eds.) *Humanity and Divinity in Renaissance and Reformation.* Essays in Honor of Charles Trinkaus. 1993
52. REEVE, A. (ed.) and SCREECH, M. A. (introd.) *Erasmus' Annotations on the New Testament.* Galatians to the Apocalypse. 1993
53. STUMP, Ph. H. *The Reforms of the Council of Constance (1414-1418).* 1994
54. GIAKALIS, A. *Images of the Divine.* The Theology of Icons at the Seventh Ecumenical Council. With a Foreword by Henry Chadwick. 1994
55. NELLEN, H. J. M. and RABBIE, E. (eds.). *Hugo Grotius – Theologian.* Essays in Honour of G. H. M. Posthumus Meyjes. 1994
56. TRIGG, J. D. *Baptism in the Theology of Martin Luther.* 1994
57. JANSE, W. *Albert Hardenberg als Theologe.* Profil eines Bucer-Schülers. 1994
59. SCHOOR, R.J.M. VAN DE. *The Irenical Theology of Théophile Brachet de La Milletière (1588-1665).* 1995
60. STREHLE, S. *The Catholic Roots of the Protestant Gospel.* Encounter between the Middle Ages and the Reformation. 1995
61. BROWN, M.L. *Donne and the Politics of Conscience in Early Modern England.* 1995
62. SCREECH, M.A. (ed.). *Richard Mocket, Warden of All Souls College, Oxford, Doctrina et Politia Ecclesiae Anglicanae.* An Anglican Summa. Facsimile with Variants of the Text of 1617. Edited with an Introduction. 1995
63. SNOEK, G.J.C. *Medieval Piety from Relics to the Eucharist.* A Process of Mutual Interaction. 1995
64. PIXTON, P.B. *The German Episcopacy and the Implementation of the Decrees of the Fourth Lateran Council, 1216-1245.* Watchmen on the Tower. 1995
65. DOLNIKOWSKI, E.W. *Thomas Bradwardine: A View of Time and a Vision of Eternity in Fourteenth-Century Thought.* 1995
66. RABBIE, E. (ed.). *Hugo Grotius, Ordinum Hollandiae ac Westfrisiae Pietas (1613).* Critical Edition with Translation and Commentary. 1995
67. HIRSH, J.C. *The Boundaries of Faith.* The Development and Transmission of Medieval Spirituality. 1996
68. BURNETT, S.G. *From Christian Hebraism to Jewish Studies.* Johannes Buxtorf (1564-1629) and Hebrew Learning in the Seventeenth Century. 1996
69. BOLAND O.P., V. *Ideas in God according to Saint Thomas Aquinas.* Sources and Synthesis. 1996
70. LANGE, M.E. *Telling Tears in the English Renaissance.* 1996
71. CHRISTIANSON, G. and T.M. IZBICKI (eds.) *Nicholas of Cusa on Christ and the Church.* Essays in Memory of Chandler McCuskey Brooks for the American Cusanus Society. 1996
72. MALI, A. *Mystic in the New World.* Marie de l'Incarnation (1599-1672). 1996
73. VISSER, D. *Apocalypse as Utopian Expectation (800-1500).* The Apocalypse Commentary of Berengaudus of Ferrières and the Relationship between Exegesis, Liturgy and Iconography. 1996
74. O'ROURKE BOYLE, M. *Divine Domesticity.* Augustine of Thagaste to Teresa of Avila. 1997

Prospectus available on request

E. J. BRILL — P.O.B. 9000 — 2300 PA LEIDEN — THE NETHERLANDS